MAYA JASANOFF graduated from Harvard before earning her M.Phil. at Cambridge and her Ph.D. at Yale. The recipient of numerous prizes and fellowships, she spent two years in the Society of Fellows at the University of Michigan, and is now Assistant Professor of History at the University of Virginia. This is her first book.

Visit www.AuthorTracker.co.uk for exclusive information on your favourite HarperCollins authors.

From the reviews of *Edge of Empire*:

'Jasanoff is brilliant, perceptive and writes like a dream; almost every page contains startling new insights and makes you look afresh at subjects and ideas you thought you knew well. With this ambitious, imaginative and mould-breaking book, she has shown herself to be a major new star in the historical firmament' WILLIAM DALRYMPLE

'An extraordinary debut. Maya Jasanoff is one of the most exciting historians to emerge in years. Her crackling prose and outstanding research have resulted in a ground-breaking book . . . a must read'
AMANDA FOREMAN, author of *Georgiana: Duchess of Devonshire*

'A clever and wonderfully researched and written book which illuminates French as well as British experience, artifacts and culture, and which looks at all the actors involved in a vivid and nuanced fashion'
LINDA COLLEY, author of
*Captives: Britain, Empire and the World 1600-1850*

'Curiosities from the East – both human and artistic – fill Jasanoff's fascinating *Edge of Empire*. By focusing with such flair on the colourful business of collecting antiquities in 18th- and 19th-century India and Egypt, she finds an exciting new way to understand what Empire – British or French – meant to its collaborators and its victims'
BOYD TONKIN, *Independent*

'Captivating ... Jasanoff has produced a fascinating book, packed with information and insights and written in vibrant, mellifluous prose' CHANDAK SENGOOPTA, *Literary Review*

'[A] sparklingly original book ... Jasanoff casts new light on the growth of empire. Her account introduces a perceptive and original historian' ANTHONY SATTIN, *Sunday Times*

'I really loved Maya Jasanoff's gorgeously written *Edge of Empire*: cultures coming together in unexpected ways in India and Egypt'
SIMON SCHAMA, *Guardian*

'[A] remarkable first book which offers an original take on debates about the British empire. The drama of Jasanoff's stories and her infectious enthusiasm make this a consuming read'
ANDREW HOLGATE, *Sunday Times*

'Jasanoff triumphs in this memorable debut ... This is partly because, mirroring her subject, she has adopted a vivacious methodology that defies category. It is an exhilarating cocktail of history and travelogue ... Jasanoff's investigation of the world that made her evokes the midday sun, the unforgettable stench and blare of the East, but populates it with characters to whom the reader can relate, as strange as fiction but actually found in real life' ROBERT MCCRUM, *Observer*

'This is a historical tour de force, with wonderfully original material moulded into a convincing new narrative. Britain's empire will never look the same again' RICHARD GOTT, *Guardian*

'A remarkable debut ... By means of a series of anecdotes and vignettes, *Edge of Empire* brings the world where "enduring cultural, social and political boundaries between East and West were taking shape" to life, with an imagination few could hope to match'
ANTHONY PAGDEN, *London Review of Books*

MAYA JASANOFF

# EDGE OF EMPIRE

*Conquest and Collecting in the East*
*1750–1850*

HARPER PERENNIAL
London, New York, Toronto and Sydney

Harper Perennial
An imprint of HarperCollins*Publishers*
77–85 Fulham Palace Road
Hammersmith
London W6 8JB

www.harperperennial.co.uk

This edition published by Harper Perennial 2006
2

First published in Great Britain by Fourth Estate in 2006



A catalogue record for this book
is available from the British Library

ISBN-13 978-0-00-718011-0
ISBN-10 0-00-718011-X

Set in Fournier MT with Burlington Display

Printed and bound in Great Britain by Clays Ltd, St Ives plc

*For my parents, border crossers*

# Contents

## PART TWO
## Imperial Collision, 1798–1801

### CHAPTER FOUR: INVADING EGYPT



### CHAPTER FIVE: SEIZING SERINGAPATAM



### CHAPTER SIX: THE OBJECTS OF VICTORY



## PART THREE
## Egypt, 1801–1840

### CHAPTER SEVEN: RIVALS



### CHAPTER EIGHT: REMOVALS

CHAPTER NINE: RECOVERIES

# EDGE OF EMPIRE

INTRODUCTION

# *A World of Empires, an Empire of the World*

It was a clear autumn morning in Calcutta, shortly after the holiday of Durga Puja. At the end of a narrow lane towered a giant image of the white ten-armed goddess, Shiva's female incarnation, which had been built for the festivities out of bamboo slats, papier-mâché, and a considerable quantity of lurid paint. Earlier, I had walked through what appeared to be Calcutta's central banana depot, where whole branches of cascading bananas were being unloaded by the truckload and stacked as high as firewood outside a mountain cabin. Another turning led into a street thick with the toasted smell of cooking oil, where men sat rolling and frying bright yellow sweets called *laddoos*, heaping them up, once cooked, in tall cones. But there, ahead of me, was the most unexpected sight of all: a vast Palladian villa, set off by a pair of wrought-iron gates, rising behind the cramped alleys like a painted stage set.

The Marble Palace, as this place is called, is only partly a house. Ever since it was built, in 1835, its owners, an orthodox Hindu family named Mullick, have filled their mansion with art and objects from all over Europe and have opened it to visitors—which makes the Marble Palace India's "first museum of Western art." I would learn more about the contents and the history of the Marble Palace on another day. But that morning, as I walked past the baroque fancies in the front garden and up the shallow steps, I had the feeling that I was wandering into an alternate, wonderfully unknown world. I sat on a high, cracked leather banquette in the Billiard Room. Plaster and marble images of Greek gods peered out from the walls, and ceiling fans like the propellers of World War II bombers loomed overhead. Though the honking city was just a few hundred feet away, the only sound here was birdsong, from a veritable aviary of wire cages in the courtyard beyond. It was like Dickens gone native.

It is so easy to dwell on the sheer cultural oddity of this kind of place, plainly the creation of individual sensibilities, and so at variance with its surroundings. But what if one tries to make sense of it on its own terms? I visited the Marble Palace in the course of my research on the cultural history of the British Empire. Most of what I had read about empire and culture drew a detailed if rather insidious picture of white European colonizers trying to supplant, appropriate, or denigrate the non-European peoples and societies they encountered. More attention was paid to how Europeans responded to non-Europeans than vice versa, and emphasis tended to be placed more on conflict than on convergence. But here was something quite different: a site genuinely embedded in the cultures of both East and West, and a vestige of empire still very much alive. What would it be like, I wondered, to enter imperial history through a gateway like this? What would empire look like from the inside out?

The Marble Palace was just one of many unexpected juxtapositions of East and West that I encountered while writing this book. There was the heart-stopping moment of finding the Mughal emperor's letters in the back room of an archive in the French Alps, folded into narrow strips and bunched into a battered metal chest, as if untouched since being read by their Savoyard recipient two hundred years before. There was my discovering, one sun-baked noon in the deserted ruins of an Egyptian temple, the name of a long-dead English diplomat scratched feebly into the stone—a sad grasp at immortality. Then there was spotting his arch rival's signature in New York, of all places, carved on an inner wall of the Temple of Dendur, beneath the glass ceiling of the Metropolitan Museum of Art. There was visiting an impeccably Tuscan villa on a hillside at the edge of Florence, only to find in it a sword with a tiger-headed hilt, seized in 1799 from the South Indian city of Seringapatam during one of the British Empire's most dramatic battles.

None of these scattered testaments—ranging across Europe and even America, as well as Britain and its former empire—is the kind of evidence that figures in most books about the British Empire. That history tends to be impersonal, sometimes doctrinaire, and often leaves out the wider context of Europe and the rest of the non-imperial world. At the heart of this book, by contrast, are these material remains and the stories behind them. Each one of these vestiges was left by a person who lived in India or Egypt, on the eastern frontiers of what became the British Empire, at a time when enduring cultural, social, and political boundaries between East and West were taking shape. These are the legacies of men and women who engaged with foreign cultures in tangible ways: as collectors of objects. Collectors bought, commissioned, traded, plundered, stole, captured, quested; they preserved and at times destroyed; they moved and coveted; they lost and remembered. In their lives and legacies, they bridged East and West, and make beguiling escorts into an intimate, little-known history of empire.

They also hold up a mirror to the larger story of how Britain itself collected an empire, in India and beyond. The century from 1750 to 1850 was a formative one for Britain and the British Empire. In 1750, Britain was an island in a sea of empires—a small island: with a population of eight million, it was only half the size of its historic enemy France, an imbalance that provoked tremendous national anxiety.[1] Britain's colonial empire was also comparatively modest. In the Atlantic world, Spain and Portugal remained major powers. France posed a greater challenge. Though Britain's North American colonies dwarfed neighboring New France (boasting 2.5 million settlers to New France's paltry 70,000), France threatened to link up its settlements in the Great Lakes with those along the Mississippi, choking off the thirteen colonies and laying claim to the beckoning West. In the Mediterranean and Middle East, Britain's presence was minimal compared with that of France, Spain, or the Italian states. In India, it was just one of several European nations—including Portugal, the Netherlands, France, and Denmark—to maintain "factories," or trading outposts, along the coast. The Spanish, Portuguese, and Dutch dominated trade to east and southeast Asia (the Netherlands controlled the valuable spice islands of modern-day Indonesia); and the South Pacific, later a region of intense Anglo-French rivalry, would not be seriously explored by Britain until Captain James Cook set off on his first voyage, in 1768.

But by 1850, the world, and Britain's position in it, looked dramatically different. Britain had become the world's first and largest industrialized nation, with a population almost three times larger than in 1750 and now heavily urban. Unlike almost every region of Europe, it had escaped the devastations of invasion, revolution, and civil war. Within Europe, Britain enjoyed unprecedented diplomatic and political authority, as well as industrial, commercial, and financial preeminence. Overseas, few of Britain's former imperial rivals could compete. Of the old colonial powers, France alone offered some counterweight, its empire relaunched with the invasion of Algeria in 1830. But at midcentury, the greatest challengers to British global power were still partly in the making: the United States and Russia, empires both, each racing toward the Pacific. The British Empire in 1850 encompassed a quarter of the globe, stretching from Ottawa to Auckland, Capetown to Calcutta, Singapore to Spanish Town. One in five people in the world was Queen Victoria's subject; many millions more (in Argentina or Portugal, for instance) lived in states bankrolled and indirectly steered by Britain. With this tremendous geographical expansion also came consistency of purpose, personnel, and culture, linking the empire's many and disparate parts. The British Empire would always have its critics, at home and abroad; it would also always be more coherent in name (or on a map) than in practice. But by 1850, many Britons had come to see the empire as a fundamental part of what Britain itself was about, a key component of national identity. The imperial sun had risen, and seemed unlikely to set.

This book chronicles Britain's rise to global power along two eastern frontiers, in India and Egypt. Those regions were to become the geopolitical gateposts of Britain's empire in "the East," where British influence expanded most dramatically after 1750. They were also the cornerstones of a Western conception of "the Orient," where Europe's encounter with cultural difference was at its most varied and complex. My narrative unfolds at the edge of empire in time as well as in space—before the formal limits of British rule were fixed, and from the perspective of people and places on the margins of metropolitan power. This history of British imperialism is very much a history of French empire, too, and of the role played by Anglo-French rivalry in determining the shape of both nations' interests in the East. But most of all, this book is about how real people experienced imperial expansion from within. How did it feel to live in this vast and changing world? And how does that world look different when seen through the eyes of collectors?

By investigating imperial expansion through a practice and those who indulged in it—collecting and collectors—I am deliberately taking an unconventional approach. This is partly to recover new profiles and experiences from the past. But these personal encounters also offer a different perspective on the relationship of culture and imperialism more generally. I do not interpret collecting as a transparent or programmatic expression of imperial power, the playing-out of an "imperial project." Rather, the history of collecting reveals the complexities of empire; it shows how power and culture intersected in tangled, contingent, sometimes self-contradictory ways. Instead of seeing collecting as a manifestation of imperial power, I see the British Empire itself as a kind of collection: pieced together and gaining definition over time, shaped by a range of circumstances, accidents, and intentions.

The men and women who populate these pages are not, for the most part, the sorts of people who usually appear in history books. For one thing, they are not defined by conventional social attributes, such as occupation, religion, class, or even ethnicity or nationality. Instead, they shared a habit and interest that cut across imperial society: from princes, officers, functionaries, and traders, through to tourists, wives, artists, and adventurers. Imperial collectors ranged from household names of imperial history, such as Robert Clive and Napoleon Bonaparte, to fringe unknowns such as the minor English diplomat Henry Salt or the eccentric Irish-born soldier Charles "Hindoo" Stuart. Inevitably, who counts as a collector is somewhat arbitrary—and though some of the figures I describe here were passionately dedicated to acquiring objects, others were collectors more by circumstance, hanging on to artifacts that had crossed their paths. But they all shared one crucial characteristic: all of them used objects to advertise, hone, or shape their social personæ. Collecting was a means of self-fashioning.[2] In fact, the connection between collecting and self-fashioning was itself a cross-cultural phenomenon, extending from Europeans who valued art collecting as a sign of their being true gentlemen, to Indian princes who collected objects from far-off lands to enhance their personal charisma.

Imperial collectors reached across the lines of cultural difference. It is easy to speak of a "clash of civilizations" when cultures are distilled to the point of abstraction. But real people in the real world do not necessarily experience other cultures in a confrontational or monolithic way. What the stories of imperial collectors make clear is how much the process of cultural encounter involved crossing and mixing, as well as separation and division. Recovering the sheer variety of life "on the ground" in an empire, and its points of empathy, seems especially important now, when theoretical and ideological discussion of empire is prevalent but the willingness to engage with and understand other cultures often is not.

These stories also counterbalance the tendency in postcolonial scholarship to portray Europe's imperial collision with the rest of the world as a fundamentally oppositional, one-sided affair: the sad, sordid tale of how Western powers imposed hegemony—technological, economic, military, and cultural—over non-Western societies. From Edward Said's groundbreaking *Orientalism* (1978), which emphasizes the capacity of Western discourse to define and dominate an Eastern "other"; to the influential Indian journal *Subaltern Studies;* to more recent work on forms of hybridity—much academic energy has gone into tracing how "the West" exerted and expressed its power over "the rest."[3] To be sure, that is in large part what European empires tried to do. But imperialism is not a one-way street, and power and culture do not always march in lockstep. Alongside trying to understand how European power got asserted over others, one should also consider how others changed and challenged it.

The archives are bursting with as-yet-untold stories of people living on the eastern edges of empire—camp followers, for example, or interpreters, or even common soldiers (about whom surprisingly little has been written), or women and children—whose experiences all warrant research. Collectors make excellent guides across imperial frontiers because of their active, tangible engagement with other cultures, and their preoccupation with status and self-fashioning. Furthermore, by moving objects to Europe, they played an active role in representing foreign cultures to a wider Western public. Many major museum collections of Indian and Egyptian objects—so often assumed to be the product of institutional plunder and appropriation—actually owe their origins to the acutely personal tastes and ambitions of individuals profiled here.

Just telling their stories, then, is the central goal of this book. But like the little mirrors stitched into an embroidered Gujarati cloth, these stories reflect back many features of the larger world in which they are set. How does the big picture look—and how does it look different—when you start small? Next to, and through, these personal histories, I also consider how the broader trajectory of British imperialism in the East was a more complex and uncertain process than traditional narratives suggest. Here, too, the image of empire that comes into view may look unfamiliar.

There was a time when people recounted the rise of the British Empire as a triumphal progress: "heaven's command," a sure thing, and a good one.[4] Indeed, some still tell the imperial story in this way. Equally one-sided, though of an entirely opposing political cast, were the portrayals of empire by postcolonial nationalists, who represented the British Empire as an insidious behemoth. Neither of these attitudes earns unqualified support from serious scholars today. Yet there is still more than a hint of teleology in discussions of empire, a sense that the end was inevitable: the white man won, the burden was shouldered, the colonized shut out.[5] This book, by contrast, stresses the obstacles to Britain's imperial success. British expansion was hotly contested both by indigenous powers and by European rivals, notably France. It was also only questionably "British," since Britain depended heavily on continental Europeans, and increasingly on imperial subjects, for manpower and support. Seeing the cracks and insecurities in British power helps explain why and when the empire took the peculiar forms it did.[6]

Where most accounts of British expansion tend to say little about Britain's rivals and opponents, the overarching narrative offered here concerns the wider global context in which British power was forged, and challenged. First, the history of the British Empire must be understood together with the history of France and its empire—and specifically, as a history of

Anglo-French war. For the nearly six decades between the beginning of the Seven Years War in 1756 and the Battle of Waterloo in 1815, Britain and France fought for more than three. This was the eighteenth-century equivalent of modern "total war." In Britain, war with France dominated politics, finance, and culture.[7] In France, war with Britain had catastrophic consequences for the state, the economy, and ultimately the monarchy. It was also global war. Fought on multiple continents, in defense of imperial interests, it decisively affected the pace, motives, and direction of British and French imperial expansion. Even after Waterloo—when Britain's global hegemony reached its height—France continued to influence British imperial expansion and imperial desires. In the Ottoman Empire, coveted by both powers, France, if anything, seemed to have the upper hand. Even in India, where conventional wisdom holds that French ambitions died by the 1760s, some French policy makers harbored dreams of renewal, through allies in the Punjab. In short, to write the history of the British Empire without including France would be like writing about the United States during the cold war without mentioning the Soviet Union. France vitally influenced the shaping of the modern British Empire.

The second way my big picture of the British Empire differs from most rests in its emphasis on locations where British power was *informal* and in the making, rather than on sites that Britain openly conquered, occupied, and ruled. *Empire* is a flexible term, and interpreting it in a flexible way lets one understand the whole range of mechanisms by which European powers sought and built empires over time. Egypt did not officially join the British Empire until it was made a protectorate in 1914. Even India, considered the "jewel in the crown" of the British Empire by the late nineteenth century, was never entirely British. At the time of its independence, in 1947, a full third of the subcontinent was in the hands of nominally independent princes. And before 1857—for the whole period covered by this book—the parts of India that *were* "British" were ruled not by the British government directly but by the private East India Company, under partial parliamentary supervision.

Throughout this period, all of Egypt and much of India continued to be the preserve of long-established Eastern imperial rulers—the Ottomans and the Mughals. Though at times the Mughal and Ottoman régimes may have looked like window dressing to European empire, their persistence was significant for several reasons. It suggested, for one thing, just how much Britain, and to a certain extent France, derived its own imperial legitimacy from older, non-European reservoirs of power. It also meant, particularly in the case of India, that cultural fusions were embedded in the very workings of the imperial state, everywhere from legal systems and tax collection to rituals, ranks, and personnel. European powers inherited—and often purposely echoed—Mughal and Ottoman ways of ruling. Finally, as long as the Mughal and Ottoman figureheads endured, the game was not up between European powers, who continued to struggle among themselves for behind-the-scenes influence. In all these respects, British rule in Mughal and Ottoman domains took shape as something far less "British" and less formal than its later incarnations might suggest.

Over the century from 1750 to 1850, Britain "collected" an Eastern empire in India and beyond, beginning with Bengal and adding other domains from there. This is certainly not to say that there was no system, no grand narrative, to imperial expansion. Britain did not simply acquire its empire, as the Victorian historian J. R. Seeley famously remarked, "in a fit of absence of mind."[8] If anything, and as Seeley knew, it did so in a fit, many decades long, of war with France. But by characterizing British imperial expansion in this period as collecting writ large, I also want to suggest that it was more piecemeal, contingent, uncertain—and in many ways collaborative—than the familiar language of an "imperial project" would suggest.

Britain itself resembled an imperial collector in two important respects. Like the individual collectors described here, Britain was in some senses marginal. It was marginal to Mughal, Ottoman, and other indigenous régimes, whose material and technological resources rightly gave it pause and whose manpower easily outstripped its own. It was also, and certainly felt itself to be, marginal to other European rivals, chiefly France.

And, like other collectors, Britain used collecting to reinvent itself, to define its sense of imperial purpose. In 1750, the British Empire had been primarily Atlantic, colonial, and mercantile, bolstered by an ideology of Protestantism and liberty.[9] This was self-consciously different from the land empires of Catholic Europe, "the Orient," and even ancient Rome, which were widely critiqued as tyrannical, despotic, and autocratic.[10] Yet the empire Britain had come to possess by 1850 was just that: a transcontinental entity formed by conquest and entailing direct rule over millions of manifestly foreign subjects. What was more, many Britons—so skeptical of land empires only a few generations before—were proud of this. For if war against France had effectively won Britain a new empire, it had also consolidated a new understanding of what Britain stood for, both as a nation and an imperial power.[11] Early-nineteenth-century British liberals began to articulate a new political ideology that encompassed both nation and empire in a shared set of terms.[12] Liberal reforms ensured that by the time Queen Victoria ascended the throne, in 1837, her Catholic subjects could sit in Parliament; her indigent subjects could be fed and housed (albeit not pleasantly) at state expense; and her middle-class subjects, most of them for the first time, could vote. Crucially, with the abolition of slavery in 1833, no Briton would ever again legally own—or be—a slave.

The imperial ramifications of the liberal ideal were set out most clearly in a neo-Roman vision of a British imperium that would embrace all subjects in a fold of "British" rights. This was the note so ringingly sounded in 1850 by Lord Palmerston, Britain's Anglo-Irish, Scottish-educated, fluently multilingual, and outspokenly imperialist foreign secretary, when, leaping to the defense of an abused British imperial subject, he proclaimed: "As the Roman, in days of old, held himself free from indignity, when he could say *Civis Romanus sum;* so also a British subject, in whatever land he may be, shall feel confident that the watchful eye and the strong arm of England will protect him against injustice and wrong."[13] Who was the British subject in question? Don David Pacifico, a Portuguese Jew, born in Gibraltar (and thus British) and living in Greece.

There was more than a little political theater in this, to say nothing of self-righteousness. Nevertheless, Palmerston and his peers recognized a truth about imperial expansion that is easy to lose sight of now, when so much emphasis is placed on the ways in which the British Empire worked to exclude various others from an essentially white, male, Christian, empowered mainstream. Empires *include* people and cultures.[14] When their boundaries grow, no matter how rigid they become, they contain more within. Indeed the central challenge for nineteenth-century Britain to survive as an empire, and as a nation, was to find ways of accommodating difference, especially overseas. Of course there were paradoxes here. But imperial expansion, Britishness, and cross-cultural inclusion were joined at the hip—and however awkward, stumbling, and painful their progress, they hobbled along together.

This does not mean that the British (or any other) Empire was somehow immune from racism, repression, violence, or prejudice of all kinds. But the "white man's burden" attitude of the late nineteenth century should not be imposed over this earlier, denser, more complicated entangling of human experiences.[15] The chauvinistic ethos popularly associated with the British Empire did not *drive* imperial expansion in the East. On the contrary, it hardened only after Europeans had for generations accrued influence in Eastern domains. It hardened in the context of global Anglo-French war. And this imperial ethos was a misleading and inaccurate construction to boot, because British hegemony was never as total as its cheerleaders (or many of its critics today) tended to suggest. Indeed, to some extent the "white man's burden" was a piece of wishful thinking, a way of justifying and compensating for, with rhetorical and moral purpose, the fundamental vulnerabilities and contradictions embedded in British imperial rule.

I have organized my narrative of how Britain collected its Eastern empire into three chronological sections, moving from India to Egypt; they could loosely be considered to address places, powers, and personalities, in turn. The first third of the book describes in detail the sheer cosmopolitanism of late-eighteenth-century India, beginning with the East India Company's acquisition of Bengal, and the uphill struggle of its great generalissimo—and collector—Robert Clive, to make a place for himself in British society. It then visits the vibrant North Indian city of Lucknow, just beyond the bounds of Company control, which flourished as a haven for collectors and cultural chameleons of all kinds. The middle three chapters focus on a pivotal moment in British imperial collecting: the French invasion of Egypt in 1798 and the British capture of Seringapatam, in South India, in 1799. Though fought on different continents, and against two different Muslim opponents, these campaigns were in fact linked fronts in the same Anglo-French war. Together they marked a shift in British imperial policy toward one of active conquest, of "collecting" territory along India's frontiers and borders. In these years, Britain and France also became imperial collectors of objects as never before; notably, the campaigns yielded the first imperial trophies to go on public display in Britain. The last portion of the book traces collecting and empire in early-nineteenth-century Egypt, where ongoing Anglo-French rivalry for political influence was channeled into an open war to collect antiquities. Finally, I reflect on some of the ways in which, even in an age of more rigid cultural stratifications, collecting on imperial frontiers—by individuals and by the imperial state—continued to subvert, manipulate, and distort cultural boundaries to enduring effect.

So familiar is the late-nineteenth-century empire of crowns and trumpets (or, more accurately, pith helmets and bagpipes), of white church steeples among the palm trees, gin and tonics on club verandas, and rubicund Englishmen attended by bevies of native servants, that it is sometimes difficult to think back to an earlier period before the ideology of an imperial "civilizing mission" was in place. This book endeavors to do just that. It steps back into a time and into places where people lived, loved, fought, and identified themselves in ways considerably more complicated than later imperial chauvinism, or even many present-day treatments of empire, might suggest.

Most of all, this book is a plea for bringing a human dimension to imperial history, a topic that is often treated in the abstract, whether by sweeping chroniclers of conquest or by postcolonial critics of imperial discourse. These collectors and their world have vanished. But the objects they collected, moved, and brought together still tender proof of their passion. In Britain and its former colonies—indeed, around the world—the artifacts give hard evidence of the human contacts that underpinned the otherwise intangible quantities of globalization and empire. In no way do I wish to make an advertisement or an apology for empire, past, present, or future. But empires are a fact of world history. The important question for this book is not whether they are "good" or "bad," but what they do, whom they affect, and how. To the extent the history offered here seeks to reflect on a newer age of empire, it is to make an appeal for remembering the essential humanity of successful international relationships: for borrowing, learning, adapting, and giving. For collecting, and for recollecting.

PART ONE

# INDIA

1750–1799

CHAPTER ONE

# *Conquests*

## 1. War of the World

Most histories would begin the account of Britain, France, and their empires not in the East but in the West: in North America, where Britain's thirteen colonies and New France commanded the Atlantic seaboard, and where the two powers had been vying for dominance since the early 1600s. Their competition reached its climax in the middle of the eighteenth century, during the Seven Years War. The focus of their antagonism was access to the alluring expanse of land beyond the Pennsylvania frontier. With that struggle, Britain and France were effectively fighting for the future of North America: who would win the right to shape it, and whose empire would thrive. Perhaps this story should begin in the West, too, on the banks of the St. Lawrence River, in the summer of 1759, where the best-known eighteenth-century scene of Anglo-French imperial war unfolded—the battle of Quebec, whose set-piece quality brought recurrent patterns of British and French conflict vividly to life.

Since the declaration of war in 1756, British attempts to advance into New France had been frustrated. But in the early summer of 1759, a British offensive advanced into Canada along the lower St. Lawrence, arriving at the key French city of Quebec. All summer long the British lay camped by the river, besieging the heavily fortified town perched on the cliffs above. But the

French, secure in their position and numbers, remained implacable, while British attempts to attack the city from below were repulsed. In September, British commanders fixed on a plan to strike Quebec from above and so lure the enemy out to battle on the Plains of Abraham, to the north. It was a bold maneuver: the cliffs were steep, the city was strong, the British severely outnumbered. But now, three months into the siege, it was time for such a move. On the night of September 12, 1759, a silent flotilla of British boats crossed the perilous St. Lawrence River and landed nearly five thousand men, who scrabbled up the beetling cliffs in a thin red line.

With the sun rising in a low mist, the black, pungent smell of waterlogged soil, damp, but no more rain: it was as good a day as any for battle. Behind Quebec's thick stone walls, the sleepless French commander, the Marquis de Montcalm, had heard cannon fire in the night and knew that some sort of trouble was at hand. In the morning, he gathered his men and trooped out of the city to see what had happened. Perhaps the British had managed to squeeze a few hundred men up the cliff? Instead he confronted a stunning sight. There, not one mile ahead of him, stood the entire British force, thousands of redcoats like beacons in the mist. There was no choice but to attack. At ten o'clock, the French charged, only to be cut down, just forty paces from the British line, by a barrage of musket fire. Through the clearing smoke and chaos of bodies, the British began their counterattack; the French, confused and terrified, scattered before them. "They run; see how they run!" cried a British soldier. "Never was a rout more complete than that of our army," reported a Frenchman. At nine o'clock that very night, the French began to retreat from Quebec, leaving the city—and the keys to French Canada—in the hands of their British foes.

What had been months, even years, in the making, was over in a matter of hours. So were the lives of the French and British commanders. The Marquis de Montcalm took a ball in the torso late in the action, and was carried back to the town, bleeding profusely and saying, "It's nothing, it's nothing." Through the long night of retreat, he lay dying; his burial the next day, in the words of the historian Francis Parkman, "was the funeral of New France." Out on the Plains of Abraham, the young British general James Wolfe aimed to achieve a more glorious death. While he was leading the charge against the French lines, his wrist was shattered by a bullet; still he rushed, till two more hit him in the belly and the chest, and he fell to the ground. Some officers said that on the river crossing the previous night, Wolfe had been reciting Thomas Gray's "Elegy Written in a Country Churchyard." If so, one line would have particularly resonated: "The paths of glory lead but to the grave." As if on cue, Wolfe expired near the battlefield, while his men charged to victory around him.[1]

General Wolfe's victory at Quebec is one of the grand scenes of British imperial history, a rare individual battle that really did (seem to) turn the tables. And like so many acclaimed victories, its drama rested in part on a string of depressing defeats that had preceded it. Now, three years into the fighting, Britons finally had something to celebrate: voices were raised in hymns and prayers of thanksgiving, church bells rang, fireworks exploded. Wolfe's fatal heroism was applauded and retold in popular ballads, stage plays, published firsthand accounts, paintings and prints.[2] By far the most famous representation appeared a full decade later, however. *The Death of General Wolfe*, painted by an up-and-coming Pennsylvania-born artist called Benjamin West, was exhibited at the Royal Academy in the spring of 1771. Promptly reproduced in a bestselling etching, relentlessly emulated—and satirized—the painting became an instant icon of British art. Part of its appeal lay in an arresting immediacy: rarely if ever had a grand-manner history painting depicted its protagonists in modern dress rather than classical togas.[3] But more lay in its subject matter. This was the ultimate clash of civilizations. The Seven Years War is known in America as the French and Indian War, and those were the villains: effete French aristocrats, Jesuits, natives of blood-curdling savagery. Arrayed against them, in West's picture, stood the best of the British Empire: bluff John Bulls in their red coats, tartan-wrapped Scots,

Benjamin West, *The Death of General Wolfe*, 1771.

sturdy colonials from New England farms, and a pensive, statuesque Indian fresh from the Ontario woods. (The Indian, among other things, was a pure invention of West's; none fought with Wolfe.) This was the British Empire of the 1760s as it liked to be seen. No accident that it was painted by a colonial—and at a tense moment in Anglo-American relations, at that.

Thanks partly to its flattering misrepresentations, West's painting conveyed two key points about the Seven Years War: this was a war between Britain and France for imperial power, and a war that Britain triumphantly won. Yet the painting's enduring popularity takes attention away from what, in retrospect, may well have been the defining imperial battle of this defining imperial war. For while Wolfe at Quebec seized the imagination of his peers (and many since), it was a near-contemporaneous victory on the other side of the world that would ultimately have more effect on the shape of the British Empire. It had been won two years earlier, at Plassey, on the steamy banks of the River Hooghly, in Bengal. There, in 1757, East India Company troops under the command of Robert Clive defeated the nawab of Bengal and asserted military dominance in a territory larger than Britain itself.

Distant though it was from the European and North American flashpoints of the Seven Years War, and an Anglo-French battle only by proxy (the nawab was said to be cultivating French allies), the victory at Plassey set in train a series of events that affected Britain's global position as profoundly as the defeat of the French in Quebec. With the nawabs beaten and an East India Company puppet installed instead, the Mughal power structure in Bengal was decisively dislodged. The Company sealed its victory in 1765, when the emperor granted it the right to collect Bengal's valuable tax revenue, the *diwani*. From this point onward, the East India Company took on the functions of a state in addition to those of a merchant body. Soon it was India, not the thirteen colonies, that would claim the heart of the British Empire.

If one had to announce a time and place for the birth of the modern British Empire, then it would be in the far-flung contests of the Seven Years War. Many of the consequences of that conflict, such as a strengthening of British imperial patriotism, had long antecedents. And many of the changes wrought by the war were in some ways merely a prologue to the epochal upheavals of the Revolutionary-Napoleonic Wars to come. Nevertheless, the Seven Years War marked a watershed in the history of the British and French empires.

In territorial scope alone, the war surpassed previous conflicts. Since 1689, Britain and France had fought three long wars already, on the European continent and increasingly overseas. But this was the fiercest, most expensive, and most *expansive* war that Britain and France had waged to date. They clashed everywhere, from Montreal to Martinique, from the mouth of the Gambia in

West Africa to the sudden rock outcroppings of South India. And almost everywhere, Britain won. The scale of British victory surprised even the victors. The prime minister William Pitt the Elder, who trumpeted patriotism as his watchword, dubbed 1759 his annus mirabilis: in that year alone, Wolfe secured British dominance in Canada; the French navy was demolished and Britain won access to the Mediterranean; and at Minden, in Hanover, British forces helped score that most precious of feats, a decisive land victory over France. Less than a year later, Sir Eyre Coote continued to rout France in India with his victory at Wandewash, in the south. The Americas, the Continent, and India: it seemed as if the whole world was falling into British hands, and at France's expense.

But victory had its price. After peace was signed in the Treaty of Paris in 1763, Britain faced an empire that was larger, costlier, and more far flung than ever before. Manpower had to be found to defend it, manpower for which Britain regularly turned to its margins and colonies—Scotland, Ireland, America, and increasingly India. Money had to be found to pay for it, money that Britain also looked to its colonies to provide. The notorious Stamp Act, passed in 1765, imposed a tax on printed material in the thirteen colonies. In 1767 followed the Townshend Duties on various British imports in America, including tea, which had fast become a staple of imperial trade and of the Anglo-American palate. Britain could justify these duties in part as a way of asking the colonists to contribute to the costs of their own defense. To some colonists, however, the taxes seemed to be little better than the despotic measures of the Oriental tyrants in the empires of the East. If the Seven Years War won Britain a greater empire than ever, it also touched off the financial and political crises that would cause the thirteen colonies to break away not twenty years later.

The Seven Years War had a profound effect on Britain's imperial geography, winning Britain important footholds around the world but also fatally weakening its ability to rule the thirteen colonies. These changes in *where* Britain had its empire were accompanied by changes in the *kind* of empire it now possessed. Historians used to treat the American Revolution as a dividing line between two distinct eras of British imperial history: a "first" British empire that was Atlantic, colonial, and mercantile; and a "second" empire, based in Asia and characterized by conquest and direct rule. The opposition of these two misleads. For what the Seven Years War heralded was the emergence of a British Empire that could be both Atlantic *and* Asian, commercial *and* conquering. It marked the beginning of a modern British Empire that was global and land-based, one that needed enormous resources—human, economic, and cultural—to keep it going.[4]

The Seven Years War also had tremendous significance for the French empire—but not, as conventional wisdom would have it, simply by ringing its death knell. (Almost no historians write about the overseas French empire between 1763 and the invasion of Algeria in 1830.)[5] Indeed, though France lost the war, it pursued its ongoing struggle with Britain with renewed vigor. The ink was hardly dry on the peace treaty before Louis XV's shrewd chief minister, the Duc de Choiseul, began to prepare for the *guerre de revanche*. France reformed and modernized its army, and substantially increased the size of its navy—a navy that performed against Britain to devastating effect at Yorktown in 1781, precipitating Britain's surrender in the American Revolution. It built up its continental alliances, and its Caribbean commerce flourished. Finally, France turned its imperial eyes keenly toward the East. Choiseul and his successors actively researched the possibility of invading Egypt—the stepping-stone to India—and sent Admiral Bougainville scouting for new colonies in the Pacific, thus provoking Britain. Because French history is so often divided up by political régimes (the Ancien Régime, Napoleon's First Empire, the Restoration, and so on), continuities across periods often get neglected.[6] But if one looks at French imperial policy, a more unified picture emerges. Notably, some of Choiseul's undertakings would find echo under Napoleon a generation later. French imperialism did not die after the Seven Years War; it just changed its tune.

Rather than put an end to Anglo-French imperial rivalry, then, or tip the scales definitively in Britain's favor, the Seven Years War opened a new chapter in the history of both the British and French empires. It signified a turn toward territorial gain and, with it, direct rule over manifestly foreign subjects. It also, critically, marked a swing to the East as a site of imperial desire. From this point on, the history of British and French imperial rivalry would unfold there, and in India in particular. Over the course of the next century, British power dramatically expanded in India and steadily reached beyond it, to Egypt, China, Afghanistan. France dedicatedly worked to thwart British expansion in India and to build its own influence in the Middle East and North Africa, where by 1900 it would be the dominant European power. In short, the Seven Years War fueled an Anglo-French competition for Eastern empire that would burn on and explode, in India and Egypt, more than thirty years later.

So what did the British Empire look like viewed from the mango groves of Plassey, instead of from the Plains of Abraham? In many ways, rather different. Unlike Quebec, Plassey was not fought for the open conquest of territory, nor was it fought explicitly against the French. It was chiefly fought not by Crown troops but instead by the private army of the East India Company and its native Indian troops, or sepoys, in defense of commercial interests. And to stand in contrast to the youthfully gallant (if also neurotically self-absorbed) Wolfe of Quebec, Plassey cast into the public eye an altogether more complicated and more equivocal hero: Robert Clive, who, while hailed by some in Britain as the "heaven-born general," would also find himself, and the empire he represented, the target of public attack. The history of British imperial collecting in the East began with the battle of Plassey and with Robert Clive. For it was there that Britain began to collect its empire in India and began the process of its own imperial refashioning, from a mercantile, Atlantic-based, colonial power to a global territorial ruler and an imperial nation-state. It was also at Plassey that Robert Clive became British India's first major imperial collector, acquiring a vast personal fortune that he would use to transform himself into the greatest—and most reviled—potentate of Britain's emerging empire in the East.

## II. Trade to Conquest

The British presence in India actually had its formal beginning one hundred fifty years before the age of Clive, Plassey, and the Seven Years War. It dated back to the last day of the sixteenth century, when Queen Elizabeth I, by then a frail old woman with thick face paint and frizzed curls, granted a royal charter to the "Company of Merchants of London, Trading to the East Indies." It was among the final acts of her reign, and one of the most significant. The charter granted the East India Company, as it was known, the right to operate a monopoly of English trade with India and the spice islands of the East. In form, the East India Company was a joint-stock company, made up of investors who bought shares in trading ventures. There were many such companies, pursuing Britain's commerce with every corner of the globe: the Levant Company, the Muscovy Company, the Royal African Company, the Massachusetts Bay Company, and the South Sea Company—whose "bubble" burst in 1720, bringing the fortunes of thousands down with it. France and the Netherlands also conducted overseas trade through monopolistic companies of this kind. The Dutch East India Company (VOC) was founded in 1602; the French East India Company, which had been established by Colbert in 1664, was revamped and consolidated as the *Compagnie des Indes,* both East and West, by the brilliant Scottish financier John Law in 1719.

These were companies; their goal was profit. But securing profits in distant, unfamiliar, and potentially hostile domains required more than business acumen and willing investors. It called for diplomats and strong defenses. Winning a charter back home to trade was only the first step. Actually carrying on that trade meant winning partners and permissions overseas. In the Mughal and Ottoman empires, Europeans needed the consent of local authorities and merchants to establish trading outposts, or "factories." And since all the European companies were competing with one another for the same markets, their representatives constantly jockeyed for position with local rulers, plying them with gifts, promises, favors, and bribes. This was the experience of Britain's first ambassador to India, Sir Thomas Roe, who traveled to the court of the emperor Jehangir in 1615. When Roe raised the subject of trade and tax concessions for Britain with the emperor,

> He asked me what Presents we would bring him. I answered . . . that many Curiosities were to bee found in our Countrey of rare price and estimation. . . . He asked what kind of curiosities those were I mentioned, whether I meant Jewels and rich stones. I answered, No: that we did not thinke them fit Presents to send backe, which were brought first from these parts, whereof he was chiefe Lord . . . but that we sought to finde such things for his Majestie, as were rare here, and unseene, as excellent artifices in painting, carving, cutting, enamelling, figures in Brasse, Copper, or Stone, rich embroyderies, stuffes of Gold and Silver. He said it was very well: but that hee desired an English horse.

Unprepared for the emperor's wishes, Roe instead found himself outmaneuvered by the Portuguese, who gave Jehangir "Jewels, Ballests and Pearles with much disgrace to our English commoditie."[7] In 1618, however—a full three years after he first sought an audience—Roe's persistence was rewarded by an agreement with the emperor "for our reception and continuation in his domynyons."[8]

For the next century and more, the East India Company evolved into one of the most profitable, stable, and progressive corporate bodies in Britain. It was still very much a business: its charter, unlike those of the companies settling North America, did not invite it to establish colonies, nor, before the 1740s, had it begun to build a substantial army of Indian sepoys.[9] By 1750, the East India Company's factories stretched from Basra on the Persian Gulf to Bencoolen in Sumatra. The Company establishment in India centered on three coastal settlements, later the "presidency" towns, or regional capitals, of British India. On the west, or Malabar, coast was Bombay, which England received from Portugal in 1661 as part of the dowry of Charles II's bride, Catherine of Braganza. By that time, Madras on the east, or Coromandel, coast was a flourishing settlement of about forty thousand, with a fort and (from 1680) the first Anglican church in India, poised on a rise above the crashing breakers of the bay. Calcutta, later the most important of the three towns, was also the newest, founded in 1690 by the Company factor Job

Charnock at a swampy site eighty miles up the Hooghly from the Bay of Bengal. Charnock had chosen the spot, it was said, "for the sake of a large shaddy tree," a choice that confounded most, for "he could not have chosen a more unhealthful Place on all the River."[10] Mosquitoes buzzed insistently, miasmatic vapors thickened in the air, and the nullahs, slow, fetid canals, lay across the settlement like breeding grounds for disease. So many of those who went to eighteenth-century Calcutta died there that "it is become a saying that they live like Englishmen and die like rotten sheep."[11]

Against disease little could be done, but against armed opponents, there were more concrete forms of protection. Right from the start, the search for profit in the East was laced with violence. European traders defended themselves and their factories with gates, guards, and guns. In part, inspired by prudence as well as paranoia, they did it to protect themselves from the locals. In Egypt, for instance, incidental attacks on Europeans were so common—or at least so feared—that Europeans were advised (if not required) to wear Eastern dress. Throughout the cities of the Levant, Europeans (like Jews, Greeks, and Eastern Christians) lived in gated districts, known as Frankish quarters, at least partly for their own security. Reading the records of early French and British traders in Egypt, one turns up a steady stream of complaints about harrassment and *avanias*—"outrages"—incidents in which Ottoman officials levied extortionate duties or demanded bribes. In 1767, Ottoman authorities even seized the chief French dragoman (interpreter) on the Alexandria waterfront and imprisoned him on the charge that he was a renegade subject of the Sultan. After nearly a year of merciless captivity, chained up in the bowels of an Ottoman slave galley, the doomed dragoman died, "broken by suffering and worry," in the slave prison of Constantinople.[12]

But the chief goal of European defenses was to protect themselves from one another. Nowadays, "trade wars" are costly but generally bloodless. In the seventeenth and eighteenth centuries, they were not. Violent altercations, particularly with the Portuguese and the Dutch, pepper the early history of the East India Company.[13] An especially vivid incident of intra-European rivalry overseas occurred in Java in 1623, when the East India Company factory at Amboina was attacked by Dutch VOC soldiers and ten Englishmen were tortured and killed. Promptly dubbed a "massacre," and the subject of intense public outrage in Britain, the Amboina episode had the effect of turning English traders away from the spice islands—where Dutch power was now paramount—and concentrating them on the Indian subcontinent. By the mid-eighteenth century, Portugal and the Netherlands no longer posed a major military threat to the British in India. But a new and far more dangerous rival appeared on the subcontinent instead: France.

Alliances and conflicts between European powers cast a long shadow over the global expansion of European trade. In the late nineteenth century, at the height of the scramble for Africa, the German chancellor Bismarck memorably remarked that his map of Africa lay in Europe. A hundred years earlier, his maps of Asia and the Middle East would have been there instead. Wars in Europe triggered conflicts between factions of Europeans abroad, and overseas incidents between groups of Europeans could touch off conflicts on the Continent. At the same time, Europeans were enlisted and manipulated by local rulers. On the coasts of West Africa, for example, European slave traders involved themselves in struggles between regional powers, not least because African prisoners of war constituted a major source of slaves.[14] In North America, the famous tale of Captain John Smith's "rescue" from execution by the "Indian princess" Pocahontas was in fact probably a ritual ceremony staged by her father, the powerful chief of the Powhatan Indians, to co-opt the strange white newcomers as subordinate tributaries.[15]

The result was a complex map of loyalties, on which national, ethnic, and even religious groupings overlapped in curious ways. Who was friend and who was foe, and how could anyone tell the difference? Even the national labels of "French" or "British" were flexible categories at best, particularly when it came to accommodating Catholics and Protestants (respectively) of other nationalities. The East India Company army, like the British Crown army, relied heavily on continental European volunteers—at times drawing as much as half its strength from non-British nationals. The French East India Company was also a hybrid creation, chaired by a Scot and manned (like the French army) by a range of Europeans, including Scottish Jacobites and Irish Catholic "wild geese" who had flown across the Channel in search of opportunities denied them in Protestant Britain. The boundaries between ally and opponent were not, and could not be, defined exclusively in ethnic or racial terms. After all, as *The Death of General Wolfe* suggested, the native North American was a truer friend to Britain than the Frenchman.

Perhaps nowhere in the mid-eighteenth century did European and indigenous rivalries cross with greater consequence than in India. Much had changed since the days of Sir Thomas Roe, when the Mughal emperor commanded three-quarters of the subcontinent, bound together by a brilliant, effective system of revenue collection and military organization. Now the Mughal Empire was racked by invasions and civil war. In 1739 the Persian warlord Nadir Shah sacked Delhi, carrying the emperor's celebrated Peacock Throne away with him as a trophy. The emperor was also steadily losing control over his vassals. Where once he had had the power to appoint and remove regional governors—and to prevent them from amassing too much power for themselves—now many provinces were governed by essentially independent rulers, who turned their offices into hereditary positions and no longer regularly delivered their tax revenues to the emperor. In the 1720s, for example, the Persian Shiite military commander Safdar Jang took control of the province of Awadh and made it effectively a hereditary kingdom for his family. In Bengal, in the east, Nawab Alivardi Khan ruled as a virtually independent sovereign from 1740 to 1756. In the south, wars of succession in Hyderabad and Arcot split the old establishment and sucked neighboring rulers into the fray. From the west, the Marathas pushed into Mughal domains, capitalizing on imperial disarray. In short, the Mughal Empire was fragmenting, and eager hands reached in from all sides, grasping for the pieces.[16]

Among the powers bidding for influence in late Mughal India were the British and French East India Companies, each of which aimed to improve its position at the other's expense. The outbreak of Anglo-French war in 1739, coinciding with a succession crisis in the South Indian region of the Carnatic, gave both their chance. (Both also, for the first time, enlisted Indian sepoys to supplement their otherwise relatively small forces.) Under the visionary expansionist François Dupleix, the French captured Madras in late 1746. Ultimately, however, it was the British who prevailed when their ally Muhammad Ali Walajah succeeded in claiming the title of nawab of the Carnatic. (Madras was returned to Britain under the Treaty of Aix-la-Chapelle in 1748.) One of the commanders instrumental in Britain's victory was a young East India Company clerk turned soldier called Robert Clive. He was rewarded with a promotion to colonel. Dupleix, however, was recalled by Versailles in 1754. With him, some have said, disappeared French ambitions for a territorial empire in India—but, in fact, French influence in South India would simmer for decades to come.

While the battle for ascendancy between Britain and France raged in the south, a new obstacle to British trade appeared in Bengal to the north. From their capital at Murshidabad, the nawabs of Bengal presided over the richest province of the Mughal Empire. Cotton cloth, raw silk, saltpeter, sugar, indigo, and opium—the products of the region seemed inexhaustible, and all the European merchant companies set up factories to trade in them. Traveling downriver from Murshidabad was like traveling across a mixed-up map of Europe: there were the Portuguese at Hughli, the Dutch at Chinsura, the Danes at Serampore, the French at Chandernagore, and, of course, the British at Calcutta.

In April 1756, the venerable nawab Alivardi Khan died and was succeeded by his nephew and adopted son, Siraj ud-Daula, then about twenty years old. Siraj was described by a contemporary British historian as a "man of the most vicious propensities," suspicious, stubborn, and violent—toward the East India Company, at any rate, a central target of his animosity.[17] On coming to power, Siraj ud-Daula promptly requested cash gifts from the European trading companies (which was customary), and asked them to disarm themselves. The Dutch and French complied. The British, however, flagrantly refused to pay and continued to build up their establishment at Fort William, in Calcutta. Convinced that the Company was plotting against him, and determined to make it submit, Siraj marched on Calcutta within weeks of ascending the throne. He seized the little settlement in the space of one day. On the night of the capture, the nawab locked approximately one hundred fifty of Calcutta's European residents into the garrison dungeon, or "black hole," as such military prisons were often called. By morning, some sixty of them were dead, suffocated in the stifling, airless space. The incident, still remembered in Britain as "the Black Hole of Calcutta," quickly became one of the most emotive and sensational episodes in the history of British India. Company propagandists played up the tragedy as a way of justifying their employer's conquests in Bengal to a potentially critical British audience. But this defeat by an Indian ruler also served as a cautionary reminder of British (and European) weakness in the face of attack, and their sheer smallness of numbers.[18]

When news of Calcutta's fall reached Madras, nearly two months later, the Company promptly launched a punitive expedition. To command it, they appointed Colonel Robert Clive, recently returned from a short leave in Britain. At thirty-one, Clive was a tough, war-hardened veteran, to outward appearances all self-confidence and swagger; few could know that he was also prone to punishing bouts of depression and had attempted suicide twice. Clive and his force of about twelve hundred landed in Bengal in December 1756, just as word arrived that Britain and France were again, officially, at war. The news, long expected, injected new strength and purpose into Clive's mission. He was now there not only to reassert the East India Company's strength in Bengal and bring Siraj ud-Daula into line, but to try to eliminate the French, Britain's chief competitors for trade and influence, and the nawab's possible allies.

After a day of intense fighting, with high losses—another reminder that the balance of power was by no means in European favor—Clive retook Calcutta in early February.[19] He then moved upriver, to the French settlement of Chandernagore, capturing it in late March. This, too, was a tough fight, for the city was well fortified and Clive's men outnumbered; losses on both sides were heavy, and in return for their exertions, Company troops violently plundered the town. (Though "the Dutch [as usual] have secured all they could get," one officer snapped.)[20] Clive moved into the final phase of his campaign: to depose

Siraj ud-Daula and install a new, pro-British nawab in his stead. For some weeks Clive and the nawab traded letters and ultimatums; Company demands included the full restitution of trading privileges and the expulsion of the French. But by early June it was clear that a confrontation was at hand. The nawab joined his army at Plassey, south of Murshidabad, and on June 13, Clive's modest army of 3,000 men (2,100 of them sepoys), with just eight small cannon, set off north from Chandernagore to fight him.

They reached Plassey nine days later, on June 23, 1757. It was almost exactly a year after the fall of Calcutta, and—like the night of the Black Hole—a day of punishing heat, before the monsoons, when summer is at its most intense and the air is a thick, still fug. Clive had headquartered himself in a hunting lodge belonging to the nawab called Plassey House; most of his men camped in a nearby mango grove, hidden from view by the dark, waxy leaves and a high mudbank. One mile away lay Siraj ud-Daula's vast encampments. With him were thirty-five thousand infantry, fifteen thousand cavalry—many of them able, well-armed Pathans—and more than forty pieces of heavy artillery, superintended by a team of French experts.[21] The Company was outnumbered almost twenty to one, and severely outgunned. In terms of equipment and manpower, to say nothing of familiarity with the terrain, there was no contest.

Yet like so many of Britain's early Indian adventures, the battle of Plassey rested on a foundation of lies, spies, and betrayal. For, during his one year on the throne, Siraj ud-Daula had alienated not only the East India Company but many of his own subjects, particularly those who did business with the Company. A powerful contingent of bankers, merchants, and courtiers had joined forces with Company agents to oust the nawab. Bengal hummed with rumor and conspiracy. At the heart of the plots was one of Siraj's top commanders, a nobleman named Mir Jafar. Through a series of backroom maneuvers, the Company signed a treaty with Mir Jafar in which he agreed to grant the Company huge cash rewards and privileges in exchange for its assistance in toppling Siraj ud-Daula and installing him as nawab of Bengal instead. At the battle everyone now expected, Mir Jafar agreed to "stand neuter," if not to lead his troops away from the fight. In effect, Plassey was won before it was even fought.[22]

Early in the morning, the pounding from the nawab's heavy artillery began, with an attack on one portion of the Company line. Most of the Company soldiers huddled behind their mudbank, hoping to hold out till nightfall, when they could make a counterattack. Clive, standing on the roof of Plassey House, could see the great mass of the army he faced, commanders on elephants, resplendent formations of troops, brilliant tents, and the gaudy pennants and banners of war. He could hear the great and sustained firing of the guns, and watched nervously as they battered his tiny group of men. Yet he could see no sign from Mir Jafar. Had Clive been betrayed, too?

Then a sign arrived, unexpectedly, from above. It began to rain. The monsoons were coming—and coming to the Company's rescue. For as the rain pelted down, soaking the men (Clive, drenched to the skin, stepped inside Plassey House to change his clothes) and spilling off the trees around them, water saturated the enemy artillery: gunpowder turned to mush, the fuses into useless strings. The firing—so fatal just moments before—fizzled out. And through the rain, the soldiers in the mango grove watched their enemy dissolve. To the right Clive and his men saw a huge contingent of cavalry move down the river and away from the fighting; it was Mir Jafar leaving the scene of the battle, as promised. On the field ahead, the nawab's men began to scatter and flee. For six miles they were chased by Company soldiers, who scooped up abandoned cannon, equipment, and stores along the way. The next day, Mir Jafar met with Clive, then traveled straight on to Murshidabad, "took quiet possession of the Palace and Treasures and was immediately acknowledged Nabob."[23] Siraj ud-Daula, who had fled the city "disguised . . . in a mean dress, . . . attended only by his favourite concubine and . . . eunuch" was captured some days later and executed by Mir Jafar's men.[24]

The battle of Plassey was a setup, not a set piece. Quite unlike the battle of the Plains of Abraham, it does not make for very glorious retellings, nor did it at the time. Yet somewhere in that swamp of conspiracy, heat, and cannon fire in the mango grove, something new coalesced about the nature of the British presence in South Asia. It was not until 1765 that Clive would consolidate his victory in Bengal by gaining the *diwani* from the emperor, thereby putting the reins of Bengal government directly into the Company's hands. But there is a reason that 1757 serves as the conventional starting date for the history of "British India." It was at the battle of Plassey that the East India Company irrevocably and victoriously asserted itself as a military and ruling power in the Mughal domains.

Plassey's central significance for the Company was to marry territorial conquest and, from 1765, administration, to trade. But two further elements in the events of those months would remain part of the imperial landscape in India for decades to come. First, rivalry with France had acted as a spur and pretext for Company attack. It was rather beside the point whether the French threat to British interests was genuine or whether it had been exaggerated. What mattered was that Francophobia and Anglo-French war formed the framework within which Company expansion took place. The Seven Years War has often been seen as the end of France's bid for empire in India, but the specter of a French resurgence—fomenting in the courts of anti-British Indian princes—haunted British rhetoric and plans right into the nineteenth century.[25]

A second enduring feature of the events surrounding Plassey was that alliances and enmities cut across ethnic, cultural, and religious lines. The Company owed its victory to a partnership with Mir Jafar, the Jagat Seth banking family, and other Calcutta merchants.[26] Siraj ud-Daula's strength, in turn, depended in part on assistance from the French. Crying "collaborator" in such a sea of interest groups is meaningless. Indeed, in Bengal as well as in the raging conflicts of southern India, it was, if anything, the animosity between the British and the French (however malleable these groupings themselves were) that helped define who was friend and who was foe.

In the short term, Plassey was the making of East India Company Bengal. With the compliant Mir Jafar now installed as nawab, the region was fair game to Company profiteers. Calcutta boomed, quickly replacing Madras as the East India Company's social and political capital. Fort William, on the east bank of the River Hooghly, was rebuilt in brick, heavily moated, and studded with six hundred cannon.[27] In 1756, the old Fort William was manned with two hundred European troops; by 1765, the garrison was two men short of sixteen hundred.[28] Outside the fort's walls, the number of civilians grew so fast that house-building could barely keep up. The new town, as one visitor described it, was "so irregular that it looks as if all the houses had been thrown up in the air, and fallen down again by accident as they now stand."[29] Those who could afford it (and many could) began to carve out plots in the jungle south of town for the "garden houses" of their dreams.[30] From 1767, the many victims of Calcutta's climate found a shady enclosure of their own, in the Park Street Cemetery.

Fantastic wealth, tremendous opportunity, the seeds of a new colonial society: it was as if Plassey had brought the East India Company an empire overnight. But what were Britons to make of it all? In Bengal lay profit for many. Yet there also lay great and unknown responsibilities, in the hands of an untested, unsupervised, largely unregulated Company government. While some Britons welcomed the opportunities presented by the Company's conquest, others worried about its costs, its dangers, and, indeed, its morality. Whatever else, ruling Bengal was risky business. And nobody would appreciate both the rewards and the risks of this new empire more acutely than its conqueror himself: Robert Clive. For Plassey was also the making of Robert Clive—and he was determined to make it in Britain next. In India, Clive had committed himself to empire-building for the Company, but in Britain he used his Indian fortune to start building a vast material empire for himself.

## III. Clive of India, Clive of Britain

The life of Robert Clive lends itself to telling as a parable about the founding of empire. More biographies have been written about him than about any other figure in the history of British India, if not, indeed, the British Empire. In the formulation of the early Victorian historian Thomas Macaulay, Clive's history and the history of Company rule were effectively one and the same. "From his first visit to India," Macaulay wrote, when Clive scored major victories over France in the Carnatic, "dates the renown of the English arms in the East." "From Clive's second visit to India"—Plassey—"dates the political ascendancy of the English in that country." And "from Clive's third visit to India," Macaulay continued, when he received the grant of the *diwani*, "dates the purity of the administration of our Eastern empire."[31] This is the man known quite simply as "Clive of India," great man of empire par excellence.

But Clive had been dead more than sixty years by the time the ardently imperialist Macaulay wrote this 1840 appreciation. In his own day, Clive had also seemed to personify Britain's new Indian empire, but to considerably less welcome effect. Contemporary Britons saw Clive as the greatest in a growing band of "nabobs" (an Anglicized form of *nawab*) who were returning from Bengal flush with ill-gotten gains.[32] While the nabobs fattened themselves on Bengal's revenues, as many as one in three Bengalis may have starved to death in the famine of 1770—a terrible contrast that moved the architect Lancelot "Capability" Brown, seeing a chest of gold in Clive's house, to wonder "how the conscience of the criminal [Clive] could suffer him to sleep with such an object so near to his bedchamber."[33] Worst of all, the nabobs' "Indian" corruption threatened to infect Britain itself. In Pitt the Elder's resonant words, "The riches of Asia have been poured in upon us, and have brought with them not only Asiatic luxury, but Asiatic principles of government."[34] Corrupt, corrupting, maybe even criminal: both Robert Clive and the empire he helped to build were perceived by many Britons as dubious at best. And if Clive of India's overseas exploits offered a synopsis of the "rise" of British rule in Bengal, his career in Britain provided another, rather different perspective on the founding of Britain's Asian empire. This other Clive, Clive of Britain, is rarely profiled, yet it was perhaps his truer face, creased with the tensions and insecurities of early Company rule.

Robert Clive was the first imperial collector of British India. He had assumed that mantle in Bengal, in a metaphoric sense, by acquiring territory and resources for the East India Company. He had also collected a tremendous fortune for himself. Clive returned to Britain after the battle of Plassey, the socialite Horace Walpole sniffed, "all over estates and diamonds." Rumors of egg-size gems and chests of gold followed him through the capital.[35] In fact, "Mr. Clive," as his wife, Margaret, called him ("I am trying to break myself of calling him Colonel") had gotten £234,000 as a personal gift from Mir Jafar, as well as a valuable *jagir,* an annual pension of £27,000.[36] (*Jagirs* were land grants awarded to Mughal officers, who received the land revenue as salary.) Ten years later, by his own meticulous calculations, Clive was worth more than half a million pounds—the equivalent of some £40 million now.[37] It was the first, and possibly the greatest, rags-to-riches story of the British Empire.

But it was in Britain that Robert Clive became an imperial collector of a type that would obtain for collectors across contexts and through generations—as indeed for the East India Company and Britain itself. He turned to collecting as a way to reinvent himself. Like most of those who sought careers on imperial frontiers, and like most imperial collectors, Clive, the son of a Shropshire lawyer, was an outsider to metropolitan power structures. He was provincial, middle class, and nouveau riche. As a collector he set out to make up for all that. With his Indian fortune, Clive systematically bought all the trappings of a British aristocrat: property, political power, great houses, fine art, stylish furnishings. Though his collecting agenda ranged from the abstract (power) to the particular (Old Master paintings), every acquisition was made in quest of the same glittering prize: a British peerage, and the social and dynastic security that came with it. Clive had scoffed at receiving the mere Irish barony of Plassey in 1761, which did not bring him a seat in the House of Lords. He wanted to be "an English Earl with a Blue Ribbon, instead of an Irish peer (with the promise of a Red one)."[38] It was, as one of his intimates put it, "the only object you have in life."[39] To win social acceptance and political influence, to replace the nabob with a British aristocrat: these were Clive's goals as a collector.

Clive began his program in the notoriously dirty pursuit of political power. In Clive's day, well before the 1832 Reform Act, seats in Parliament were frequently filled by men with money, property, and connections. And though nabobs like Clive were singled out by critics for buying their way into Westminster, they were certainly not alone.[40] "Rotten boroughs," sometimes with just a handful of constituents, would elect members of Parliament who had been essentially handpicked by local grandees; votes were often effectively purchased. Clive had made his first foray into politics as early as 1754, by standing for election as a protégé of the Earl of Sandwich in the rotten Cornish borough of Mitchell.[41] After Plassey, Clive used his wealth to begin building up a parliamentary faction, or "party," of his own. In 1761, he was elected as member for Shrewsbury and also managed to get seats for his father, Richard, and for his close friend John Walsh; two years later, his cousin

George Clive was returned in a by-election. In 1768, he sponsored the election of three more close personal associates, thus making a parliamentary party of seven, which he maintained until his death.[42]

Clive needed a foot in Parliament (or fourteen feet, as the case may be) in order to secure his Indian interests in general, and specifically to prevent his enemies—of which he had many—from moving to block him from accepting his *jagir* payments from Mir Jafar, which they considered a kickback. But this Westminster fiefdom—a sort of human collection—was also tied up in Clive's perennial quest for a British peerage and a seat in the House of Lords. After the 1761 election, for example, he threw in his bloc of votes behind the Duke of Newcastle, a leading contender for prime minister, hoping to be rewarded for his loyalty with an earldom. Much to his chagrin, he received only the Irish peerage and the Order of the Bath. For the rest of his life, Clive remained convinced that by spending more money and cultivating more connections he could win the title he so craved.

The parliamentary seats were also related to another part of Clive's empire-building: his accumulation of land. Land was the absolute foundation of power and prestige in Britain at the time. Clive knew it; so did generations of "gentlemanly capitalists," who made fortunes in the City—often in imperial trade—and invested them in land.[43] Beginning in the mid-1750s, Clive began to stitch together a green quilt of property along the hills and ridges of his native Welsh borders, including the 6,000-acre estate of Walcot, which became the family's favorite rural retreat, and Oakly Park, which he bought from the Earl of Powis. To his tens of thousands of acres in the border country, Clive joined the splendid Surrey estate of Claremont, in 1769.[44] Many of these estates effectively controlled parliamentary seats: Walcot came with two seats for nearby Bishop's Castle; Oakly Park controlled the seat of Ludlow; another land purchase, Okehampton, brought Clive a seat in Devon.[45] But equally important, land bought status. Any reader of Jane Austen knows how precisely a man's social value might be measured by his acreage. One social benefit of Clive's purchases was to strengthen his relationship with the Earl of Powis, the leading peer of the borders region, and a political ally. First a patron, then a colleague and neighbor, the earl would posthumously become a relative of Clive's. In 1784, Clive's eldest son, Edward, married the earl's daughter, Henrietta; and *their* son would go on to inherit the Powis title and estates. Thus, in the space of three generations, the Clive family moved from rural English gentry to established peers of the realm, successfully marrying imperial money to noble blood. The strategy had worked.

Of course, there was not much point in having so much land if one didn't live on it in style. In London, the Clives established themselves in a handsome gray Palladian town house in up-and-coming Berkeley Square. They hired Britain's premier architect, Sir William Chambers, to renovate the London house and their country house at Walcot. In fashionable Bath, where Clive often retired to take the waters for his troubled digestion (one of India's less welcome gifts), he bought a grand mansion that had previously belonged to Pitt the Elder. But all these dwellings paled before Clive's grandest estate of all, Claremont, in Surrey. Clive had bought it from the Duchess of Newcastle for £25,000 (bargaining her down from an asking price of £45,000)—about £2 million in today's terms—and intended to make it his main country seat. (Had he received his coveted earldom, he would surely have taken the title Clive of Claremont.) Claremont truly was fit for a lord, with a distinguished house built in the reign of King George I, by Sir John Vanbrugh, and gardens laid out in the 1730s by the innovative William Kent.

But Clive's first act as owner of Claremont was to tear the whole thing down. The building, he thought, was too damp. He summoned Capability Brown, Britain's best landscape architect, to rebuild the property. A statement of work to be done in 1772 gives some impression of the degree of magnificence Clive sought:

> Principal Floor . . . with very neat Mahogany Sashes, Best Plate Glass, Silk Lines, inside Shutters double hung, the mouldings of which . . . to be richly Carved, the Architraves, Base and Surbase mouldings also to be enrich'd with Carving . . . the Doors to be made of fine vaner'd Mahogany with the Mouldings to the Pannels enriched, Best Mortice Locks with ornamental furniture with rich Frizes and Cornices over each, the Chimney Peices to be made of rich Marbles finely Carved, Statuary Slabs, Black Marble Covings, and back Slips, and bright steel hearths.

For the "Eating Room," Clive's plans were especially grand. He commissioned a set of four history paintings from Benjamin West, each one to commemorate a different scene of his Indian achievements. To be sure, such splendor came at a price. A 1774 invoice from Capability Brown "for building the New House and other Works done at Claremont" billed Clive for almost £37,000, and still the house was not done—nor would it be when Clive died later that year.[46]

As Claremont rose on its high foundation (to keep it above the damp), Clive turned his attention to a final area of acquisition. He began to collect fine art. Of all Clive's many purchases, his art collection most transparently attested to his desire to cultivate an aristocratic persona. By the mid-eighteenth century, Old Master paintings and classical antiquities had become de rigueur props for British gentlemen. Privileged young men would start collecting on the Grand Tour, the long ramble around Europe's cultural capitals that served as a sort of finishing school for the British male elite. The focal point of the Grand Tour was Rome, where the ancient and the Renaissance met. There, dozens of art dealers supplied "Grand Tourists" with everything they were expected to take home with them, from Mannerist paintings and Piranesi prints, to Etruscan pottery and Roman busts. Dozens more artists earned their livings by painting flattering Grand Tour portraits, the essential "I was there" record of the experience, in which Grand Tourists posed soulfully against backdrops of ruins, caressing antiquities in their hands.[47]

A Grand Tour had been well beyond the reach of young Robert Clive, who had had neither the money nor the leisure to pursue one. He would discover the art and culture of the Continent only later in life, though he made sure to send his son Edward on a Grand Tour at the appropriate age. By the time Clive became interested in art, however, the opportunities to collect it in London itself were greater than ever before. In the decade from 1765 to 1774, more than ten thousand paintings were brought into Britain from the Continent, almost double the number imported during the (admittedly war-torn) decade before.[48] A testament to, and encouragement of, the widening market for continental paintings in Britain came in 1766, with the founding of Christie's auction house. (Sotheby's had been founded in 1744 but chiefly sold books.) Between 1710 and 1760 there were perhaps five to ten art auctions per year in all of London. Throughout the later eighteenth century, Christie's alone held between half a dozen and a dozen major sales of European paintings annually.[49] Aristocrats, connoisseurs, and middling sorts alike came together in James Christie's "Great Room" to gape at and bid on canvases by Europe's most admired painters: Nicolas Poussin, Claude Lorraine, Sebastien Bourdon, Guido Reni, Salvator Rosa, Peter Paul Rubens, David Teniers.

Robert Clive knew nothing about paintings, but he knew that they were things he ought to own. As he freely confessed, he "was no Judge of the Value or Excellence of Pictures and . . . left the Choice and Price of Pictures to others who understood them. . . ." If paintings "fit for my Collection can be picked upon by Gentleman to be depended upon I have no Objection."[50] In 1771, Clive called in several experts to advise him: Benjamin West, a Scottish connoisseur named William Patoun, and possibly his cousin Charles, who was a painter himself.[51] Then, with the same blitzkrieg prodigality he invested in his lands, his houses, and his person (he ordered his shirts in batches of two hundred), Clive formed a major collection of Old Master paintings almost overnight.[52] The record of Clive's art purchases in the first half of 1771 alone is staggering. In February and March, he spent some £1,500 on paintings at Christie's, either attending auctions himself or appointing agents to buy for him.[53] In May, he contracted to buy at least six canvases for £3,500 from the courtier and dealer Sir James Wright. He planned to spend a further £2,500 on paintings Benjamin West had picked out for him in Brussels.[54] "You will think me picture mad," Clive wrote to his confidant Henry Strachey; he had bought some thirty paintings in four months.[55]

As these numbers suggest, Clive's purchases were not cheap. At a time when certainly no more than one in ten paintings sold at auction cost more than £40, two of the ten paintings Clive personally bought at Christie's in 1771 cost nearly that, and three others considerably more, notably a landscape by Salvator Rosa, "clear and beautiful, touched with great spirits and freedom, and one of the most transparent and brilliant that any where can be found," for which Clive paid almost £100.[56] Some of Clive's most treasured and valuable acquisitions, such as a pair of seascapes by Claude Joseph Vernet, set him back the stratospheric sum of £455 2s. 7d.[57] This was a drop in the bucket for a man whose total wealth in 1771 and 1772 ran to well over £600,000.[58] The real issue was what his extravagance showed the outside world. As a piece of pure, pricey conspicuous consumption, Clive's art collection delivered the strongest evidence yet of his social ambitions. Horace Walpole, always armed with a put-down, sneered at the "learned patrons of taste, the Czarina, Lord Clive, or some Nabob," who were completely ignorant about the real value of art.[59] (A fine comment coming from Walpole, considering that "the Czarina" Catherine the Great was soon to acquire most of his father Robert's Old Master collection, considered the finest in Britain, for the Hermitage in St. Petersburg.)[60] But to Clive, it was hardly of consequence whether or not he liked the art himself.[61] What mattered most was that his collection be admired by connoisseurs, and "seen to great advantage" at Berkeley Square or Claremont.[62]

Clive's Old Masters put the finishing touches on the aristocratic profile he had worked so hard to cultivate. As a collector of art, he acted out the role he had defined for himself by "collecting" parliamentary power, estates, and houses. Buying up intangible commodities such as these may not usually be characterized as "collecting" in the way that buying up paintings is. (Typically, accumulating power and property gets called empire-building instead.) But the motives—and the money—behind all Clive's various kinds of acquisitions were identical. His art collection simply captured in miniature his systematic collection of everything else that a British aristocrat should have, from status symbols to raw power. Call it a collection, call it an empire: it was effectively both, amassed in his search for a place among Britain's ruling elite.

What did this self-made creation, Clive of Britain, look like? Clive's aristocratic ambitions are captured in a little-known portrait, painted in 1764, shortly before he sailed to India for his third and final time. The portraitist was his cousin Charles Clive, an artist much less famous (and less talented) than the fashionable society painters Clive usually patronized. Nevertheless, the image Charles produced was every bit as flattering as Robert could have wished.[63] Clive stands out from the murky canvas in vivid scarlet, larger than life. (Scarlet, the hue of military uniforms, was definitely his color, and he had himself painted in uniform by some of Britain's leading artists, such as Thomas Gainsborough and Nathaniel Dance.) But this scarlet is no soldier's coat. It is the ruby velvet of a baron's robes, trimmed with ermine, cuffed with brocade, garlanded with gold braid. Nor is there any of Clive's usual military swagger. He poses instead with the mincing elegance of a nobleman. That is

Robert Clive, painted by his cousin Charles Clive in 1764.

because he *is* one, ennobled in 1761 as Baron Clive of Plassey. On the table next to him sits his coronet.

A further curious detail pulls together this image of aristocracy. Hanging over Clive's shoulder on the wall behind him is a profile of Mir Jafar, his Bengal ally. What accounts for this portrait within a portrait? Nothing is known about the circumstances in which this canvas was produced, but a letter from Clive's wife, Margaret, of February 1764—about the time the work must have been painted—suggests that it may actually have been intended for Mir Jafar, a "Present as a mark of our lasting Sense of his Favors."[64] (The exchange of portraits between rulers was a common means of cementing alliances.) Perhaps this picture was a celebration of a remarkable symbiosis. Clive made him, and he made Clive: nawab and baron, transcontinental peers.

Portraits are revealing documents of the sitter's self-image. This was Clive as he wanted people to see him: stately, prestigious, powerful, noble. The soldier is entirely absent; he has been absorbed into the aristocrat. But portraits are also often deceiving, and this was no exception. Clive's peerage was of course an Irish one, not the English one he craved, a slight he railed against to the end of his days. Furthermore, his association with Mir Jafar, far from crowning his achievements, cast a black shadow over them in the minds of many of his contemporaries. So if this painting broadcasts an image of Clive as he wished to be seen, it also contains allusions to the very sources of insecurity that propelled his refashioning in the first place. Would Clive of Britain be able to efface the darker image of that other empire-builder, Clive of India?

## IV. Empire Unmasked

Many of those sitting in the audience of the Theatre Royal Haymarket in the spring of 1772 might have recognized a quite different image of Clive in Samuel Foote's new satire, *The Nabob.* The play follows the adventures of Sir Matthew Mite, a nabob modeled on Robert Clive and his peers. Mite has returned from India glutted with wealth, and promptly tries to purchase the hand, and the status, of a neighboring baronet's daughter. In one scene alone, he and his henchmen plot ways to increase their influence in East India Company elections; scheme about forcing an aristocrat to sell Mite his ancestral estate; and plan to rig two parliamentary seats for the pointedly named borough of Bribe'em. Another scene features Mite's election to the Society of Antiquaries, a prestigious club of gentlemen connoisseurs, membership to which he has earned by presenting the society with a ludicrous assortment of artifacts, and delivering a learned discourse on Dick Whittington's cat. This is an unlovely character. Yet for all that Clive might have cringed at the caricature, he would have been forced to empathize with his alter ego's parting words: "Now-a-days, riches possess, at least, one magical power, that, being rightly dispensed, they closely conceal the source from whence they proceed."[65]

How successfully had Clive managed to "conceal" the dubious source of his own wealth, and assimilate himself into the British elite? In external respects, eminently so. By 1772, he was one of Britain's richest men and a leading landowner. He controlled seven parliamentary seats. He played a major role in East India Company affairs. He had been ennobled and decorated with the Order of the Bath, and he consorted with some of the wealthiest and most powerful figures in the land. He divided his time between three substantial and fashionable houses, and was in the midst of building himself a veritable palace. He owned valuable paintings appreciated by connoisseurs. He was a household name.

But he was also a notorious one. For as Foote's satire made clear, the more power and possessions Clive amassed, the more he seemed to embody everything that critics deplored about the East India Company and its Bengal empire: corrupt, unprincipled, unregulated, new. Clive became the focal point in a rising public outcry against Company rapacity. These challenges came to a head in 1772, when a parliamentary select committee was appointed to investigate the state of Company government in India. The inquiry was at one level a broad—and the first—appraisal of the Company's transformed position in Bengal. At another level, it was a direct challenge to Robert Clive himself and to the legitimacy of his Indian actions and fortune.

The inquiry led to the passing of the Regulating Act of 1773, the first attempt to bring East India Company government under a measure of parliamentary control. The act also established a central administration for India, in the form of a governor-general and council, to be based in Calcutta. It did not, however, put an end to the continued perceptions that the East India Company government was corrupt and unprincipled. Challenges to Company rule arose just as quickly as the Company's empire had, and would endure in some quarters just as long as the Company itself. The controversies of 1772–1773 foreshadowed the debates leading to the India Act of 1784, which established a formal supervisory body in Parliament to oversee East India Company affairs. Its ad hominem focus on Robert Clive also anticipated the theatrical attack on the East India Company empire that would unfold in 1788, with the impeachment trial of Warren Hastings, governor of Bengal.

Openly charged in Parliament by his enemies with having "illegally acquired the sum of £234,000 to the dishonour and detriment of the State," Clive found his mask of British gentility suddenly stripped away. He offered dramatic and moving testimony in his own defense: "Leave me my honour, take away my fortune," he cried on the last day of the debate, the tears welling up in his eyes.[66] His eloquence worked. He emerged from the ordeal with both his honor and his fortune more or less intact. In late 1773, he set off on a long trip to Italy, as if making up for the Grand Tour he had never had, avidly collecting art along the way. But though he had been exonerated by Parliament, the strain of the past year's events had taken its toll. The black clouds of depression began to thicken. His health deteriorated. The parliamentary inquiry led indirectly, many have said, to Clive's untimely death.

He did it, some morbidly supposed, with a penknife. Others suspected a pistol, which he had tried twice before, in his early days in Madras, before concluding that fate was saving him for a grander future. The likeliest truth, or at any rate the least gruesome, was an overdose of laudanum, which Clive regularly quaffed to soothe his tortured stomach. Whatever the means, the end was the end. After a lifelong battle with depression, Robert Clive committed suicide in his house at Berkeley Square on November 22, 1774. He was buried quickly, silently, and secretly, in an unmarked grave in the parish church of tiny Moreton Say, in Shropshire. The mourners were few.[67]

Clive's eldest son, Edward, studying in Geneva after his time at Eton, was not among them. "Ned" came of age four months later as the heir of one of Britain's richest men, and his inheritance was vast. There were all the estates and the political power that they conferred. There were the East India Company shares and the voice in Company administration those shares commanded. There were the several great houses—Claremont, still under construction, among them—and the quantities of art and fine furnishings that filled them. There was, of course, the title.

Among all the legacies that awaited the new Lord Clive when he returned to England from Geneva in 1777, there was one chest that had been specially set aside for him. In it, Edward found some of his father's personal effects and valuables: a gold watch and buttons, topaz shoe buckles, a broken agate snuffbox. The chest also contained two of Clive's dress swords and his complete costume as a Knight of the Bath, from its precious jeweled collar right down to the special ribbons for his shoes. Were these things—the props and furbelows of an English gentleman—the items Robert Clive had particularly wanted his son to have? But then Edward discovered the main contents of his father's memorial chest: "Indian Curiosities." Hundreds of them.[68]

Going through the container must have been like unpacking a treasure chest. There were turban ornaments, jeweled bands with spiked brooches set with emeralds and diamonds. There were gorgeous hookahs encrusted with brilliant enamels, their ornamental snakes wrapped with gold wire, mouthpieces studded with gems. These were only the most obviously valuable objects. They might well have been given to Clive by his rich and powerful Indian associates, in keeping with ritualized conventions of diplomatic gift-giving. (And not exclusively, as Clive's enemies would have charged, as shameless bribes.) Alongside these objects, Clive had also packed away various smaller accoutrements of his residence in India. Filigree boxes, silver bowls, golden scissors, betel-nutcrackers, ivory combs, brightly enameled bottles for rose water, and shallow jade bowls polished to a hard, glassy finish: the chest was stuffed full of the precious everyday objects of a privileged Mughal life. Unlike the ostentatiously splendid pieces, these were things Clive may very well have used and kept as personal effects. Somewhere in the chest, Edward even found his father's set of ivory playing cards, painted with fair-skinned princesses, and princes on elephant-back shooting tigers.

Then there were the weapons. Many European officers brought weapons back from India, not least because they had many opportunities to collect them. Besides, as a visit to any armory in the world will rapidly confirm, displaying an enemy's weapons involves no small share of triumphalism. But Europeans collecting Indian weapons were not moved to do so only out of imperial arrogance. They were *beautiful*, these things, elegantly and richly decorated. They were also often technically sophisticated, and appealing because of fascinating workmanship and unusual design. And they were exotic, or so Edward must have thought when lifting a scimitar out of the chest, with its cruel, enchanted blade inscribed with verses from the Koran. There were steel daggers curving out of shining hard-stone hilts. There were matchlocks with barrels a yard long, inlaid with silver. There were battle-axes and spears of a kind long gone from European battlefields in this age of cannon and musket.[69] All these things were foreign to Edward. But to Robert, their collector, they would have been as familiar as the sword he hung at his hip—perhaps the part of India's material culture that he, a soldier, would have known best.

In the chest of "Indian Curiosities," Edward discovered another side of his father's life, hidden as carefully as it was preserved. *Curiosities* was something of a misnomer. For these were not curiosities like the gifts Robert Clive had once delivered from the Mughal emperor to King George III, flashy diplomatic presents that would be seen and admired once, as exotic novelties, before being tossed into a storehouse and forgotten.[70] Nor were they curiosities like the miscellaneous objects, found and made, that filled up eighteenth-century cabinets of curiosities, token emblems of distant parts. These objects were the record of Robert Clive's Indian life: the things he had surrounded himself with, the things he had chosen to preserve as a collection. As Edward picked through the gifts, trophies, souvenirs, and ornaments that his father had so neatly kept for him, he handled the most intimate existing archive of Clive of India. Edward had never gone with Robert to India—they had lived in separate countries for nine years, and under the same roof for no more than five. In these objects, he was touching a father he barely knew.

Robert Clive devoted his life in Britain to concealing his questionable Indian career behind a British façade. Yet in death, his legacy to his son Edward served to emphasize just how entangled the Indian and British parts of his life had always been. Whether it was acquiring political power, estates, houses, or fine art, Clive used collecting to fashion his British persona as a plutocrat and a connoisseur. In this sense, he formed an emphatically British collection, consisting of objects and status symbols designed to win him a place in British elite society. Yet this was an inescapably Indian collection, too—at its most elementary, because it was bought with Indian money, but in inspiration also, because it was supposed to echo in Britain, as well as compensate for, the fame and power that Clive had earned in India. In his collections, as in so much else, Clive of India and Clive of Britain were one and the same.

Clive's own collecting project, to use his imperial fortune to refashion himself, distilled the larger process in which he had also played his part: the East India Company's acquisition of Indian resources, and attempt to shape a ruling image for itself. Robert Clive's death coincided with the end of the first chapter in Britain's Indian empire. The East India Company had begun to rule as well as trade; military and fiscal control were asserted; the seeds of British government were planted. Britons back home began to confront and come to terms with a new, and in many respects unwelcome, form of empire. This was no longer a principally Atlantic, maritime empire of settlement and trade. It now included large, populous territories in Asia, acquired by conquest. It took shape under the nominal aegis of an extant and legitimate indigenous power, the Mughal Empire. And it was enmeshed in global war and rivalry with France.

These were all to some extent the legacies of Robert Clive, overseas empire-builder. There would also be consequences of Clive's more personal legacies. In 1804, Edward Clive fulfilled his father's dearest ambition: he became an English earl. But there was to be another way in which Edward built on his father's foundations—and another place for the Clives in this book. In 1798, Edward traveled to India himself and served for five years as governor of Madras. There, he and his own family became Indian collectors, acquiring Indian art and artifacts with an enthusiasm and purpose that Robert had invested in European objects instead. When Edward came into his inheritance he had no intention, and still less desire, of following Robert to India. But could it be that as he looked through his father's Indian chest, the idea of going there first crossed his mind? Could it be that the end of one collector's vision contained the beginning of another's?

# CHAPTER TWO

# *Crossings*

## 1. Beyond the Frontier

In 1768, an East India Company officer took up his pen to sketch a panorama of Calcutta. It had been only eleven years since Plassey, and just three since the Company secured the Bengal *diwani*, but already Calcutta had all the bulk and bustle of an established, modern commercial town. Or at least so this Company officer's drawing—which extends to a full eight feet—aimed to suggest. Waterfront perspectives like this were popular in part because it was from the water that the engines of British trade and power were seen to best advantage: docks, customs houses, cargo ships, men-of-war, fortifications. At the left of the picture are the Kidderpore docks, primed to load and unload the East Indiamen, the Company's vessels, from their six-month voyages across the seas. Next comes Calcutta's growing municipal center, anchored by a row of Palladian buildings and the long, low wall of the old fort. Church steeples are not much in evidence (the only one here belongs to the Armenian Church), but behind the old fort one can just make out the obelisk commemorating the victims of the Black Hole, erected by the incident's most vocal survivor, John Zephaniah Holwell. Dominating the southern end of the city is the new Fort William, its stone points jutting over the Hooghly. This was the first major structure you would see approaching Calcutta by boat, and it was duly impressive—"reminding me of Valenciennes," one visitor wrote in 1771, "regular, majestic and commanding."[1] Rowboats and canoes skim over the water; great oceangoing ships stand gracefully at anchor. The Union Jack flies high. This is Calcutta as a merchant, a soldier, and a patriot would have liked to see it.

Detail of Antoine Polier's panorama of Calcutta, 1768.

All of these visual flatteries were definitely intended by the soldier-artist, Major Antoine Polier, who presented his handiwork to high-ranking patrons in the East India Company. Polier had good reason to celebrate the Company and its newest capital. He had sailed to Madras in the year of Plassey, joining the Company army as a lad of sixteen. His first years in India were spent at war, fighting under Clive in the triumphant campaign against the French in the south. In the meantime, Polier specialized as a military engineer. Promotion was swift. Transferred to Bengal in 1761, he soon found himself in charge of redesigning Fort William as a state-of-the-art military installation. His panorama, with the new fort dominating the scene, was effectively a piece of self-advertisement, and it worked. As the painter William Hodges cooed some years later, this "considerable fortress . . . superior to any in India . . . reflects great honour on the talents of the engineer—the ingenious Colonel Polier."[2] By 1766, Polier was chief engineer to the Bengal Army and a major, at the tender age of twenty-five.

In many respects, Antoine Polier's rapid ascent echoed the rising stature of the Company he served. But there was one crucial fact about him that did not fit the conventional image—as even he drew it—of an emerging "British" empire in India. For Polier himself was not British but rather Swiss, born in Lausanne into a family of Huguenot émigrés. Both his ancestry and his mother tongue were French. And though he had glided up the ranks thus far, his foreign birth and connections now became an obstacle in a way they had never been before. Pressure was mounting in the Company against non-British officers. In 1766, the same year Polier was promoted to major, the Company passed a decree that no foreign soldier could rise above that rank. Polier was only in his mid-twenties, and already it seemed his career was coming to an end. "I now despair ever of seeing merit or long Service, the allowed qualifications to a candidate for preferment," he would later complain.[3]

But elsewhere in India, opportunity beckoned. Across the native courts, from Mysore in the south to the Maratha kingdoms of the west, and in the Mughal provinces of Hyderabad and Awadh, European officers and technicians were in high demand: to design fortifications, develop arsenals, and drill troops able to rival those of the west. Compared with East India Company service, the pay was excellent, the lifestyle easy and permissive, the possibilities for personal advancement tremendous. If there was no future with the British Company, then Polier would seek one somewhere else. In 1773, he crossed the western frontier of Company-controlled Bengal and entered the province of Awadh, to work for its nawab, Shuja ud-Daula. For the next fifteen years Polier made his home in Lucknow, Awadh's capital, inserting himself into a large community of European expatriates and a thriving regional court. He would never be British again. In Lucknow, he earned a small fortune, prominent friends, and recognition in European and Mughal circles alike. He also formed a large manuscript collection that anchored him firmly in both communities. Polier was one of many who discovered in Lucknow the means and chance to collect and cross borders. His friends Claude Martin, Benoît de Boigne, and even the nawab of Awadh himself, Asaf ud-Daula—who ascended the throne vacated by his father, Shuja, in 1775—did the same. Their stories bring a remarkable and little-explored side of imperial culture into view.

By the time Antoine Polier moved to Awadh, British rule in India was taking root. In Bengal, the Company began to develop tools and institutions with which to govern its vast and unfamiliar new territory and subjects. To gather taxes, for instance, it needed data about population, agricultural production, and trade—to say nothing of knowledge of India's basic geography. In 1765 the first survey of India was undertaken by Major James Rennell; his map "Hindoostan," published in 1782, offered the European public its first coherent and detailed image of "India" as a geographical unit.[4] To defend and control its territory, the Company recruited more and more Indian sepoys, which meant that officers had to learn local languages and how to accommodate the needs and expectations of high-caste Hindu troops (its preferred constituency). Warren Hastings, governor-general of Bengal from 1773 to 1785, set efforts to "know" India at the center of his governing program. Where Robert Clive tried to live India down, Hastings and his peers made it their mission to lift India up, searching through its past for ways to guide its future. Wanting to rule India according to its "own" traditions, Hastings sponsored projects ranging from the translation of Persian histories and the Sanskrit *Bha-*

*gavat Gita*, to the compilation of Hindu and Muslim legal traditions; from supporting a madrasa (Muslim school) in Calcutta and the first Bengali printing press, to promoting exploratory missions to Tibet. Alongside these Company-funded Orientalist projects, "amateur" Orientalism flowered in Calcutta's Asiatic Society of Bengal, founded in 1784.

Meanwhile in Britain, a skeptical public was learning about and fitfully coming to accept this new kind of overseas dominion, so different from the settlement colonies of the Americas. The paranoia over nabobs had subsided. East India Company propagandists worked to foster an image of the Company as a benevolent, fair-minded ruler. The Company did have its critics, and always would. The most eloquent was Edmund Burke, who in 1788 would lead the charge to impeach Warren Hastings for corruption and abuse of power. Owing not least to Burke's intervention, the Hastings Trial (at least during the first of its seven years) would pose a higher-profile, more sweeping, and vastly more dramatic challenge to Company rule than the 1772–1773 Clive inquiry had done. But while Burke, and Whigs led by Charles James Fox, opposed the abuses of empire on moral grounds, they were mainly attacking Company "despotism"; the fact of British rule in Bengal was widely acknowledged and accepted. In the event, Fox's radical East India Bill of 1783—which would have brought the Company under full parliamentary control—failed; William Pitt's more moderate India Act of 1784 established a parliamentary Board of Control, which jointly supervised Indian government with the Company's Court of Directors. (Hastings, whose sad, distinguished figure in the dock had won him more sympathy than opprobrium, was acquitted by the House of Lords in 1795.)

This, then, was the "British India" that Robert Clive had helped to build: an *actual* empire of conquest and direct rule administered with a blend of rapacity and paternalism, and an *idea* of empire gradually being woven into British government and society. Yet there were two significant respects in which late-eighteenth-century India was far from British. The first lay with men like Antoine Polier: the thousands of non-British Europeans who lived and worked under the East India Company banner. Throughout the 1750s and 1760s, the East India Company army—like the British Crown army, and the armies of many other European powers—relied heavily on recruits from across Europe. In 1766, for instance, the year of the Company's decree on foreign promotions, only three in five white soldiers in the Madras army were actually English or Welsh. Continental European troops composed almost 15 percent of the army—more than the Irish (13 percent) or the Scots (11 percent). At the end of 1800, the ratios were still more pronounced: one in every five soldiers in the Madras army came from the Continent, while only half the army was English or Welsh. And if the Company's white soldiery was by no means fully British, neither was it uniformly Protestant. Though most of these continental troops hailed from the stalwart Protestant regions of the north—the Netherlands, the northern German states, and Scandinavia—large numbers of French and southern Europeans, combined with the Irish Catholics, made for a substantial Catholic presence.[5]

Even Calcutta, that most British of Indian cities, was a lot less British than images let on. Popular aquatints produced in the 1780s by the uncle-nephew team Thomas and William Daniell showed a polite and well-tended city, where swift phaetons flew over the streets as sepoys paraded past. But north of the wide avenues and clean white colonnades of the city center twisted the narrow lanes of Calcutta's Bengali districts, home to anywhere from one hundred thousand to four hundred thousand Bengalis.[6] Also outside the frame were the Armenian and "Portuguese" (often a synonym for mixed-race or Indian Catholics) quarters, each with long-established communities. (When Siraj ud-Daula marched on Calcutta in 1756, more Portuguese and Armenian militiamen were on hand to defend the city than regular European troops.)[7] And according to a "List of Inhabitants Residing in Calcutta," drawn up in 1766 for Clive, only 129 out of 231 European men—more than half—were formally British, that is, English, Welsh, or Scottish. Twenty were Irish, another twenty from German states, and the rest from virtually every corner of western Europe. They included discharged veterans, resettled émigrés from French Chandernagore, and a wide range of enterprising souls, such as John Richard, Calcutta's French pastry chef; John Davour, "Lord Clive's German musician"; and Laurens Orman, a Swede who lived in Calcutta from 1759 to "keep a Punch house with permission."[8] Probate records offer evidence that communities mixed: Bengalis, Armenians, Portuguese, Britons, and continental Europeans regularly encountered one another at estate sales and auctions.[9]

The other way in which "British India" was far from British lay in regions such as Awadh, in the areas under at best indirect control, beyond the frontiers of formal Company rule. Fifteen years after Plassey, British Indian towns remained coastal toeholds on the very edges of the Mughal Empire. Company territory consisted chiefly of Bengal, Madras, and Bombay—a triangle of significant possessions, yet together just a tiny fraction of a massive and contested land. The vast majority of the subcontinent remained in the hands of the Mughal nobility and other Indian rulers. The nawabs of Awadh and the nizams of Hyderabad governed the two largest and richest Mughal provinces—just to the west of Bengal and Madras, respectively, and thus just on the border of Company domains. Other important regional rulers included the confederacy of Maratha leaders in the west, and various independent rajas and sultans in the south, notably Haidar Ali and Tipu Sultan of Mysore. None of these states would fall into direct British control for decades to come; many never would.

Nor did many Britons want them to. Possessing Bengal certainly encouraged some top figures in the East India Company to acquire more. There were new commercial and strategic interests to protect, new desires to satisfy, new and neighboring territories to bring into line with Company ends. But old imperatives remained. The Mughal emperor still sat on his throne. It was probably beyond the Company's ability to topple him; it was definitely beyond its strategic and economic interests. The Company was still a company. It needed to turn a profit for its shareholders, as well as abide by its charter and the dictates of Parliament's Board of Control. Further costly armies, expensive conquests, and showy heroics were undesirable; to many, having to administer Bengal was bad enough.

This meant that the Company walked a fine line between trying to consolidate and extend its influence, and trying not to incur extra commitments and costs. It was a tension that nagged the Company right up to its demise in 1858. The best way around the problem was for the Company to pursue its ends behind the scenes: to develop an informal empire of influence and manipulation, rather than a formal empire of conquest and direct rule. Across the native courts of the subcontinent, a web of British residents, advisers, and spies worked to promote (and often shape) Company policy from within.[10] The Company also forced Indian rulers—particularly the nawab of Awadh and the nizam of Hyderabad—to take in large numbers of Company troops, ostensibly to defend their states from outside attack. In return, the rulers had the pleasure of footing the bill for the troops' expenses. Through this brilliant, nefarious system (known as the subsidiary alliance system), the Company was able to preserve the nominal autonomy of native states while embedding itself within them, and to increase the size of its army at low cost.

In the three decades after Clive left India, there was absolutely no doubt that British power was spreading across the subcontinent. The Company consolidated its rule in Bengal and pushed its influence outward into Awadh and other provinces. Nor was there any doubt that the social life and personnel of Company India was becoming in some sense more British, particularly in the army. The Company's 1766 decree indicated wariness about welcoming continental Europeans—with their suspect loyalties—into its officer corps. The composition of the ranks also shifted. Embarkation lists of Company troops sent to India during the years of the American Revolution indicate a strong and growing reliance on Irish manpower. Of the 1,683 soldiers sailing to India on Company ships in the 1778–1779 season, a full third were Irish; of the 777 soldiers embarked the following season, the Irish made up 38 percent; and in 1780–1781, Irishmen accounted for 45 percent of embarkees.[11] Though of course it would never be exclusively "British," the white soldiery of the East India Company would never be as mixed as in the days of Robert Clive.

But this was still a far cry from the raj of crowns and trumpets, and there was no way anybody could even anticipate it would become that. For the generation after Clive, "British India" remained more a concept than a fact. Who was to be included among the British and who was not was up for debate: where did continental Europeans such as Antoine Polier fit? What was British and what was not—how would one characterize zones of informal empire such as Awadh?—was similarly far from settled. This was an empire under cover and in the making, and it required a fabulous assortment of cultural fusions and illusions to hold it together. As long as the ruse of Mughal authority remained, so did the need for Company agents to learn and abide by, however imperfectly, its workings, rituals, and language. (The East India Company only stopped using Persian as an official language in 1835.) As long as large numbers of continental Europeans remained in India, either in Company or in native service, the Company remained anxious about where exactly those Europeans' loyalties lay. Was it with Britain? With native states? Or, worst of all, with France? Within the borders of Company territory, the lineaments of a British Empire in India might be taking discernible shape. But beyond the frontier, crossings and collaborations—between Europeans and non-Europeans, as well as between different kinds of Europeans—were a defining fact of life.

Nowhere in late-eighteenth-century India would one experience the pains and pleasures of life beyond the frontier more acutely than in Lucknow, capital of Awadh. Bengal's immediate neighbor, rich, large, and strategically significant, Awadh was a prime object of Company desire. Warren Hastings and his successors worked hard, and effectively, to turn the province into a puppet state. (Indeed, Hastings's behavior in Awadh ranked high among the charges at his impeachment.) Yet even as Awadh's political importance faded, Lucknow blazed into cultural prominence. Under the reign of the nawab Asaf ud-Daula, the city emerged as India's most cosmopolitan and dynamic center. Frontier regions have a way of attracting drifters, pioneers, and outcasts—people on the margins, people on the make. Lucknow's ranks swelled with figures such as Antoine Polier, who were lured by the prospect of the fame and fortune that eluded them elsewhere. It quickly became home to some of the eighteenth century's most unlikely "imperialists" and most remarkable profiles in self-fashioning.

Polier and his Lucknow peers were border crossers, social climbers, chameleons—and collectors. For it was as collectors and patrons of art that many Europeans in Lucknow cemented their newfound social positions. In Polier's case, collecting manuscripts put the final touch on his stunning double persona as gentleman Orientalist and Mughal nobleman. His best friend, Claude Martin, performed a more extravagant reinvention. A French-born officer who considered himself British and had lived and worked in Lucknow for twenty-five years, Martin amassed one of eighteenth-century India's greatest fortunes, and collections. In a staggering assemblage that rivaled those of the major European connoisseurs, Martin re-created an exquisite Enlightenment world in the heart of India. Lucknow even worked its transformative magic on the nawab of Awadh himself, Asaf ud-Daula. Asaf was universally reckoned a laughingstock as a ruler—if not worse, since it was during his reign that the Company established indirect rule. Yet as a collector and patron of art—European, as well as Asian—the nawab attained a stature and degree of autonomy he was otherwise denied.

These men's stories reveal, in wonderfully personal detail, what it was actually like to live in an expanding, changing world. From Calcutta, or from London, empire might have looked a bit like Antoine Polier's panorama: coastal outposts of ships, forts, and British flags. But from Lucknow, Polier's adopted home beyond the frontier, it all looked rather less ordered.

## II. Chameleon Capital

The modern history of Lucknow began in January 1775, when the young prince Asaf ud-Daula succeeded his father, Shuja ud-Daula, as the nawab of Awadh. Shuja had been a true warrior-king, the grandson of a noble Persian soldier who had worked his way up the Mughal ranks to claim control of the province. Shuja's reign had not been easy. All around him the Mughal Empire lay in disarray, racked by Afghan, Maratha, and now British incursions. As a vassal of the Mughal emperor, Shuja ud-Daula was expected to fight for Delhi; and fight he often did, leading an army he had built up with support from European advisers and technicians, Antoine Polier among them. At the same time, Shuja confronted the steady encroachment of his greedy and aggressive eastern neighbor, the East India Company in Bengal. In a showdown at Buxar, in Bihar, in 1764, Shuja ud-Daula, together with armies of the emperor and the nawab of Bengal, was defeated by the Company—a critical sign of the limits of Mughal power.

Pressed between empires, Mughal and British, Awadh needed a strongman and a strategist like Shuja at its head. Asaf ud-Daula was neither. Fat and dissolute, the prince seemed barely to have stirred from the banquet table when he was called to the throne. Asaf's first move as nawab was away from politics, which he disliked, and away from his mother, whom he despised. He summoned his chief steward, Murtaza Khan, promoted him to the highest offices in the state, and left him free to run the government. Asaf then paid off his father's retainers, packed up the old court at Faizabad, and moved west, to the small provincial town of Lucknow. There he settled into an abandoned old palace, far from his manipulative mother and the tiresome affairs of state.

It was hardly an auspicious beginning. In one fell swoop, Asaf had managed to antagonize his rich and powerful mother, Bahu Begum, alienate most of Awadh's nobility, turn the administration on its head, and shatter the autonomy so carefully cultivated by his father. The East India Company, quick to take advantage of the weak new ruler, "speedily initiated" the nawab "into their modus operandi."[12] Just months after coming to the throne, Asaf ud-Daula signed a devastating treaty that forced him to cede territory to the Company—and with it, some half of his revenue—and to pay a higher subsidy for Company troops. He was also asked to expel from Awadh all Europeans "unauthorized" by the Company, notably his father's continental military advisers—further indication of the Company's growing anxiety about the presence of non-British Europeans in India.[13] Trends that would continue throughout Asaf's twenty-two-year reign were established in its very first months. For the next two decades, his province would be split by bitter feuds between his mother's faction in Faizabad and the Lucknow court. It would be paralyzed by Company pressure on its borders, treasuries, and policies. And it would be ruled by a nawab who didn't much want to govern.

But Asaf ud-Daula's move to Lucknow signaled change for the better in one substantial way. He may not have cared about administration, but he adored the arts, and had plenty of money to indulge in them. And though as a ruler he was weighed down by Company demands, responsibilities to the emperor, and his father's legacies, Asaf ud-Daula enjoyed complete control, for once, over cultural matters. By establishing a new capital for himself, he could look to the great Mughal emperor Akbar as a model. As a young ruler, Akbar had abandoned Delhi, the capital of his ancestors, in favor of Agra and the new city of Fatehpur Sikri, where he assembled the very finest talents in the arts, sciences, philosophy, and letters. What Akbar had done for Fatehpur Sikri, Asaf now set out to do for Lucknow. With a stupendous program of monumental building, patronage, and court entertainments on a scale so lavish they put Orientalist fantasies to shame, Asaf ud-Daula transformed Lucknow into the new cultural capital of North India.

Asaf ud-Daula's Lucknow: the Asafi mosque from the roof of the Bara Imambara.

And it was a melting pot. Asaf ud-Daula was a Persian Shiite, ruling largely Hindu and Sunni Muslim subjects, and welcoming a fat payroll of Europeans into his service. Drawing on his Persian inheritance, he sponsored Shiite religious scholarship and festivals, and erected Lucknow's most important shrine, the Bara Imambara. He also actively patronized the arts and letters of Mughal India. Finally, and perhaps most visibly, he cultivated ties with Europeans that influenced everything from the food on his table to the design of his many palaces. The result was a city so vibrant and various that descriptions of it erupt with adjectives. Overripe, sophisticated, seedy, magnificent, voluptuous, glittering, wicked, melancholic, battered, cosmopolitan, faded, dynamic, bittersweet: Lucknow was all these things and more; a "curious and splendid city," in the later words of the British administrator Sir Henry Lawrence, where the sublime and the ridiculous folded into one.[14] Lucknow, in a word, was an experience. And you either loved it or hated it.

To the many Europeans and Indians who hated Lucknow, the city was debauched, corrupt, and extravagant. One needed only to look at Asaf ud-Daula for proof. The obese nawab, coiled and quivering with fat, positively oozed debauchery. As one French officer put it, disgusted by the "monstrously fat" young man, "one would never imagine in Europe that depravity could be taken so far. . . . [I]n no country of the world and in no history would one find examples of turpitude equal to those which this man daily presents to his court and capital."[15] Asaf's marriage, it was said, had never been consummated. He moved from wine to hashish to opium; from women to boys and back again (said some; others insisted he was impotent); from chickens fed on musk and saffron to gleaming pilaus where each grain of rice was dyed a different jewel tone.[16] He may merely have been conventionally self-indulgent, rather than criminally voluptuous. (And a fitting contemporary for Britain's famously gluttonous Prince of Wales, the future George IV, another disempowered royal and patron of the arts.) But to those on the lookout for signs of Awadh's decline and fall, encountering the debauched nawab was omen enough.

"There must be much that is 'rotten in the state,' whose chief city, the residence of the sovereign, presents such an appearance," declared one British visitor.[17] You could see signs of corruption just by walking down the street: poor people shoved into swilling gutters while persons of privilege lumbered past on caparisoned elephants. The court was rife with nepotism; royal favorites fed on state offices like vampire bats. "There was no low or low-minded class, barbers, green-grocers, butchers, mule-vendors, elephant-drivers, sweepers, and tanners," hissed another critic, the embittered Awadh nobleman Muhammad Faiz Bakhsh, "but some of them rose to opulence and rode proudly through the market-places in fringed palankeens, on elephants with silver litters, or on state horses."[18] Still worse, as far as the British were concerned, was the worry that this corruption could be catching. It infected them, too. Even Warren Hastings—who was impeached in part for his extortions in Awadh—was appalled: "Lucknow was the sink of Iniquity. . . . It was the school of Rapacity. . . . What will you think of Men receiving the Wages of Service from the Nabob, and disclaiming his Right to Command it; and what of a City filled with as many independent and absolute Sovereignties as there are Englishmen in it?"[19] Thus European and Asian voices joined in deploring the corrupt capital, where British civil servants were "orientalized" and the Indian ruling classes shamelessly aped the West.

In short, Lucknow seemed to be awash in extravagance and excess. The fact that half of Asaf ud-Daula's revenue was sucked up in payments to the East India Company only made his profligacy look worse. He spent money everywhere: on his eight hundred elephants (in days when a decent elephant cost £500) and his thousand horses ("kept merely to look at," as he was too fat to ride them); on his hunts, gargantuan processions a thousand animals long, weighed down with everything from his mistresses to ice blocks for his drinking water. He spent money on his wardrobe, banquets, dances, and cockfights. He spent money on his army—of servants, that is, to trim his mustache, snuff out his candles, and feed his pigeons.[20] He spent money on his art collection—so much, some estimated, as to rival all his other expenses combined. And he spent money on his city. The nawab's "building mania," ranted another Awadh notable, Abu Talib Khan, cost the state coffers some £100,000 per year. To make matters worse, hundreds of poor townspeople would be evicted every time a palace went up; and yet the nawab generally abandoned his new palaces after spending just a few days in them. Even noblemen suffered in a display-obsessed court culture that forced them, "on the principle of 'like master, like man,' " into a bankrupting contest of conspicuous consumption.[21]

Debauched, corrupt, extravagant, to contemporary critics Lucknow seemed to be "the true image of despotism," a city of sin of almost biblical proportions.[22] And yet alongside this image, there gleamed a picture of the city equally vivid, if strikingly different. As ardently as some abhorred Lucknow, others adored it. Their beloved city was a place of perfumed orange groves and cool marble palaces, eloquent conversation, and exquisite banquets accompanied by the thrum of sitars. Their Lucknow was refined, dynamic, and generous.

To achieve perfect refinement in all things seemed to be the city's collective ambition. Even ordinary pastimes were raised to the level of high art. Sporting pigeons, trained and flown in flocks of up to nine hundred, were carefully plucked and then painstakingly "re-feathered" with multicolored plumes. Kites were fashioned into human form and lit up inside with lanterns, to ghostly effect.[23] Animal fighting, another favorite hobby, reached such a "pitch of perfection"—according to Lucknow's greatest rhapsodist, the late-nineteenth-century writer Abdul Halim Sharar—that meek, spindle-legged stags were set against one another, just so spectators could admire how elegantly they fought. It was claimed that in Lucknow even everyday Urdu speech had been raised to its highest degree of perfection. "The masses and uneducated people" were said to "speak better Urdu than many poets . . . of other places," and outsiders were too intimidated to open their mouths. In the celebrated salons of Lucknow's noblewomen and courtesans, conversation flowed with such grace "it seemed as though 'flowers were dropping from their lips.' "[24]

Lucknow was buzzingly dynamic. In a self-conscious effort to echo the lost glory of Akbar's India, Asaf ud-Daula patronized writers, musicians, artists, craftsmen, and scholars on an imperial scale. Leading Urdu poets such as Mir Taqi Mir fled the crumbling Mughal capital and came to Lucknow instead, where they developed a distinctive style and school of poetry.[25] Modern Urdu prose literature originated in Lucknow, and Persian, the language of status and learning, flourished. As a seat of Shiite scholarship, Lucknow rivaled the religious centers of Iran and eastern Iraq.[26] It also attracted European artists: the well-known London painters Johan Zoffany and Ozias Humphry each spent several years there, drawn by the promise of lucrative commissions from the nawab. Across the arts, a "Lucknow style" emerged—a style defined by hybridity. Urdu writers blended different traditions so seamlessly that it was often impossible to tell whether they were native Persian or Hindustani speakers, Muslim or Hindu.[27] European artists influenced local painters. Lucknow's architecture—much of it designed by the nawab's European employees—fused European and Indian elements.[28]

Refined and dynamic, Lucknow was also marked by the nawab's tremendous generosity. Maybe generosity is just profligacy by another name. Still, even Asaf ud-Daula's harshest critics conceded that there was some virtue in his most extravagant building project, the Bara Imambara. This shrine to the imams Hassan and Hussein was Asaf's most important architectural legacy (and, incidentally, his only building not influenced by European models). It was a massive undertaking: one Englishman (albeit one given to rash estimates) put the cost at a million pounds.[29] But it was also a massive piece of public welfare. Started during the crippling famine of 1783–1784, the project employed perhaps as many as forty thousand people, and paid them with food.[30] It was even said that the nawab had pieces of the structure torn down every night, in order to prolong the undertaking. Apocryphal though this story may be, it was just one of the many tales of Asaf ud-Daula's generosity to work its way into poetry and folklore. According to the poet Mir Taqi Mir, "the great Asaf" was "renowned . . . for his generosity and benevolence."[31] "All his natural faults were effaced under the cover of his generosity," wrote Abdul Halim Sharar. "In the opinion of the public he appeared not as a dissolute ruler, but as a selfless and saintly guardian."[32] More than a hundred years after Asaf's death, Lucknow shopkeepers were still remembering his generosity every morning, opening their stores with the couplet: "If one does not get from God, he receives from Asaf ud-Daula."[33]

Debauched, corrupt, and extravagant? Or refined, dynamic, and generous? Which was the real Lucknow? Indeed, the leading historian of the city asks, "Given the weight of all these foreign elements, can the 'real' Lucknow be said to have existed at all?"[34] Yes. It lay in the combination of all of them at once. Whether one loved it or hated it, the defining fact was inescapable: Lucknow was the most cosmopolitan city in India. Not only was its population diverse; diversity was a way of life. Hindus and Muslims shared state positions, celebrated each other's holidays, borrowed from each other's literary and artistic traditions. Europeans caroused and hunted with the nawab, and talked, traded, and intermarried with his subjects. For people of all backgrounds—and from social margins everywhere—Lucknow held out the promise of reinvention in its cosmopolitan embrace.

Johan Zoffany, *Colonel Mordaunt's Cock Match*, 1784–86.

This mixed society is captured in glorious Technicolor by Johan Zoffany's *Colonel Mordaunt's Cock Match,* painted between 1784 and 1786 for Warren Hastings, and later copied for Asaf ud-Daula. Bustling, populous, energetic, the composition was an unusual one for Zoffany, who had made his name in Britain as a painter of elegant conversation pieces and staged theatrical scenes. Indeed if anything, its microscopic detail and flat perspective lend it the feel of a Mughal miniature—a style Zoffany certainly knew and just might have been echoing.

At first glance, the painting plainly seems to illustrate a world of luxury, lassitude, pleasure, and indulgence.[35] This is an image, above all, of the *exotic:* of Europeans "going native" and of decadent Asians, of lush temptations and shameless self-indulgence. But it is easy to forget, looking at the picture today, just how *familiar* it all would have been to the people who appear in it (most of whom are identifiable historical figures). They were not merely playing at being exotic. Around the time this was painted, in fact, Colonel Mordaunt's cockfights—to say nothing of banquets, festivals, weddings, and many other occasions where Europeans and Asians came together—were practically weekly events. Of course artistic license is at work here, and the scene is not without violence, or divisions, or barriers. Nevertheless, the painting exposes the genuinely multicultural possibilities of Lucknow. Who you were, with whom you associated, and how you wanted to live were not either-or choices. You could bridge the boundaries.[36]

And many of the people shown in the painting did. Antoine Polier is not in attendance, but his best friend, Claude Martin, is, sitting on the sofa in his East India Company uniform. A Frenchman and, like Polier, an outsider to the Company hierarchy, Martin was Lucknow's premier self-made man, transforming himself there into a British country gentleman and connoisseur. Or consider the two central figures. Mordaunt, standing tall in virginal white underclothes, was the bastard son of the Earl of Peterborough, and traveled to India to get away from social stigma at home. Asaf ud-Daula, for his part, was impotent and heirless, as well as politically disempowered, and thus especially concerned with finding posterity by alternate means, such as cultural patronage. It is a crude joke—this cock match between the illegitimate and the impotent—but also an astute comment on two men who both came to Lucknow to escape the social margins. As, in his own way, had Zoffany. Austrian by birth and British by adoption, he arrived in Lucknow to find fortune after losing the support of his patroness, Queen Charlotte. Snubbed by British royals, he showed himself, at the top of the painting, sheltered by a green umbrella: a traditional Indian emblem of royalty.

*Colonel Mordaunt's Cock Match* is a splendid snapshot of a working world at play. But perhaps the fullest picture of Asaf's Lucknow in its heyday emerges, instead, from the scrawled sepia entries in a young Englishwoman's diary. Beginning on January 1, 1787, and continuing into October 1789, the diary of Elizabeth Plowden is a rare and wonderful document: a young mother's unpublished account of living, traveling, and rearing children in Calcutta and Lucknow. Elizabeth Plowden had first stayed in Lucknow as a new bride in the late 1770s, when her husband, Richard Chicheley Plowden, was serving alongside Mordaunt in Asaf ud-Daula's bodyguard. In 1781, the Plowdens moved to Calcutta, leaving Lucknow, like many Europeans, with an outstanding debt from the nawab. Richard waited in vain to be paid. And money was tight. With seven children born in almost as many years, the Plowdens barely had enough money to send the eldest back to Britain for school, let alone to return themselves (in the style they would want to, that is). Elizabeth even had to ask her mother "to be an Economist," "to buy nothing for the House," and to stay with friends until their fortunes revived.[37] In late 1787, the Plowdens went back to Lucknow with their two youngest children—baby William, just a few months old, and toddler Trevor Chicheley—in a last-ditch effort to get their £3,000 from the nawab. They stayed on for a year.

"Miss Brown and myself with the Gentlemen went to Col Mordaunts Cockfight," Elizabeth scribbled in her diary on June 15, 1788. "The Nabob [was] there, we dined with him at a little after 9. He did not keep the fast of Remyan [Ramadan] but eat [*sic*] very heartily," she noted, and "ask'd me a great many questions about my little ones and said William could not be flesh and blood, he was certainly form'd of Wax and Cotton." Attending blood sports, feasting on curries, chatting with kings, and nursing an infant in between: it was not how most Englishwomen spent an evening. But to read Elizabeth's Lucknow diary is to discover just how ordinary such seemingly extraordinary cultural mixtures were. All the pillars of Lucknow society were her old friends—Asaf ud-Daula, Antoine Polier, Claude Martin, and many others—and she was quickly swept up into a whirl of social engagements, across the lines of East and West. Often she brought her children with her, always a sure way of winning Indian hospitality. Asaf ud-Daula doted on them and gave them toys; the emperor's son, visiting Lucknow, "helped little Chichely to tea asked his name and took a great deal of notice of him." Zoffany, for his part, "declared he would like to paint them both without any regard he was so taken with them."[38]

In Calcutta, Elizabeth Plowden's social life had revolved around the city's Western-style entertainments: plays, masquerades, balls, carriage rides. In Lucknow, she walked into a quite different world. There were days she passed in the company of European friends around town, or in her friends' country houses nearby. On others, she breakfasted or dined with the nawab and his courtiers. She might steal a few hours between engagements to study Persian or Hindustani with her *munshi* (teacher). But her greatest passion was for Indian music. Whenever Elizabeth heard appealing Persian or Hindustani airs, she made sure to get copies of them for her substantial collection of sheet music—a process that in itself involved cross-cultural communication on several levels. At the nawab's one morning,

> the Entertainment as usual Notching [dancing] I desired them to sing the song of 'Jo Shamshere Serey Allum Decktey.' His Excellency told us the Poetry of this song was his own composition. As I had not a correct copy I sent Mirza Golam Hossein to request permission of sending my Monshy to the Nawab's Ostand [*ustaad*] for a Copy. The Nawab said he would repeat the words to the Mirza who would write them down if I pleas'd.[39]

She also learned to sing many Hindustani songs, and entertained her Indian and European friends by performing them, often to the accompaniment of a harpsichord given to her by Claude Martin. All told, it was a glorious and relaxing year: of nibbling on "Grapes Pomegranates Oranges dates Pistachio Nuts and other dry fruits" while watching elephant fights and fireworks in the nawab's perfumed gardens; of seeing a palace at night, lit up for Muharram "with Glass Lustres Wreathes of Silver and Gold flowers and colour'd Lamps," as black-clad mourners chanted in memory of the martyred imams; of spending afternoons with friends, sifting through Indian miniatures and the latest prints from Britain, or quiet evenings at home, with a nautch (dance performance) after dinner.[40]

Obviously there were limits to how deeply Elizabeth ever could—or would want to—immerse herself in Indian society. But in a small and remarkable way, she was invited into it. In June 1788, Asaf ud-Daula presented her with a unique testament to their friendship: a Mughal sanad (deed of grant) awarding her the title of begum (queen or noblewoman).

> We have conferred upon Sophia Elizabeth Plowden, who is specially gifted with exceptional devotedness, and rare fidelity, high titles and honourable address: She is the 'Bilkis' of her age and the Begam among the nobility and the aristocracy, with high distinction and exalted fame among her peers and contemporaries.[41]

European men's receiving Mughal titles, generally in recognition of military service, was not unheard of, but the granting of such a distinction to a European woman—particularly when her husband was not especially high-placed—was unusual to say the least. It is hard to know what prompted it, but the text remains an intriguing artifact of a city shaped by cultural crossing.

Richard Plowden was also fortunate: he got his money. (Unlike many. Poor Ozias Humphry spent years hounding the nawab for his money, and pestering friends in Britain to help him, to no avail.)[42] In late 1788, the Plowdens left Lucknow for good, and returned to Britain in 1790, where they set themselves up in style in London's Devonshire Place. They left warm memories behind. "I never passed More happy day in my Life but when you was in Lucknow," Claude Martin wrote to Elizabeth in his broken English, eight years after their last meeting:

> Those happy days, I never Can forget, your Company Enlivened the place tho there was many other family in the place, your lively and amiable Manner attracted Every body to your home, Your house was My Magnet. I never visited so much, as I did to you, we have had many Good Lady here, but none that I wisited with so real pleasure as I did you.[43]

Nor did the Plowdens forget India. Little William and Trevor, along with all their brothers, went on to have careers in India; and there would be Plowdens in India for generations to come.

A shimmering cosmopolis beyond the frontier, Lucknow offered Europeans and Asians alike terrific chances to make money and spend it, to cross cultural lines, and to become self-made in all senses of the word. They were living out the Lucknow dream—of fame, fortune, and self-fashioning. Even for Elizabeth Plowden, the middle-class wife of a middle-ranking Company soldier, Lucknow was a site of reinvention: she arrived as Mrs. Richard Plowden, and she left a begum, formally ennobled by order of the Mughal emperor. She also left with her music collection, thickened with offerings from European and Indian friends. A full participant in Lucknow's cosmopolitan high society, Elizabeth Plowden straddled cultural lines to a degree she had not, or could not, in Calcutta. For her male friends in Lucknow, such possibilities were greater still. And for three in particular—Antoine Polier, Claude Martin, and the nawab himself—the Lucknow dream became real in the most extravagant, unexpected of ways. It is to them, to further tales of collecting and cultural crossing, that the story now turns.

## III. Orientalists?

You could find yet another sign of Lucknow's cultural preeminence by visiting the city's bazaars. Thread your way into the narrow lanes of the chowk—among vendors toting giant trays of sweets, mangoes, and coconut wedges, past the flower stalls laced with garlands of jasmine and marigold—and you would find the Orient for sale. In the spice market, there were cones of magical colored powders and sacks of Persian cashews, East Indian cloves, obscure roots and aromatic barks; in the jewelers' shops, pearls and Golconda diamonds, emeralds from the New World mines, lapis lazuli from the snowy reaches of Afghanistan. There were kite-makers and metalworkers, potters and tobacconists; cloth merchants selling bolts of fabric woven stiff with gold *zari;* and stalls where the celebrated Lucknow embroiderers sat bunched over yards of muslin, their intricate designs taking shape under a blur of moving hands. The perfumers could sell you another local favorite, pure attar of roses, or mix any scent you liked from the mysterious essences that lined their shelves.

It was in these bustling bazaars that you might also buy fine art and rare texts. Here, dealers did a lively trade in manuscripts, calligraphy, and paintings old and new. To sift through the paintings on sale would be like looking into fantasy worlds, where skies were celadon, skins were blue, and peacocks sat on parapets in the moonlight. The dealer would turn them over to read the price, marked in a coded script, called *raqam,* that only he and his colleagues could decipher. Forty rupees, one hundred rupees. Two pounds, five pounds. A mere trifle compared with the finest illuminated manuscripts, licked onto paper with brushes no thicker than a single hair, every page bordered by a network of flowers and birds. Those could cost a thousand pounds.[44] In the bazaars you could also buy individual specimens from Lucknow's famous calligraphers, in flowing swirls and scoops of nastaliq script. But a single *letter* in the hand of the best of them, Hafiz Nur Ullah, would cost you one rupee (two shillings), so the text had better be short.[45]

Lucknow was the art capital of India, a Rome of the East. The reason for its thriving trade was sad but simple. In Delhi and the Mughal heartlands, the old aristocracy was in terminal decline. Their lands ravaged and their incomes no longer secure, many were reduced to selling off their family heirlooms—libraries and art collections included. In Lucknow, though, there was a nouveau riche elite ready and able to buy. Dealers, calligraphers, and artists left Delhi to find a better market among Lucknow's new consumers. Manuscripts and paintings were prized in Mughal India in much the way that libraries, antiquities, and Old Master paintings were valued in contemporary Europe.

So it made good sense that Asaf ud-Daula and his courtiers—many of them, like him, relative newcomers to affluence and power—should wish to buy the trappings of the Mughal nobility. As collectors and patrons, they were doing in Awadh just what Robert Clive had done in Britain: buying cultural capital to bolster their social positions.

And many Europeans in Lucknow followed suit. Antoine Polier was probably the most vigorous manuscript collector; others included Nathaniel Middleton, East India Company resident from 1777 to 1779; John Wombwell, appointed paymaster to the Company troops in 1782; and Richard Johnson, who lived in Lucknow as head assistant to the resident from 1780 to 1782. Johnson collected about as avidly as Polier, and his collection, preserved almost intact today in the British Library, attests to the range—and sheer beauty—of items circulating in the Lucknow art market. He bought many of his books in the bazaar; some of them still have prices marked in *raqam.* (In fact, since owners often stamped manuscripts with their seals—the Indo-Persian equivalent of a bookplate—it is sometimes possible to reconstruct the movements of a single manuscript over a period of several hundred years.) Johnson was also an active patron. During his two years in Lucknow he commissioned more than two hundred fifty paintings, including five complete *ragamala* series, which illustrate Indian musical modes. Johnson's commissions to poets and writers included works not just in Persian—India's premier literary language—but also in Urdu, which was rapidly gaining literary stature, thanks not least to the support of Asaf and his court.[46]

What drew Europeans into this rarefied world? Plain curiosity, to some extent. They had come of age in Enlightenment Europe, and many approached India with a broad interest in the human and natural sciences. They were Orientalists in the traditional sense of the word: amateur students of Indian history, languages, religion, music, medicine, or whatever else their intellectual predilections steered them toward. Of course, Orientalism has come to mean something quite different since Edward Said's pathbreaking book of that title. By no means a mere pastime, Said argued, Orientalism was bound up in the pursuit of imperial power. Gathering knowledge about the Orient was a prerequisite, and sometimes a substitute, for gaining authority over it. Legal codes, maps, political intelligence, population statistics, history books, religious texts—all of these helped imperial rulers infiltrate the cultures they confronted, and devise ways of governing them. By collecting knowledge, the East India Company really was collecting an empire.

Warren Hastings was a prime specimen of the Orientalist in both the contemporary and the postcolonial senses of the term. Wellborn and well educated, steeped in the classics, tending toward deism, and convinced of the intrinsic merits of ancient cultures, Hastings was a dedicated and accomplished student of the Orient. He knew Urdu and Persian, took an interest in Sanskrit and in Hindu doctrine, and, not coincidentally, collected manuscripts. Not for show alone was he invited to become the first president of the Asiatic Society; and though he graciously deferred the honor to Sir William Jones, he gladly accepted the title of patron instead. But as governor of Bengal, Hastings also harnessed scholarship to imperial rule. A good case in point was his patronage of Nathaniel Halhed, whose *A Code of Gentoo Laws* (1776) came to serve as a foundation for Company-administered Hindu courts. The aim was to rule India by its own laws, but the effect was to impose a British interpretation of what those laws were, to split Bengal's (and later India's) population into rigid categories, to essentialize cultural difference, and to sow the seeds of religious communal division.[47]

Antoine Polier and the other Lucknow collectors were Orientalists in both senses too, devoted students of Indian culture as well as agents embedded in the workings of imperial expansion. While Hastings, however, was born a gentleman and became a governor, Polier and his friends stood closer to the margins of social and political power. Orientalism, for them, included a powerful dose of frank self-interest. Sentimental aesthetes these men were not. They were hardheaded careerists on the make. (Not for nothing was Richard Johnson's nickname "Rupee"—more, it must be said, for his talent at making rupees for others than for earning them for himself.) And as a trip to the bazaar would quickly show, collecting seriously was a very expensive business. This was certainly not just a hobby. But neither was it part of a job, or a wider program of imperial rule. Collecting was a personal, social investment. And for Polier, its rewards were of two striking, and dramatically distinct, kinds.

The Janus-faced profile of Lucknow Orientalism is beautifully captured by two portraits of Antoine Polier at home. The first, by Johan Zoffany, offers a fine glimpse of the erudite society that flourished among Lucknow's European residents. Painted in 1786, shortly before Polier left Lucknow, the canvas shows *Colonel Polier and His Friends*—Claude Martin, John Wombwell, and Zoffany himself—relaxing one cool morning at Polierganj, Polier's Lucknow house. Martin eagerly leans behind Wombwell to point out a detail in a watercolor of the Lucknow house he had designed for himself some years earlier. Zoffany is painting away at his easel. And Polier, looking over some of his beloved Indian manuscripts on the table beside him, has just been distracted by his gardeners, who are bringing in the morning produce for his inspection. Legs splayed, belly protruding from his uniform jacket, Polier surveys the fruit of his land with proprietorial care. Cabbages, onions, mangoes, papayas,

Johan Zoffany, *Colonel Polier and His Friends*, 1786.

tomatoes, bananas: his eye roams; his hand dangles loosely from its long lace cuff; and he points, delicately, at his choice. This, Zoffany seems to say, is a true lord of the manor. And a nabob from the neck up; with his drooping mustache, sagging jowls, and fur hat, Polier looks uncannily like his employers, the nawabs.

Altogether, the picture resembles the British conversation pieces for which Zoffany was known (if, that is, one can look past the turbaned Indian servants, the scampering monkey, and the huge branch of bananas on the floor). Like those paintings, which often posed families in front of their rolling, well-tended acres, this picture celebrates comfort, comradeship, property. Polier lived richly and well. Nudged out of Company service in Bengal, he had found lucrative employment in Awadh as a military engineer under Shuja and then Asaf ud-Daula. He even received, in 1782, a courtesy appointment as brevet colonel from the East India Company (though with the stipulation that he not serve in any corps). He had rank. He had land, the critical indicator of social status. And, of course, he had a collection.

The painting also pays tribute to gentlemanly erudition, a theme Zoffany had addressed some years earlier in a well-known picture of the leading antiquarian Charles Townley. Antoine Polier was definitely an Orientalist. Not long after this painting was finished, Elizabeth Plowden "saw a very curious collection of all 3 Gods which Col. Polier has procured paintings of," and noted that "he has also inform'd himself of their history which he has an idea of putting in some persons hands for publication. It will be a very curious and interesting compilation and is to be embellished with prints from the ninety he has in his possession."[48] Polier had been studying Hindu texts with the aid of his pandit (teacher) Ram Chand, and did eventually commission a book on Hinduism. (Ram Chand was Sikh, not Hindu, but he "had two Brahmins always attached to his suite, whom he consulted on difficult points.")[49] Polier also contributed to Europe's "Oriental Renaissance" by sending the first full copy of the Sanskrit Vedas (ancient sacred Hindu texts) back to Europe.[50]

Polier's intellectual interest in Indian religion was not altogether surprising given that one of his uncles, a leading Protestant theologian in Lausanne, was a correspondent of Voltaire's and a contributor to the *Encyclopédie;* at least two of the same uncle's daughters, Polier's cousins, would follow their father into the world of letters. And there was an obvious respect in which collecting opened doors for Polier. Shut out from Company hierarchies because of his foreign (Swiss) birth, Polier could use collecting and connoisseurship as an alternate way up the ladders of India's European society. He had the same pandit as the illustrious Orientalist Sir William Jones, whose discovery that Sanskrit shared a common parent with Greek and Latin (Indo-European) helped to raise the stature and status of Indic studies in the west. Polier's taste for rare Asian manuscripts brought him close to Warren Hastings. He was on friendly terms with both men, and cannily sent them gifts of "fine Oriental writings"—"as a small token," he told Hastings, "of my gratitude and regard."[51] It also could not hurt that he was a friend and patron of Zoffany. Polier must have been delighted to be voted a member of the Asiatic Society of Bengal just two weeks after its founding.[52]

But there was another way in which Polier's collection was a social investment, a form of self-fashioning. This second face of Lucknow Orientalism comes to life in a strikingly different image of Polier relaxing at home, a 1780 miniature by the Lucknow painter Mihr Chand. It is evening now, and out on the verandah Polier rests against the plump cushions of a yellow settee. A pair of dancers performs for him, accompanied by four musicians. The warm, low light of glass lanterns turns the dancers' bodies into elastic shadows beneath their violet and crimson skirts. The sky behind them is alive with fireworks and whorls of ocher smoke. Polier, though, is not distracted. He nurses his hookah and studies the dance. His crisp muslin robes are edged with heavy golden embroidery, his scarlet turban banded with a jeweled *sarpesh* and spiked with a bristling black feather ornament. His face is the plump, serene profile of a Mughal nobleman.[53]

Mihr Chand's miniature is an exact parallel to Zoffany's painting: a celebration of Polier's gentility. It is also, if anything, more accurate. Polier may have studied Hindu scriptures and Sanskrit, and traded manuscripts with his European friends. But he led his everyday life in Lucknow, in Persian, with his two Indian wives, a daughter, and two sons. His Persian name, given to him by Emperor Shah Alam, was Arsalan-i Jang (Lion of Battle). His *jagir* (revenue-producing land grant) was near Aligarh. He was a Mughal nobleman.

The details of Polier's life in Awadh appear with marvelous intimacy in the pages of his surviving Persian letters, the *I'jaz-i Arsalani*, bound into letterbooks according to a Persian literary convention.[54] They lead the reader into a world where personal relationships across cultural lines not only were a part of professional life in India, or even (as they had been for Elizabeth Plowden) after-hours sociability, but also infused every aspect of private affairs. Many of the letters gathered here were fired off to a wide network of Indian agents (Hindu, Muslim, and Christian), all across Awadh and Bengal. On Polier's instructions, these men would buy and sell for him everything from guns, elephants, and steel, to opium, oranges, gold lace, and dried fruits. While Polier was on campaign with the nawab in the winter of 1774, his agent Mir Muhammad Azim sent him such essentials as tobacco, wine, paper, and ink, while in the meantime getting his mirrors polished, supervising the embroidery of a tent and an elephant canopy ("the embroiderer is a bastard," Polier wrote, "please be strict with him and have it sent soon"), searching out sugar candy "of high quality, oil free and crystal clear," and traveling to Faizabad bearing hookahs, shawls, and birdcages for Polier's household, and a bag of toys for his young son.[55]

Mihr Chand, portrait of Antoine Polier, 1780.

These agents also supplied him with various items for his collection. "I have learnt that a boat full of books and other papers and a *wilayati* chariot with musical instruments for me have gone astray towards Chunar," he complained to two deputies from Calcutta. "As soon as you receive this letter, send a *harkara* [messenger] to bring this boat from there to Faizabad. Unload it and keep my things in place."[56] Some months later, he wrote to thank another agent for sending a copy of the famous Persian poem the *Gulistan* and a fresh batch of pictures—as well as some chutney and mango pickle. "I relished the [chutney and pickle]," he said, "and enjoyed reading the book and going through the album. You write that there are other good pictures in Murshidabad. I would like to have a look at them on my arrival there." In place of the rather formal officer of Zoffany's painting, one can just imagine Polier lounging around in his long muslin *jama*, nibbling on pickles and Indian snacks, while thumbing through the pages of his latest Persian book.[57] One can imagine also, reading Polier's letters to Mihr Chand, a little of what it may have been like to work for him. "I fail to understand why you are sitting idle," Polier chastised Mihr in one letter. "Prepare some more similar portraits if you have finished the ones you were engaged with so far. This . . . is your work, and it is meaningless to sit idle." On another occasion he ordered Mihr to "prepare a draft of the painting of the dance. I will see the draft when I come back and then you can finalize it as per my instructions."[58] Could this be the very painting that still survives?

The *I'jaz* also recorded deeply personal matters. Polier had two Muslim wives, about whom little is known beyond their names, Bibi Jawahar and Bibi Khwurd. (Even here there is some disagreement: Claude Martin referred to them as Jugnu and Zinat.) But in his letters to them, and to his household steward, Lal Khan, it is possible to peer into a cross-cultural domestic ménage of a kind not often opened to view. There was nothing at all unusual about a European man living with one or more Indian mistresses, or *bibis*, during this period. (The best-known relationships involved men, and often women, of high rank; but these were merely the most visible.) It was also not considered particularly scandalous. Even Elizabeth Plowden—a white Englishwoman, whom one might expect to be "protected" from knowledge of such things—knew about Polier's half-Indian family and visited his children at Claude Martin's house. While she was in Lucknow, another of her friends and his *bibi* had a baby girl; Elizabeth went to see them, too, pronouncing the baby "the fairest and smallest Child I ever saw born of an Hindostauny Woman."[59] (Tragically, the infant died two days later.) These relationships were a normal feature of European society in India right up until the late eighteenth century, especially in Lucknow and Hyderabad, outside the more segregated society of the presidency towns.[60]

Later generations responded to interracial liaisons with such horror—and tried so vigorously to cover up their traces—that it is still often difficult to get a sense of these families as living, breathing, feeling groups. But Polier's letters nicely animate his own domestic sphere. On learning that Bibi Khwurd, the younger of the two women, had been suffering a difficult pregnancy, Polier instantly wrote to Lal Khan to insist that she have constant attendance, fresh clothes, and a clean room. Bibi Jawahar got a sound scolding for not telling him about her co-wife's discomfort. "Your welfare is linked to hers. I therefore write to you to remind you that it is your responsibility to take care of her. Make sincere efforts to please her. I will be delighted if she is comfortable and if I hear anything contrary to this I will keep her separately. Since I love you," he concluded, "I am happy that you have now made up [with her]. Rest assured that I am fond of you, and forget the heart-burn."[61] Tension between the wives lingered for some months but evaporated when Bibi Khwurd had her baby: a girl.

Polier was a devoted father, constantly concerned about the health and well-being of his children. When they were ill, he called not on Lucknow's European doctor, William Blane, but on local hakims who practiced traditional *yunani* medicine. While he was away on business trips, he sent his children a regular stream of small gifts, sweetmeats, and paternal instructions. "My dear son," he wrote to his eldest boy, Anthony,

> it is necessary that you go for horse riding and for strolls in the garden to enjoy the greenery and the beautiful flowers. You should visit Captain Martin two to three times a day without fail. Sit with him for some time and introduce yourself to whoever comes there so that you get used to interacting with people. It is not proper to stay indoors for long. This is a must.[62]

It is plain from this letter that Polier wanted his son to become familiar with European society and learn to move in it; he may well have hoped to send Anthony into the East India Company army, a common career choice at the time for officers' half-Indian sons. And yet, of course, it was not in English that Polier and his son corresponded, but in Persian, their family language.

Looked at full on, Antoine Polier's two faces blend into an extraordinary hybrid: the image of a man who had managed to make it in both European and Mughal society at the same time. As a collector and patron of Indian art—a practice valued in both cultures—he scored a double coup. Some would argue that imperial collecting of any kind is fundamentally an acquisition of power. Maybe so. But with Polier, as with Robert Clive and many of Polier's Lucknow peers, this was power of a very personal kind. A Swiss-born foreigner in Indian service, Polier was not an "imperialist" like Governor Warren Hastings. It was specifically because he was *excluded* from the East India Company hierarchy that he needed to find a different way in, other routes to fame and fortune. Orientalism wove Polier into an elite group of Europeans in India, and underscored his position among them as a man of property, learning, and talent. Yet if Polier was an Orientalist, he was an Oriental, too. For as a collector and patron, he was also acting out the role of the Mughal nobleman that he was. From the moment he left Company Bengal in 1773, Polier lodged his career, his affections, his money, and his interests in Mughal India. He worked for Indian rulers, started an Indo-Persian family, acquired a title and a *jagir,* and adopted the way of life of a member of the Mughal elite. Collecting was a sport of princes in Mughal India, too, and Polier cemented his status in Lucknow by indulging in it.

None of this meant that he renounced his European friends, gave up his political allegiances and desire for promotion, or abandoned the idea of returning to Europe. (How, why, and with what consequences he left Lucknow behind is for the next chapter to tell.) But as long as Polier lived in Lucknow, capital of cultural crossing, he could keep up both personæ. And he was by no means the only, or even the most conspicuous, collector to reinvent himself in Lucknow, to cross the lines. For while Polier and others were delving into the world of Mughal cultivation, Claude Martin and Asaf ud-Daula were managing between them to make Lucknow a center of European connoisseurship as well.

## IV. Connoisseurs?

One day in the hot early weeks of May 1760, Claude Martin gave up. He abandoned his post in the bodyguard of the Comte de Lally, France's commander in chief in India, climbed onto his horse, and trotted out of the French settlement of Pondicherry. It was the height of the Seven Years War. All around the town the East India Company army under Colonel Eyre Coote lay encamped, besieging the French into submission. As far as Martin was concerned, the time had come. He crossed the hedge of prickly pears that bounded the settlement and surrendered himself into the hands of a nearby British detachment.[63]

Colonel Coote was used to defections like these. (The East India Company army was hardly immune from defections itself.) Since he had routed Lally at the battle of Wandewash in January, the situation of the French in

South India had grown desperate. While Coote and his men ringed Pondicherry to the west, Admiral Pococke brought seven warships into the waters to the east, completing a blockade around the settlement. Inside the city walls circumstances were still worse. No provisions, no money, no defenses, no ships, and no morale: all that the starving, defeatist French population had, and all that united them, was passionate hatred for Lally, who would later be tried and beheaded in France for his troubles. So many French soldiers deserted during those terrible months of 1760 that Coote decided to create a "Free French Company" in the (already multinational) Madras army to contain them. It was to this regiment that Coote attached Martin, who brought his new masters eight years' experience soldiering and some technical skills as an engineer. In 1763, the young Frenchman was formally commissioned ensign in the East India Company army. There was no going back. From that day on, Martin was a Frenchman by birth but a Briton by choice.

When Martin stumbled out of the cactus hedge and into the Company army, he knew that he was moving still farther from the medieval streets of Lyon's Presqu'île, where he was born—away from his family's vinegar business and a good bourgeois life. This, he knew, was a step not just away from France but away from the French. Yet not even Martin could have predicted that his path with the British would take him to Lucknow, to a fortune of

Claude Martin.

almost half a million pounds, and to a future as one of the eighteenth century's greatest collectors. Where Polier had made himself an Orientalist and an Oriental, Martin took advantage of Lucknow's opportunities—to make money, among other things—to reinvent himself as a Briton, a gentleman, and a European connoisseur.

After many years in North India, fighting and working as a surveyor under James Rennell, Claude Martin arrived in Lucknow in 1776 to take up a new job as superintendent of the nawab's arsenal. His appointment was due to the Company's increased military presence in Awadh; the arsenal would be casting guns for the Company's own troops. It also hinted at the Company's rather ambivalent position toward continental Europeans: having forced Asaf to dismiss his father's "French" advisers, here it was inserting its own French-born agent instead. Martin, at any rate, a keen opportunist, had lobbied hard for the posting and welcomed the chance to get rich off the concessions and soft money that abounded in Awadh.

Martin had no more compunctions than anybody else about milking the nawab for favors. But he owed his tremendous fortune primarily to a natural talent for business, and relentless energy in exercising it. He drew rent on more than a dozen properties in Lucknow, including the Company residency, and various estates around Awadh. He also earned a hefty interest income by lending money to various Europeans, to say nothing of the profligate nawab. Martin invested some of his money in Company stocks and bonds; mostly, though, he pursued an export business, which ranged from small ventures in sugar, shawls, and lapis lazuli, to a sustained private trade in piece goods and indigo. From 1791, Martin manufactured and exported the blue dye himself, at his Najafgarh estate.[64]

In 1800 Martin's net worth was over £400,000 (40 lakhs of rupees), which made him about as rich as the great nabobs of the 1770s, and quite possibly the richest European then in India. Like a latter-day Robert Clive, he plowed his money into land, houses, and political influence. His estates stretched over a vast reach of northeastern India, from Lucknow to Cawnpore, Benares, Chandernagore, and Calcutta. At Najafgarh (which he bought from Polier in 1786), Martin was a gentleman farmer, tending his indigo fields and growing roses for attar. In Lucknow, he based himself in a lavish house of his own design, the Farhat Baksh, which ingeniously channeled water from the River Gomti to cool its rooms. This was only one of many buildings Martin designed in and around Lucknow. During the last years of his life, he built his own equivalent of Claremont: the sprawling mansion of Constantia, on the outskirts of the city. Also like Clive, Martin recognized that he needed to protect his fortune with friends in high places. On the one hand, he made sure to cultivate connections with Warren Hastings and a range of top East India Company officials. On the other, he stayed close to the nawab Asaf ud-Daula, who had the power to grant him lucrative concessions, just as Martin was able to supply the nawab in turn with ready cash. Theirs was a marriage of convenience: they did not especially like each other, but they knew they would be worse off alone.

Unlike Clive, Martin does not seem to have been interested in power simply for its own sake. But he was interested in virtually everything else. Soldier, trader, banker, entrepreneur, farmer, inventor, architect, Claude Martin really was one of those Enlightenment jacks-of-all-trades for whom nothing was too dull or difficult to try. Curiosity sparked in him. And for every interest, there was an object to own. Most of all, Claude Martin was a passionate collector. Acquisition was his addiction. The best surviving testament to Martin's obsession resides in an inventory of all his belongings, compiled when he died. Five or six pages would be more than enough to list all the possessions that the average European in India owned. For Martin, it took *eighty.* In column after column of this inventory, what comes through so powerfully is the sense of a man whose life was lived in and through objects. Every one of Martin's interests is reflected in his things—and none more conspicuously than his quest for European refinement.[65]

Some of what Claude Martin owned would not have been out of place in Robert Clive's Indian chest: the keepsakes of a soldiering career, acquired in the line of duty. While on campaign in Bhutan in 1773, for instance, he picked up some "Bootan books pictures reliques etc." by rather proactive means—according to a French officer, who later saw "many rarities that [Captain Martin] appropriated to himself by pillage from several temples of the Bhutanese. He even gave me several manuscripts that he pulled from the hollows of statues. . . ."[66] Like his friends Wombwell and Polier, Martin also collected Indian manuscripts in Lucknow, of which he owned some five hundred. Indeed it was even said—by a critic, who accused Martin of doing all this for the sole purpose of finding things to bribe people with—that Martin "ransacked the remotest tracts of Cashmere, Nepaul, Candahar, and other regions, from the frontiers of Oude to the confines of Tartary" for objects, using "Catholic missionaries, Hindoo merchants, Mussulman caravans" as his agents.[67]

But the really unusual items in Martin's collection came from a more distant, if less exotic, source. For Martin did not acquire only the sorts of weapons, manuscripts, paintings, and decorative objects that many Europeans collected in India. He also managed to collect everything that a European gentleman connoisseur would possess back in *Europe*. It was a staggering assemblage. There were enough paintings to fill two houses, to say nothing of the thousand-odd fashionable prints and caricatures or the extensive assortment of coins and medals. Martin decorated his rooms with Wedgwood medallions, marble busts (of Louis XVI and Marie Antoinette, no less), and a gleaming array of mirrors, clocks, and chandeliers. He owned cutting-edge scientific apparatus and a substantial cabinet of natural history specimens. And alongside his collection of Indian manuscripts, Martin could set what was probably the largest European library in India, some 3,500 volumes in English and French. In short, Claude Martin had all the trappings of a European connoisseur and man of fashion. Only he had them in Lucknow.

Four or five times a year, in an office on a Bloomsbury side street, William and Thomas Raikes, agents, would break open Martin's wax LABORE ET CONSTANTIA seal, decipher his erratic syntax, and set about fulfilling their client's latest wishes. Raikes and Company sold Martin's indigo, bought him East India stock, handled his bills of exchange, and managed his cash account. They also fulfilled his insatiable demand for objects, shipping him everything from "some caricature prints to the amount, as by invoice, about ten pounds sterling. And also some colored prints of the best sort . . ."; to glass lampshades: "Send me about forty dozens," Martin ordered. "My servants break one with another about 30 to 40 per month, what makes about that number for the year."[68] On Martin's orders, Raikes often handed twenty or thirty pounds to Johan Zoffany (who had returned to Britain from Lucknow in 1789) to pick up "any curious thing he may think curious to buy for me." Zoffany also vetted scientific instruments for his old patron, which were invariably the most troublesome items on Martin's wish lists. A pair of Herschel telescopes arrived in Lucknow missing "the terrestrial apparatus . . . which without I can't make any use of them." A "philosophical instrument for making oxygene air" had "no book of instructions with it; by what mean, I must find out how to make it." As for the steam engines Martin ordered, "I can't manage to make the two you sent me to play at all." There was one serious drawback to being the only man in Awadh with such equipment: nobody was around to show Martin what to do with it. (But Martin did manage to launch hot air balloons in Lucknow in 1785, just two years after the first balloon ascent by the Montgolfier brothers in Paris.)

Zoffany, and other Lucknow friends who had returned to Europe, did more than send Martin collectibles. They invited him into an international network of connoisseurs. Through them, through letters, and through the constant traffic of objects across the seas, Martin was able to join an elite brotherhood of collectors, even at thousands of miles' remove. That the noted antiquarian Charles Townley was one of Martin's correspondents and suppliers shows how high his contacts reached. (Townley, for his part, owned several pieces of medieval Hindu sculpture, which made him one of only a handful of British connoisseurs collecting Indian objects—though antiquarian interest in ancient India was to be heightened by Jones's discovery of Indo-European.) If Martin had brought his collection back to Europe, speculates his biographer, he might have been another Sir John Soane, the early-nineteenth-century architect and magpie collector, whose vast and various collection can still be seen, virtually unchanged, in his house in London's Lincoln's Inn.[69]

Yet in Lucknow Martin remained. As an archetypal man of the Enlightenment on an imperial frontier, Claude Martin invites comparison with another inveterate collector and polymathic gentleman: Thomas Jefferson, who carved out his own patch of Enlightenment on the edge of Virginia's Blue Ridge Mountains. It was the sheer anomaly of the setting—this island of European connoisseurship in the center of India—that made Claude Martin's collection so remarkable. He lived at a time when it took an average of six months for letters to pass between Calcutta and London, and longer still from Lucknow, several hundred miles inland, which was neither on the Ganges nor the Grand Trunk Road. If, that is, they got there at all. Ships could sink. (Lloyd's of London—and with it, the modern insurance industry—was founded for just this reason.) They could be wildly blown off course. Cargo could be jettisoned in storms. And if the rats and weevils didn't get to it, perhaps the water would. Even if you were lucky enough to receive your chests, you might unpack them only to find a mess of sea-stained splinters and shards. Yet in spite of all the hazards and delays, transcontinental crossing went on regularly, vigorously, and profitably. Claude Martin's collection offers splendid material proof that "globalization" of a sort was alive and well centuries before the word was coined.

A Frenchman in British and Indian service, and a newcomer to wealth, Claude Martin was another of those men on the margins for whom collecting provided a means of reinvention and made a public statement. Martin did not collect in the way that Antoine Polier so remarkably had, effectively living like a Mughal aristocrat. His own ambitions more closely resembled Robert Clive's, in that he sought the life and status of a European nobleman instead. Nevertheless, Martin also very consciously intended to make his collection work for him within India as well as among Europeans beyond it. "Here I am at present among the Great Ones," he boasted to the Bengal councillor Philip Francis in 1780: general Sir Eyre Coote, who in 1760 had held the renegade young Frenchman's fate in his hands, was now Martin's houseguest.[70] And while collecting helped make Martin a king among his peers, it bound him ever more closely to the king next door: Asaf ud-Daula.

Claude Martin's collection would have been impressive even in Europe;

encountering it in Lucknow left some visitors rubbing their eyes in disbelief. But the incongruity of Martin's collection was nothing compared with the greatest museum in town: Asaf ud-Daula's own. To enter the Aina Khana, or "Mirror Hall," of the nawab's palace was to encounter yet another of those fabulous Lucknow fusions. From floor to ceiling, the place was packed with "English objects of all kinds—watches, pistols, guns, glassware, furniture, philosophical machines, all crowded together with the confusion of a lumber room."[71] Giant mirrors multiplied every twinkle of the chandeliers overhead. The space was alive with the whir, tick, and chime of dozens of clocks and watches.

Stunning it absolutely was—and to most Western visitors, in stunningly poor taste. Nobody doubted the quality of some individual items. But taken together, the collection was remarkable chiefly "for its ridiculous assemblage of finery and trumpery jumbled together."[72] "He is fond of lavishing his treasures . . . above all, on fine European guns, lustres, mirrors, and all sorts of European manufactures, more especially English," explained one Englishman,

> from a two-penny deal board painting of ducks and drakes, to the elegant paintings of a Lorraine or a Zophani; and from a little dirty paper lantern, to mirrors and lustres which cost £2000 or £3000 each. . . . Asuf-ud-Dowlah is absurdly extravagant and ridiculously curious; he has no taste and less judgement. . . . [B]ut he is nevertheless extremely solicitous to possess all that is elegant and rare; he has every instrument and every machine, of every art and science; but he knows none.[73]

This particular observer reckoned that Asaf ud-Daula spent some £200,000 *per year* on his collection. (The observer, for his part, collected a tidy annual salary of £1,800 from the nawab with "nothing to do but to enjoy his frequent entertainments of shooting, hunting, dancing, cock fighting, and dinners.") Altogether, the Aina Khana offered yet another sign—as if any were needed—of the nawab's excess.

But what most European visitors did not know was that the Aina Khana wasn't just an expression of what they saw as Asaf ud-Daula's incurable childish whimsy. It was part and parcel of the culture of Indian kingship. Kings make collections, and collections make kings. To own rare, precious, sacred, or just plain numerous things is a virtually universal emblem of royal power.[74] In many parts of the Muslim world, collecting meaningful and valuable objects enhanced a sovereign's personal charisma, or *barakat*, and with it, his ability to command the loyalty and admiration of his subjects. In much the way that European princes assembled cabinets of curiosities, the Mughal emperors formed libraries and treasure-houses, called *toshkhana*. Elsewhere in India, regional rulers followed suit; the nizams of Hyderabad, for instance, started a *toshkhana* in the eighteenth century that would develop into India's finest collection of jewels.

Never one to be modest where immodesty would do, Asaf ud-Daula embraced the genre with characteristic extravagance. Elaborate weapons crammed his armory, his jewel house shimmered with gorgeous stones. In his library, album after album of miniature paintings confirmed his princely cultivation. "Most of them are antique productions," noted one British visitor, who generously allowed that "though widely different in manner from European matters, neither taste nor elegance are wanting to these compositions."[75] For £1,500 (about twenty times the price of an expensive Old Master painting in contemporary London), the nawab acquired one of the finest Mughal illuminated manuscripts ever produced, straight out of the Delhi imperial library: the *Padshahnama*, a history of Shah Jahan's rule, made for the emperor Shah Jahan himself. In 1797, Asaf ud-Daula presented the sumptuous manuscript to the new governor-general, Sir John Shore. "It was fit for a Royal library," said Shore, declining the gift for his own collection; he forwarded it to King George III's library at Windsor, where it remains today.[76]

Asaf ud-Daula was certainly not the only Indian ruler to collect European objects. As early as the 1750s, for instance, the Maharaja of Bhuj, in Gujarat, built an extraordinary "European" palace (in truth, about as European as chinoiserie was Chinese) in order to house a collection of European art. The collection had been formed for him in part by his chief artisan, who had studied painting in Holland, and returned there several times to buy art for the king.[77] Tipu Sultan of Mysore, also questing for *barakat*, had European objects in his *toshkhana*, too. But Asaf was surely the only Indian ruler to see a major European collection up close, and that, of course, was Claude Martin's. From cladding his walls with paintings by Zoffany to enthusiastically acquiring clocks and mechanisms of all kinds, Claude Martin was Asaf ud-Daula's closest model, and one of the nawab's key suppliers. He was also Asaf ud-Daula's greatest rival. Collecting seems to have been something of a competitive sport between the nawab and the nabob. The nawab, it was said,

> could never bear to hear that any person possessed any thing superior to his own. He had a large room filled with mirrors, amongst which were two of the largest size that could be made in Great Britain. . . . The Colonel [Martin] seeing them, immediately wrote to France where plate glass is cast of larger dimensions . . . and procured two of

> the largest size, which he sold to the Vizier at a very extraordinary high price.[78]

Asaf ud-Daula had good reason to compete with Claude Martin, a king of his own minting. He had to show the world who was *really* king.

So maybe the nawab was not such a dupe after all. Most kings collect to assert and display their power. Asaf ud-Daula collected to compensate for his *lack* of power. His hands were tied by the Company in virtually everything else, but in the sphere of art and culture he was free. Collecting was also a way to put Awadh on the map. Attracted by talk of the nawab's lavish acquisitions, "merchants of large property from all parts of India" swept into Lucknow with curiosities to sell.[79] Even in distant Europe, Asaf's desires were attended to: the Raikeses sent him objects, at Martin's request; Polier procured him an elaborate organ, "a precious and rare gift in India, which in the hands of inexperienced people will go [to] waste."[80] When his ministers chastised him for spending so much, Asaf ud-Daula smiled wanly and said, "how could he refuse one who had taken the trouble of travelling all the way to Oudh having heard of his generosity!" After all, he had a reputation to uphold.[81]

In the eyes of some outsiders, Martin and Asaf personified everything that was wrong with Lucknow. They, and their collections, were like the city itself: debauched, corrupt, extravagant. One civil servant (a thoroughly pompous young man of nineteen) found it "impossible to see without pain and shame the evidence which the Inah Khanah alone afforded of the weakness and extravagance of the Vizier, and of the dishonourable cupidity and deception with which this injurious dissipation was encouraged principally by British subjects. . . ."[82] Asaf ud-Daula could not possibly be a connoisseur because he was ignorant about European taste, value, and art—because, in a word, he was Indian. Claude Martin did not even have that excuse. He was accused not just of taking criminal advantage of "the Nawaub's idiotical propensities" by selling him objects at usurious rates. In the words of his most savage critic, the aristocratic traveler Viscount Valentia, who visited Lucknow three years after Martin's death:

> With affluence to which he had never been brought up, and which, of course, he knew not how to enjoy, he never did a generous act, and never had a friend. . . . [I]f he is handed down to posterity as a man who raised himself to riches and power . . . it will also be added, that his riches were contaminated by the methods employed in obtaining them, and that his character was stained by almost every vice that can disgrace human nature.[83]

Martin was no connoisseur because he was unscrupulous, opportunistic, and a crook—and, above all, because he was nouveau riche. (So, incidentally, was Valentia, who will reappear in these pages.)

And yet, Martin and Asaf also personified what was right about Lucknow. For behind its sybaritic, eccentric exterior, something quite amazing was unfolding there. The game of empire was afoot, the Company was moving in. But some of the underdogs were winning. Despite the obvious differences among them, Claude Martin, Asaf ud-Daula, and Antoine Polier were all outsiders to the mainstream of imperial power—displaced persons, and disempowered ones. Yet living on the edge of empire opened up splendid opportunities. In Lucknow, as a collector, each managed to remake himself in extravagant style. Just as Polier collected manuscripts in the manner of a Mughal nobleman, so Martin and Asaf collected European objects to advertise their own Lucknow personæ: self-made combinations of power, wealth, and status. None of them, to be sure, was the typical representative of his own native culture. Yet neither did any of them completely adopt the ways of another culture. Rather, they were partners in a kind of third world, where an Indian environment absorbed European influences, where Europeans assimilated Indian ones. What was right about Lucknow was that it could, at once, be both. The only question was, how long could it last?

CHAPTER THREE

# *Compromises*

## 1. Going Un-Native

As the monsoon rains sheeted down over Lucknow in 1786, Antoine Polier wrote to his benefactor, Warren Hastings, with a surprising and wonderful piece of news. For ten years Asaf ud-Daula had been in Polier's debt, owing him loans and interest payments amounting to the staggering sum of twenty-seven lakhs—about £270,000 then, at least £20 million today.[1] Polier had been waiting for so long he must scarcely have believed he would ever be paid. But now, he informed his patron, "in consequence of the arrangements, you took when last with us, and your recommendations in my favour, I have already received a considerable part of my debt from the Vizier, and am in a fair way of realizing the whole before November next, if no sinister accident intervenes." The money was Polier's ticket home. "I am now enabled by this event to follow my inclination, which has long pointed out to me a trip to England, as a thing of absolute necessity; I therefore intend, God willing, to quit this Country by one of the early ships of this season. . . ." This would mean a hurried departure, just a few months later, "but having it now in my power to retire," he concluded, "I should think myself deserving of all the ills I have suffered and do still suffer was I any longer to remain as I am."[2] Thus Antoine Polier, Arsalan-i Jang, prepared to return to Europe, after an absence of thirty years. Little did he know that he was soon to suffer the cruelest truth of empire: you could never go home again.

How long would cosmopolitan Lucknow survive? Only as long as Polier's generation of border crossers and collectors remained there. For if entrepreneurial Europeans had discovered in Lucknow the chance to make money, to span cultural borders, to collect, and to reinvent themselves, leaving Lucknow threatened to break their fusions catastrophically apart. Even Polier must have known that his departure for Europe would have serious consequences for his cross-cultural household. What he could not know was that it would also test the limits of his European identity in a dramatic and quite unpredictable way. And his experience was not unique. A foil to Polier's predicament would be provided by Benoît de Boigne, one of his and Claude Martin's closest friends. De Boigne, a Savoyard, was another Francophone European in British and Indian service, and a sometime denizen of Lucknow. An active soldier, he spent too much time in the field to immerse himself in Lucknow the way Polier and Martin had; but he, too, made his Indian home there, with his beloved Muslim wife and their children. Like Polier and Martin, he also was a collector, recording his Indian life in objects. For both him and Polier, choices about when, where, with what, and with whom to leave Lucknow would yank the foundations out from under a delicate assemblage of European loyalties and Indian commitments.

The obvious question, of course, was why—given the depth of their Indian attachments—such figures opted to leave at all. Indeed, Polier had several times risked unemployment and Company disapproval in order to *stay* in Lucknow. But dreams of return were usually what had lured officers and civil servants to India in the first place: the dream of returning richer, more secure, better established, than they had left. To be sure, the rampant fortuneering of the Clive era was less and less common. By the late 1780s, under the administration of Lord Cornwallis, Company servants were not allowed either to accept "gifts" or to engage in private trade. (Awadh and Hyderabad were such appealing postings partly because it was easier to skirt those regulations.) Still, even the midranking soldier Richard Plowden returned to Britain £33,000 richer than he had departed—in today's terms, he was a millionaire several times over—bought a stylish London house, frequented distinguished circles, and set up all four of his sons as East India Company writers, or junior clerks.[3] The East was becoming a career.

Few, of course, would be so lucky. The vast majority of the forty thousand or so Europeans in India by 1800 were enlisted soldiers with limited chances of returning to Europe: one in four would die in India.[4] A walk among the moss-caked obelisks and mausolea of Calcutta's Park Street Cemetery impresses one with the scale of civilian loss. These monuments are *huge*, as if sheer mass of bricks and mortar could stand in for lives ended too young, "on distant shores from Kindred dust removed." They are also insistent. THIS IS LAWRENCE GALL'S TOMB, pronounces one: IT WAS THY FATE, O GALL, TO LIVE LONG ENOUGH TO SEE THYSELF NEGLECTED BY THOSE FRIENDS WHO OUGHT TO HAVE SERVED THEE. TO THEE AND THINE FORTUNE HAS BEEN UNKIND. Another epitaph summarizes the life of Richard Becher, who had actually made it out of Bengal once alive, in 1771, returning to Britain a successful nabob; but he met ruin in London, and traveled once more to Calcutta, where UNDER THE PANG OF DISAPPOINTMENT AND THE PRESSURE OF THE CLIMATE, A WORN MIND AND DEBILITATED BODY SUNK TO REST. He died in 1782. What also comes through so poignantly is how many of those who returned to Britain were emotional survivors, too, leaving loved ones beneath Indian soil. Becher had already buried his wife, Charlotte, in the graveyard of St. John's Church, who died AFTER SUFFERING WITH PATIENCE A LONG ILLNESS OCCASIONED BY GRIEF FOR THE DEATH OF AN ONLY DAUGHTER. Poor Philip Hunt had three graves to tend: in 1801 he lost his twenty-one-year-old wife Harriet, only to be bereaved again just three years later, with the deaths of his second wife and his infant son. HER WAYS WERE WAYS OF PLEASANTNESS, / AND ALL HER PATHS WERE PEACE.[5]

To return, then, was to be fortunate. But it was also to confront sometimes painful dislocation. Most Europeans arrived in India as teenagers; if they left, it was usually in middle age. No matter how much they prayed, planned, and waited for it, nothing could overcome the fact that they would be returning to a place they might barely recognize. "It is not to be conceived how very remote from reality are the imaginary ideas of this country, which, while abroad are insensibly established on the mind of a person who has passed 20 years of his life in India as you and I have done," one old India hand wrote from Scotland in 1798, to warn a cousin who was considering return. "Be assured, it requires no small portion of philosophy to become unaturalized [*sic*], by far the greater number find it impossible they are therefore rather miserable in spite of their wealth." And the worst part was not even that these "Indians" (as Britons who lived in India were styled) were still, forty years after Plassey, regarded as "miscreant delinquents" by the British public at large. It was that "they find themselves exotics" in a land they had once called home. Some returnees were said to have lost command of their mother tongues or to have acquired permanently darkened skin. Others had taken on incorrigibly "Asiatic" ways, and pined for the hot, bright tropics of their youth. Home had changed, and they had changed, and the two might no longer suit.

Leaving could mean losing, in both concrete and emotional terms. What would you take with you? What would you leave behind? At one level, these were practical questions. But they also touched directly on the way people remembered, and represented, their time abroad. For collectors in particular, to whom objects were a way of recording and recasting experience, the question of what to take cut to the quick. On the one hand, it mattered for personal, aesthetic, and highly individual reasons. On the other, as many collectors, to say nothing of ambitious imperialists—witness Robert Clive—were keenly aware, it also mattered in terms of public image. Warren Hastings, for instance, weighed both private and public considerations as he packed up his own belongings before leaving India in late 1784. "I will carry nothing to England with myself that I shall care to lose, or [be] ashamed to shew," he wrote to his wife, Marian.[6] To "care to lose" betrayed a quite personal concern. When a ship went down (as about one in thirty did), the financial effects could be disastrous; but if you had a personal investment in the cargo—if you *cared* to lose it—the loss could be emotionally devastating as well. To be "ashamed to shew" implied a more public preoccupation. Hastings had last been in Britain in the late 1760s, at the height of the nabob scare, and rightly worried about how his objects might affect the way he was perceived.

Warren Hastings came from old if impoverished stock, and had gone to India partly to earn enough money to buy back his family's ancestral estate, Daylesford in Worcestershire. He had a clear home to which to return. For Polier, de Boigne, and other continental Europeans in British service, however, the choice about where to go was less obvious—and less safe. Polier returned to Europe on the eve of the French Revolution. In June 1789, at the meeting of the Estates General in Versailles, the Third Estate broke with the king's authority to form themselves into the National Assembly. Three weeks later, the people of Paris expressed their support for the change by storming the Bastille prison; and by the end of October, a constitutional monarchy was in place. Up to this point, the Revolution was widely welcomed abroad, including in Britain, for putting an end to absolutism. But events soon took a more radical turn; and with radicalism came war. In early 1793, France declared war on the Dutch Republic, Spain, and Britain, beginning an Anglo-French conflict that would continue virtually unabated until 1815.

As the shadow of Anglo-French war lengthened again over the Continent and the world, it forced Europeans of previously ambiguous loyalties—such as Polier, de Boigne, and Martin—to take sides. Polier and de Boigne would find themselves sucked up in the turmoil of revolutionary Europe with traumatic immediacy. And their fates in war-torn Europe in turn influenced their friend Claude Martin to arrive at perhaps the most unexpected choice of all. Martin had spent so much of his life trying to escape the limitations of Lucknow. Yet, in the end, informed by his friends' unhappy departures, he decided never to leave Lucknow at all, but to stay on there, to die there.

Taken together, the entangled endings of these three friends and collectors record in miniature a bigger narrative about the relationship between Britain, Europe, India, and empire. An age of fusions was ending. The next generation of Europeans in India would find it harder and less attractive, politically as well as socially, to cross the lines between East and West. They would also find it almost impossible to blend British and European loyalties in the way Polier, de Boigne, and Martin so remarkably had. In a world polarized and unsettled by conflict, relationships once flexible and mixed would be cut up and classified in new ways. And each of these men crystallized the wider transformations of their world in a final, significant way. What happened to them personally would be reflected and recorded in their collections. There, too, previously coherent wholes would be disrupted and transformed.

It was Antoine Polier who first tasted the bittersweet realities of leaving Lucknow, and whose experiences framed this larger set of fractures and change. He was just sixteen when he came to India from Switzerland, armed with little more than his wits and expectations. Now forty-six, he had lived in Awadh for fifteen years, "more," he said, "with the natives of the country than with the Europeans."[7] Measured either by European or by Indian standards, he was surrounded with the possessions of an extraordinarily privileged life:

A page from one of Antoine Polier's books.

he had two wives, three children, property throughout the region, two houses, business relationships, friends galore, and a massive collection of manuscripts. How much of this would he be able, or would he choose, to take back to Europe with him?

First and foremost, he took what was by now an enormous collection of manuscripts, chiefly in Sanskrit, Persian, and Arabic. These were not "manuscripts" in the sense one might imagine: thin loose-leaf sheets. Many of them were chunky, heavy, ornate, leather-bound books, and Polier had at least six hundred, which now had to be packed into chests. Each chest, in turn, would probably be hauled out of Lucknow by oxcart to the nearest Ganges port, then loaded onto a riverboat and taken to Calcutta. Once in Calcutta, they would then be loaded onto an East Indiaman for the six-month voyage around the Cape of Good Hope to Europe. There, each of Polier's containers would be tugged back inland again, over the Alps, to Lausanne. Moving the manuscripts was expensive, cumbersome, and time-consuming. The fact that Polier took the manuscripts with him at all afforded powerful proof of how much they mattered to him. In Lucknow, his manuscript collection had embodied and sustained his double persona, Mughal nobleman and Enlightenment gentleman rolled into one. By taking them out of Lucknow, Polier seems to have expected them to retain social and personal (and perhaps financial?) value in Europe.

Along with the manuscripts, Polier took with him another part of his cross-cultural life: one of his sons (probably the elder, who would have been about fifteen) and his daughter; but he left "a fine stout boy" in Lucknow, in Claude Martin's excellent care. His wives, too, he left behind with Martin, where they disappear from history's view, in the commodious zenana of the Farhat Baksh.[8]

Then, of course, he took his own "Asiatic" self. When Polier returned to Lausanne in 1788, he would have been completely unrecognizable to many of his family, including a first cousin, Marie Elizabeth de Polier, Canoness of the Reformed Order of the Holy Sepulchre, lady-in-waiting to the Court of Saxe-Meiningen.[9] To Marie, this unlikely kinsman brought a wonderful whiff of the exotic, to say nothing of the forbidden, into the devout confines of her Alpine world. She was captivated. In Polier she saw Asiatic dissipation thrillingly personified. She could see it in his soft brown face, and in his long mustache, which seemed to droop with all the lassitude of India. She could see it in his behavior. "For along with Oriental luxury," she observed, "he had brought from his long stay in India all the indolence of Asia, and he had lost the ability to express himself correctly in French and English." And she could see it, above all, in his things. Shivering with regret for the lost warmth of

Lucknow, Polier lamented the friends he had left behind, and leafed through the paper microcosms of his collection, with Marie at his elbow. Eagerly she pressed Antoine to explain, to translate, to publish. No, he answered frankly, "I am too lazy, and not a writer at all." He left the job to her instead.

Using Polier's manuscripts, and the notes he had made in Lucknow, Marie compiled a two-volume book entitled *Mythologie des Indous,* framed as a dialogue between Polier and his pandit, Ram Chand. This is one of the earliest treatises on Hinduism in French, and quite possibly the first work of scholarly Orientalism authored by a woman. (It was not, however, the first book written by Marie, whose novels and translations included such titles as the 1792 treatise *Le Club Jacobin, ou l'Amour de la Patrie.*) Through Marie's book, Polier's manuscripts contributed to the growing Orientalist archive of knowledge on and about India. Yet this was effectively Orientalism by accident; left to his own devices, Polier would not have bothered. While he was in India, Orientalism had granted him entrée to elite European society, and friendship with the likes of Warren Hastings and Sir William Jones. But back in Europe, Polier did not seem to think it worth the effort. If he wanted to act like an aristocrat there, he would have to find another way to do it.

Indeed, even the manuscripts themselves, which had formed so large a part of Polier's Lucknow life, appeared to have lost their value to him in Lausanne. For while the canoness plugged away at the papers, Polier's attention was engaged elsewhere. He cultivated a new friend in the person of a local nobleman called Baron von Berchem. And he discovered a new object of desire, in the person of von Berchem's fetching young daughter Anne, known as Rosette. The old soldier was smitten—yet he held back from making any advances. Would she find him too old? Would she feel "repugnance at the title of step-mother to his [half-Indian] children"? Marie argued down his objections, and served as his go-between. In 1791, Polier and Rosette were married, and settled down together in Lausanne.

But Polier was restless, and not altogether happy with his cold Alpine home. Then, with von Berchem, he discovered a new enthusiasm. Over the border, in France, amazing events were unfolding. The French Revolution was now in full swing: Louis XVI ruled subject to a new constitution; the Declaration of the Rights of Man and Citizen had been issued; feudalism had been abolished; and privileges of the Church and the aristocracy had been revoked. Both Polier and his father-in-law embraced the principles of the Revolution, which seemed to promise utopia. And utopia was right next door. Together, the two men decided to move to France, and bought themselves adjoining estates near Avignon.

Polier was ancestrally French—his Huguenot forebears had emigrated to

Switzerland after 1685—but this latest border crossing was singular, to say the least. Throughout his career in India, Polier had fought the French, informed against them, and repeatedly sought to prove "my atachement to the service of the Company and the Nation" of Great Britain.[10] And though many people in Britain and elsewhere had welcomed the early phase of the Revolution as a challenge to absolutist despotism, by the time Polier moved to France it was already clear that the movement was radicalizing fast. France under the egalitarian Jacobins was hardly the most congenial spot for a man who had spent the last fifteen years of his life actively cultivating the persona of an aristocrat. Maybe Polier was terribly misinformed; perhaps he was merely naïve. At all events, his desire to move again—and to move to France in particular—spoke eloquently to his ongoing search for a home. This time, he left his manuscripts behind.

The land was cheap, the sun was hot. Polier was back in his element. Ensconced in his new Provençal estate, he feasted and entertained on a lavish scale, opening his house to all. "In adopting the chimerical ideas of equality which then reigned in France, M. Polier could not relinquish his Asiatic splendors," commented Marie. In a rather touching respect, his life in Avignon was just as hybrid as his life in Lucknow had been. There, he had adjusted his small-town Swiss manners to the opulence of the Awadh court. Here, he brought the habits of a sumptuous Indian lifestyle into the French provinces. There, he had enjoyed domesticity Indian-style, in the polygamous enclave of Polierganj. Here, he cherished his young bride, looked attentively after his in-laws, and promptly fathered an heir. Here as there, Polier settled down as a foreigner at home.

But the year was 1792, a supremely bad time to buy a French chateau. While the Jacobins were seizing power in Paris, trouble was stirring in rural France. Bandit gangs, inflamed by hunger and fierce ideology, terrorized the countryside from Normandy, across central France, and right down the Rhône, to Provence. One of these groups, the notorious Bande d'Orgères, numbered more than a hundred members and counted seventy-five murders to its name before it was rounded up in 1798. They were also approaching Polier's part of the country. Counterrevolutionary violence against Jacobins was mounting in the south, compounded by a long-standing hostility to the Protestant minority in the region.[11] Yet Polier—a soi-disant Jacobin and a Protestant—full of "the generosity, goodwill, and Asiatic insouciance that formed the basis of his character," went banqueting on, a little too conspicuously for the times.

It was past dark on a February evening in 1795 when bandits came for Polier's Indian treasure. They had known that the Poliers would be out that day, and the unbolted doors gave way immediately at their touch. Quickly they rounded up the servants and locked them out of the way. In the kitchen, they mixed up a paste of flour and water and smeared it over their faces, disguising themselves behind ghoulish white masks. Then they went to work. Polier's Asian wealth was famous for miles around; surely there must be a fortune hidden in the house. By torchlight, they smashed, ripped, and broke their way through anything that might hide a secret trove of money and jewels. But as the burglars rifled on, with mounting violence, no treasure appeared. Crashing into a bedroom upstairs, they found Rosette's mother and sister cowering in fright. The women handed over what jewels they had. But still this was no hoard—not the Indian magnificence the thieves had been led to expect.

The lookout party on the road intercepted the Poliers' carriage on its way home. "Robespierrist!" the bandits shouted, yanking Polier out of the coach and shoving him to the ground. They had come to arrest him, they claimed, and demanded all his money and valuables in the name of the law. Bewildered and terrified, Polier staggered through the wreckage of his house, surrendering whatever things of value he could find. Yet still there was no treasure trove. Then the burglars pushed him down the cellar stairs, into the last unexplored corner of the house. Would it finally yield diamonds and gold? No again. All they had was in front of them: Indian luxury personified, battered and whimpering, fat with good food and offensively well dressed, pleading with them like an empty-handed beggar. They cut him down with sabers till he fell to the flagstones, writhing. Then they fired muskets at him until he stopped moving. Polier was dead. Dead, as he had lived—an aristocrat and a foreigner.

It could have been worse. The manuscripts, left in the devoted custody of Marie de Polier in Lausanne, survived. So did young Rosette—with the son she was carrying, born four months later.[12] At the trial, Madame de Polier looked through her black veil and recognized that some of the accused had been guests at her husband's table.

Back in Lucknow, Claude Martin heard of his best friend's awful death before the year was out. He was devastated. In a letter to his old friend Elizabeth Plowden, he wrote: "I reely lament and very much the fate of Polier, how unfortunate he has been, he was an Excellent good man, and the life of Society where he was. . . . I have been very unhealthy to lose him and I fear his Children [*sic*]."[13] The news from Europe weighed heavily on Martin. For he, too, had hoped to retire in Europe—if not in his native France, then in his adopted country of Britain, a homeland he had never seen. Yet the tumult of revolutionary Europe and Polier's murder finally extinguished Martin's thoughts of return. Instead, he pressed ahead with construction of his intended last retreat, the country house Constantia, on the outskirts of Lucknow. Its central barrel and rotunda rose directly above the space Martin had designated in the cellars for his own empty, expectant tomb.

## II. Settling

In the late spring of 1797, a brown, dark-haired boy, somewhere in his early teens, stumbled into London for the first time. Like many adolescents wandering out into the teeming capital, he must have been bewildered, probably excited, and perhaps afraid—for it had been a long journey for him from India, his native country, and the new life in Britain that lay ahead was unpredictable at best. But "Col. Polier's son is also arrived safe and in good health," Benoît de Boigne assured his Calcutta agents in July of that year. "He is now to the school, as well as my own Children."[14] The lad was none other than Antoine Polier's "fine stout boy," who had been left living until then in Lucknow with Claude Martin. "I will Endeavour to send [him] to . . . [Polier's] wife," Martin had promised the previous summer, "as the Education of India is so bad, that I never would advise any body to let their Children receive it in such a Country, where they learn Every kind of evil by Black Servant."[15] Now, and for some years to come, "Master Polier," "George," would be schooled in England, under Benoît de Boigne's care.

The surfacing of George Polier—surely Antoine's younger son Baba Jan—in the papers of the Savoyard general Benoît de Boigne is more than coincidence. It is gripping evidence of the close networks that bound together Europeans in India, and of the deep commitments they maintained, not just to one another but also to the families they formed. De Boigne's intimate connection with Polier underscores the many characteristics that the two men, together with their mutual friend Claude Martin, already shared. Like Polier and Martin, de Boigne was a European opportunist on the make, who spanned Indian, European, and British cultures both professionally and personally. His decisions about where to retire and what to take with him stand in counterpoint to the tragedy of Antoine Polier, and expose another intimate tale of how individual people experienced the pains and pressures of an imperial world in flux.

In the spring of 1797, de Boigne himself had only just arrived in England for the first time, and by a circuitous route. He was born Benoît Leborgne in 1751, in Chambéry, Savoy, the third son of a furrier.[16] But like his Lucknow friends—both from the same general French-speaking Alpine region—

Benoît de Boigne.

de Boigne imagined a life beyond the mountains. In 1768, he joined the Clare regiment of the French army's Irish brigade. With the Clares he changed his name from Leborgne to the pseudo-aristocratic "de Boigne"; he also paid his first visit to the East, spending a year in Mauritius, and gained an excellent command of English. And he grew bored. Garrisoned through the winter of 1772–1773 in the bleak, soggy lowlands of northern France, de Boigne decided to resign his commission and seek adventure with the Russian army in the eastern Mediterranean. Equipped with a letter of introduction to the legendary Russian commander Count Alexis Orlov, he landed a captaincy in a Russian-allied Greek regiment. On his very first military action, however, he was captured by the Turks—hardly an auspicious start. But it was during those months of Turkish captivity in 1774 that de Boigne arrived at a critical decision: "Seduced by the brilliant pictures people had drawn him of India and the assurances of rapid advancement that could be had in the service of England," he decided to push onward, to India.[17]

With the help of the East India Company's man in Alexandria, George Baldwin, de Boigne sailed for Madras in 1777.[18] There he joined the Madras infantry—and narrowly missed being beaten with them by Haidar Ali of Mysore and Haidar's Savoyard commander, Lallée, at the battle of Pollilur, in 1780. But de Boigne was nothing if not restless. Resigning his commission again in 1782, he drifted from one scheme to another: should he scout out an overland route to Europe, or take service with an Indian prince? An appealing opportunity came his way in 1786, when he was offered the chance to raise troops for the Marathas, who were then allied with the Company. So it was, almost by accident, that Benoît de Boigne stumbled into his last and greatest military command: recruiting, training, and leading an army for the Maratha warlord Mahadji Scindia, one of the most powerful men in Hindustan.[19]

De Boigne's army under Scindia began as two fairly modest battalions of 850 men each, whom he led with distinction into battle against the Muslim warlord Ismail Beg, at Agra and Delhi in 1788. He raised a further eleven battalions (about 6,600 men) in 1790; by the following year his army had swelled to 18,000. At the head of the sepoys marched a veritable league of nations. De Boigne's officer corps included Captain Perron, a villager from the Orléanais, who would later succeed him in command; Captain Drugeon, a fellow Savoyard; Lieutenant Sutherland, a Scot; an English captain named Gardiner; Lieutenant Pohlman from Hanover; the "Portuguese" soldiers Ensign Manuel and Cannoneer Francisco; and even an American, John Parker Boyd, "late a Captn. Lieu[tenant]. in the army of the United States of America," who would go on to fight against Britain with distinction in the War of 1812.[20] All told, it was such a "spurious, and motley assemblage of Franks," one of de Boigne's friends (half) joked, that "your best friends are apprehensive that even the Genius of Cesar or Zenophon could not draw much credit, or much use" from them.[21] But holding these men together did not really take genius. It took regular pay, which is what de Boigne gave them.[22] He also gave them a tightly disciplined and orderly camp, good care for the wounded, smart red coats, and a regimental band.[23] Like the future Duke of Wellington, Arthur Wellesley, who came to India as a young colonel in 1797, de Boigne realized that these were the things a good "Sepoy General" (as Napoleon scornfully put it) was made of. A natural soldier he may have been, but a bookkeeping bourgeois he was born.

Soldier in four armies; traveler on three continents; prisoner of the Turks; possibly an agent for the Russians; mercenary to Indian kings—de Boigne sounds more like a character out of the swashbuckling novels of G. A. Henty or H. Rider Haggard than like someone out of the archives: the life and adventures of a freebooting "sword for hire."[24] To this extent, he was temperamentally different from his friends and fellow European adventurers in India, Polier and Martin, for whom career advancement also involved staying put. De Boigne clearly enjoyed the excitement of an uncertain future, sought out adventure, avoided commitments, and traded allegiances as easily as uniform coats. His only surviving statement of loyalties is contained in a delicate letter to Lord Macartney from 1782, in which he asked to resign his East India Company commission: "not," he insisted, "with a view to serve with the French, as some bad-intentioned men may suppose. I am not of that Nation, nor inclined towards them, having always had the most perfect attachment to the English Government and proposing myself to be for ever in the same opinion."[25] It sounds disarmingly frank, but it was distinctly disingenuous, for de Boigne had of course begun his career in the French army; and the Maratha force that he went on to build would soon be considered a major threat to the British. Whatever sincerity there was in de Boigne's "perfect attachment to the English" was self-serving at best.[26]

Yet, however transient his political loyalties, it seems unfair to reduce de Boigne to a one-dimensional soldier of fortune. For a start, that would mean neglecting the scale of his accomplishment at the helm of a formidable Maratha army.[27] Such European officers may have been swords for hire, but they were sharp and menacing, and could cut to the quick. By training Indian soldiers and introducing European technology, quite small numbers of European mercenaries could significantly increase the military capacities of indigenous armies. These European-trained forces posed a considerable challenge to the encroaching British—a challenge that the British were inclined, if anything, to overestimate.

It would also mean ignoring de Boigne's entire personal life, and with it, a remarkable—if by now partly familiar—story of cross-cultural relations. For it was here that this otherwise freewheeling soldier made his most enduring commitments. He was thirty-seven years old in 1788 when he met Nur Begum, daughter of a "Persian cavalry commander," then a girl of about fifteen. She was beautiful, it was said, and fair. Her sister Faiz un-Nissa was the *bibi* of William Palmer, de Boigne's friend and confidant in Lucknow, and it is surely through Palmer that they met. De Boigne fell in love. He resigned his commission (yet again) and settled down with Nur in Lucknow, to enjoy, for the first time, the comforts of domestic, civilian life. De Boigne had already spent time in Lucknow, in 1783, and formed a fast friendship with Antoine Polier and Claude Martin. Then, Polier had helped de Boigne learn Urdu and Persian; now, Claude Martin introduced him to the world of Indian business, assisting him in investing the income of his *jagirs* in indigo. It was through Martin, chiefly, that de Boigne began to build a great financial network that would sustain him for the rest of his life.[28] He also began to build a family: at the end of 1789, Nur and de Boigne had a daughter, Banu Jan; in the winter of 1792, a son, Ali Baksh.

De Boigne's stint out of uniform was characteristically short-lived. In 1790 he reentered Scindia's service and fought his greatest battles, at Patan and Merta, against the renegade Mughal commander Ismail Beg and the Rajputs.

But his domestic responsibilities followed him. From the front lines, he oversaw the welfare of his Lucknow ménage through the good offices of Joseph Queiros, Claude Martin's faithful Spanish steward, whom de Boigne deputed to look after Nur and the children. "You have in your Lady a Treasure my good friend," Queiros said, beaming:

> She has no will of her own, and [I] never heard a woman be contented with so little—indeed she has surprized me by telling [me] that a house of less rent than 20 Rs. might do for her, while she is alone—and is exceedingly afraid of making expences—I have told her however what was your Intention and that she should not be so œconomical at present she has charge of two dear children of yours, who for the sake of saving a few rupees ought not to be exposed to the danger of too close lodgings.[29]

Of course, Nur's self-abnegating devotion could also have been a way of telling de Boigne to take her with him; in which case, she eventually succeeded.

At the end of 1794, a nineteen-year-old civil servant called Thomas Twining visited de Boigne in his camp at Aligarh. Young Twining was immediately captivated by this tall, craggy officer, who fed him a lavish dinner of pilaus and curries, took him on an elephant ride, and told him gripping stories of war. After breakfast the next morning, de Boigne called for his hookah and "said he must introduce his son to me." Little Ali Baksh, just short of three years old, came trotting out "dressed much as the child of a prince of the country would have been—a turbaned cap, similar to what his father wore, and sandals, worked with gold thread on his feet." Like many an Indian prince, de Boigne proceeded to hold a *darbar* with his son and heir, the *Sahibzada*, by his side. As the visitors filed in, they offered a customary tribute of gold coins to de Boigne and another to the little boy, so that soon "there was a small heap of gold mohurs and rupees before the child, who went through this early initiation in Eastern manners very readily."[30]

This picture of the de Boignes is a happy one, and de Boigne would gladly have seen it endure—notwithstanding the death of his Maratha employer Mahadji Scindia in 1794. Unfortunately de Boigne's health simply did not agree. By the end of 1795, he was suffering badly from fever and "the flux." He was so constantly sick that his survival was in question. It seemed there was only one cure for it: if he wanted to live, he would have to return to Europe. This was bitter medicine, and went against all his inclinations and desires. "Try Europe, as I am going to do," his friend Doctor Blane in Lucknow had earlier advised, "and if we do not like it, which is extremely possible, we can come out together—but do not graft yourself entirely upon India, and vegetate and wither a Marrattah."[31] Like Martin and Polier, de Boigne had rooted himself personally and professionally in India. But leaving the country would now bring the costs and consequences of his cross-cultural life vividly to the fore.

De Boigne set off after his last parade at Agra, on Christmas Day 1795, with "four elephants, 150 camels and bullock-wagons laden with his effects" trailing on behind him to Lucknow.[32] Many of those possessions made their way into ten camel-skin trunks, which were loaded onto the Danish ship *Cromberg*, which de Boigne would take passage on. Three of the trunks contained his personal effects: "Persian [and] Indian clothing, for men and women," "bed cushions, Indian tobacco chest," "Eight Chinese metal spittoons, a copper tea-maker, one of iron, a fly-whisk for elephants from cow horn from Tibet, mounted in silver, a copper powder-flask, a silver handle for a water pot, a box of mother-of-pearl chips and tokens, etc. etc."[33] These were the sorts of things that surrounded de Boigne every day, and he had no intention of leaving India without them.[34] Another trunk held "books, papers, maps, etc." This would have included his grants of *jagirs* and titles—he was called both I'timad ud-Daula (Stay of the Empire) and Shamshir-i Jang (Sword of Battle)—and his Persian and Marathi correspondence, which ranged from letters of praise from Maratha chiefs to petitions for help from the emperor Shah Alam himself.[35] It also contained his small collection of Indian miniatures and a folio-size drawing of the Taj Mahal. The Taj is now the quintessential symbol of India, but de Boigne was one of the first Europeans to take a special interest in it, making sure to guard the building from shelling in 1788, and advocating restoration work on it some years later.[36]

Two more chests contained a different record of de Boigne's Indian life: a collection of eighty-six swords, guns, daggers, shields, and bows. Reading the inventory of this substantial collection, which survives among de Boigne's papers, is like reading de Boigne's curriculum vitæ. Each phase of his military career in India is represented. An English copper-handled saber, for instance, might well have been the first "Indian" weapon he wielded, as a young soldier in the Madras infantry. Most of the other pieces he had acquired while serving with the Marathas. From the Mughal armories of North India and the Deccan, there were Persian swords, damascened and chased with Koranic inscriptions along the blades. Weapons from Hindu kingdoms—less common in collections of the period than Indo-Persian arms, but probably more familiar to de Boigne—included a sword "with the gods of their mythology on the handle and on the blade," and a cutlass "gilded with a mythological emblem."[37] Of all the keepsakes of his military career, perhaps the most precious were swords belonging to de Boigne's two most dangerous foes, Ismail Beg and the Rohilla chief Ghulam Khader, now forever retired in their black and red velvet sheaths. Finally, there was an emblem of the rank de Boigne had attained: "2 commander's batons *à l'indienne* in engraved silver." From East India Company ensign to Mughal commander in fifteen years—it was a stunning rise to the top, chronicled in objects.[38]

The camel-skin trunks went down into the hold of the *Cromberg,* but de Boigne kept his most important belongings close to him, up above. In his cabin he had "a square wooden Chest with a Padlock and tied up with Ropes . . . containing a Gold smoaking Ouka with all his apparatus, a sylver one, and many other things of value."[39] And in or near his cabin he kept one of the most precious things he had in the world: his beloved wife, Nur, soon to be known by the English name Helen. Their two children also traveled with them on the *Cromberg,* and had provisionally been given European names as well: Banu Jan would be called Helena, after her mother; and Ali Baksh would become John Baptiste, after de Boigne's father.

It was not uncommon for mixed-race children to be sent to Europe at this time, but for Nur herself to accompany de Boigne was quite unusual. For the most part *bibis*—particularly women of such high status—stayed behind in India, usually with some kind of financial settlement. (This is what Polier had arranged with his two *bibis.*) According to the conventions of the time, de Boigne could have set up Nur with a house and a generous pension, and walked away with his conscience quite clear. In fact he did precisely that in 1796, for two other *bibis* he had been keeping in Delhi, "Zeenett Begum, daughter of the late Nawab Mahommed Beg Khan Stammandary . . . and Meroo Nissan Begum, adopted daughter of the late Nawab Najaf Kooly Khan."[40] He cared little for his Delhi women; one, he said, was:

> a girl whom I have never touched . . . having been, in regard of this girl, taken in by her mother Fattima Begum who twice permitted me to see her Daughter only at a distance, when painted in white, red, and black, which I have discovered when mine, and in her true colour and form, which has turn'd out to be very inferior to the beauty, as supposed to be.[41]

But nowhere in his papers is there anything to suggest that he considered abandoning Nur or their children. Nur occupied an altogether different place in de Boigne's affections: she was the anchor in his roving mercenary's heart.

The *Cromberg* sailed in January, and on May 31, 1797, de Boigne and his family disembarked at Deal. The general was in a bad way. He had "been continually ill" on the voyage, and remained so "sick . . . at the time of my landing, [that] in the end to have no troubles with the Custom House's Officers, I took absolutely nothing with me; but few changes of old cloths and linnen."[42] The chests traveled on, with Captain Tennent and the *Cromberg,* to Copenhagen, where de Boigne expected to have his goods stored until he could return to the Continent himself. The de Boigne family, in the meantime, went straight to London, where, "thank God!" de Boigne wrote. "Having put myself as soon [as I] arrived in London in the hands of able Physicians I find my self already a great deal better; so much so that I have great hopes of recovering my health; but having been so long time ill, my recovery must in consequence be slow; no matter, best later than never."[43]

But his health was just about the only thing de Boigne felt happy about. For he had just received a devastating piece of news. The *Cromberg* had gone down in a storm in the Baltic, just off Elsinore—with all de Boigne's belongings on board.

The news hit him "with the greatest grief and affliction." With the ship's sinking, he lost everything. "I had a great property on Board the said Ship," he reported—forty-five bales of textiles, in particular—for which he was "only insured for the sum of 80000 S[ic]ca Rupees," a fraction of its actual value.[44] "What change in fortune have I experienced since I left Bengal, I left it possessing a large fortune, a rich man in every sense of the word, I have since made such heavy losses, and my affairs are so much embroiled that I don't know how it will end, and what will remain me of my great fortune."[45] Yet the money was the least of it. The really shattering part was losing everything else. "In my baggage I had the most rare, curious and rich articles that I could collect in the course of twenty years residence in India, and which no money or wealth can reemplace the like . . . so I find my self at the moment as destitute of every Indian articles, as if I had never been in India."

Gone was the wooden chest with the "Gold Ouka with all it's apparatus, a sylver do. Three Gold watches, and many other sylver's furnitures, the Chest to be worth about £6 and 700." Gone were "8 Camels Thrunk." Gone, in them, were "all my sylver plates." Gone were the "8 China's white Brass Pickdannys or spitting furniture." Gone was the "large chest of arms as Persian Swords, Match's locks, Bows, Arrows, Poigniards etc." Gone, in a word, was de Boigne's life. He groped for consoling words, inadequately, clumsily: "Everything is for the best and luck is the best and only security we can depend upon as every days we see things happening which no human wisdom could foresee." But the hollow remained; and he could only say it again: "I find my self at the moment as destitute of Indian articles as if I [had] never been in India. Enstead of possessing, if the sad accident had not happened, the finest collection of as curious rare and valuable articles that any man did ever possess."[46]

"As destitute of Indian articles as if I had never been in India." It was poignant, moving testimony of the emotional significance of his collection. It was also slightly misleading. What about his family—Nur, Banu Jan, and Ali Baksh? They lived together with de Boigne in London, under the name of Bennett (an Anglicization of de Boigne's first name, Benoît). All three were baptized Catholic, and renamed Helen, Ann Elizabeth, and Charles Alexander. Ann went to school in Hammersmith, and Charles in Westminster; Polier's son George, too, was fully supported by de Boigne. And despite his losses on the ship, de Boigne was still a fantastically rich man—worth, he reckoned, £255,415 2s. 6d., to be precise. According to a will he drew up in mid-August 1797 (with his old Lucknow friends and fellow collectors Nathaniel Middleton and Richard Johnson as executors), he intended to leave £100,000 to his son and £60,000 to his daughter—fortunes that would have kept them both in luxury for life. And although "to the Begums Mother of my two Children, if she stay's in Europe or returns to India Encluding her passage and Jewels" he proposed to leave a far smaller legacy of £2,500, this was a respectable provision (more, for instance, than he left his sisters), particularly if he expected Charles and Ann to help support their mother. He also specifically stipulated that "The Mother to be permitted to see her Children; but not confided to her [i.e., in her custody]." It is a little difficult to interpret this partial concession, since it was so unusual for a man of de Boigne's stature to bring back his Indian wife—and even rarer for a woman of Nur's stature actually to come. What is plain, though, is that he had no intention of neglecting her upkeep.[47]

The truth was that though de Boigne felt physically better, he was profoundly out of place in England. Losing his belongings was like the last twist of the knife. Just five months after his return, he wrote:

> I am not without much inclinations of visiting the East once more,
> Europe has no relish for me, and I have been much disappointed.
> Indeed, it must be said also that the French cursed Revolution
> having much altered the face of Europe and the mind of the people
> for the worst, which circomstance make's me much regret India and
> I am afraid I can't be happy; but in ending my days there.[48]

By January 1798, "already much tired of Europe," he was of "the firm belief that no person having lived 20 years in India, can never [i.e., ever] accommodate himself to it [i.e., Europe], the mode of living, the manners, the people and the Climate not being of an engaging nature, I am confident that the voyage alone detain's the greatest numbers of those visiting Europe."[49]

He was even less at home than Polier. France held no allure whatsoever. But England was no place for him, either: cold, gray, and dull, as foreign to him as he was to it. De Boigne was not French, nor was he a friend of the French. But French was his native language, as anybody speaking to him or seeing his name would know. And Britain was again at war with France, fighting more intensely by the year. De Boigne even risked being interned.[50] So why not go back to India? "Your brigades are in a very good condition and everyone wishes very much to see you again," Claude Martin reported, encouragingly, "all the Marratta Chiefs and all the rajas of Scindias, even the Court of Dhely. . . . You need not fear that you will not be well received, people ardently desire it, I have always hoped for your return, I have told you so before. . . ."[51] Why not cut his losses, gather up the Bennetts, and head east again, to the sun, to his friends, to his army, and to fame and fortune anew?

Because a new chapter of his life—and ultimately the saddest—was just starting to unfold. One spring evening in 1798, his old Lucknow friend Richard Johnson took de Boigne to a party, a musical soirée at the house of some French émigrés, the Marquis and Marquise d'Osmond, and their pretty sixteen-year-old daughter, Adèle. D'Osmond had once been a Versailles courtier, and the Marquise a favorite of Madame Adélaïde, Louis XVI's aunt. Now destitute in London, they lived hand to mouth on the charity of friends and distant relations. (D'Osmond's forebears, as the name hints, were Irish Catholics.) De Boigne had a weakness for titles, and for young women who had them. Adèle sang Italian duets, and he was hooked. It was as if he heard in her voice the sound of another choice calling, the chance to move past the wreckage of his Indian life and start afresh in Europe. Within a matter of weeks, he tendered a proposal of marriage; twelve days later, in June 1798, he and Adèle were married.[52]

The general thought he was in love. "Loving for the first time" (he later told her) "I abandoned myself to the feeling. . . . If I had only one other wish, it would be to have a bigger heart, in order to love still more."[53] He gave her Indian jewels: "An aigrette called Kalkuy and Cheupes given to me by the Mogul emperor being a distin[c]tive insignia of my Rank," "1 large Emerauld given to me by the Jeypore's Rajah as a Keep Sake," and a "Green Shawl quilted being a kind of curiosity to me." He gave her an embroidered rug, of the kind that would be spread across a royal throne.[54]

But Adèle's were siren's songs. As far as she was concerned, the marriage was a financial contract, no more; she agreed to marry de Boigne only when he consented to give her parents a generous annual allowance. Far from the tender girl he had fancied, he found her disdainful, cold, and mean; she recoiled at his touch. Adèle was no Indian princess. And de Boigne, despite his name—and as his wife learned to her dismay, after marriage—was no French aristocrat. "He deceived me on his whole background," she said, "his name, his family, his past life." She knew about the Bennetts; that did not bother her.[55] De Boigne's personality did. He was miserly, controlling, filled with "Oriental jealousies"; "an immoderate use of opium" had "paralyzed his moral and physical faculties" (by which she might have been implying that he was impotent).[56] In short, the couple despised each other. In less than a year, he packed her back off to her parents.

Yet the damage had been done. While de Boigne and Adèle moved into a fancy Adam-designed house at Portland Place, the Bennetts were hidden away in Soho. By October 1798, de Boigne had revised and drastically reduced his financial provisions for them, allowing now a mere £200 annuity for Nur/Helen, and £200 to be divided among the three children, Ann, Charles, and George Polier.[57] Still, in some ways, he stayed close to them. In bunch after bunch of receipts, de Boigne monitored and chronicled every detail of their daily lives. He knew when Charles had his hair cut and when he went to see the panorama; he bought him schoolbooks, a slate, and a "Mug to drink water in school." He spoiled Ann from a distance, with frequent trips to the theater, dancing lessons, and a rented piano; and, as she was still just a girl of ten or eleven, a doll, a skipping rope, and a checkerboard. "Mrs. Begum's" allowance was supplemented by expenses like trips to the dentist for "drawing teeth" or to the apothecary for "doses of powders." The whole family, it seemed, suffered from chronic colds, for which he bought them a steady supply of "black carrant lazinges" and "barley sugure draps in different tinnes for cough."[58]

In 1798, de Boigne was made a British subject, which protected him from possible internment during the ongoing war with France. With Adèle there would be reconciliations. During one of them, in 1801, de Boigne planned to buy a country estate, as befitted a man of his wealth and position. Scouting around England for a suitable property, he fell upon a splendid choice: Robert Clive's Claremont, unfinished at the time of Clive's death a quarter century before, but now complete on its high foundations—waiting for its nabob. But de Boigne and Adèle soon separated again, and the deal for Claremont fell through.[59] When peace came between Britain and France in 1802 (short-lived, in the event), de Boigne left Britain to settle in Savoy—alone.

During his five years in Britain, only one thing really came out well: it turned out that the losses on the *Cromberg* were not so bad after all. Many of de Boigne's rarities had been dredged up from the sea, including the wooden chest from his cabin with the valuable gold and silver hookahs, and most of his treasured weapons. He asked his Copenhagen agents to have "all the armes cleansed, being afraid that the rust may spoil them such as to render them unserviciable, or less valuable to the Eye, which is much more in the rarety or curiosity of them than in the intransic value of them." Wiped down "with the Graisse of fowls," they were like new again.[60]

## III. Staying On

"I could not, my good friend, be more pleased that you have found a treasure in a young, charming and amiable Companion, endowed with the best qualities, as you said, and from such an honourable family, as you said, you are happy, my good friend, I congratulate you from the bottom of my heart. . . ." Thus Claude Martin wrote to Benoît de Boigne in the late summer of 1799, to congratulate him on his marriage. But Martin's heart must have been heavy, too. Just a year earlier he had been so confident that his friend would soon return to India that he instructed him to bring "about a thousand or two of nice curiosities from Europe, things of little value, but in great numbers," and gleefully anticipated establishing a Masonic Lodge "here when you arrive, where you can serve the Grand Master in my new Chateau."[61] Now, though Martin still tried to tempt de Boigne back—"you will always be received with open arms and you can be assuredly the Commander of Hindustan, where the rupees will rain down into your hands"—he knew that de Boigne's marriage had effectively foreclosed the possibility of his return.[62] De Boigne was gone. Polier was dead. And Martin stayed on in Lucknow, alone.

The vibrant, cosmopolitan Lucknow of the 1780s had been vanishing. For many years already, Martin had talked of leaving the place about which he now complained so much: what had once been full of friends and rewards now seemed provincial, isolated, uncomfortable, unfashionable, with only "blacks" and the dregs of a once-flourishing European society for company. (Though "having always the good company of a mistress by me"—his *bibi* Boulone, whom he nicknamed Lise—"with my Zenana I spend some agreeable moments.")[63] By the mid-1790s, as Martin entered his seventh decade, his closest friends had left, and his health was steadily declining. Another reminder of his mortality, and probably the greatest transformation of the Lucknow world Martin had known, came with the death of Asaf ud-Daula in 1797. Yet it was in those years of loneliness and change that Martin embarked on his last, his greatest, and his most paradoxical act of self-fashioning. He decided to die as he had lived: an English gentleman, in Lucknow. Like a latter-day pharaoh, Claude Martin began to build his own tomb.

Maybe it was the sudden violence of Polier's death that made Martin prepare for his own with such scientific precision. "When I am dead," he instructed, in a meticulously detailed will,

> which I suppose will happen in Lucknow . . .I request that my Body may be salted or put in spirit or embalmed, and afterward deposited in a leaden Coffin made of some sheet lead in my Godown and this Coffin is to be put in another wooden one of Sissoo wood of thick plank of two inches thick and this to be deposited in the Cave of my Monument or house at Lackparra called Constantia in that Cave and in the small round Room North easterly to erect a Tomb of about Two Feet elevated from the Floor and to have the Coffin deposited in it and the Tomb to be coverd with a marble Stones and Inscription . . .

Its wording, naturally, he specified himself: MAJOR GENERAL CLAUDE MARTIN BORN AT LYON THE [5th DAY OF] JANUARY 1735 ARRIVED IN INDIA A COMMON SOLDIER AND DIED AT——THE MONTH OF——IN THE YEAR——AND HE IS BURIED IN THIS TOMB. PRAY FOR HIS SOUL.[64]

But Martin's one-line autobiography was misleading on several counts. First, he may have been "born at Lyon," but he had renounced his French loyalties in 1760 and considered himself British from then on. In 1785, he requested naturalization as a British subject. When he talked of returning to Europe, it was Britain, not France, that he had in mind. "Europe is certainly the country where to enjoy life," he wrote to Ozias Humphry in 1789, "and England Most Particularly for me, who have no other friend and acquaintance, but in England, and"—a significant declaration, this—"who may say is an Englishman having spent more than Life of a man among them. . . ."[65] Second, if Martin had "arrived in India a common soldier," he went on to attain there the money and stature of a prince. Amassing a fortune of over forty lakhs of rupees, or nearly half a million pounds, Martin not only became one of the richest Europeans in India, but also would have numbered among the richest men in Britain, too. And anyone reading his brief epitaph would have had evidence of both his wealth and his self-made social status right before their eyes. For "this tomb," which he designed himself, was nothing short of a palace: Constantia, set in the countryside southeast of Lucknow, "my reason for having built it wanting at first to make it for my tomb or Monument." *This* was Claude Martin as he meant the world to see him.

Constantia resembled its builder: there was nothing modest about it. In its scale, conception, and style, the house easily rivaled contemporary British stately homes. In character it far surpassed them. Statues decked its terraces: sphinxes, head-shaking mandarins, and gaping lions (a joke on Martin's birthplace, Lyon), with lantern eyes that glowed red into the night. Sweeping colonnades embraced a huge swath of parkland, sloping down to the Gomti River. At the back of the house was perched a row of cannon, cast in Martin's own foundry, including the *Lord Cornwallis,* which had pointed menacingly at the fortifications of Tipu Sultan's Seringapatam in 1792. Now it faced off against a tall, fluted column rising over an ornamental pool. Just maybe, standing under the arches of Constantia's cupola four stories up, you would see a touch of India in the distance—palm trees or spindly minarets in the low orange haze. But you would have to look for it.[66]

Martin might have been lonely, but he was not idle. Every morning he rode out of Lucknow to supervise the building work. Every afternoon, heavy with dinner, he rolled back in a carriage to check it again. "That building I think improve my health by Making me take plenty exercise," he joked.[67] He hung his paintings in its picture gallery, a suitable place at last for his collection of about seventy European oil paintings and at least as many more by Indian artists working in the European style. Into his elegant new library he moved about five thousand volumes from his overflowing townhouse, the Farhat Baksh. He also made room at Constantia for his scientific instruments, and for all the curiosities he had accumulated over the years. His salons were fitted

Constantia, Claude Martin's last retreat.

with Wedgwood cornices, great sash windows, and marble floors; and he decorated them with chandeliers, mirrors, fine carpets, and Gobelin tapestries. Out on the grounds, Martin finally put his steam engines to work, to power dancing fountains.[68] And he planned a European garden, asking de Boigne to send him seeds of "raspberries, strawberries of all kinds, large currants, little red and white currents . . . onions, . . . tulips, hyacinths, buttercups, . . . apricots, peaches, sweet-chestnuts . . . cardoon [artichoke], salsify, and others that we don't have here."[69] Building Constantia "will keep me long at it and perapse as long as I live . . ." said Martin cheerfully, "or otherwise I will have the happiness to see it finishd and to hear people praise it, as they do my present one."[70]

Without a doubt, Constantia was a glorious advertisement of Martin's self-made success. It was for Martin what Claremont was for Robert Clive: enduring proof of its builder's immense wealth, taste, status, and talents. A connoisseur, collector, and architect, an English gentleman, and a man of the Enlightenment: Claude Martin had made himself all these things and more, and his house brashly broadcast it. Yet it was founded on a paradox. For if Martin was so committed to living like a European gentleman, and to letting everybody know it, then why did he not go to Europe and do it properly? He had the money to retire, in bucketfuls; he was childless; he had friends and connections there aplenty.

Some of the answers are plain. There could be no question, for Martin, of returning to France in the 1790s. Polier's murder in 1795, by which Martin was so "extremely affected," brought the danger and destructiveness of the Revolution into painful focus.[71] Britain was the only real possibility, yet there, too, were obvious obstacles. For one thing, like all nabobs, Martin would have worried about how actually to remit his money home—a difficult business at the best of times, now even harder given the war in Europe and the disruptions in Awadh following Asaf ud-Daula's death. Nobody could guarantee, either, that Britain would be immune from the infectious radicalism of those years, or indeed, from a full-scale French invasion, which was widely (and to some extent justifiably) feared in 1798. Given "the wildness of the times . . . [and] the insecurity of every part of Europe," Martin's friends advised him, it was simply safer, financially and personally, to stay put in Lucknow.[72] Then, too, though Martin might call himself a Briton in Lucknow, it would be a lot harder to do so in London. His name was French (if easily Anglicized), his national origins were well known, his English was broken and heavily accented. As de Boigne could have told him, this was hardly the best moment for a Frenchman to try to integrate himself into British society. Even some of the British in Lucknow had made cutting allusions to "renegade Frenchmen" in their midst.[73]

All these factors—instability, war, Polier's death, de Boigne's disappointments—would certainly have encouraged Martin to remain in Lucknow. And to all these, Martin must have added one more, the only reason that can explain why he had begun to plan his mausoleum as early as 1792. For Claude Martin understood something his friends did not: you can't take it with you. By making himself a soi-disant English gentleman in Lucknow, he anchored himself just as firmly in India as had Antoine Polier by becoming a Mughal nobleman, or as had Benoît de Boigne by becoming a Maratha warlord. Martin earned the social and economic freedom in Lucknow to emulate the European lifestyle he so admired. Yet his was a replica and no more. Founded on self-made wealth, French origins, and Indian opportunities, the copy would never be able to stand up to the real thing. In short, for all that his social ambitions were directed toward Europe, they could not have been transplanted there with anything like the success he enjoyed in Lucknow. Somewhere deep inside him, Claude Martin must have known, even before the examples of Polier and de Boigne could prove to him, that exporting his Lucknow identity was impossible.

Staying in Lucknow was a hard decision for Martin, and it did not make him happy. Still, he comforted himself that it was the right one. "It doesn't matter," he said to de Boigne, that people were envious of his wealth or that enemies muttered character-smearing rumors behind his back:

> "After me the end of the world." However I shall try to leave sufficient to get me a place in the bosom of our good mother earth to whom we will all return, and as we are nothing but travellers on the Globe try to live in the best mansions and there to live the best that we can [and] do the best that we can think of, without meanwhile being uncomfortable.[74]

Thus he consoled himself, and went on building his mansion.

But he was in great discomfort. His was a lingering, tortured death, under the triple afflictions of venereal disease, a swollen prostate, and an ulcerated bladder. The pain was so excruciating at times that he grew half-mad with it, waking in agony every hour. Maybe it was this that made him, notoriously impious though he was, call for a priest in his final hours. Yet the old sinner had eschewed and insulted Padre Banton in the past, and now the padre returned the favor, by refusing to come to Martin's deathbed. On the night of September 13, 1800, Claude Martin returned to "the bosom of our good mother earth," an unconfessed Catholic—a death, like his life, between identities.

He was interred, according to his instructions, in the bowels of his house, and the inscription placed over his remains reads just as he drafted it. For in the end, that was his reward. Staying on in Lucknow gave Martin a rare and priceless luxury: to write his own epitaph, to build his own tomb. And in their twin messages, of humility and arrogance, of Frenchness and Britishness, in this brash re-creation of Europe in the heart of India, Claude Martin could show the world exactly what he had achieved in it.

## IV. Legacies

"After me the end of the world": Martin's words were entirely apt. The thriving, hybrid Lucknow he had known was finished. In early 1798, six months after Asaf ud-Daula's death, the Company unceremoniously ousted the nawab's hostile and supposedly insane heir, Wazir Ali, to install their preferred candidate, Asaf's half-brother Saadat Ali Khan. Where Asaf had blended European elements into a fundamentally Indo-Persian court culture, Saadat Ali, who had been raised and educated by the British in Calcutta, tended toward straightforward assimilation instead. The new nawab dressed in nankeen breeches and velvet riding coats, spoke some English, was "highly gratified by any comparison between himself and the Prince of Wales," and kept India's finest pack of foxhounds. When Viscount Valentia dined with him in Lucknow in 1803—on a French meal prepared by Saadat Ali's French cook, served on the finest European plate and crystal, and accompanied by an English regimental band—"the scene was so singular, and so contrary to all my ideas of Asiatic manners," the viscount said, "that I could hardly persuade myself that the whole was not a masquerade."[75]

Of course, it *was* a masquerade: behind the scenes, and increasingly in front of them, the Company was controlling Awadh's economy, military, and policy more than ever. In retrospect, it looked as if from Saadat Ali onward, the Company and the nawabs joined hands and together walked the road to their own destruction. In 1801 the Company annexed half of the province outright. Eighteen years later, it encouraged the nawab Ghazi ud-Din Haidar to break entirely with the Mughal emperor—and in effect align himself openly with the British—by crowning himself padishah.[76] In 1856, the Company annexed the rest of Awadh, a critical provocation for the Indian Mutiny-Rebellion of 1857–1858. It was to be in Lucknow, where East and West had once mixed to a greater degree than virtually anywhere in Asia, that some of the mutiny's first and most savage acts were played out; the ruins of Lucknow's British residency still stand as a skeletal reminder of that violent year. After the mutiny, the Company was replaced by the direct rule of the British Raj. Much of the architecture of the nawabi capital vanished, as British planners razed the city's riot-prone, disease-ridden, corrupt, and corrupting lanes.[77]

All of that was for the distant future, to be sure. But Martin's death in 1800 fell at a threshhold. He died at the end of a period in which the cultural, social, and political boundaries between British, European, and Indian were relatively permeable. His own layered profile—a Frenchman who called himself English while living in a semi-independent Mughal province—was something the next generation would find more difficult to pull off, or condone. (Recall Viscount Valentia's vitriolic condemnation of him as nouveau riche.) Martin's death also coincided with a significant moment of transition in British imperial expansion: the outbreak of the Revolutionary-Napoleonic Wars, and Anglo-French conflict on the imperial stages of Egypt and India. As Polier and de Boigne experienced firsthand, this new imperial and global war made certain kinds of border crossing harder and rarer. Returning to Europe, they found that the personæ they had pieced together in India did not map neatly back over European social and national borders. They had come "home" only to find themselves strangers in strange lands.

What do these three individual experiences of loss and compromise reveal about the larger historical scene of which they were part? Single lives plucked from a sea of millions, their stories help give some sense of how ordinary people could be caught up in events much greater than themselves. Yet each of these men also made a mark on their world. They left material remains behind. They left collections. In their legacies, it is possible to trace out some of the changes in how Britain, Europe, India, and empire would interact in the decades to come.

The first legacy to consider is specifically tangible, and best addressed through the fate of Antoine Polier. What happened to collections when they were taken to Europe? And what became of them when their owners died?

Returning to Europe was in some ways as disastrous for Polier's manuscripts as it was for Polier himself. Taken out of Mughal India, the manuscripts were stripped of the social value that had encouraged Polier to acquire them in the first place; this was surely in part why he lost interest in them himself. Polier was unusual in that he had a relative, his cousin Marie, who cared about his strange Indian papers. Even so, his collection, like so many others, would be scattered after his death.[78] Most of the time, a collector's heirs would have "no use" for manuscripts in tongues they could not decipher, and the pieces were "in danger of being neglected, and at length in a great measure lost to Europe as well as India." So common was "this injury to letters" that the East India Company itself, in 1798, decided to step in and establish a "Public Repository [in Britain] for Oriental writings."[79]

The Oriental Repository, later called the India Museum, opened in the Company's London headquarters, on Leadenhall Street, in 1801. It was a milestone in the history of imperial collecting: the first institution in Britain (and probably Europe) explicitly dedicated to non-European collections. At one level, the museum was an institutional heir for a dying generation of collectors; in its first decade, for instance, it was enriched by manuscripts collected in Lucknow by John Wombwell, Richard Johnson, and Warren Hastings.[80] But it was also something more. "By such a collection," the Company hoped, Indian literature "may be preserved in this country, after, perhaps, it shall, from farther changes, and the farther declension of taste for it, be partly lost in its original seats."[81] Appeals to preservation are widely made today, but at the time this language was quite novel. By appointing itself the custodian of India's literary traditions, the Company was wrapping itself in the mantle of the Mughals, assuming a guise of patron and protector that would live on, in varying incarnations, until the end of the British Empire in India.

Virtually all collectors of Indian manuscripts in the eighteenth century had lived in India themselves. This, too, was changing. At Christie's, not a single collection of "Oriental" manuscripts was sold between the firm's founding in 1766 and 1800. In the first decade of the nineteenth century alone, however, the house sold three major collections of Indian manuscripts. This sudden burst of activity in the market revealed both new sources of supply—the estates of deceased collectors—and a new kind of demand. Now, an "Orien-

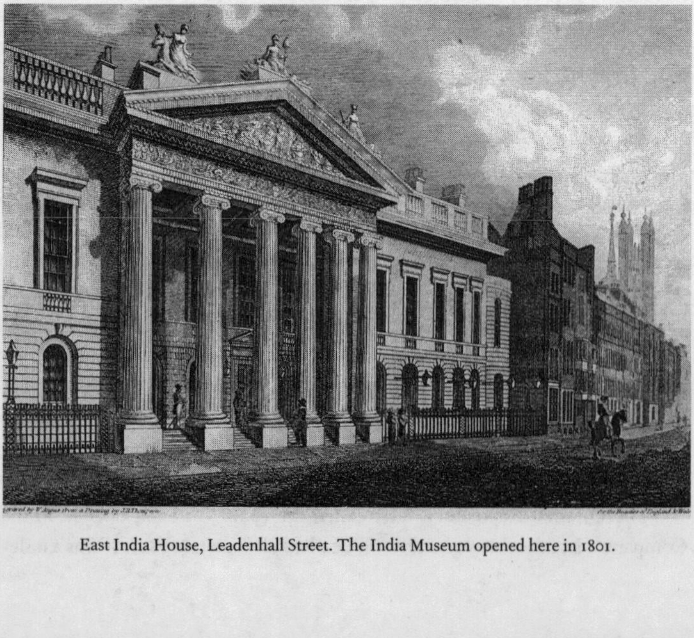

East India House, Leadenhall Street. The India Museum opened here in 1801.

talist" circle was taking shape in Europe.[82] At its center were former East India Company servants, like the Sanskritist Charles Wilkins, or the Persophile brothers Sir William and Sir Gore Ouseley. But it also embraced aesthetes and young Romantics with no personal connection to India, such as the writer and fanatical collector William Beckford, whose extravagant neo-Gothic house, Fonthill Abbey, was a fantastic statement of self-fashioning if ever there was one. Beckford, in fact, acquired some of Antoine Polier's albums of paintings, which was only fitting since he, too, was performing a cosmopolitan fusion: plowing his family's West Indian sugar fortune into a collection of Eastern curiosities.[83] Beckford was a new kind of imperial collector, using imperial money to buy imperial objects, but without having to leave the imperial capital, London, to do it.

A widening fissure was coming to separate actual *objects*—weapons, metalwork, jewelery, textiles, carvings, and so on—from manuscripts. The former, often brought home as personal keepsakes, were still generally kept in private, family hands. (Robert Clive's collection, for example, is on display today in the house of his heirs, Powis Castle; and the de Boigne family owns many of Benoît's weapons.) Manuscripts, however, might pass into "public" precincts such as libraries or the India Museum. As those collections were dispersed, they were also categorized in radically new ways. Where Polier himself had collected manuscripts in a range of languages, making little evident distinction between "Hindu" and "Muslim" writings, after his death his Sanskrit manuscripts would end up staying mostly on the Continent, while his Persian and Arabic manuscripts went to the libraries of Eton and King's College, Cambridge, to be studied by future generations of Indian civil servants. Once divided, and along religious and linguistic lines in particular, the collection that Polier had formed—united by the social environment of Asaf's Lucknow—was forever lost.

A second legacy of the Lucknow generation had a human face, as de Boigne's fate revealed in poignant detail. What happened to people of mixed allegiances once they returned to Europe? And what happened to those who accompanied them?

As the Peace of Amiens settled over Britain and France in 1802, Benoît de Boigne made his way back to his beloved "snowy mountains of Savoy."[84] He returned to Chambéry more than thirty years older—not the Leborgne he had left it, but now General de Boigne, a man of stature and substance—and bought himself a grand, gray mansarded house on the hills above the town, Le Buisson Rond. Yet all was not right with his world. For some four centuries Savoy had been an independent duchy, but it was now effectively a French colony, invaded, occupied, and annexed by revolutionary forces in 1792.

When Britain and France resumed hostilities in 1803, de Boigne was once again caught wrong-footed. "The English General Boyne" (as he had been called in French newspapers) was in Paris on a British passport, and could potentially be interned.

Precisely how he eluded arrest is not clear. But the price of freedom was collusion, or at least rumors of it, with Savoy's French masters. In 1803, Napoleon supposedly wrote to the veteran, asking him to help lead a joint Franco-Russian invasion of British India. Word quickly reached the ear of the governor-general of India, Richard Wellesley, that "M. de Boigne . . . is now the chief confidant of Bonaparte. He is constantly at St. Cloud. I leave you to judge why and wherefore." London papers buzzed with libels against the "French" de Boigne.[85] As it happens, de Boigne never met Napoleon, but the moral of this story is clear. In a Europe divided by war, multiple loyalties could not stand. It was manifestly impossible to be both British and French when Britain and France were at war. Only with the reestablishment of the House of Savoy in 1815 could de Boigne again navigate a third way between them, a Savoyard once more—and a count, ennobled by Victor Emmanuel in 1816.

On the domestic front, de Boigne's return to Chambéry in 1802 was no more satisfactory. Adèle was not with him, which suited both parties well enough. But he was lonely in the Buisson Rond, and his thoughts returned again, often, to his first family, left behind in Britain. He kept up with their doings through mutual friends, and an infrequent correspondence with Nur. "Helen Bennett"—or as she was sometimes referred to, "Mde. Begum Bennet" (a wonderfully polyglot set of titles), or simply "Mrs. Begum"—now lived on an annuity of £250, in a house de Boigne had bought for her in Surrey. She was received in local society as his legitimate wife.[86] Ann, aka Banu Jan, a pretty girl of "a very pleasing color to the eye, though born of an Indian mother," went to Mrs. Barker's school in Hammersmith. Charles, Ali Baksh, a gangling adolescent, studied diligently at St. Edmund's College in Hertfordshire.[87] In 1804, when Ann was fifteen, de Boigne decided to bring her out to live with him and preside over his household. That September, she sailed for Holland and traveled down through Belgium to meet her father in Paris. They had been apart two years at least, perhaps as many as six. He was overjoyed to have her back.

But Ann had been ill all the way from Brussels, and though her father whisked her off to Beauregard, his estate outside Paris, "she arrived . . . only to take to her bed and to die in my arms twelve days later." De Boigne was devastated. He cursed himself for his selfishness: "she would still be alive had I thought of her happiness rather than of my own. . . . She is happy but there will be no more happiness for me." Helen, too, was shattered. "I don't know what to write upon my misfortune," she said. "I dare say you did love her as much as I did. . . . She is happy, an angel in heaven who prays for us." Across the many barriers that separated them, the parents shared an unspeakable grief.[88]

It took ten more years for de Boigne to reach across the Channel again. Charles, during these years, had grown into a young man of ability and purpose, and was studying law at Lincoln's Inn. He often saw his mother, who had moved to Sussex; and he wrote sometimes to his father, though he was often upset by long silences he received in response. But when peace between Britain and France came again, in 1814, de Boigne asked Charles to come and join him. In the early summer of 1815 (just as Napoleon was preparing to meet the British at Waterloo), twenty-two-year-old Charles Bennett landed at Boulogne. De Boigne had not seen him since the boy was at most ten years old. The young man who now came out to greet him looked unmistakably like his father: tall, and with the same long nose, cleft chin, and gaunt, high cheekbones. But where the father's hair was gray and thin, the son's was full and black. His skin was distinctly brown. He spoke and behaved like the young English gentleman he was.[89]

De Boigne legitimized Charles in 1816, making him heir to the great and growing de Boigne fortune and to the new family title of count. Later that same year, Charles married into one of Savoy's most distinguished families. When de Boigne went to his grave in 1830, aged eighty, he died confident of his son's material, social, and dynastic success. He left behind a financial empire that stretched from Italy to Denmark to the United States, real estate in multiple countries, a position of great influence in Savoy, and a hereditary title. Thus it was that his own mixed identities came together, with his heir, into a single version: a Savoyard aristocrat.

It was also through Charles that another piece of de Boigne's life, unexpectedly, fell into place. Adèle, whose disdain for her husband only increased with the years, took a surprising shine to his son, only seven or eight years her junior, and the two kept up an amiable acquaintance throughout Charles's life. (She, for her part, presided over a glittering salon in Restoration Paris and left her own legacy in the observant, acute *Mémoires de la comtesse de Boigne*. In its two volumes, she makes little mention of her detested husband and none at all of her half-Indian stepson.)[90] From his own mother, however, Charles grew more distant. Helen Bennett stayed in England, living in a lodge down a woodland path in St. Leonard's Forest. "The Black woman," as she was known, smoked hookahs, went to Mass regularly, and outlived her son by some months. In 1853 she died at the age of eighty-one, and was buried in the churchyard like the good Catholic she was. But her grave, unlike all the others, pointed south. Was it meant to be facing southeast, toward Mecca, an allusion to her Muslim and Indian origins? Or was it a renunciation of them, a way of eschewing the East in death, as she had in life?[91]

It is tempting to see the apotheosis of Benoît de Boigne as a "what if" rewriting of Polier's tragic end. Where Polier was murdered for trying to live as both an aristocrat and a Frenchman, de Boigne persevered through revolution and war, and ultimately prevailed, winning both title and nationality back in his native Savoy. But perhaps the truer comparison lies not between their lives but between their legacies: de Boigne's family and Polier's manuscript collection. The de Boigne family, like many a collection, had been displaced and broken apart in Europe: Helen died in Britain and Ann in France; Benoît and Charles found their last homes in Savoy. Each, too, had been fitted into new categories. As for de Boigne himself, returning to Europe meant grappling with conflicting ambitions and loyalties—to Britain, France, Savoy, and India. It meant risking freedom and happiness; it meant, most of all, repeatedly having to compromise. If his was a success story, it was also, in the end, like Polier's, a tale of loss.

The third and final question raised by these figures and their cosmopolitan age can best be considered through the legacy of Claude Martin. What remained behind, in India?

In the months following Martin's death, a team of clerks superintended by the trusty Joseph Queiros fanned out across the rooms of Martin's two great houses, the Farhat Baksh and Constantia. Their job was to inventory all the contents, a long and involved task indeed. They probed every chest, opened every drawer, inspected every shelf, counted, described, and recorded, in a seemingly endless column of sloping sepia words. The inventory, when they finally finished it some six months later, ran to seventy-six pages. It remains in the archives today, like a balance sheet of Martin's life, a biography in objects. Little is known of the fate of his enormous, extravagant, eclectic collection—little, that is, beyond the familiar story of dispersal. Most of it was packed up and sent to Calcutta, where it was sold off by the city's leading auctioneer, William Tulloh. The governor-general Richard Wellesley bought Martin's chandeliers and mirrors for his new Government House, and many of Martin's possessions may have found their way into non-European houses, too.[92] Back in Lucknow, the nawab Saadat Ali Khan bought the Farhat Baksh, on account of its "very commodious zenana."[93] And so the material world of Claude Martin vanished, into the salons of Calcutta and beyond.

Constantia, of course, remained. The house, with his body buried inside it, was completed according to his designs; over his tomb presided "Two Molla at 20 Rs. p. month or one Priest at 50 Rupees per month" (a fine piece of cultural interchange) and four plaster sepoys. And he had further plans for the house. Martin had never fathered children, but he nevertheless wanted to have an heir—or better yet, as many heirs as possible.[94] He decided to make Constantia "a house for School or Coledge for learning young Men the English language and Christian Religion if they find themselves inclined." In his will he endowed three secondary schools: one in the great house in Lucknow, another in Calcutta, and a third in Lyon, all to be named La Martinière, after him. La Martinière students in Calcutta and Lucknow were taught English and Persian, and were attended (like Martin's tomb) by Muslim mullahs as well as Catholic priests. Every September 13, the students raised a glass to Martin's memory.[95] His legacy is an important reminder that not all fusions and mixtures vanished with the nineteenth century. Even he, expatriate and adoptive Briton, remembered the city of his birth and his French relatives in his will. His lavish European mansion still stands outside Lucknow, and Indian students there and in Calcutta continue to receive an English-language education in his name.

And yet, if being an "Indian" in Europe was difficult, as returnees had been discovering for generations, being a "European" in India *à la* Claude Martin—French by origin, British by preference, European by lifestyle—was becoming impossible. Martin's Lucknow persona rested in part on a broadly European profile of the cultivated gentleman, one in which distinctions between British and French meant little and mattered less. But in India as in Europe, after 1789, Anglo-French rivalry and war divided the European population into opposing camps with new vigor. By staying on in India, Martin escaped the ludicrous predicament of de Boigne, a French citizen in London and a British subject in Paris. He managed to remain suspended in between. Many of his fellow Francophones would not.

At the time of Martin's death, continental Europeans could be found across the subcontinent, in the service, like him, of Indian princes. So could Britons, as a perusal of de Boigne's officer lists shows; Irishmen, such as the famous adventurer George Thomas; and Anglo-Indians such as Hyder Jung Hearsey and James Skinner.[96] But Company expansion, in the context of Anglo-French war, put pressure on the relationship of Europeans to Indian states. While the Company invited Anglo-Indians and British "renegades" back into the fold of its army, it became increasingly suspicious of continental Europeans outside it, often labeled as "French."[97] In Hyderabad, the nizam's infantry marched behind a Frenchman, Raymond, who flew a tricolor at their head. In northern Hindustan, de Boigne's Maratha army continued to drill and fight under the command of the French general Perron and his European subordinates. In Mysore, most visibly of all, Savoyard-trained troops fought for Tipu Sultan, whose successful adaptation of European military and legislative techniques rendered him the most dangerous opponent of British expansion in South India.

All these powers, and Tipu Sultan especially, were believed to be pro-French by anxious British authorities at the end of the eighteenth century. But it was not only the Company that drew lines between British and French, friend and foe. From France, too, the rallying cry was sounded: French officers and veterans from Indian armies were invited, or in some cases volunteered, to turn their experience and resources against the Company. Whether or not Napoleon solicited de Boigne's help for an invasion of India in 1803, the plans were nevertheless developed; French soldiers in, or formerly in, Indian service were available, and many of them were prepared to help.[98] What remained behind in India after the days of Claude Martin and his friends, in short, was a European society, and a European relationship with Indians more generally, that would be significantly reshaped around lines of nation and culture in the decades to come.

A single theme runs through all of these lives and legacies. Each one suggests how mixtures, fusions, and collaborations that were developed during the late eighteenth century were divided into new categories in the nineteenth. It happened to objects. When cross-cultural collections were displaced or dispersed, they were regrouped under new headings, in new hands. It happened to people. When individuals who had joined together various loyalties moved on, into new contexts, they were forced to make choices, to abandon or revise their mixed identities. And it happened, in a manner of speaking, to states. When war between Britain and France extended with new intensity into Asia, indigenous powers and Europeans within them aligned themselves around the combatants in starker and clearer terms than ever before. That realignment would take place in the last years of the eighteenth century, and its flashpoints would flank the Indian Ocean: in Egypt and the South Indian kingdom of Mysore.

PART TWO

# IMPERIAL COLLISION

1798–1801

CHAPTER FOUR

# *Invading Egypt*

## 1. A New War, a New Empire

The new phase of Anglo-French imperial rivalry began in Paris, with the killing of a king and the start of another war. Hours before dawn on January 21, 1793, the condemned king Louis XVI prepared for death. He confessed to his Irish priest; removed his wedding ring, to be delivered, with a packet of locks of family hair, to his grieving wife, who would follow him to the scaffold some months later; and climbed into a closed carriage, which drove him slowly through silent streets, from the Temple prison to the Place de la Révolution. There, at ten o'clock, Citizen Louis Capet mounted the steps to the scaffold—facing the empty plinth where an equestrian statue of his grandfather once stood—protested his innocence before a crowd of twenty thousand, and lost his head to Dr. Guillotin's *rasoir national*.[1]

The execution of Louis XVI marked a point of no return in the sequence of events that had unfolded in France since the storming of the Bastille in 1789. As long as the king remained on the throne, the French Revolution had appeared to consist mostly of implementing a British-style monarchy bound by law, and dismantling many of the hoary privileges of the Ancien Régime aristocracy and clergy. As such, it had been welcomed at first by liberal French aristocrats such as the Marquis de Lafayette, and by many Britons. But in August 1792, when a mob stormed the Tuileries Palace, it became evident that things were about to get a lot more revolutionary. The National Assembly was replaced by a republican government, the Convention, in which the radical Jacobins soon took power; the monarchy was abolished outright; the king and queen were tried and executed. No more king, no more establishment, equality for all: Louis XVI's execution signaled the start of an entirely different order of things. It also commenced a new chapter in the age-old animosity between Britain and France.

News of the regicide electrified Britain. In the words of a contemporary chronicler, "Every sentiment of abhorrence towards the French republic was kindled to a flame, on the intelligence of the condemnation and public execution of the unfortunate Louis. . . ."[2] As a matter of course, the French ambassador in London was dismissed; and on February 1, 1793, after months of bellicose talk and provocations, France declared war on Britain and the Dutch Republic. Even King George III, who had been deeply opposed to war ever since the disastrous loss of the thirteen colonies ten years earlier, was moved to aggression by Louis's fate. "Indeed," he wrote to his prime minister, William Pitt the Younger, the day after France's declaration of war, "my natural sentiments are so strong for peace that no event of less moment than the present could have made me decidedly of the opinion that duty, as well as interest, calls on us to join against that most savage as well as unprincipled nation."[3]

Little did he or anybody else then know that the war now started against France would continue virtually unabated until the Battle of Waterloo, in 1815. And if the French Revolution marked what is still widely considered to be the beginning of a "modern" political age, so too the wars that accompanied it marked the beginning of a new kind of conflict. Its profoundly shocking start was just one of several ways in which the Revolutionary-Napoleonic Wars differed from the five long Anglo-French wars that had been fought since 1689—even from the Seven Years War, which had itself been a watershed. Out of this struggle would come not only great human loss, great political change, and a heightened sense of national identity, but also a new configuration of world power, a new kind of empire.

First, as the king's execution made plain, the ideological proportions of this conflict were dramatically greater than those of Britain's wars against Bourbon France. Earlier conflicts had pitted British liberty, British Protestantism, and British-style monarchy against the perceived despotism of French absolutism and Catholicism. From 1793, however, the clash was no longer between two different models of crown, church, and state; it was between two drastically opposing visions of society. In British eyes, this was a struggle to defend the familiar social order against the kingless, godless, egalitarian republicanism of the Reign of Terror. To the French revolutionaries, the conflict pitted reason, equality, and liberty against religion, privilege, and tyranny. The strength of these ideological convictions made the Revolutionary-Napoleonic Wars stand in relation to the Seven Years War in something like the way World War II later would to World War I. The Seven Years War had been fought for power, land, and security; now Britain and France were fighting to defend and extend their very ways of life.

They were also fighting on a vastly greater human and capital scale. This was the second way in which the Revolutionary-Napoleonic Wars differed from earlier Anglo-French conflicts. Almost double the size of the fighting forces of the Seven Years War, the "People's Armies" of the French Revolution were made up of 500,000 to 750,000 men; 300,000 alone were raised in desperate levies in March and August 1793 alone.[4] At its peak, Napoleon's army verged on a full million men, two-thirds of whom would march with him to Russia in 1812. Britain, perennially worried about its small size in relation to France, had much to fear from these massive armies. It is no coincidence that the first British national census was undertaken in 1800, at the peak of the war. Yet while many Frenchmen fought against their will—some 16,000 to 24,000 twenty-year-olds were conscripted each year under Napoleon, and stood at best a one-in-three chance of ever coming back alive—Britain's armies were smaller but arguably more resolute. Widespread (and entirely justified) fear of French invasion prompted some one in twenty British men to join volunteer corps and militias for home defense: 116,000 in 1798, swelling to at least 380,000 in 1804. A roughly equivalent number served in the armed forces, which reached about half a million men at their height.[5] These numbers matter not just to show that huge armies now faced off on the battlefield; they suggest what a high percentage of each country's young male population was drawn by war directly into the service of the state.

Fervently ideological and waged on a spectacular scale, the Revolutionary-Napoleonic Wars marked the beginning of something new. These were explicitly *imperial* wars, far surpassing previous colonial conflicts in scope and clarity of imperial purpose. To be sure, all Anglo-French wars since 1689 had been fought in, and to an increasing extent about, overseas colonies. This was patently true in the Americas, where the first shots of the Seven Years War had been fired, where Montcalm and Wolfe had met their deaths, and where Britain's most recent war with France, the American Revolution, had been fought and lost. The imperial consequences of Anglo-French war had also been manifest in India, where throughout the 1740s and 1750s the British and French East India companies had vied for ascendancy. But from 1793, overt state-driven conquest of territory, both beyond and within Europe, stood at the very center of French and British war efforts.

Historical treatment of the Revolutionary-Napoleonic Wars so overwhelmingly focuses on Europe that the global dimensions of the struggle tend to get lost and its overseas episodes crowded out. Yet for both Britain and France, the wars were infused with imperial significance. For the French revolutionaries, conquest formed part of an imperial *mission civilisatrice*, or "civilizing mission," designed to spread republican and Enlightenment ideals across Europe.[6] Napoleon began his own imperial career under the tricolor of the French Revolution, leading republican "armies of liberation" into Italy (1796) and Egypt (1798). Britain did not enter the wars with as explicit an ideological posture, but the conflict sharpened the nation's imperial policy. Where Britain had been reluctant to undertake aggressive and preemptive conquests in the past, it now pursued campaigns in South Asia, the Caribbean, Africa, and the Mediterranean—to say nothing of incorporating Ireland under the Act of Union in 1801—as part of a worldwide effort to prevent and counteract French success. A further impetus to imperial expansion was provided by the military stalemate in which the powers were caught. Britain's naval supremacy alone could not vanquish France; nor could France's superior land strength by itself defeat Britain. The key to victory for either side might well lie abroad, in the acquisition of commercial and strategic dominance overseas.[7] War with France was more than a convenient excuse for British empire-building, as has sometimes been suggested. Imperial consolidation and expansion were believed to be vital to the security of Britain.[8]

James Gillray, "The Plumb-Pudding in Danger," 1805. The British prime minister William Pitt and Napoleon carve up the world between them. Note that Napoleon greedily slices off a tranche of land in Europe, while Pitt cuts through the Atlantic Ocean, suggesting Britain's naval dominance.

The eighteenth-century British Empire had not come into being as a single "project" plotted by London schemers; nor was it united by a homogeneous culture, ethnicity, or national identity. How much did the wars change that? The short, obvious answer is: a very great deal.[9] For a start, by encouraging an active approach to territorial expansion, the Revolutionary-Napoleonic Wars provided the closest thing to a state-sponsored imperial agenda that had hitherto been evident. The wars also significantly transformed the parameters, purposes, and public perception of empire. After Waterloo, the British Empire was much larger in extent than before, and expanding unequivocally in Asia and Africa instead of in North America. Developments that had been anticipated by the Seven Years War gained fuller expression. Now more than ever this was an empire of conquest and direct rule as well as settlement, an empire of security as well as commerce. It was an empire that looked more and more like the sort of territorial dominion so many Britons had been wary of, and often opposed to, in the past. At the same time, the wars helped consolidate a wider sense of support for and identification with empire, and a clearer vision of what imperial rule was intended to achieve. The new British Empire would come to turn domination over non-white, non-Christian peoples into its mission and justification, and it would be confidently, proudly, and assertively "British" as never before.

These years proved vital to the forging of British national and imperial identity.[10] This is not to say that the British Empire suddenly consolidated overnight. In significant and defining ways, it remained permeable to and dependent on outsiders. Boundaries hardened between different kinds of *Europeans*—British and French most of all—as men such as Claude Martin, Antoine Polier, and Benoît de Boigne experienced firsthand. Yet at the same time, the expansion of empire relied upon a capacious understanding of who and what was to be considered British or French.

A glimpse into the sheer variety embraced under those national labels could be found within the ranks of their huge armies. The British military remained heavily dependent on Irish enlistment: more than a third of the army was made up of Irishmen during the Napoleonic Wars; the East India Company army was even more substantially Irish. Catholic and Protestant alike, the Irish were builders and beneficiaries of the British Empire at the same time that they were its rebels and victims.[11] The East India Company army, by 1815, counted 200,000 Indian sepoys to a European officer corps of 30,000.[12] A similar dependence on imperial subjects existed in Napoleon's armies, a full third of whose strength came from the newly annexed territories of Savoy, northern Flanders, and the Rhineland; a further third was composed of mercenaries and new imperial subjects, largely from central and eastern Europe.[13] The

French army even included a brigade of Egyptian Mamelukes—whom Francisco Goya vividly depicted slashing Spanish patriots in his masterpiece of anti-Napoleonic resistance, *The Second of May*.

Armies are not necessarily national microcosms, but the enlistment of imperial subjects to secure and extend empires points to one way that boundary crossings were needed in order for nations, and empires, to survive. The hardening of imperial purpose plainly involved developing ways of justifying British superiority over foreign subjects; exclusionary definitions of "otherness" were taking shape, based on race, religion, ethnicity, or a culture's perceived level of civilization. At the same time, however, the expansion of empire also brought about a vast increase in the number of foreign subjects to be incorporated into the fold of British rule. How they were *included* in the rhetoric and systems of empire has been much less carefully explored. The collaborations and cosmopolitan assemblages familiar from the eighteenth century were not wiped out; they were reconfigured.

So it was that in this epochal struggle, British and French imperial interests were shifted, extended, revised. Much of the newly nationalist (for lack of a better word) imperial ideology to emerge in this period was formulated and exercised on the European continent, the heartlands of Napoleon's French Empire—which is worth recalling, given the tendency to think of empire as an overseas phenomenon, involving white rule over nonwhites. In the Western Hemisphere, the decades of war witnessed the scaling-back of the Spanish and Portuguese empires, as the British and French juggled support for Latin American claims to independence with the desire to sustain or develop informal empire. But nowhere were the tensions of inclusion and exclusion, empires new and old, formal and informal, of more palpable and lasting significance, than on Europe's eastern imperial edges, on the overlapping grounds of Ottoman, Mughal, British, and French power. Two key linked events within this great if unacknowledged world war brought cross-cultural conquest and entanglement into sharp focus. They unfolded in Egypt and India.

In the summer of 1798, Napoleon Bonaparte invaded Egypt, beginning what would be a three-year occupation by France. Quite unlike European expansion in India or Indonesia, for example—which originated in internecine conflict between European trading companies, perched on the edges of Eastern powers—the French invasion of Egypt was a bald grab for territory on a scale no European nation had yet undertaken outside the Americas. It thus stands as one of the first and most overt "imperial" conquests in modern history. According to Edward Said, who famously identified the invasion as the first "Orientalist" project, it also initiated a new *kind* of extra-European conquest, legitimated by a rhetoric of Western superiority, and harnessing institutions of knowledge and culture to the state. Most of all, it was a perfect example of the globalization—and imperialization—of Anglo-French war: Napoleon's stated goal was to challenge British dominance in India.

And it was to be on the other side of the Indian Ocean that the second series of events played itself out. In 1799, the East India Company launched a war against Tipu Sultan, ruler of the South Indian kingdom of Mysore, and captured his capital, Seringapatam. For thirty years Tipu Sultan and his father, Haidar Ali, had challenged British forces in southern India; 1799 represented the fourth in a string of armed contests between the Company and Mysore. Spearheaded by a new governor-general, Richard Wellesley, the 1799 campaign exemplified Britain's own turn toward active expansion, and marked a fundamental shift away from the earlier East India Company reluctance to pursue expensive and potentially entangling conquests. Wellesley's offensive militarism would continue with fierce wars against the Marathas, commanded on the field by Wellesley's more famous younger brother, Arthur, the future Duke of Wellington, who later recalled them as the hardest he had ever fought. It also resulted in a series of informal acquisitions and annexations, and in what was then the largest (and only the second) overseas campaign by the East India Company: a counterinvasion of Egypt in 1801.

Waged on different continents and, on the face of it, against quite separate indigenous powers, the French invasion of Egypt and the British capture of Seringapatam were in fact two fronts in a single Anglo-French war. Because British and French histories are so often treated in isolation, and because the overseas clashes of the Revolutionary-Napoleonic Wars are often overshadowed by those on the Continent, few historians have paid much mind to the connection between Egypt and Seringapatam. But the campaigns had tremendous significance for British and French ambitions in the East. Together, they represented an abrupt collision between imperial expansion and Anglo-French war, and a "what if" moment that might have left Indians today speaking French, not English, as their first Western language. The years around the turn of the century marked the last concerted bid by France to win a foothold in India. They witnessed the first major British attempt to secure and protect India from abroad, and Britain's first territorial entry into the Ottoman world. And they opened a new sphere of British informal empire—of influence and control behind the scenes—in the Middle East.

Against these changes in global geopolitics and the practice of European expansion, the campaigns in Egypt and Seringapatam also reflected an enduring feature of imperial cultural politics on the ground. Both Britain and France depended on, and constructed, definitions of friend and foe that bridged East and West. In Egypt, French success or failure hinged on France's ability to win some degree of Egyptian acquiescence and support; without it, the severely outnumbered and isolated French army could be rapidly overcome. In an extraordinary series of cultural overtures, Napoleon tried to woo the Egyptians by playing up his affiliations with Islam. In India, in the meantime, British war against France was caught up in long-standing discourses about the "otherness" of Indians, and of Haidar Ali and Tipu Sultan in particular. Yet in many respects Tipu Sultan was remarkably Western and was dangerous precisely for this reason, as well as for his cultural and military ties with France. These cross-cultural relationships, though rarely taken seriously, were to have important effects on the shape and nature of the nineteenth-century British and French empires.

Finally, the campaign belonged to an enduring pattern of imperial collecting and reinvention, both metaphorically and literally. A state's forcible acquisition of land, people, and resources—imperialism—is "collecting" on a scale different from an individual collector's acquisition of an object. It involves collecting human beings, with deeply significant cultural and moral consequences. Nevertheless, British and French expansion in these years resembled collecting in suggestive ways. These campaigns stemmed from emerging, increasingly centralized programs of acquisition. And if collecting is a kind of reinvention, then these conquests also fitted into an agenda of reinvention by the British and French imperial states. For France, the invasion of Egypt was the first expression of the revolutionary *mission civilisatrice* beyond Europe. For Britain, and for the East India Company specifically, the capture of Seringapatam helped cement a new image of the British Empire as an empire of conquest as well as of trade.

The invasions also involved collecting of a tangible kind. Both campaigns yielded the largest hauls of Eastern *objects*—trophies, souvenirs, plunder, curiosities—that had yet been brought to Europe by conquering states. It was Napoleon in Egypt who most famously pushed the art of state-sponsored collecting to a new level, by bringing with him a corps of more than one hundred scholars, known as the savants, who would study Egypt in the army's victorious wake. The savants spent the three years of French occupation pursuing a mandate to collect. Antiquities, artifacts, natural specimens, plans, drawings, music: their trove of information ranged across ancient and modern Egypt, nature and culture, and would later form the basis of one of the nineteenth century's greatest publishing projects, the *Description de l'Égypte*. From the other front of the war, in India, objects also appeared in the service of state conquest. Using a range of trophies from the fallen kingdom of Mysore,

Richard Wellesley presented the British public and British officials with a splendid, self-confident image of the East India Company as an imperial ruler. In close parallel with the savants' researches in Egypt, the East India Company undertook its first surveys in Tipu Sultan's captured domains. Yet while some Seringapatam objects underscored the Company's power, others, in private hands, would reveal how wide the range of British representations and engagements with India continued to be.

Collecting territory and collecting objects, invasions and reinventions: Egypt and Seringapatam together marked a turning point in French and British imperial expansion in the East. With these campaigns France and Britain collected territory with a heightened sense of imperial purpose. The imperial states also emerged as collectors of objects, using and manipulating them to cultivate ruling self-images. In short, it was during these years of war that the foundations were laid for a larger and more assertive—yet diverse and diffuse—British Empire in India and the Middle East. To understand how that Eastern empire came into being, it is time to look westward from India: to Egypt, the new frontier.

## II. Westward Bound

There were no great omens or long histories to anticipate British imperial involvement in Egypt. Actually, there were disasters. One day, in June 1779, on the outskirts of Cairo, a group of villagers saw a white man approaching. He came out of the desert like a dead man walking: naked and skeletally thin, his skin encrusted and erupting with ulcers, half-blind eyes glazed over, lips glued shut. His name, it later emerged, was Saint-Germain, and his gruesome story encapsulated both the troubles and the temptations facing would-be European imperialists in Egypt.

Saint-Germain had been the commandant of the French East India Company's factory at Dhaka; his brother was stationed in the factory at nearby Kasimbazar. Upon the outbreak of Anglo-French war, in 1778, both brothers were taken prisoner by the British, but in a concession commonly granted to officers, they were then released on parole and allowed to return to France. They took passage from Bengal on a merchant ship, the *Nathalia*, sailing under Danish colors and bound for Suez. There the *Nathalia* was to unload its cargo of "calicos, pepper and other drugs" and its passengers, who would cross the Isthmus of Suez in caravan, and board another ship at Alexandria for Europe.[14]

After the Suez Canal opened in 1869, virtually everyone traveling between

Europe and India would go via Egypt, but in 1778, this was an extremely unusual route. Red Sea navigation was perilous and the winds unfavorable, blowing from the north for six months of the year, north by northwest for the other six. A further serious obstacle was presented by Ottoman authorities, who were wary of allowing European ships in their waters, especially so close to the holy cities of Arabia. Indeed, just weeks before the *Nathalia* set off, the sultan issued an order to Egypt's ruling beys (its Ottoman-appointed governors), insisting that: "We absolutely will not suffer Frank Ships to come to Suez. . . . The Sea of Suez is destined for the noble Pilgrimage of Mecca. To suffer Frank Ships to navigate therein, or to neglect opposing it, is betraying your Sovereign, your Religion, and every Mahometan. . . ."[15]

Yet for Europeans, and Britons in particular, the allure of the Suez route was tremendous. Weather permitting, it could reduce the average travel time between India and Europe from six months to a mere two. The commercial benefits were clear. In 1775, Warren Hastings had negotiated a treaty with the Beys permitting the East India Company to trade at Suez at a lower duty than that levied at Jeddah. There were also strategic advantages to the route, which had been demonstrated as recently as April 1778 by George Baldwin, an entrepreneur and self-designated British representative in Egypt. Learning of the renewed war between Britain and France, Baldwin sent rapid word of the conflict to India, thereby—as he saw it—enabling the East India Company to score an important first strike against the French.[16]

The *Nathalia,* in the event, would break no speed records; after "a tedious and perilous passage of near five months," it reached Suez in late May 1779.[17] Cargo and sea-weary passengers were duly unloaded and, a fortnight later, set off into the desert in caravan, toward Cairo. They traveled through the cool night, either riding on horseback or curled up into baskets on camel-back to catch some rest. But at dawn on their very first day, they were abruptly awakened by a party of Arab raiders riding toward them from the desert in attack. The Arabs came to plunder and to punish: if the Europeans were going to defy the sultan's orders, they would pay for it. Robbing the caravan with brutal efficiency, the raiders disappeared back into the desert with the ship's entire cargo, leaving the *Nathalia* party stranded, stripped even of the clothes from their backs. Some managed to flee early during the melée and get back to Suez. They were the lucky ones. Eight more—the brothers Saint-Germain among them—decided to make their way on foot toward Cairo.

On the first day, a major investor in the *Nathalia,* Captain Barrington, fell, and his companions were forced to walk on without him, leaving him to a miserable fate of dehydration and death. The next day, two more dropped of exhaustion and were in turn abandoned. On the third day, Saint-Germain's brother collapsed, and Saint-Germain left him, too, with two dying black servants, continuing on with the only remaining survivor, an Armenian interpreter named Paul. The interpreter was the last to die. Saint-Germain staggered through the desert alone, bitten by flies and lacerated by sand, racked by fever, reduced to drinking what urine his body could still produce. The Egyptians who found him carried him to the house of a French merchant in Cairo, where assiduous nursing and the ministrations of a European doctor slowly returned him to life. He was haunted by his experiences, "ever lamenting the cruel fate of his unhappy brother, whom he always loved with the tenderest affection." Only later did he learn that Suez, and safety, had been just thirty miles away from where they started their march.[18]

Plainly, this was a cautionary tale. "This melancholy example ought, certainly, to discourage the English, in India, from frequenting any more these Countries," concluded one European resident in Cairo, reporting the tragedy to Sir Robert Ainslie, British ambassador in Constantinople.[19] Ainslie, for his part, was irate: by openly violating the sultan's orders—to say nothing of orders against private trade in the Red Sea issued by the East India Company—the *Nathalia* merchants had placed him in a very awkward position with Ottoman authorities. To Ainslie and the British Foreign Office, there was no question that the sultan's good favor was far more important than the obstreperous desires of a handful of "exasperating . . . People in India."[20]

Yet while the *Nathalia* disaster discouraged many from further excursions into the Red Sea and Egypt, it also gave ammunition to advocates of an opposing view. If Egypt was vital to British trade and contact with India, well, then, Britain should conquer Egypt, too. This was the position tirelessly and prolifically advocated by George Baldwin, the same man who had demonstrated the utility of the Suez passage in 1778 by sending prompt news of war to Bombay. Baldwin had worked as a silk merchant in the Levant for some years, and had become so enthusiastic about the commercial and strategic potential of an Egypt-India link that he settled in Cairo from 1775 in order to develop and promote his scheme.[21] (During this period he also acted as a sort of unofficial British consul, looking out for travelers and merchants. It was in this capacity that, in 1777, he helped and befriended another European in transit between Egypt and India: Benoît de Boigne.) Baldwin's argument rested on a crucial diplomatic development. In 1774, the Ottomans lost a six-year-long war with Russia; in the peace treaty of Küçük Kaynarca, the sultan, for the first time in Ottoman history, had to cede some of the empire's heartlands to an enemy power. Many Ottoman provinces were already semiautonomous, including Egypt, which was ruled by a group of Mameluke beys. (Mamelukes were not Arabs; they were, or were descended from, Turkish slaves, trained to fight in

Muslim, often Arab, armies. Now, with the Ottoman concessions of 1774, it seemed as if the sultan's once-impregnable domains might come apart entirely. Austria, Russia, and France made little secret of their ambitions to grab its pieces. Baldwin urged Britain to do the same.

Conquering Egypt, he said, would be profitable and quick. Not only would securing access to the Red Sea immeasurably speed up contact between India and Egypt—with all kinds of positive consequences—it would also bring the East India Company untold wealth in the coffee trade and other lucrative commerce. The time was right. Egypt's government was riven by factional infighting between the beys, and toppling them would have little bearing on Ottoman stability more generally, for this "hydra-headed government," Baldwin said, was "neither a dependent, nor independent State, yet, is nominally subject to the Ottoman Yoke, and virtually independent."[22] And it was time to act fast. If Britain didn't move quickly to conquer Egypt, France would beat them to it. "The power of annoying England has been ever a predominant argument with France for the adoption of any design," he warned:

> France in Possession of Egypt would possess the Master Key to all the trading Nations of the Earth. Enlightened as the Times are in the general arts of navigation and commerce, she might make it the emporium of the World. She might make it the Awe of the Eastern World by the fertility she would command of transporting her Forces thither by Surprize in any number and at any time; and England would hold her Possessions in India at the Mercy of France.

"Either by fair means, or by force," Baldwin declared, "it behoves the India Company to secure that passage, though it should involve them in a War with the whole Turkish Empire."[23]

Of course, to many Britons in government in 1779—with the American Revolution raging—the idea of becoming entangled in yet another theater, especially one so large and complicated as the Ottoman Empire, was far from desirable. Though other European powers were looking for ways to pounce on Ottoman weakness after 1774, British diplomats favored bolstering the sultan's authority—not least so as to prevent their continental rivals from seizing the lion's share in the event of complete Ottoman collapse. (It might be noted, too, that Sir Robert Ainslie particularly despised George Baldwin and saw the *Nathalia* episode, which resulted in Baldwin's having to flee Egypt, as comeuppance for this troublesome figure.) Furthermore, the rewards of a British toehold in Egypt were not necessarily as clear to others as they were to Baldwin. Although, when looking east from Europe, one might see Egypt as the natural point to cross into the Indian Ocean, looking westward from India, one would see other routes presenting themselves, notably the Persian Gulf. Long-standing Indian Ocean trade networks linked the Malabar coast with Basra and Bandar Abbas, for instance, where the East India Company opened a factory in 1623; by the 1720s, the Company dominated European trade in the Gulf.[24] In light of episodes such as the *Nathalia* disaster, the dangers of Red Sea navigation, and the larger aims of British foreign policy in the Ottoman world, it is hardly surprising that the British government and East India Company directors paid little mind to the prospect of establishing a colony in Egypt.

But what the *Nathalia* incident and Baldwin's insistent schemes brought vividly to the fore was how Egypt was ineluctably bound up in an imperial geopolitics, whether or not authorities in Whitehall or Westminster cared to act on it. Little has been written about British commitments in the Middle East and the Mediterranean during this period, and the pipe dreams and might-have-beens of imperial history—which is exactly what a British conquest of Egypt seemed to be in 1779—rarely get much notice. Nevertheless, the genealogy of British imperial interest in Egypt forms a key part of the larger history of British empire-building in and around India. It also resembles many of the developments that marked British expansion in India in the first place: the same general shift from trade to conquest as the object of intervention; the same sometimes awkward relationship between private initiative and public policy; the same marriage of convenience between indigenous authorities and behind-the-scenes European rule. Most of all, the history of British intervention in Egypt is a textbook case in how Anglo-French rivalry catalyzed commercial interests and transformed them into a drive for open conquest.

Baldwin's warnings about the French were slightly melodramatic, but they were also prescient. By the late 1770s, Egypt had begun to loom large in France's expansionist imagination. In 1785, a French envoy successfully negotiated a treaty with the Ottomans that gave France unprecedented rights to trading in the Red Sea. Some prominent British officials became alert to the commercial and strategic potential of the Egypt route, notably Henry Dundas, president of the newly established Board of Control, which supervised East India Company affairs in Parliament. Sponsored by Dundas, George Baldwin returned to Egypt in 1786, this time with an official appointment both as British consul and East India Company agent. "The great end of Mr. Baldwin's Residence at Cairo, is the opening [of] a communication to India through Egypt," Dundas said. In addition to securing a trade treaty for the East India Company, Baldwin was also instructed to "make it an object of your constant Attention to discover the motions of the French."[25]

Baldwin kept close watch on his hated rivals. "I watch" the Egyptian political scene, he said, "as Sir William Hamilton does Vesuvius, and hear its subterraneous grumblings, and understand its symptoms as well. I am not afraid of it."[26] "They know the Value of Egypt," Baldwin wrote darkly of the French to Dundas in 1787, "and if it appears to them that nothing can save the Turkish Empire from ruin, will their delicacy, their national faith, deter them from partaking? I have strong suspicions, sir, that they will do more than passively look on. . . . I believe their resolution is taken."[27] He was closer to the truth than probably even he knew. Schemes for conquering Egypt had been aired in France as early as 1672, when the philosopher Leibniz wrote a memorandum to Louis XIV urging the step. France, of course, is a Mediterranean nation, and had always been bound into the crosscurrents of trade and culture that linked the shores of that sea. When Baldwin settled in Cairo in the 1770s, he was one of the only Britons even *in* Egypt, and he was the first British consul ever to be appointed there. The French, on the other hand, had maintained steady diplomatic representation in Egypt since the seventeenth century; operated factories at Alexandria, Cairo, and Rosetta; and lived in small but long-established communities in the country, complete with a French baker and several Jesuit and Capuchin friars.[28] In contrast to the somewhat dilettantish Baldwin, the leading figures of the French community were a Provençal merchant called Charles Magallon, who had lived in Egypt from the 1760s, spoke fluent Arabic, and was friendly with numerous high-ranking officials; and his wife, a conspicuous figure in her own right and a particular intimate of the wife of Murad Bey.[29]

And where Baldwin was virtually the only figure openly to advocate a British invasion of Egypt in this period, at least a dozen formal proposals for conquering Egypt were presented to the French government between 1774 and Napoleon's 1798 expedition—plans that have not been seriously investigated by historians for almost a century.[30] Drawn up by military officers, consuls, merchants, and independent entrepreneurs—some of them openly sponsored by the French state—these plans can be found today in the archives of the French navy, army, and foreign ministry, which suggests what a wide official audience they reached. The most detailed scheme was developed by the Hungarian-born baron François de Tott, a former military adviser to Sultan Mustafa III. In 1777, de Tott was sent by the French government on an official inspection tour of factories in the eastern Mediterranean. He also had secret orders to collect intelligence for a potential French invasion of Egypt. (He was later advised to mask his real mission by telling people he was "making astronomical observations for the Academy of Sciences, research on natural history, corals and other madrepores, and whatever other plausible pretexts you can find.")[31] He and his aide, the Chevalier de la Laune, drew maps and coastal profiles, took soundings in Alexandria's harbor, and assessed Egyptian defenses. Like many schemers, de Tott also advocated cutting a canal across Suez.[32]

To French colonial strategists, Egypt held particular appeal as a substitute for the American colonies they had lost after the Seven Years War; this rationale was explicitly outlined to Louis XV by the Duc de Choiseul in 1769. Egypt's agricultural potential was tremendous, it was argued, suitable for growing rice and wheat, as well as the valuable cash crops of sugar and indigo.[33] Then there was its location. "One need only cast an eye over the map of Egypt to see, in its position relative to Europe, Asia, Africa, and the Indies, the entrepot of a universal commerce," de Tott pointed out.[34] If France held Egypt, he and others suggested, it would no longer matter that Britain had the upper hand in India, because through Egypt "France can exclusively procure all the commerce of India. . . . We shall deliver their Indian commerce the most fatal blow without using the means of arms."[35] Thus it was argued in peacetime. When war broke out again between Britain and France, Egypt was seen as a springboard for attacks on British India.

Yet while France schemed, Britain slept. Not only were Baldwin's urgings unheeded by most persons of influence in Britain; just days after Britain and France went to war in 1793—exactly when Egypt's strategic importance should have impressed itself on British minds—the Foreign Office sent a letter to Baldwin closing down the consulate.[36] For aside from questions of Britain's Eastern policy, its geographic and cultural distance from Egypt, there may have been a further reason that British official interest never really awakened to the imperial value of Egypt. That reason was George Baldwin himself. While in one dispatch Baldwin was sending accurate accounts of French maneuvers, in others he was proffering observations on a range of increasingly improbable subjects. In July 1791, for instance, he wrote to Dundas with word of his miraculous cure for the bubonic plague. Rub plague victims down with olive oil, he promised, and they would be hale and hearty in no time.[37] (Baldwin was evidently a great believer in the curative powers of olive oil, later counseling his friend Benoît de Boigne to "take now and then a spoon full of good olive oil" for his asthma.)[38] He also offered remedies for flatulence, deafness, colds, and "gravel." And from 1795 to 1797, he spent most of his time holed up in his great house in Alexandria recording the "magnetic dreams" of an Italian mesmerist called Cesare Avena de Valdieri, which he later published.[39] (Valdieri was apparently known to be a charlatan: as a nineteenth-century reader penciled into the margin of the British Library's copy of Baldwin's book, "it should be known that he magnetised all the money out of Baldwin's pocket into his own.")[40]

Baldwin never received the Foreign Office's 1793 letter closing down the consulate. In fact it took four years for him to learn, by duplicate copy, that his office had been ended. (Another testament to the unreliability and slowness of communications in this period: though he had noticed that his salary was not being paid, he had apparently not thought much of it, and presumably supported himself by trade or other means.) By then, late in 1797, Baldwin was sick and heartily disgusted. "Forced to abandon my post, my property, and most of my correspondence, and to quit the country for a chance of life in another scene," he left Egypt for Italy in the winter of 1798.[41] But it was an extraordinary piece of poor timing, for all Baldwin's prognostications were soon to be borne out in the most extravagant of ways. No longer were the French merely probing, researching, and scheming in Egypt. The time of plots was over. The time for invasion had come.

## III. Empire by Design

In February 1798, Charles-Maurice de Talleyrand, foreign minister of France, received a report from Charles Magallon, the Cairo merchant who for the last five years had also been serving as France's consul in Egypt. The theme of Magallon's "Memoir on Egypt" was familiar to anybody who had been following French policy for the region: why France should conquer Egypt, and how it could most effectively do so. Magallon's arguments were clear and to the point, backed up with detailed firsthand observations (he even suggested sailing dates for a French fleet) of a kind one might expect from a man who had lived in Egypt for some forty years, who knew Arabic well, and who had "acquired friends in all stations"—friends, he confidently asserted, who would receive the French "with glee [*avec transport*]." The larger objectives of the conquest, especially at this time of intense Anglo-French war, were by now evident. "Once our government has Egypt," Magallon concluded, "it can regard it as a conquest taken from the English." From Egypt, the army could move on to India, where by making contact with "the enemy . . . whom [the British] fear the most . . . Tippoo Saïb, son of Hyder Aly, who is constantly at war with them," France could fight Britain out of the subcontinent.[42] Forceful, specific, compelling, Magallon's memoir was more than just a generic proposal. It was a blueprint for invasion—and it had been commissioned personally by Talleyrand, who intended to put it promptly into action.[43]

War had been going very much in France's favor of late. In Italy the previous year, the talented young general Napoleon Bonaparte had led the revolutionary armies to resounding victory over the Austrians and had marched into Rome. Trophies from his Italian campaign would soon be paraded through the streets of Paris in triumph, and later installed in the Louvre.[44] France's enemies on the Continent were making peace one by one. Britain, in the meantime, was being harassed by the French in the Caribbean, where a major British offensive of 1796 met with yellow fever, malaria, and some fourteen thousand deaths.[45] Despite the steadfast leadership of William Pitt the Younger, many in Britain felt vulnerable, overstretched, and deeply anxious about their own capacities; a French strike in the right place might bring them to the bargaining table. An "Armée d'Angleterre" was massed in northern France with a view to a possible invasion of Britain. In the same month that Magallon's report reached Talleyrand, Napoleon (now commander in chief) and his top generals made a quick tour of Channel ports, to survey preparations and set the wheels in motion for an invasion.

Due chiefly to problems of naval transport, Napoleon decided that an outright invasion of England would have to wait.[46] But the Armée d'Angleterre could be turned against Britain in another sphere instead: it could be sent east, to Egypt, to challenge British power in India. Cribbing directly from Magallon's text—modifying it only with heavy lashings of revolutionary rhetoric—Talleyrand presented the Egypt scheme to the five-man Directory, France's top executive body. They responded enthusiastically to the idea. Napoleon, for his part, welcomed the plan both for its evident strategic merits, of which he was convinced, and for its appeal to his own sense of grandeur: Alexander the Great had conquered Egypt at just the same age, twenty-nine. And like Alexander, Napoleon—who, to his particular satisfaction, had recently been elected a member of the prestigious Institut National—aimed to be a cultured conqueror as well. As soon as the plans were in train, Napoleon set about recruiting savants to study Egypt while he conquered it.

To its Paris planners, the invasion of Egypt seemed like a sure thing. The country's defenses and military capacity had been reconnoitered in advance; each step in the campaign and in the establishment of a new régime had been considered; knowledgeable advisers such as Magallon and the veteran Ottoman interpreter Venture de Paradis were on hand to assist. In fact, far from an improbable fantasy scheme, this was a mature piece of foreign policy, developed and refined over the course of decades. It traced an important line of continuity between the policies of Ancien Régime and revolutionary France. Its strategy and aims, outlined in the official orders of April 12, 1798, were crystal clear: to gain control of the eastern Mediterranean, to cut off Britain from Asia, and to prepare the way for a French offensive in India. Nor were they implausible. Egypt seemed ripe for the taking; allies in India, Tipu Sultan in particular, were ready and waiting. It was only a matter of time.

The French force, more than thirty thousand strong, sailed from the Mediterranean port of Toulon in mid-May. "You are one of the wings of the Armée d'Angleterre," Napoleon told them, not dishonestly, for they were indeed off to fight Britain, if only by proxy. On June 9 they reached the central Mediterranean island of Malta, for centuries the stronghold of the crusading order of the Knights of St. John. Occupying a key strategic position and boasting one of the finest harbors in the Mediterranean, Malta was a valuable prize to seize en route. The knights surrendered with barely a contest. (It helped that of the five hundred fifty knights, more than two hundred were French, and dozens too old or sick to fight.)[47] The army paused in Malta for one week—during which Napoleon dissolved the medieval order and set about turning the island into a French colony—before setting sail again. It was only now that most of his troops learned their ultimate target. "Soldiers!"

Antoine-Jean Gros, *Bonaparte Haranguing the Army Before the Battle of the Pyramids, July 21, 1798*, 1810.

Napoleon announced to his men, henceforth known as the Armée d'Orient: "You are about to undertake a conquest whose effects on civilisation and world commerce are incalculable. You will deliver England the surest and most painful strike, while waiting to give them the death blow."[48]

On the night of July 1–2, the first French troops pushed through strong, high breakers onto Alexandria's beach. After two days of fighting, the city leaders signed a peace accord with the French. Napoleon moved rapidly onward, sweeping down the Nile Delta toward Cairo and the inevitable confrontation with the main body of Mameluke forces. Nearly three weeks later, on July 21, 1798, the French and Egyptian armies met on the west bank of the Nile, opposite Cairo. The French formed squares to face the attack of Murad Bey, who was leading twelve thousand Mameluke cavalry and forty thousand infantry. Against the horizon, the pyramids of Giza were dimly visible. "Go!" Napoleon yelled to his troops, "and think that from the tops of these monuments forty centuries are watching us!"[49] Within two hours, the battle had been fought and won. Murad Bey disappeared south into the desert, taking three thousand of his crack cavalry with him but leaving perhaps as many as two thousand men behind, dead, in the swirling dust and the lapping waves of the river.[50] The Armée d'Orient started entering Cairo the next day, bearing a proclamation from Napoleon: "I have come to destroy the Mameluke race, protect commerce and the natives of the country. . . . Fear nothing for your families, your houses, your property, and above all for the religion of the Prophet which I love."[51] Napoleon moved into the lavish new house of the Mameluke leader Alfi Bey at Ezbekiyya, just completed and never occupied—"as if," the Cairo notable and historian Abd al-Rahman al-Jabarti remarked, "it had been built expressly for the French general."[52]

Napoleon had seized Alexandria and Cairo in exactly three weeks: to all appearances a stunning validation of the invasion plans. Yet the success of this apparent blitzkrieg was illusory. For a start, although casualty figures suggested that the Battle of the Pyramids was a decisive French victory (only three hundred French troops were killed), Murad Bey's escape with some of his best cavalry amounted to a serious failure. Strategic retreat was a key Mameluke tactic, and as long as Murad remained at large, the French conquest was by no means finished. Later, in August, Napoleon would dispatch General Desaix with nine thousand men (and the artist Vivant Denon, who recorded their voyage in a best-selling book) into Upper Egypt after the Mamelukes. The beleaguered French troops spent nearly six months alternately harassed and eluded by an enemy they outnumbered three to one—and they still never captured Murad.

A more immediate threat, however, lay to the north, from Admiral Horatio Nelson's British fleet in the Mediterranean. Though in peacetime British policy makers had paid little attention to the eastern Mediterranean, war there had changed that. Ever since the French had left Toulon, in mid-May, Nelson had been cruising the Mediterranean trying to track them down. Were they heading for Malta? The Peloponnese? Corfu? He gathered intelligence from Cadiz, Naples, Sicily, Smyrna; he watched the winds; he waited and he calculated. By June 17—several days before even Napoleon's generals knew their final destination—Nelson had worked out that they must be on their way to Egypt: "I therefore determined . . . to go to Alexandria, and if that Place or any other part of Egypt was their destination, I hoped to arrive time enough to frustrate their plans. . . ."[53] He pointed the *Vanguard* south from Naples and led the fleet through the Straits of Messina on June 20, the day after the French had sailed out of Valletta. The next day—in an extraordinary case of ships passing in the night—the two fleets glided by each other at a distance of twenty-two leagues, beyond telescope range. Nelson arrived off Alexandria within a week and sent an officer ashore to speak with George Baldwin and discover whether the French had been seen. (The officer instead discovered that Baldwin had left two months earlier.)[54] Hearing no news of the French, on June 29 Nelson set course for Cyprus. Little did he know that that very same day, the French fleet drew within five leagues of Alexandria—sketching distance for the artist Vivant Denon, who traced a fine coastal profile from the deck of the *Junon*.[55]

The French thus landed unimpeded, but it was only a matter of time before the British navy returned. Sure enough, on August 1, Nelson discovered the French fleet in Aboukir Bay, a shallow and poorly sheltered dip in the coast east of Alexandria. Napoleon had failed to order the fleet to a more secure location, and it floated there in the open water like so many sitting ducks.[56] Nelson seized his chance. Boldly maneuvering half his ships between the enemy and the shore, surrounding the head and center of the French line, he opened fire shortly after six o'clock in the evening. On the face of it, the numbers were tilted slightly in French favor: thirteen French ships of the line and four frigates, versus fourteen British ships of the line; 1,182 French guns to 1,012 British.[57] The results were anything but in French favor. At about ten that night, a massive explosion rocked the center of the French line: *L'Orient*, Napoleon's flagship and the largest of the fleet, blew up, taking the French commander Admiral Brueys with it. For a full half hour the guns were silent, as sailors on both sides, "stupefied," watched the great ship erupt, flaming into the sea, pouring cascades of splinters over the hundred or so of its crew members lucky enough to leap off in time.[58] When, at the end of the battle, the following afternoon, the guns at last stopped again, the scene was no less dramatic. Only four French ships had survived destruction or capture; their commander, Admiral Villeneuve, lived to be beaten by Nelson again, at Trafalgar. More than three thousand French sailors had been killed or wounded, and a further three thousand taken prisoner.[59] The Battle of the Nile, as the British triumphantly dubbed it, was an unmitigated success. Nelson got a peerage and lasting glory.

For Napoleon, the consequences were dire. One month to the day after landing in Egypt, the Armée d'Orient was marooned. All those Ancien Régime invasion schemes, so confident of quick success, were quite useless now. Nobody had planned for this. The news reached Cairo on August 15, and the soldiers were stunned: "Here we are, abandoned in this barbaric country, with no means of communication and with no hope of going home!" Napoleon was prompt with reassurances: "We have an obligation to do great things," he said, "we will do them; to found an empire: we will found it. The seas, of which we are not the masters, separate us from our homeland; but no ocean separates us from Africa or Asia. We are numerous, and we will not lack men to recruit into our corps."[60] But he knew that his plans needed revising—radically.

These were more than just soothing words. His navy was destroyed, his men demoralized and under constant threat and stress, trapped in a hot, profoundly foreign country and surrounded by unknown enemies. Mutiny was a very real risk. To hold his army together it was essential that he reach some kind of modus vivendi with the Egyptian people. He also needed to produce a new exit strategy. The destruction of the fleet meant that the only immediate way for the army to leave Egypt was to push onward, either overland through Palestine or by sailing east into the Red Sea—"for strange as it may appear at first sight," Nelson himself had pointed out, "an Enterprizing Enemy if they have the force or consent of the Pacha of Egypt may with great Ease get an Army to the Red Sea, and if they have concerted a Plan with Tippoo Saib to have Vessels at Suez three weeks at this Season is a common passage to the Malabar Coast when our India Possessions would be in great danger."[61] Indeed, far from ringing the death knell to French plans to march onward to India, to some extent the Battle of the Nile infused them with new urgency.

Some Britons might have believed that the threat posed by the French in Egypt was at an end. Yet it was now that the most striking and in many ways the most frightening part of the campaign was to unfold. For Napoleon needed to do more than secure Egypt. He needed to seduce it. So it was that in these weeks of hardship he improvised a daring way forward. He expounded, in increasingly radical terms, on his devotion to the principles of Islam. In a series of gestures so remarkable they seem almost fantastic, Napoleon worked to persuade the Egyptians that he was a pro-Muslim liberator—indeed, to persuade them that he was a Muslim himself—and to enlist Egyptian support in his quest to move onward to India. His strategy had two parts. On the one hand, he redoubled efforts to win Egypt by winning over the Egyptians: he promoted a pro-Islamic, anti-Ottoman rhetoric, and sought allies in the Egyptian Arab (that is, non-Ottoman) elite and among the *ulama*, the religious leaders. At the same time, he promoted the idea of a march to the East—which was now, practically speaking, his clearest way out—in overtly imperialist terms infused with visionary purpose.

Little of this, of course, was in the original plans. Napoleon's invocation of the language of pan-Arabism and nationalism, and his challenges to the authority of the Ottoman sultan (who was also the caliph, the supreme leader of Islam) were to have considerable long-term impact on the political configurations of the region.[62] In the short term, his cross-cultural overtures correlated so closely with his military setbacks that the two can be charted virtually day by day. As the invasion of Egypt diverged from its pre-written script, Napoleon launched a bold experiment in cosmopolitan fusion—an attempt to merge East and West not just for propagandistic effect, but for outright survival.

## IV. Abdallah Bonaparte

Propaganda, though, was an art form that many leaders of revolutionary France excelled at, and none more so than Napoleon. Cruising toward Alexandria in the last days of June 1798, the interpreter Venture de Paradis sat on the flagship *L'Orient* and drafted a "Proclamation to the Egyptians," which was printed onboard on what was soon to be Egypt's first Arabic printing press.[63] Immediately after landing, Napoleon dispatched messengers—many of them Muslim prisoners he had freed in Malta—to carry the text into the towns and villages of the Delta.[64] People assembled to hear their muftis and sheikhs read Napoleon's words aloud. "O Egyptians!" the proclamation began:

> You have been told that I have come to this land only with the intention of eradicating your religion. But that is a clear lie; do not believe it. Tell the slanderers that I have come to you only to rescue your rights from the hands of the oppressors. I, more than any Mamluk, worship God, glory be to Him, and respect His Prophet and the great Quran. . . . O you *shaykhs*, judges, *imams*, *jurbajiyya* [cavalry commanders] and leading men of the country, tell your nation that the French are also sincere Muslims. A confirmation of this is that they

entered Rome and there destroyed the throne of the Pope, who had always urged Christians to combat Islam. Then they marched to Malta, whence they expelled the knights, who claimed that God, exalted is He, sought of them that they fight the Muslims. Moreover, the French continued to be sincere friends of His Excellency the Ottoman Sultan and the enemies of his enemies. . . . All Egyptians must be grateful to God . . . for the termination of the dynasty of the Mamluks, saying loudly "May God perpetuate the paying of honour to the Ottoman Sultan, may God perpetuate the paying of honour to the French army, may God curse the Mamluks, and may He ameliorate the condition of the Egyptian nation."[65]

These were the words of a liberator—and an apparently Muslim one at that. He swore allegiance to the sultan and the Prophet. He began and ended his address, as a French officer in Rosetta recorded, with "that remarkable phrase from the Koran, which flattered and seduced a great number of Muslims. *God is Great and Muhammed is his Prophet*."[66] Was there any particular reason to think that Napoleon's promises, delivered to Egyptians in the voices

بسم الله الرحمان الرحيم لا اله الا الله لا ولد له ولا شريك في ملكه

Napoleon's "Proclamation to the Egyptians," adorned with revolutionary insignia.

of their local leaders, were completely unbelievable? According to the same officer, the townspeople of Rosetta certainly did not find them so: "As soon as they heard that the French army had no other intention than to fight the Mamelukes and to deliver all Egyptians from their odious yoke; the fanatical rage of this populace, as barbaric as ignorant, suddenly changed into mad joy, and cries of the most boisterous elation replaced those of the most terrible fury."[67] Even the French officer thrilled to the Arabic cadences, and "infinitely regret[ted] not having been able to get a copy of this proclamation." He saw the tricolor snapping in the hot Nile wind; he thought of the Rhine, the Tiber, of the Romans and Carthage; and he swelled with patriotism, admiration, and purpose. Napoleon was already a revolutionary hero. If, as it seemed, the people of Rosetta found his call to arms compelling, couldn't he be a Muslim messiah—a Mahdi—too?

Not everyone was convinced, of course. The broadside reached Cairo a week later, and in a city abuzz with news of Alexandria's fall, it aroused a passionate response. The Egyptian historian Abd al-Rahman al-Jabarti, who left a vivid eyewitness chronicle of this interlude in his region's history, was so stirred that he immediately copied the text into his journal. Al-Jabarti had seen revolutions in Egypt before, notably in 1786, when the Ottomans tried to reassert authority over the wayward beys. Then they had issued similar proclamations promising to free the Egyptian people from Mameluke tyranny.[68] But *this*, al-Jabarti found as he looked over Napoleon's Arabic speech, was something new—and distinctly unwelcome. At least he could have had the grace to phrase it grammatically! "Here is an explanation of the incoherent words and vulgar constructions": "His statement *fahadara* (Therefore has come) there is no reason for this *fa* here. Good style would require *wa-qad hadara* (it has come)." "Proof of ungrammatical language": "His statement *wa-bayn al-mamalik*, the word *bayn* is out of place and makes the language even more corrupt." And "base ignorance": "His statement *fa'l-yuwarruna* (let them then produce), this is a colloquial word which is not in accordance with Arabic style." For al-Jabarti, bad usage was tantamount to telling lies. "Then he proceeds to something even worse . . . may God cast him into perdition, with his words: 'I more than the Mamluks serve God . . .'. There is no doubt that this is a derangement of his mind. . . ."[69]

Yet this speech, the first in a series of similar addresses to the Egyptian people, was more rational than not—what now would be considered a "psychological operation," an attempt to win hearts and minds.[70] In a 1787 invasion scheme, in fact, the French consul Mure had specifically suggested that upon landing, a French army "should publish in the city and in all the villages where they will go, that they have only come to the country to deliver it from the tyranny of the Beys and the foreigners attached to their service."[71] During the trying months ahead, Napoleon's appeal to Egyptian Arab sensibilities, and to the rhetoric of Islam, would take on startling significance. But as the response to the "Proclamation" suggested—favorable in some areas, downright offended in others—Napoleon would meet with only partial success.

A series of three festivals coming on the heels of the disaster at Aboukir Bay offered Napoleon an important chance to cultivate ties between the French occupiers and the Egyptian people. The first was the Festival of the Nile on August 18, 1798, which celebrated the river's annual flood with the ceremonial breaking of the dike on Cairo's canal. The rites had been observed since antiquity, and Napoleon, appearing at the nilometer with his generals and the city's civic and religious leaders, stepped into the role of pharaoh with aplomb. He rained fistfuls of coins over the crowd below, wrapped the Cairo notables in pelisses and kaftans, and paraded back through the city to the music of a French band. In the Ezbekiyya Square, according to the new French newspaper the *Courier de l'Egypte*, Egyptians "sang the praises of the Prophet and the French army, while maligning the Beys and their tyranny. Yes, it was said, you have come to deliver us by the order of almighty God." They called it the best flood in a century.[72]

Three days later, the celebrations of the Prophet Muhammad's birthday began. The French learned that Cairo's sheikhs and ulama, in a gesture of passive resistance, were not planning any public observance of the occasion. Napoleon promptly lavished attention and money on festivities, in order to insist that he was a true friend of Islam. The streets came alive with singers, jugglers, monkeys, and dancing bears; oil lamps flickered through the night along the walls of the mosques, souks, and mansions. Napoleon visited Cairo's great al-Azhar mosque—the most important religious center in Egypt, and one of the most significant in the Muslim world—where he listened to Koranic recitation. Afterward one of the leading sheikhs held a banquet in Napoleon's honor, at which the French officers manfully dispensed with cutlery and braved a succession of heavily spiced dishes. Then they watched fireworks and congratulated themselves on their fraternity with the Muslims.[73]

Fraternity was the theme of the third festival that season: the Festival of the French Republic, on September 21. The date—the anniversary of the abolition of the Bourbon monarchy in 1792—was in effect the national day of revolutionary France and was celebrated in elaborate ceremonies across the nation, where patriotic festivals played a major role in helping to shape a secular, republican French identity. Now similar rituals were performed in France's newest colony—presumably as much for the edification of the

French troops as for the Egyptian people.[74] It was certainly a neat coincidence that so many French revolutionary motifs were Egyptian in the first place, as the decorations erected in the Ezbekiyya Square reflected. A wooden obelisk, ringed by columns and triumphal arches, loomed at the center of the square, emblazoned in gold French and Arabic letters A LA REPUBLIQUE FRANÇAISE, L'AN VII and A L'EXPULSION DES MAMELUKES, L'AN VI. In the modest provincial capital of Atfyeh, Janissaries and members of the diwan (Muslim council) marked the occasion by swearing "an oath of friendship and attachment to the French Republic and the Grand Seigneur." In Rosetta, the tricolor flag of revolutionary France was flown off the highest minaret in the city.[75]

The festivities of Republic Day rounded off a neat triad of public holidays: one Egyptian, one Muslim, one French republican. It also had an extra political significance, for just two weeks earlier, the Ottoman sultan had proclaimed a jihad against France. This dealt a further serious blow to the French cause. From the "Proclamation to the Egyptians" onward, Napoleon had attempted to portray the French as being allied *with* the Ottomans, working to expel the disobedient Mamelukes. The sultan's declaration of holy war, and the flood of Ottoman propaganda that accompanied it, gave the lie to all Napoleon's assertions. No longer could he sustain the illusion of Franco-Ottoman alliance, or nurse the hope that the Ottomans would passively accept French occupation of Egypt. The call to jihad forced another marked shift in French policy and rhetoric, another approach to the Egyptian people.[76]

Turning away from his appeal to a common enemy, Napoleon began actively to promote a new vision of Franco-Egyptian solidarity. Republic Day had provided a good opportunity to fuse French and Egyptian political identities in symbolic ways; it was now time to try to fuse them in practice. A week later, Napoleon asked Egypt's premier sheikhs to send a letter to the sultan and to the sharif of Mecca, the two most important leaders of the Muslim world. The text of the letter—copied down by al-Jabarti with characteristic skepticism—laid out all the ways in which the French had demonstrated their respect for Islam, and was promptly printed and pasted up around the country.[77] On October 7, Napoleon moved toward establishing a full colonial administration, by convening Egypt's highest fiscal and civic authority, the general diwan. "The French people," he told them, "have longed in their soul to deliver [Egypt] from its circumstances and to free its people from the masters of this overwhelmingly ignorant and stupid [Ottoman] dynasty."[78]

The diwan worked obediently and efficiently to French instructions. It wiped out the old system of tax collection, reorganizing taxation around fixed, property-based rates, and ordered a census to assess individual dues. All of this seemed a tidy compromise between the financial demands of the French army and the vested interests of Egypt's influential revenue farmers. But ordinary Egyptians were infuriated. In the Ottoman Empire, only non-Muslims were subjected to an individual poll tax (called the *jizya*), and the new French system seemed to be treating Muslim Egyptians themselves like subordinate minorities. The census offended still more. Violating the sanctity of private homes, French soldiers entered houses, fingered belongings, and might even have caught glimpses of unveiled women, ordinarily unseen by men outside their families. Who knew what might come next? Could the massacre that Ottoman propaganda had warned of be about to take place?[79]

So the people of Cairo struck first. On October 21, 1798, the bazaars shut down: a sure sign of trouble. A mob soon massed around the house of the chief *qadi* (judge) to demand a stop to the census. When he hesitated, the crowd attacked him. Violence escalated fast: French officers were lynched, houses pillaged, fires lit. Rebels clashed with troops throughout the streets, and the next day more than seven thousand protesters attacked the main French battery. Muezzins (criers) mounted the minarets and called for the extermination of the infidels, casting battle cries across the city.[80] "May God let Islam triumph!"[81] The Cairo uprising (or *fitna*, in Arabic) was a genuinely popular protest, an attack against both the French and their allies among the Egyptian elite. (Thus, for example al-Jabarti, a member of the elite himself, had only limited support for the rebels, despite his unswerving animosity toward the French.) It was also overtly religious, organized chiefly by the middling rank of clerics, and fueled by older sectarian tensions. (Syrian Christians and Copts, notably, remained "loyal" to the French.) It was, in effect, a riot in the language of jihad.

But a riot was something that Napoleon, fresh from the turbulent streets of revolutionary Paris, knew well how to suppress. (As the savant Geoffroy Saint-Hilaire coldly observed three days later, "The miserable inhabitants of Cairo forgot that the French are the world's teachers for . . . fighting insurgents.")[82] Napoleon ordered a relentless bombardment of all the insurgent districts, and kept it up until, on the evening of October 22, the rebel leaders came to plead for peace. By the next morning, all was quiet on the streets. The bodies of up to three thousand Egyptians were gathered, bathed, shrouded, and buried. Some three hundred French soldiers had also been killed. With them died another of Napoleon's attempts to govern the Egyptians by their own accord. In the most notorious act of the entire French occupation, he ordered General Bon to sack the al-Azhar quarter and the mosque in retaliation for the violence; French cavalry rode into the courtyard of the holiest mosque in Egypt and harnessed their horses to the *qibla*.[83] The Armée d'Orient now plainly lived in the houses of its enemies—and with inadequate supplies, demoralized, vulnerable men, and no chance of reinforcements, it was clear Napoleon could not fend those enemies off forever. Another rhetorical reinvention was due.

In December 1798, a story began to wend its way through the alleys of Cairo. A holy man, it was said, had seen a vision of Muhammad. The Prophet stood on the northern shore of Egypt, looking out over the calm sea. A thin row of black spots flecked the horizon, and lengthened and swelled as he watched. Soon he saw that they were warships, flying tricolors: it was a French fleet, and it was coming to invade Egypt. Muhammad was furious, and stormed off to Destiny and berated it. "Thankless wretch!" he spat, "I made you the sovereign arbitrator of the world, and you want to hand over to the French the most beautiful of the lands under my law!" But Destiny answered calmly back: "Muhammad, the order is written, it must come about. The French will land on Egyptian soil, and they will conquer it. I no longer have the power to stop it. But listen," Destiny continued, "and console yourself. I have decided that these conquerors will become Muslims." Muhammad was comforted by these words, and went away well pleased.[84]

It was never clear who started the story, nor did the holy man's vision seem terribly plausible. Yet it captured currents in the air that December, for it must have been then that a parallel story, left to posterity by Napoleon himself, also unfolded. In his memoirs, Napoleon later reported that he went to the al-Azhar mosque to meet with the sheikhs. He spoke to them bluntly: "These disorders must be stopped. I need a fatwa . . . that orders the [Egyptian] people to take the oath of loyalty." The clerics jumped at his request. "[If] you want Muslim Arabs to rush behind your flags . . ." they suggested, then "make yourself Muslim! 100,000 Egyptians and 100,000 Arabs will come from Arabia, from Medina and Mecca, to follow you. Led and trained in your ways, you will conquer the Orient, you will re-establish the homeland of the Prophet in all its glory." Convert his army to Islam, and conquer the Middle East with local support? It was indeed an appealing vision for Napoleon. But there was a hitch—or, rather, two. His soldiers were unwilling to part with their wine, or with their foreskins: two key requirements for conversion to Islam. There were limits to what even he could persuade them to do. A meeting of sixty sheikhs convened at al-Azhar to discuss the matter; while Napoleon and his generals began to receive religious instruction.

Rumors of the mass French conversion flooded the city: "[T]he joy was general. It was spread about that the French admired Muhammed, that their commander knew the Koran by heart. . . . Already they were no longer infidels." After forty days of deliberations, the four chief muftis emerged from al-Azhar with their long-debated fatwa. They had good news for the French foreskins: circumcision, they concluded, was a "perfection . . . only recommended" for Muslims, not an essential commandment. As for wine, the soldiers were free to drink as much as they pleased; they merely would not be able to enter heaven. The fatwa Napoleon had demanded was posted around the city, and people began to prepare in earnest for the miraculous event—the conversion of the invading French troops. But Napoleon worried about the afterlife. How could he convince his soldiers to accept a religion that told them they would be damned if they drank alcohol? The muftis returned to their deliberations. After corresponding with religious authorities in Mecca, they emerged with a new fatwa. The French converts could go on drinking and *still* go to heaven, it said, as long as they made up for the sin by donating 20 percent of their wealth to charity, rather than the customary tithe. This was more acceptable. Napoleon reckoned he would be able to convince his men within about a year, and plans were drawn up for "a mosque large enough to contain the entire army."

The issuing of the revised fatwa alone seemed to achieve all that Napoleon had wished, easing relations between the French occupiers and their would-be Egyptian allies:

> Everywhere sheikhs preached that Napoleon, being no infidel, loving the Koran, having the mission of the Prophet, was a real servant of the holy Kaaba. This revolution in attitudes produced one in administration. Everything that had been difficult became easy; everything that could only be obtained before with weapons in hand, was offered in goodwill and without trouble. From this time on, pilgrims, even fanatics, never failed to offer the Sultan El-Kebir [Napoleon] the same honors due a Muslim prince; and . . . the general in chief never went into the city without the faithful prostrating themselves; they treated him as they had behaved toward the sultan.

The great march to the east, the great escape, could begin.[85]

Napoleon recounted this extraordinary tale of his army's possible conversion many years later, in exile on St. Helena, where his imagination was just about the only thing that was free. But deeply implausible though it certainly sounds, it would be wrong to dismiss the story entirely. First, that Napoleon made increasingly vigorous overtures of this kind is undeniable. (One of the most intriguing surviving vestiges of Napoleon's chameleon approach is an unattributed drawing in the French Bibliothèque Nationale, which shows Napoleon with two faces, playing-card style: one head sports a French bicorne, the other is topped with a turban.) Second, Napoleon's embracing attitude toward Islam—as laid out in his proclamations, for example—was in keeping with the deistic, rationalist bent of some French revolutionary ideology, which envisioned a kind of universal and unadorned faith that could encompass all mankind. It was with something of this spirit that one of the top French generals, Jacques Menou, did convert to Islam in 1800, so that he could marry an Egyptian woman; many other French soldiers did the same.[86] Third, the gesture was entirely of a piece with Napoleon's political strategies both in Egypt and elsewhere. As he put it some years later to the French conseil d'état, at the time of the Concordat with the Vatican: "My policy is to govern men as the majority wants to be [governed]. . . . It was by making myself Catholic that I won the war in the Vendée, by making myself Muslim that I established myself in Egypt, in making myself ultramontane that I won minds [ésprits] in Italy. If I governed the Jewish people, I would rebuild Solomon's Temple."[87]

In short, the conversion talks fit completely with the long sequence of cultural overtures Napoleon had been making in the wake of each of his military and political setbacks in Egypt. This, his most extreme gesture of self-reinvention, was performed at his moment of most serious danger. It was not an empty sign of arrogance. It was an act of desperation.

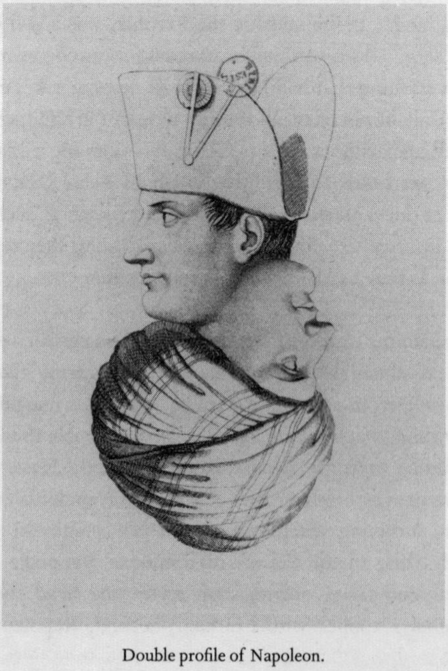

Double profile of Napoleon.

Without a doubt, the self-described Mahdi was beginning to adopt a messianic tone. At the end of December 1798, Napoleon convened the diwan again. God, he said to them,

> has decreed for eternity that I come from the West to the land of [Egypt] to destroy those who have been oppressors in it. . . . [T]he great Qu'ran makes clear in many verses the occurrence of what has happened. . . . Know also that I am able to reveal what is in every one of you because by looking at a person I can know everything about him. . . . [T]here will come a time and a day when you will see clearly that everything I have done and ordered is by irrevocable divine order.[88]

The historian al-Jabarti, of course, did not believe a word of it, and copied down Napoleon's statement staggered by the general's "pretensions of placing himself in the elite of humanity."[89] Did Napoleon believe himself? Hard to say. But the self-appointed liberator was certainly ready to lead. Throughout January of 1799, Napoleon prepared an onward march into Palestine, arranging supply lines in the Nile Delta, reorganizing chains of command, assembling artillery and troops. He packed a portable Arabic printing press so he could issue proclamations on the campaign trail. By the beginning of February, his men, a tough force of thirteen thousand veterans, were gathered on the Mediterranean shore of the Sinai Peninsula, prepared to head north into the Holy Land. On February 11, Napoleon left Cairo to join them.[90]

The French advance into Syria and Palestine would prove little more successful than the campaign in Egypt had been, and it could be seen as a desperate play by an otherwise marooned and beleaguered army. Napoleon himself was already contemplating his own return to Paris, where his friends were plotting a coup d'état against the Directory. Nevertheless, both Napoleon's personal ambitions and the fate of his army remained to a great extent bound up in the East. There was the problem of how to spread and sustain French rule in Egypt—or how to get the army out of it altogether. There was also the bigger strategic objective, which remained very much in play: how to strike at Britain; how, ideally, to get to India; how to build a French empire in the East.

With the march into Palestine, with the continuing occupation of Egypt, and with Napoleon's persistent attempts to forge a political and cultural alliance between the French and the Egyptians, the vision of an eastern French empire endured and strengthened. For as Napoleon camped on what would later be the edge of the Suez Canal—conjunction of continents and empires—his thoughts still turned to India, pivot of the imperial world. He wrote a message to the sharif of Mecca, who had responded favorably to

French overtures, asking him to forward an important letter.[91] The enclosed note was addressed to Tipu Sultan, king of Mysore in South India, long-standing ally of France and inveterate opponent of the British. United in their desire to rid India of the British, Napoleon and Tipu Sultan had much in common, and many things to discuss. And it was in the realm of Tipu Sultan that the next part of the story would take place.

## CHAPTER FIVE

# *Seizing Seringapatam*

## 1. Citizen Tipu

The days heat up fast in summer, so by six o'clock one May morning in 1797 the festivities were already well under way.[1] A large crowd had assembled on the parade ground of Seringapatam, capital of the South Indian kingdom of Mysore. Among them was Tipu Sultan, Mysore's ruler, likely dressed with habitual simplicity in white muslin and a green turban. On a signal from Tipu, a barrage of gunfire tore into the pale morning: five hundred cannon from the ramparts of the fort; five hundred rockets; a volley of more than one thousand muskets. Even if the numbers (given in a contemporary account) are exaggerated, this was certainly a show of firepower few Indian kings could muster—and Tipu Sultan knew it. In his fifteen years on the Mysore throne, Tipu had built on his father, Haidar Ali's, legacies to form one of the most technologically and strategically advanced fighting forces on the Indian subcontinent. This was what the morning's display of firepower so brazenly affirmed; and this, he hoped, would ensure his kingdom's security and further growth—particularly at the expense of his bitter enemies, the British.

The pyrotechnics served another purpose, too. They paid tribute to Tipu's coveted allies, the French. The morning's ceremonies were held in honor of one of the strangest cross-cultural juxtapositions in the annals of imperial history: the Jacobin Club of Seringapatam. The club—one of hundreds of revolutionary Jacobin organizations spread across France proper, and in French domains overseas—had been established earlier in 1797 by a French privateer, François Ripaud, and drew its approximately sixty members from the large population of French soldiers, artisans, and technicians who lived and worked in Seringapatam. Dedicated to learning about, promoting, and rejoicing in republican values, the Club also organized festivals of the kind celebrated throughout France and even in French-occupied Egypt. That day, in what may have been the most far-flung revolutionary festival ever, the Seringapatam Jacobins had gathered to raise a tricolor and to hear speeches and tributes to the principles that bound them together.

Tipu Sultan, for his part, used the occasion to advertise and affirm his long-standing friendship with France. "Behold my acknowledgement of the Standard of your country," said Tipu when the guns fell silent, "which is dear to me, and to which I am allied, it shall be always supported in my Country, as it has been in that of the Republic, my Sister!" The club members then planted a liberty tree (a Maypole-like post that was the centerpiece of many revolutionary festivals) and listened to an impassioned sermon from their president, Ripaud, on the sublimity of republican values, the "barbarity and atrocity" of the perfidious English, and the treachery of counterrevolutionary rebels.

Tipu Sultan, in a contemporary Indian portrait.

"Citizens!" he intoned in fervent climax. "Do you Swear, Hatred to all Kings except Tippoo Sultaun the Victorious, the Ally of the French Republic. War against all Tyrants and love towards your country, and that of Citizen Tippoo." "Yes!" the chorus of voices, European and Indian both, swelled enthusiastically back: "We swear to live free or die!" Another cannon salute (this time fired by a modest eighty-four guns) ended the formal proceedings, and dancing continued around the liberty tree into the night.

The image of French Jacobins earnestly celebrating the Revolution in a tiny corner of southern India seems at one level almost laughable. Yet this curious vignette of East-West fusion provides an extraordinary testament to the rich range of cultural crossings that took place on the ground of empire. Quite aside from what this remote outpost of French republican culture says about the international dimensions of the French Revolution—how, for instance, its values were transmitted to the thousands of French men and women who lived and worked overseas—the Seringapatam Jacobin Club also invites a second look at the widespread assumption that there was no meaningful French presence in India at this time.[2] Plainly, in point of human numbers and territorial power, French influence had dwindled markedly after the successful British campaigns of the 1750s. Nevertheless, Frenchmen, like other continental Europeans, remained in service across the courts of the subcontinent, and formed an enduring network of contacts that Napoleon and other French expansionists could reach out to if and as desired.

And what about "Citoyen Tipou," surely the world's only Jacobin king? The very existence of the club, to say nothing of Tipu's open patronage of it, testified to a bond between France and Mysore that was by now almost forty years old. What, if anything, Tipu shared or understood of his protégés' political message is hard to know. But without a doubt his association with the Jacobins furthered his own ambitions in an important respect. They encouraged him to hope for continued French support in Mysore's long and bitter struggle against the British.

How real was the possibility of renewed French engagement in the subcontinent? Real enough, certainly, for Napoleon's invasion of Egypt to awaken genuine fear in contemporary British breasts. It was also real enough in some Indian eyes for rulers such as Tipu to continue to turn to other European powers, and individuals, to gain military or technical support. This was why the East India Company had been so quick to expel continental European advisers when it gained informal control in domains such as Awadh. Beyond the borders of Company power, such relationships flourished. Maratha leaders like Mahadji Scindia, Benoît de Boigne's employer, deployed European and specifically French assistance to raise a massive European-style army, able to fight the British to damaging effect. In the 1790s the nizam of Hyderabad's troops marched to the orders of an Indophile Frenchman, Raymond, whose standards were topped with both a revolutionary cockade and the crescent moon of Islam. Well into the 1830s, the Sikhs relied on the support of French advisers and the prospect of aid from France in an effort to secure their rule in the Punjab, and to extend it.[3] The East India Company may have had little to fear from any given individual Indian ruler, or for that matter from a small French force, but the right combination could be fatal. And it was in Seringapatam—in the specter of a union between Tipu Sultan, the Company's most dangerous Indian enemy, and French forces arriving from Egypt—that Britain would confront that combination in its most threatening form.

The significance and the consequences of such cross-cultural alliances were more than just military. Citizen Tipu appears in many ways to be as implausible a figure as Napoleon the Muslim convert. But neither was merely playacting. Both leaders were acutely aware of the need to bridge cultures and constituencies in order to build and maintain popular support. Tipu, a Muslim newcomer to the throne (his father, Haidar Ali, had taken control of Mysore from a Hindu ruler), worked to fit himself into local Hindu traditions of kingship and, as the Jacobin Club spectacularly attests, to foster close ties to the West. Napoleon pursued and relied on assimilation of various kinds while in Egypt, in much the way that as emperor of France some years later he would blend monarchical and revolutionary influences. For both leaders, reaching across the lines of East and West was vital to the success of their political, personal, and (for Napoleon at least) imperial agendas. Cosmopolitanism, in short, was an essential technique of expansion and survival. This kind of cross-cultural alliance understandably gave the British pause. After all, Britain's overseas power depended on achieving exactly the same thing.

Mysore, in particular, had by the 1790s come to occupy a prominent place in British imperial ambitions and anxieties. Haidar Ali and Tipu Sultan fought four wars against the British (in 1767–1769, 1780–1784, 1790–1792, and 1799), which were among the most intense contests waged between the East India Company and any Indian power—further reminder that India was far from being "British." The success of the Mysore rulers inspired a vigorous literature in Britain that painted them as the quintessential bogeymen of imperial rule, in much the way Napoleon was to Britons on the home front. (They also, however, particularly before the 1790s, found some admirers, especially among critics of the East India Company.)[4] In pamphlets, plays, cartoons, stirring reminiscences by veterans, and—perhaps most grippingly of all—toe-curling narratives by Haidar and Tipu's British prisoners of war, the Mysore rulers were depicted as archetypal Muslim "others": tyrants, usurpers, and savages. Tipu's "unrelenting, unmanly, unprecedented cruelty of mind . . ." it was said, "vented itself . . . in a rooted antipathy and inveterate hatred to Europeans."[5] He was such a "Bigot in Religion," one British officer claimed, that "he urged his neighbours as a necessary duty of their Religion to league against *all Christians* the Enemies of the Mahometan faith."[6] But probably the worst charges against Tipu and Haidar were levied by their European male and female captives, of whom there were more than a thousand between 1780 and 1799, a telling indication of Mysore's strength. Many British men claimed to have been forcibly circumcised; others described being made to serve as dancing boys for Tipu, dressed, humiliatingly, in womens' clothes.[7]

This historical case of imperial villain-making has special relevance in light of more recent contests between the Anglo-American West and Muslim East. Clearly the British obsession with Mysore—for obsession it plainly was—stemmed from a range of contemporary anxieties about empire in general, and about Islam and cultural confrontations more specifically. And yet, the reason that Haidar and Tipu appeared to be so dangerous was not merely that they were alien and different. It was that they were frighteningly familiar. They developed technical innovations, such as rockets, that made their army just as "modern" as that of the East India Company. They adopted European military tactics, weapons, uniforms, and—crucially—personnel. They financed their war machine with a system of military fiscalism just like the one that drove British expansion. Most threateningly of all, they cultivated a deep and enduring alliance with France.

Mysore's long-standing ties with the French have been undeservedly sidelined by imperial historians—undeservedly in part because it was this closeness to the West, to France, that made Haidar and Tipu into such potent figures of villainy, and because it was precisely such French-Indian alliances that turned British imperial policy in India toward open territorial conquest. Downplaying the strength of the Franco-Mysorean bond also marginalizes the agency of Indian challengers to British expansion, and makes British success seem far surer and simpler than it really was. The conquest of Mysore was hard fought; and it was the French, in the end, who led to Tipu's demise. In 1799, in the wake of Napoleon's invasion of Egypt, and at the behest of the virulently Francophobic governor-general Richard Wellesley, British forces would march into Mysore, opening what was to be the second front of the war that had begun on the banks of the Nile.

The storming and capture of Seringapatam, in May 1799, resonates to this day as one of the most dramatic battles of British imperial history. It also marked a turning point in East India Company policy. Earlier campaigns, such as Clive's march to Plassey, or the Company's own earlier wars with Mysore, had been at least ostensibly retaliatory or defensive. With its final war against Tipu, the East India Company exercised a new stance as an aggressively expansionist military state. And while it signaled a shift toward militarism on the front lines of empire, victory in Seringapatam also marked a change in how the Company presented itself on the home front. Back in Britain, trophies from the fallen city (among the first Indian objects to be publicly displayed in Britain) were used to promote a new image of the Company as ruler.

East India Company propaganda after Seringapatam was so brash and comprehensive that it has become easy to interpret the British offensive as resting on trumped-up charges. But beneath the rhetoric resided a history of deep, remarkable, and quite real contact between Mysore and France. Their relationship affords a tantalizing glimpse into an India in which, had the protagonists had their way, Britain might never have managed to sustain its empire, and certainly not on its own terms.

## II. L'Alliance Française

Mysore's fatal romance with the French started around the time of Tipu Sultan's birth, in 1750, in a world of violence, intrigue, and opportunity. The Mughal Empire was racked by Afghan invasions and no longer able to command its major vassals. Succession crises in the kingdoms of Hyderabad and Arcot erupted into a free-for-all among Mughal imperial factions, various regional rulers, the Marathas, and, of course, the British and the French East India companies, which coveted these rich inland domains from their factories on the Coromandel coast.

For Europeans on the make, such as Robert Clive, the wars of the 1750s provided unprecedented chances to seek money, fame, and power. And in the kingdom of Mysore, near Bangalore in southern India, another ambitious and resourceful officer seized on the wars to advance his personal position. Haidar Ali was at that time a cavalry commander in the service of Mysore's Hindu Wodeyar king. Mysore also had been caught up in the tangled wars of succession, and it was from this vantage point that Haidar Ali had occasion to watch French troops in battle. The sight "made such an impression on his mind," a French officer later wrote, "that he was persuaded the French were capable of undertaking the most difficult enterprises."[8] Haidar devoted himself to a close study of European military methods. He explored the fortifications of Pondicherry, watched French troops drill and train, bought European flintlocks for his men, and enlisted French gunners. In 1752, he was able to study French tactics directly on the battlefield, by placing his forces right next to allied French units so "that he might learn from them the art of war. In fact," the officer went on to say,

> he was very attentive and exact in observing everything that passed in the French camp; and caused several of their evolutions to be repeated, as well as was in his power, in his own camp. This repetition caused some diversion to the French officers and soldiers, whom he was attentive to please by his politeness and good manners.[9]

View of Seringapatam.

Haidar also apparently learned to "understand perfectly all the French oaths and curse-words"; and his association with Europeans gave him a taste, it was said, for drinking wine and eating ham—though he had an unaccountable aversion toward the European fashion of powdered hair.[10]

The French were less amused by Haidar's successful recruitment of "the most active and intelligent French soldiers into his service." But following the East India Company's capture and destruction of Pondicherry in 1761—about the same time that Claude Martin and many others defected into British service—French armorers, carpenters, artillery experts, and architects streamed into Haidar's employ. By the early 1760s, Haidar had deposed the reigning raja and secured control of Mysore himself. He established his capital at Seringapatam, a small, rocky island in the Kaveri River, not far from the town of Mysore, and an excellent site for a fortified citadel. French engineers girded and barricaded the perimeter of Seringapatam with walls, redoubts, bastions, and batteries.[11] European officers, such as the Savoyard mercenary Lallée, trained Haidar's Indian commanders and led a brigade of at least four hundred European (mostly French) troops, cantoned at the "French Rocks," a few miles north of the city. Haidar terrorized his Indian enemies with tales of these "cruel people, and devourers of human flesh."[12]

The presence of European advisers, technicians, and officers in Mysore was just one instance of a pattern repeated throughout the subcontinent—and, increasingly, the Muslim world.[13] Many non-British Europeans in particular, such as Antoine Polier, found service with native princes more rewarding than the somewhat restricted options available to them in the East India Company army. Many Indian princes, in turn, gladly availed themselves of these Europeans' skills, with little intention of establishing formal alliances with European powers as such.

Yet the relationship between Mysore and France was a special one. For one thing, it was unusually sustained: perpetuated and deepened by Tipu Sultan, the connection would endure almost four decades, until the fall of Seringapatam, in 1799. It was also remarkably successful. Haidar and Tipu's adoption of European, and specifically French, techniques helped make them arguably the most visible military obstacle to British expansion in South India. To British eyes, the danger posed by European advisers in Indian states was self-evident. By sharing European methods with Indian rulers, French advisers whittled away at whatever narrow technical and tactical advantages the Company army held over its Indian opponents. Even "a very small increase of French soldiers," a British official later observed, "is a very material addition to Tippoo's strength."[14] He and his peers would have had reason to know: the Company ran its sepoy army on exactly the same principle.

But what made the bond between France and Mysore so particularly important was that it rested on more than a handful of renegade advisers. This, potentially, was a union of states. Far off in distant France, government ministers worked to cultivate ties with Mysore, seeing the alliance as one of France's best chances to reclaim territory and power in South India. In 1769, not long after France's severe defeats in the Seven Years War, the Duc de Choiseul dispatched a small party of officers to Haidar's court to develop closer connections with this up-and-coming opponent of Britain. (This was the same year that Choiseul also proposed to Louis XV an invasion of Egypt.) A full thirty years later, the prospect of formal alliance with Mysore was still very much alive for Talleyrand and Napoleon. So was the legacy of the connection. One month before leaving for Egypt, Napoleon summoned one of Tipu Sultan's veteran French advisers to join him on the expedition, in order to make contact with Mysore.[15] And though pinning down the loyalties of

European mercenaries can be a hazardous business, there is no doubt that some of these men viewed their service in Mysore as a patriotic act. "Far from making me abandon the interests of the French nation . . . ," Haidar's mercenary commander Lallée wrote, service in Mysore "excited in me the desire to prove to France my inviolable attachment"—an especially revealing assertion since Lallée was in fact a Savoyard (like Benoît de Boigne) and not formally French.[16]

No single event more painfully forced the British to confront the power of a Franco-Mysorean alliance than the battle of Pollilur, in September 1780. The battle was one of the first clashes in the East India Company's second war with Mysore, itself an offshoot of the Anglo-French war that had started in 1778. Declaring himself the guardian of French possessions in Malabar, Haidar Ali marched on the British-protected province of Arcot in July 1780, with Tipu and General Lallée by his side. At Pollilur, a few miles outside the temple city of Kanchipuram, the Mysoreans trapped a detachment of the East India Company army, commanded by Colonel Baillie. The Company soldiers resisted Tipu's attacks, anxiously awaiting reinforcements from General Sir Hector Munro. When fresh troops "clothed in scarlet . . . beating the British grenadiers' march" appeared at their rear, Baillie's men let out a shout of joy—only to discover, in horror, that the sepoys were not Munro's men at all, but Haidar Ali's.[17] Surrounded on all sides, Baillie's army closed into a square to resist the Mysorean cavalry charge. Lallée then delivered the coup de grace. Pointing his artillery toward the British ammunition tumbrils, he blew up three of them and brought British hopes to a dramatic close.

Sir Hector Munro, whose failure to arrive on the scene had been a major factor in the disaster, called Pollilur "the severest blow that the English ever sustained in India."[18] Some three thousand Company soldiers were killed, while Baillie and two hundred Europeans, fifty of them officers, were carried off to Seringapatam in chains. The captives' sufferings became an emotive theme in British representations of Mysore, and one of the Pollilur captives, David Baird, would avenge the battle personally by leading the charge against Seringapatam in 1799.

"You owe the victory to our disaster [i.e., errors], rather than to our defeat," Baillie boasted to Haidar Ali, full of Scottish pride.[19] But less sanguine observers saw it the other way around: Britain would go on to win the war and retain its place in India thanks only to its opponents' confusion. "Had the French sent timely assistance to the enemy," one analysis concluded,

> as there was every reason to expect, and had the Mahratta States, and other native persons of Hindoostan, instead of remaining quiet spec-

> tators . . . joined their confederate forces, and acted with unanimity, there could not have been a doubt but the English must have been dispposs[ess]ed of almost every settlement on the Peninsula. Had Hyder pursued his success after the defeat of Baillie considering the shattered and dispirited state of the rest of the army, there could scarcely have been a hope of its not falling together with Fort St. George, almost a defenceless prey into the hands of the enemy.[20]

In short, if Mysore had tightened its alliances, especially with France, then the results could have been a lot worse for the British.

The battle made an equally profound impression back in Seringapatam, where Tipu Sultan celebrated his victory with unusual style. He had it painted on the wall of his summer palace, the Daria Daulat Bagh. A wide-eaved pavilion about a mile outside the city walls, set in a cool enclosure of cypress avenues, the palace was Tipu's sanctuary of personal peace. Here, in this "Garden of Happiness," war was a memory, rendered in scarlet and golden paint. The mural of the battle of Pollilur covers the external length of the palace's western face and presents an unabashedly majestic scene. The Mysore army marches across the wall in splendid ranks of lance-wielding cavalry and archers on horseback, helmeted cuirassiers, infantry in brilliant turbans, and European cannoneers poised behind heavy blue guns. The British troops, in the face of this tremendous onslaught, are just two feeble rows of scissored white legs and stiff red backs. Many of the British soldiers are tipped over, dying, pierced by lances or decapitated by Tipu's saber-swinging men. Lallée,

The Battle of Pollilur, as represented by Indian artists on the walls of the Daria Daulat Bagh palace, Seringapatam.

who peers down through a telescope from his vantage point in the upper right-hand corner, has already exploded one of the British powder tumbrils, and aims his artillery straight into the Company ranks.[21]

It is a scene of vigor, violence, spectacle—and, unmistakably, of triumph. On the right, in a small opening at the center of the British square, a palanquin shelters Colonel Baillie. He sits almost invisibly in the dark wooden enclosure, wounded, biting his finger anxiously. Boxed in on all sides, he is already, effectively, a captive. At the left of the painting, by contrast, a wide clearing sets off the Mysorean commanders. Tipu and Haidar, hovering above the fray on their caparisoned elephants, ride majestically toward the battle, holding roses to their noses, unswerving, implacable. To all intents and purposes, they have already won.

No wonder the British despised the mural when they saw it (albeit with a kind of morbid fascination that led Arthur Wellesley to restore it in 1799, and Lord Dalhousie to have it repainted in 1854).[22] "[P]roof of their puerile taste . . . ," snapped one British officer, "neither better imagined nor executed than the commonest Pagoda daubing in the Carnatick done by a bad monchee man."[23] To the spirited adolescent Charlotte Clive (Robert Clive's granddaughter), who stayed with her mother and sister in the palace zenana just a year after the fall of Seringapatam, the mural seemed "very ludicrous . . . the natives having no idea of distance, or perspective."[24]

But the Scottish aristocrat Lady Hood, pausing at Seringapatam on a leisurely sketching tour of Mysore in 1812, "could not help remarking the decided differences in national character that the native artist has put into the countenances of the French and English soldiers."[25] The contrast between these two different sets of red-coated and white-trousered troops may not be as evident to a viewer today, but Lady Hood's contemporaries would have immediately spotted what she meant: mustaches—curling, silky, *Indianizing* mustaches—on every French soldier, just like their Mysore allies, and a stark contrast to the impeccably clean-shaven British. Indian observers, on the other hand, would have noted a different feature in the Frenchmen's appearance: hats, the signature accessory of a European in a land where turban was king. Here, then, is a kind of fusion in a scene that otherwise calls attention to difference. Sporting the whiskers of an Indian and the headgear of a European, the French in Mysore are at once neither, and both.

Haidar Ali died in 1782, before the war was over. He told Tipu "while dying," according to the French chronicler Michaud, "that he could conquer the Europeans by putting one nation against another; and seeing all round in Hindustan, only tottering states, and feeble monarchs, and princes who did not know how to hate the English like himself, he turned, once more, his eyes towards France."[26] Tipu developed the French alliance with dedication and purpose. In 1787, he decided to send an embassy directly to Versailles. (Two years earlier, he had ventured into overseas diplomacy by dispatching a mission to Constantinople, to ask the Ottoman sultan, in his capacity as caliph, for formal recognition as king of Mysore.)[27] It was the first embassy ever sent to Europe by an eighteenth-century Indian ruler, and a clear sign that Tipu Sultan's ambitions extended well beyond merely enlisting French mercenaries in his army. He wanted Louis XVI to sign an offensive and defensive alliance, cemented by a permanent force of ten thousand French troops to be based in Seringapatam, answerable to Mysore law and commanded personally by Tipu.[28] Tipu also asked the French king to send him a range of professionals and craftsmen to work in Seringapatam: gardeners, glassblowers, weavers, watchmakers, porcelain crafters, and, notably for the period, "printers of Oriental languages." In another remarkably forward-looking proposal, Tipu suggested sending one of his sons to France to be educated.[29]

The three ambassadors and their retinue sailed from Pondicherry in July 1787, on a French ship, flying Tipu's flag.[30] They reached Paris exactly one year later, and were received by the king in Versailles's Salon d'Hercule on August 10, 1788. Louis XVI accepted their gifts of gold, diamonds, and pearls, and listened to a long speech detailing British iniquities in India. But France was then in the midst of the economic crisis that would ultimately bring down the monarchy. The prospects of persuading the king to *extend* his commitments, spend a great deal of money, and provoke another global war with Britain were poor to say the least. Louis's ministers politely put off all of Tipu's substantive requests. The ambassadors had come to ask for sustained military assistance, but in these last, straitened days of the Ancien Régime, "the French Government could give them only shows and festivals."[31]

That, however, it did with panache. As a piece of sheer theater, the embassy was a tremendous success—and the ambassadors' colorful prominence must have played its own part in deepening French interest in India and keeping the idea of an association with Mysore alive. Crowds lined the streets to gape at the visitors as they traveled up through Marseille, Grenoble, and Lyon; when they walked in the park at Saint-Cloud, footmen had to clear a way for them between the full silk skirts of all the ladies milling around.[32] Paris loved the ambassadors: "They were the subject of all conversations, on them all eyes were fixed, and the name of Tippoo Saheb became, for a moment, famous among the light-hearted people, who were more struck by the originality of Asiatic costumes than by the importance of their possessions in India."[33] "Despite their copper complexions [they] had the most splendid features," gushed the artist Elisabeth Vigée-Lebrun, who painted a majestic portrait of one of the ambassadors, Muhammed Darwesh Khan, a stern robed figure with his fist clamped around the pommel of a scimitar. Another of his colleagues was modeled in terra-cotta; images of all three appeared on everything from Sèvres coffee cups to ladies' fans and even coat buttons.[34] Perhaps their most unusual appearance of all was in pamphlets by contemporary philosophes, where they served as mouthpieces in the debates about despotism and monarchy that were echoing through Paris's prerevolutionary salons.[35]

And the ambassadors loved Paris. In fact, it was with considerable difficulty that they were at last persuaded to leave, in October 1788. During their three months in the capital they had overspent Tipu's allowance by 50,000 livres; and with the expenses of the voyage (on a French vessel) factored in, hosting Tipu's embassy cost the French Crown over 800,000 livres (or about the same amount in contemporary pounds sterling).[36] Yet the Mysoreans returned to Seringapatam with little more than a band of ninety-eight artisans, some French seeds, and a massive presentation service of Sèvres porcelain for Tipu from Louis XVI. The set, worth over 30,000 livres, had been specially designed for Tipu without animal representations (so as not to offend his Islamic sensibilities), and included washbasins, hookahs, spittoons, and a half dozen busts of the king and queen. Tipu was furious.[37] Porcelain was no substitute for troops. But he wrote graciously to Louis XVI nevertheless, thanking him for the workmen and the porcelain. "The foundations of the good understanding and friendship that reigns between your Imperial Majesty and us are too old and solid to be shaken . . . ," he said, "despite the efforts of the English, that universal disruptor."[38]

Louis's unwillingness to commit, followed by the coming of the French Revolution, meant that Tipu had to fight the Third Mysore War (1790–1792) without French aid. For the first time in all his struggles against the East India Company, Tipu suffered humiliating defeat.[39] The British—led by Lord Cornwallis, who was making up for his embarrassment at Yorktown some years earlier—captured the eastern part of Seringapatam island itself, and imposed a punitive treaty on Tipu that forced him to relinquish half his territory, pay a substantial indemnity, and hand over two of his small sons as hostages.

Now more than ever Tipu needed French aid. In much the way that Napoleon's appeals to the Egyptian people took on new depth and urgency in the wake of defeat, so Tipu's overtures to the French state continued after his 1792 loss. He corresponded regularly with French officials in Pondicherry and Mauritius, and kept abreast of Paris's changing régimes. (A note in his handwriting shows him learning the "Names of the Sirdars (or Chiefs) of the French Nation. Five Select Sirdars, possessing the Supreme Authority in France . . ."—i.e. the Directors—"Official Designation of the Assembly of 500 Sirdars, constituting the deliberative body in France, and Subordinate to the five Sirdars above mentioned, Conseil des Anciens.") He sent guns, jewelery, and khelats (the robes typically exchanged as ceremonial gifts in Indian courts) "to the five French Chiefs, and their Wives."[40]

Throughout the 1790s, Tipu continued to dream of ten thousand Frenchmen in Mysore, and of the day when, together, they would chase the British out of India. One night in 1797, he had an actual dream about it. "It was represented to me that a Frenchman of standing had arrived," he recorded in his dream book:

> I asked him to take a seat and inquired after his health. The Christian then said: "I have come with ten thousand Franks to serve the *Sarkar-i-Khudadad* and I have disembarked them all on the shore. They are well-built, stout and young." I, thereupon, said to him, "That is fine. Here too all the equipment for war is ready and the followers of Islam are eager, in large numbers, to prosecute *Jihad*."[41]

Then he woke up.

Yet the reality Tipu did wake up to was not entirely different from his dream. For in the winter of 1797, a Frenchman *had* arrived in Seringapatam describing himself as a man of great importance. It was François Ripaud, the Jacobin, who had washed up in a shipwreck on the coast near Mangalore. Ripaud represented himself as a naval officer and envoy from the French colony of Mauritius, and told Tipu that ten thousand French soldiers were waiting there to follow him to Mysore.[42] This, of course, was exactly what Tipu wanted to hear. Despite some of his ministers' mistrust of this French "scoundrel," Tipu dispatched Ripaud to Mauritius with two ambassadors in the fall of 1797.[43] His chief request, as ever, was for men (including one "to do my French correspondence, Citoyen Ripaud does not express himself well and he is not a writer").[44] The French governor of the island, Malartic, received the Mysoreans warmly, but like Louis XVI a decade earlier, Malartic could offer Tipu little more than plants and seeds.[45] The best the governor could do was to post an announcement asking for volunteers to go and serve in Seringapatam. Just under one hundred signed up, to whom Malartic added fifteen officers, under the command of brigadier Chapuis.[46] "This motley reinforcement of naval, and military, creole, and European" arrived in June 1798—yet another disappointment to Tipu.[47]

But there was more news—inspiring news—soon to come, for in September 1798, Tipu learned about the French invasion of Egypt. Now those ten thousand Frenchmen were just an ocean away! What was more, he heard that they were planning to try to cross over and join him. Tipu was equally delighted by the East India Company's obvious discomfiture at the development. The new governor-general, Richard Wellesley, sent Tipu a "pompously detailed account" (Chapuis's words) of the Battle of the Nile, and warned him to steer clear of the French.[48] Tipu wrote disingenuously back, that the British victory "has given me more pleasure than can possibly be conveyed by writing"—and then promptly began to plan his rendezvous with Napoleon.[49] Brigadier Chapuis helped him prepare dispatches for Egypt.

Another confrontation with Britain was plainly at hand, and Tipu Sultan had every reason to look forward to it. With the support of French troops, he could reasonably hope to reverse the defeat of 1792 and make substantial further gains. The alliance with France, so carefully cultivated over decades, would, it seemed, soon reach its fruition. Tipu saw the coming of war with a prophetic eye. "The fractured mast of Ripaud's worthless vessel will cause the subversion of an empire," he is said to have anticipated.[50] But it was a Delphic utterance, for little did he know that the empire destined to be lost was none other than his own.

## III. A Dangerous Liaison

There is something titillating about reading other people's mail. At least so the British officer who read this billet-doux, taken from a soldier in the Armée d'Orient, might well have found: "I no longer know myself, o my [Justiniana]! What will become of me far from you? The burning climate of these regions, seems to attract and increase the fires that devour me."[51] This one might have been equally tantalizing to its British reader:

> [I sent you] a letter long as a book . . . [but] I don't know if that letter reached you. Accursed English! If that piece of writing has fallen into their hands . . . my vengeance will be as terrible as it possibly can.
>
> For the rest, console yourself my dearest, they will know a part of our history, but they will never know the authors. I would only be upset that you would not know all that has happened to me. . . . Your portrait lost, then refound in the hands of Turkish women, a chain of events interesting as well as painful. Beloved image! I had promised you so, never to separate myself from you. . . .[52]

But this letter would surely have been the most intriguing of all:

> You have already been informed of my arrival on the borders of the Red Sea with an innumerable and Invincible Army, full of the desire of delivering you from the Iron yoke of England.

> I eagerly embrace this opportunity of testifying to you the desire I have of being informed by you, by the way of Muscat and Mocha, as to your Political Situation. I would even wish you could send some Intelligent Person to Suez or Cairo, possessing your confidence, with whom I may confer.
>
> May the Almighty increase your power and destroy your Enemies.[53]

No misplaced love letter this: it was a letter from Napoleon Bonaparte, and it was addressed to Tipu Sultan. Unlike the majority of communications intercepted by spies, soldiers, and secret agents in wartime, this one appeared to convey genuine strategic intelligence of an important and usable kind.

Penned as Napoleon prepared to march north into Palestine, on January 26, 1799, and sent under cover to the sharif of Mecca, this letter expressed that dearest of Napoleon's hopes: to join forces with Tipu and wage successful war against the British in India. (The sharif of Mecca had replied to Napoleon in late April 1799, telling him that he had placed the letter "in safe hands," to be delivered to Tipu.)[54] The letter would also, of course, have seemed like a dream come true to Tipu Sultan, waiting anxiously in Seringapatam for his ten thousand Frenchmen. But Tipu never received it. For it was the East India Company whom this letter satisfied most of all. Intercepted by the British off Jeddah on February 17, the missive gave British leaders incontrovertible proof of the dangerous liaison between Napoleon and Tipu that many had long suspected. It provided formal justification to march on Mysore—and to do so soon.

This, at any rate, was the opinion of Richard Wellesley, who had been appointed East India Company governor-general in 1797. An Anglo-Irish Protestant peer and politician, Wellesley had spent five years engaged with Indian affairs on the Board of Control. Although married to a glamorous Catholic Frenchwoman, Hyacinthe, with whom he corresponded lovingly in French, Wellesley was Francophobic through and through—an inclination shared to some extent by his political ally William Pitt the Younger.[55] It was Francophobia above all that would guide Wellesley's policy while in India. Viewing India as another theater in Britain's war with France, he pursued a policy of aggressive expansion against numerous "pro-French" Indian princes, Tipu Sultan chief among them. Wellesley's term as governor-general has become synonymous with the shift toward preemptive expansion in India and with the rise of an increasingly straitlaced British culture overseas that proved less tolerant of East-West crossings than the generation of Warren Hastings had been.

To Wellesley, the letter from Napoleon to Tipu would have been a gratifying discovery, but in no way surprising. Wellesley sailed to India in the late autumn of 1797, preoccupied with French plots. On reaching Calcutta in May 1798, he swiftly moved to wipe out pockets of French influence in the subcontinent. The first target was Hyderabad, where Raymond's men, he said, constituted "the basis of a permanent French faction in India." He forced the nizam of Hyderabad to sign a treaty of subsidiary alliance with the East India Company, whereby the nizam promised to give up his French-officered troops and to maintain at his own cost six thousand East India Company soldiers instead.[56] (Wellesley also permitted a corps to continue under the command of the Irish mercenary Michael Finglas, arguing that "On general principles of policy, I am sensible of the danger of admitting the establishment of Corps of this description among the Country powers, even under the Command of British subjects; but the numerous military establishments of French adventurers in the service of the different states of India, suggested the necessity of opposing some counterpoise to their dangerous influence and growing power.")[57]

The French presence in Mysore, however, was far more dangerous in Wellesley's eyes, and could not be so easily defused. Learning of Tipu's recruiting efforts among the French in Mauritius, Wellesley decided that "the evidence of meditated hostility was complete."[58] With proof in hand of Tipu's communication with the French, and further reports that Tipu was also making overtures to two of the Company's most ardent Asian opponents—the Afghans and the Marathas—Wellesley drafted a minute to the secret committee of the East India Company outlining the "measures . . . most advisable for the purpose, of frustrating the united efforts of Tippoo Sultaun and of France."[59] It was his blueprint for war, and he intended to put it promptly into action. By early February 1799—as Napoleon prepared to march into Palestine—twenty-one thousand East India Company troops were massed at Vellore, poised to strike against Tipu. On March 5, under the command of General Harris, they invaded Mysore.

When Richard Wellesley's arguments are read alone, it seems obvious that the British turn toward offensive action was precipitated by Anglo-French war. The trouble is that this was precisely what Wellesley wanted his readers to think, and he was a skilled propagandist. He had actually completed his war plan, so convinced of Franco-Mysorean collusion, on August 12, 1798, a full two months *before* Company officials in India heard news of Napoleon's invasion of Egypt.[60] Indeed, at every stage, Wellesley's actions anticipated his evidence, to such an extent that it must be wondered how meaningful his evidence was.[61] And Wellesley had a special investment in stressing the French connection, because he faced opposition from his superiors in London. Provoking wars and pursuing open conquest stood at odds with the wishes of the

East India Company Court of Directors, who were wary of undertaking expensive, messy, bloody campaigns. Promptly after the invasion of Mysore, Wellesley began to write long dispatches back to London, to justify his decisions and the "heavy expense to your finances" that they entailed. "The designs of France as well as of the Sultaun," he argued to the Board of Directors, "were of a much more extensive and formidable nature, than any which have ever been attempted against the British Empire in India, since the hour of its first foundation."[62]

The obsessive, predetermined, and frankly manipulative quality of Wellesley's crusade against Tipu Sultan—his warmongering—has generally been seen as stemming more from personal paranoia and thirst for power than anything else. But situating this episode in the context of contemporary events and worldviews suggests a different reading. The dangers posed to Britain by revolutionary France appeared all too clear in 1799. At the same time that Wellesley warred and schemed, Britain itself faced the most serious invasion scare since the Armada. In 1798, a French force had actually landed in Ireland, where the United Irishmen planned a rebellion against British rule, and civilians across Britain were joining volunteer militias for home defense by the thousands. British power in India, in the meantime, was a fragile thing, resting on a sepoy army and on tenuous terms of cohabitation with dozens of armed and powerful neighbors. Nobody, in 1799, could look down the tunnel of Anglo-French global war and see through to the relative security of post-Waterloo Britain and its empire. Wellesley and his generation had been raised in a Britain shaped both by war with France and by the expansion of empire. However "justified" or not, he and many others believed that offensive moves—and the policy transformations they entailed—were essential. This sense of scale, risk, epic-making conflict—the sense that Britain itself, and not just British power in India, hung in the balance—would make the Fourth Mysore War strike a particular chord among Britons at home.[63]

The final, fateful collision of Britain, France, and Mysore was also to be a collision of three individual, and remarkably parallel, lives. Napoleon, Tipu, and Wellesley had each inherited earlier sets of political relationships. Napoleon inherited Ancien Régime scripts for an invasion of Egypt, and for a vision of imperial France resurgent. Tipu Sultan inherited his father's animosity toward the British and his friendship with the French; and he inherited a recently acquired throne, which he was almost constantly at war to protect. Richard Wellesley inherited the wounds and scars of decades of British war with France. He also inherited a government in India that many Britons had long been skeptical of, and a view of Mysore as the enemy of everything that British rule, at its best, hoped to represent.

Power brokers all three, these men shared a further defining characteristic: each felt himself to be marginal. Napoleon, the shy Corsican who spoke French with an accent, saw Egypt as another rung on the ladder up the power hierarchies of France. Tipu, the "usurper's" heir, was deeply concerned with asserting his legitimacy as a Muslim ruler in a Hindu province. Wellesley, an Irish peer, longed, like Robert Clive before him, to land himself squarely in the center of the English aristocracy, with a seat in the House of Lords.

The resemblance to Clive is not coincidental, for Wellesley, like his rivals and fellow marginals Napoleon and Tipu, was a collector. Collectors in the metaphoric sense, all three men were conquerors of territory and power. They were also collectors in concrete terms. Tipu Sultan, like his near-contemporary Asaf ud-Daula, formed a substantial library and a *toshkhana* that he filled with European objects. Napoleon and Wellesley, who shared a penchant for the personal trappings of power, both raised state-sponsored collecting to a new level, systematically acquiring art, artifacts, and specimens in the wake of conquest. The invasions of Egypt and Mysore made these men's imperial and personal agendas come crashing together. They also forced two kinds of imperial collecting to converge: the seizure of territory and the appropriation of objects.

## IV. The Fall, and After

Seringapatam, undeniably, was a beautiful target. In the words of a young colonel who had approached Tipu's capital with Cornwallis's army in May 1791, "The Country . . . served as a foil to the Island, which was then covered with the most beautiful Verdure, the City also presented itself in its utmost splendour; for the sun then shone bright upon its ramparts, and the many sumptuous buildings they surround, and his rays glittered upon the gilded domes of the palace of the Sultan."[64] "What glorious sport," he had fantasized, "to break down the doors of the tyrants Zanana, and set all his little dusky Fawns at Liberty—and what satisfaction! to return to Calcutta, with my sacks of Pagodas."[65]

Now, eight years later, to the men dug into trenches on the north side of the Kaveri, the sight of the shining city in the river must have been still more alluring. Seringapatam, by this, the British army's fourth war against Mysore, had become a city of legend. Somewhere in that fortress lurked the monster himself, Tipu Sultan, the villain they had learned through captives' and veterans' stories to dread and hate. There was treasure, too—gold and jewels beyond their wildest dreams. There were women, fair damsels and "dusky fawns," waiting to be sprung free. And food! Their food was running out so fast they would hit famine within days. After nearly four weeks hunkered down, so starved that they could almost drop with weakness and the sick pain of hunger, the hidden realm behind the walls must have seemed like the promised land itself.

The storming of Seringapatam on May 4, 1799, was ripe for mythmaking from the start. Anticipated by decades of fighting and writing over Mysore, the conflict had an epic quality. (And scale: the army was "the finest which ever took the field in India," boasted Richard Wellesley, composed of more than twenty thousand East India Company troops, supplemented by Crown forces—including Richard's younger brother Arthur Wellesley, a colonel in the thirty-third Foot—and thousands of Hyderabadi sepoys.)[66] The events of the day were also heightened with personal drama when the charge was led, at one o'clock that afternoon, by the brawny and beloved Scottish general David Baird, who himself had been held captive in Seringapatam. For more than a day, British cannons pounded away at Seringapatam's curtain wall, opening an all-important breach. Baird and his men splashed across the rocky river, under a barrage of musket fire and rockets, but in minutes they had fought their way up through the gap and hoisted British colors from the fortress walls. Following a well-coordinated plan of attack, thousands of Company and Hyderabadi troops assaulted the ramparts and swelled into the streets of the city.

Later in the evening, hours into the fighting, Baird presided over another episode in the legend of Seringapatam's fall, when reports reached him that Tipu Sultan had been killed. Baird steered his way through heaps of bodies—some dead, others hot and bleeding—to the gateway where Tipu's corpse was said to lie. In that low-arched tunnel, "the scene was altogether shocking, the number of bodies so great, and the place so dark that it was impossible to distinguish one person from another."[67] But still, "as a matter of the utmost political importance," it had to be done. They rolled the bodies off one at a time and checked the faces by candlelight. At last, they found him, slashed and shot and stripped of his jewels. In the words of Major Alexander Beatson, a kind of epitaph, "He who had left the palace in the morning a powerful imperious Sultaun, full of vast ambitious projects, was brought back a lump of clay, abandoned by the whole world, his kingdom overthrown, his capital taken, and his palace occupied by the very man, Major-general Baird, who . . . had been . . . in irons, in a prison scarce three hundred yards from the spot where the corpse of the Sultaun now lay."[68]

It must have been part of the British inclination to see their capture of Seringapatam as a matter of destiny that made them keenly interested in the details of Tipu Sultan's last day. For him, too, their sources told them, the fates had been circling. During those last days before the assault, Tipu had consid-

Sir David Wilkie, *General Sir David Baird Discovering the Body of Sultan Tippoo Sahib after having captured Seringapatam on the 4th of May 1799*, 1839. Painted four decades after the battle, this dramatic image speaks to Seringapatam's place in the canon of British imperial legends.

ered leaving Seringapatam, abandoning his capital to its fate. But no, he decided, he would not evade the inevitable. Instead he "looked up towards the heavens, and sighing deeply said, 'I am entirely resigned to the will of God, whatever it may be.' "[69] On the morning of May 4, Tipu visited his Hindu priests (though he was a devout Muslim, it was his custom to do this) and learned that the omens were against him. Despite his presenting an elephant to the temple, giving alms, and praying with the priests, there was nothing to be done but confront what events the day might hold.[70] He fought the invaders "courageous as a lion," and "drank of the cup of Martyrdom." Tipu's Persian epitaphs have a melancholy poignance:

> *"Ah! at the destruction of this prince and his kingdom,*
> *Let the world shed tears of blood."*
> *"For him the sun and moon shared equally in grief,*

> *The heavens were turned upside down and the earth darkened."*
> *"When I saw that sorrow for him pervaded all,*
> *I asked grief for the year of his death.*
> *An angel replied, let us mourn his loss with burning sighs and tears—*
> *For the light of the religion of Islam has departed from the world,*
> nuru'l islam din az dunya raft."[71]

And what of the French? Tipu's ministers had advised him against relying upon the French to defend Seringapatam, "for both these people (the English and French)," they said, "consider themselves originally of the same tribe, and they are one in heart and language."[72] But when the British stormed into the breach of Seringapatam fort, it was French soldiers they met: the Mysorean commanders had been bribed by the British to leave the way clear. (This was one reason the British were able to win relatively easily.) Tipu's last day, according to Chapuis, was spent in a tent with one of his favorites, while Chapuis himself, dutiful to the last, fought on until he was taken prisoner.[73] (Even a British officer highly contemptuous of Tipu's "motley band" of French "vagabonds" grudgingly conceded that this "elderly man . . . had something of the military vetran in his appearance.")[74] After two years in prison at Portsmouth, Chapuis returned to France and reported the events of May 4 to Napoleon, thus fulfilling "the engagement that I formally undertook with the four sons of Tipu Sultan" to plead for their salvation in the faithful hands of France. So it was that Napoleon and Tipu finally did make contact, in a way, though only when it was too late for both.

On balance, perhaps the French historian Michaud provided Tipu's fairest epitaph:

> If the Government of Mysore had historians like those the Europeans had to expose their grievances and voice their complaints, they would not have failed to reproach the English for their invasion of nations who had no quarrel with them, their violation of the most sacred treaties, and their contempt for the first laws of Nature which had given to every nation a motherland whose sanctity should be inviolable. I do not make this observation to justify the barbarism of Tippoo Saheb; but the most impartial writer cannot always get rid of a secret sympathy for an unhappy prince who had as his chroniclers only those who invaded his Empire and destroyed his life.[75]

Michaud was certainly right to decry the triumphalism in British accounts of Tipu and Mysore. Where earlier British discussions of Mysore, and of empire in India in general, had stressed the perils and pitfalls of engagement, victory over Tipu Sultan encouraged a shift toward open celebration of Company and British rule—a shift bolstered, crucially, by what was now public evidence of Tipu's collaboration with the French. After the fall of Seringapatam, Wellesley and his minions promptly seized on documents discovered in Tipu's palace—such as the splendidly incriminating proceedings of the Jacobin Club—to prove their case. Wellesley's acolyte William Kirkpatrick reviewed Tipu's Persian papers and reported gratifyingly back that they "abundantly warrant the conclusion that Tippoo Sultaun never ceased to meditate on the means of subverting the British Power in India from the moment in which he executed the Treaty of Mangalore [1784] to the hour of his Death."[76] Kirkpatrick went on to translate twenty items concerning Tipu and the French—supposedly "but a small part of the Mass of voluminous correspondence . . . manifesting the same implacable hatred, of the British Nation"—which immediately became the foundation for official histories of Mysore.[77] If history is written by the victors, in this case it was as if Wellesley sat down to compose it himself.

With victory, then, came rewritings of a particular and newly patriotic kind. But was the voice of Tipu Sultan, and with it alternate interpretations of British expansion, entirely silenced? No. In objects—trophies, prizes, souvenirs—Tipu's Mysore would reach Britain in varied and sometimes contradictory forms. For the storming of Seringapatam on May 4 was just the beginning of an imperial phenomenon whose scope extended much further: through tales, and above all, through things.

On the morning of May 5, 1799, Captain David Price limped into Seringapatam fort. The scene that confronted him inside the fallen capital, the morning after, seemed almost to defy description. Bodies, one officer wrote, "lay in such immense heaps on the Ramparts, and in the Ditch as well as in different parts of the Town, that no regular account of them could be taken."[78] British estimates put the number of Mysoreans killed between six thousand and ten thousand.[79] Whatever the number, the carnage made a profound impression on Price: "It would be scarecely possible to describe, in adequate terms, the objects of horror, the ghastly spectacle, presented to the senses, by the bodies of the slain, in every attitude, and in every direction; lying in the virandahs, and along the principal street."[80] Though Price had spent May 4 safely behind British lines, the scene was especially poignant for him: in the Third Mysore War he had lost his leg to Mysorean fire, while trying to storm one of Tipu's hill fortresses.[81]

The British could not count the bodies, but they could certainly count the treasure. Price was one of seven "prize agents" appointed by the army to add up Tipu's wealth—now theirs, by British conventions of war, to be parceled out among the soldiers in shares according to rank. He lurched through the corpse-choked streets of Seringapatam to Tipu's palace, and into the courtyard where the treasury stood. It was like stepping from a nightmare into a dream: "The wealth of the palace, which was sufficiently dazzling to the eyes of many who were much more habituated to the sight of hoarded treasures than we were, seemed, at the moment, in specie, and jewels, and bullion, and bales of costly stuff, to surpass all estimate."[82] By the end of that first day alone, Price and his colleagues had counted up almost £500,000 worth of hard cash, and still the treasure houses were full. When the counting was finished several days later, the total prize came to £1,143,216—about £90 million today—unquestionably the largest ever taken by British arms. What a turn of events it was for an army that just days before, as Tipu's courtier Kirmani wrote, "had been reduced to death's door by the want of supplies and the dearness of provisions, who had been obliged to pay . . . two rupees for a bundle of the roots of grass."[83]

For those who lived through the horrible night of May 4, the reversal of fortunes was as violent and palpable as it was complete. It was customary for British officers to turn a blind eye and allow the men some period of time for looting, before imposing discipline and sending in the prize agents. At Seringapatam, the besieging soldiers plundered with a vengeance. "What followed in the slaughter of the Musulmans, the plunder of their property, and the violation of their women had better be left untold," lamented Kirmani.[84] A stoic Colonel Arthur Wellesley was placed in charge of discipline in the fallen citadel. "It was impossible to expect that after the labour which the troops had undergone . . . they should not have looked to the plunder of this place," he reported to his brother Richard. "Nothing therefore can have exceeded what was done on the night of the 4th. Scarcely a house in the town was left unplundered. . . . I came in to take the command on the morning of the 5th, and by the greatest exertion, by hanging, flogging, &c. &c., in the course of that day I restored order among the troops."[85] Wellesley would see something like it again at Badajoz on the Portuguese border in 1812, four hard years into the Peninsular Wars, when after a month of arduous siege, the conquering British soldiers ran such riot through the Spanish town that it took three full days—and the gallows in the Plaza Mayor—to rein them in.

Nobody would ever know how much wealth changed hands during the night of May 4, but tales of luck and extravagance fast became an enduring, evocative part of the Seringapatam legend. For days afterward, it was said, "you might . . . see soldiers betting handfuls of pagodas in the streets on the issue of a cock-fight."[86] "It was . . . notorious that a quantity of the most valuable pearl was to be bought in the bazaars, from the soldiery, for a bottle of spirits."[87] One man's recklessness was another man's fortune. The best-known contemporary anecdote featured a Scottish medical officer who bought a pair of jeweled bangles from a soldier for a hundred rupees, and later discovered them to be worth over £30,000.[88] This was the scene so powerfully conjured by Wilkie Collins in the opening pages of *The Moonstone* (1868), the first detective novel in English literature, which revolves around a cursed diamond plundered from Seringapatam.

Their inherent appeal notwithstanding, get-rich-quick stories like these must have been popular for another reason as well. "Plunder" was effectively the poor man's prize, the only way a common soldier could hope to get rich from victory. Of the vast prize money—the £1,143,216—an ordinary private saw about £7 4s. if he had the good fortune to be white and just £5 if he was Indian. This was a substantial supplement to ordinary pay, though by no means a fortune for life.[89] His officers, however, walked away from Seringapatam anywhere from several hundred to several thousand pounds the richer. Arthur Wellesley, for instance, received £4,300 as his share, which was enough for him to repay his eldest brother, Richard, the price of his commission.[90] Richard Wellesley, for his part, wisely rejected an offer of £100,000 from the Company, "lest it should be said that as Governor-General . . . [he] had a direct personal interest in making war upon a Native Prince."[91] But the commander in chief, General Harris, had no hesitations about scooping up a staggering eighth of the total—over £140,000—for himself alone.[92] In 1801, he bought the estate of Belmont, in Kent, and retired as Baron Harris of Belmont and Seringapatam. Today the word *plunder* is applied so indiscriminately to any form of appropriation that its specific meaning in the context of war tends to get lost. But it is worth considering how much its pejorative cast owes to a deeply hierarchical system that made "plunderers" of the rank and file, while rewarding their officers—sometimes outstandingly greedy ones—with legitimate "prizes."

This massive transfer of wealth, to say nothing of the mayhem that surrounded it, was just one way in which, after May 4, it seemed as if the world really had turned upside down. If the fall of Seringapatam foreshadowed Badajoz in violence and havoc, the fall of Tipu's entire kingdom with it anticipated something of the hard-won finality of Waterloo in 1815. Like the Battle of Waterloo, the capture of Seringapatam put an end to a period of protracted and uncertain struggle. Britain's eventual victory over Mysore had been won at the cost of four wars over thirty-two years; and even the campaign of 1799, though quick and relatively bloodless, was nearly forced into retreat by crippling supply shortages. It is true that Tipu's kingdom, resources, and prestige had been seriously limited by his defeat by Cornwallis in 1792. But the dangers of world war with France had infused the enmity with Mysore with renewed urgency—in something of the way that the "war against terror," ten years after the Gulf War of 1991, revived American hostility toward Saddam Hussein. For decades previously, histories, war memoirs, and captivity narratives had invited the British public to tremble at the names of Haidar and Tipu—at their supposed cruelty, despotism, religious fanaticism, and destructive drive against Britain. Until May 4, 1799, Tipu was still at large, Mysore was resurgent, and France was pressing against the gates of British India. And then on May 5, Tipu was dead, Seringapatam had fallen, and the entire kingdom of Mysore was in British hands. In place of terror, there was triumph.

The storming of Seringapatam, after the panorama by Robert Ker Porter.

For all these reasons, then—because of the intense drama of the event itself; because it took so long in coming; because the enemies were so reviled; and, not least, because it was an episode of Anglo-French war—the capture of Seringapatam made an immediate impact on the British public as no Indian victory, and arguably no imperial victory on land, ever had.[93] (It helped, too, that this triumph for the army came at a time when Britain was especially concerned about its fighting capacities on land.) The storming of the city inspired at least six plays, a panorama, countless prints, pamphlets, and eyewitness accounts. Drawings made by officers on the spot reached and influenced British artists from the young J.M.W. Turner to Robert Ker Porter, who painted an enormously successful panorama of the battle, exhibited in the great room of the Lyceum in 1800.[94] Various firsthand testimonials were cobbled together—and exaggerated and dramatized—in a sensationalist pamphlet called *Narrative Sketches of the Conquest of Mysore.* Running to three editions by 1801, *Narrative Sketches* was an instant popular hit. It was sold at the panorama and, like the painting, toured Britain; its third, fourth, and fifth editions were printed in Edinburgh, Bath, and Hull, respectively.[95]

The victory reverberated throughout the empire, too. In Dublin at the end of 1799, the Indo-Persian traveler Abu Talib Khan (who was originally from Lucknow) saw "the principal events of *The Capture of Seringapatam* exhibited on the stage, by which I was very much affected."[96] In the West Indies, Creole children acted pantomimes around the same theme.[97] At the time of the union with Ireland in 1801, the British drew self-congratulatory parallels between their recently defeated Francophile enemies, "Citizen" Wolfe Tone, a leader of the United Irishmen rebellion of 1798, and "Citizen Tipu."[98]

In sum, the capture of Seringapatam marked a turning point in the history of the East India Company—and of the British Empire—for two reasons. First, because of what it actually was: an act of imperial conquest, legitimated by war with France. Mysore itself had been "collected" into the Company's empire. All Tipu's treasure was claimed by the British as prize. The Company pompously restored his throne to its supposedly rightful incumbent, the puppet king Krishnaraja Wodeyar, age five, and "of a timid disposition."[99] Tipu's domains were carved up and partly annexed by the Company. Even his herd of 250,000 draft cattle was quickly co-opted into British military service, where they helped speed up Company mobility in its next expansionist wars, against the Marathas. And in a nearly exact analogue to the researches of Napoleon's savants in Egypt, in 1800 the Company commissioned two agents, Francis Buchanan and Colin Mackenzie, to undertake comprehensive surveys of its newly conquered domains. The Mysore surveys, like the survey of India that Mackenzie later went on to direct, gathered knowledge in the service of state power. As an institution of collection and classification, the survey would become a key governing instrument of the nineteenth-century colonial state.[100]

The capture of Seringapatam also marked a turning point in how imperial victory was represented. There were certainly ways in which the portrayals of Tipu that emerged in the wake of victory fitted into a longer genealogy of representations of Muslim or Oriental "otherness." Perceptions of Tipu were equally influenced, though, by the real if exaggerated context of war with France. Perhaps nowhere was the ripple effect of the capture of Seringapatam, and the range and variety of its representations, more palpable than in the circulation of objects from the fallen city. For during that frenzy of looting on May 4 and 5, Mysore had been materially collected as well, in hundreds of objects swiped, swapped, bought, found, auctioned, and awarded from the fallen city. Seringapatam objects were acquired with unprecedented eagerness by soldiers, civilians, and the Company itself. As tangible pieces of the historic event, they achieved in a single stroke what pamphlets and pictures did at one remove: they brought direct testimony of imperial conquest into the hands of British civilians. They also reached a wider cross section of the British public than any other Indian artifacts had done before.

It was through collecting of this tangible kind that the imperial collecting of Seringapatam, in more metaphoric terms, can best be gauged. From trophies on public display in London, to Tipu's own elegant possessions, objects from Seringapatam gave material form to the conquest of Mysore. Their collectors were equally various. At one extreme was the East India Company state, which put Seringapatam trophies in its new London museum, dedicated to self-advertisement. At the other were individuals who scooped up Seringapatam objects for a variety of personal reasons. The most avid of these private collectors were none other than Lady Henrietta Clive and her husband Edward, governor of Madras, Robert Clive's son and heir. What did Seringapatam collections say about Britain's imperial persona, personnel, and opponents at a moment of change?

CHAPTER SIX

# *The Objects of Victory*

## 1. Trophies

In 1808, an object went on display in London that remains, to this day, one of the most eye-catching museum pieces of the British Empire. The object is a life-size wooden model of a prostrate European soldier—presumably British, since his coat is red—in the process of being devoured by a tiger, presumably Indian, since India is where the object is from. Inside the tiger's flank is an organ, whose "sounds," a contemporary description explained, are "intended to resemble the cries of a person in distress, intermixed with the horrid roar of the tiger." While the instrument was playing, "the hand of the European victim was often lifted up, and the head convulsively thrown back, to express the agony of his helpless and deplorable situation."[1] "Tipu's Tiger," as this remarkable item is known, was found by British soldiers in the music room of Tipu Sultan's palace. Its imagery was irresistible. Before the year was out, the Tiger was sailing toward Britain, bound for the London viewing public. (It is in fact the first documented Indian object to be specifically exported to Britain for public display.)[2] The Company exhibited the Tiger in the "Oriental Repository" it had recently opened in India House, where the beast soon received notice in guidebooks as a London tourist attraction. So many visitors came to see it, and to crank up its noisy organ, that readers in the adjacent library complained about the disruption. One of those on whom the Tiger

Tipu's Tiger. The provenance of the object is unknown, but the organ is of European manufacture.

made a lasting impression was the young poet John Keats, who later described a "Man-Tyger-Organ" in verse, as the plaything of a despotic Eastern ruler.[3]

Unquestionably, Tipu's Tiger was put on view as a piece of imperial propaganda. "This characteristic memoreal of the arrogance and barbarous cruelty of Tippoo Sultaun," as the Tiger was described in a pamphlet that accompanied it to Britain, reinforced at a stroke all that the British had been told about Mysore's Muslim bogeyman. Tipu "frequently amused himself" (it was said) "with the sight of this emblematical triumph of the Khodadad [God-given state] over the English Circar."[4] The object was "emblematical" for Tipu because he had adopted the tiger as his personal symbol. Famous for his boast that "he would rather live two days like a tiger, than two hundred years like a sheep," Tipu was widely known as the "Tiger of Mysore."[5] He surrounded himself with tiger motifs to an almost obsessional degree: his throne was ringed with gold and crystal tigers, his calligraphic cyphers resembled a tiger's face, and a stylized tiger stripe adorned everything from the uniforms of his soldiers to the plastered interior of his mausoleum.[6] Now shifted to India House, the Tiger was "emblematical," instead, of Britain's success: the tiger slain, the European victorious. It is probably no accident that the Seringapatam medal, distributed to veterans by the Company in 1808—the same year Tipu's Tiger was put on display—directly echoes, and inverts, the image of the Tiger. It shows a powerful British lion mauling a prostrate tiger. Above them flutters a banner, whose Arabic lettering reads, ASAD ALLAH AL-GHALIB: "the *lion* of God," not the tiger, is the conqueror.[7]

Today, Tipu's Tiger is a popular draw at the Victoria and Albert Museum, where it seems to epitomize what is now identified as a dated, objectionable form of imperial arrogance. For those wishing to point fingers at the prejudices and plunders of empire, this is a prime target. And to an extent, of course, that reaction is justified: those were exactly the attitudes that its captors wished to project. As such, the Tiger—the first Indian trophy to be exhibited in this way—underscores how the Seringapatam campaign more generally represented a turning point in imperial expansion: attracting wide public notice, it fed a rhetoric of Oriental brutality on the one hand, while promoting a patriotic association with the Company and British arms on the other.

But like all propaganda, Tipu's Tiger was also in part a fraud. By using the Tiger to emphasize Tipu's sadism, his monomania, and his sheer "otherness," the Company also obscured the many ways in which Tipu was actually surprisingly similar to Europeans, and not only in his military techniques or love of technology. The Tiger was more or less the only Seringapatam object in Britain that *did* so explicitly appear to reveal Tipu Sultan's "savage" side. The vast majority of Seringapatam objects attested, rather, to his aristocratic tastes and cultivations. Furthermore, the Tiger was displayed in the East India Company's own premises in India House, and not, as some officers had originally proposed, in the royal precincts of the Tower of London. No small part of the Tiger's propaganda value lay in the fillip it gave to Company power specifically, not to British power in general. It bolstered the image of an armed, conquering Company, shaped, as the Wellesley-worshipping Viscount Valentia put it, "with the ideas of a Prince, not with those of a retail dealer in muslins and indigo."[8]

Though the Tiger may have reinforced an image of Tipu Sultan's brutality, the other trophies Richard Wellesley chose to send back to Britain worked primarily to promote the image of the Company as a ruler, and to narrow the gap between Company and Crown. Arguably the most evocative of these objects was Tipu Sultan's gorgeous gold throne. There is something particularly symbolic about seizing a vanquished enemy's throne (as demonstrated, for instance, by the Persian ruler Nadir Shah, who carried off the celebrated Peacock Throne of the Mughals in 1739, or indeed by King Edward I of England, when he seized the Stone of Scone from Scotland in 1296 and set it beneath the Coronation Chair in Westminster Abbey). Wellesley promptly latched on to the idea of presenting Tipu's throne to King George III, "so splendid a trophy of the Glory of the British arms in India" was it. Unfortunately, by the time Wellesley learned of its existence, the prize agents had already auctioned off its decorations and peeled off its gold cladding to dole out in prize shares to the subalterns. The Company was thus put in the some-

Tipu Sultan on his throne, as imagined by the Clive family governess, Anna Tonelli.

what embarrassing position of having to buy back from its own officers as many of the fragments as it could.[9] But expense notwithstanding, Wellesley's wishes prevailed: the Court of Directors and the King received a gold tiger's head each; the magnificent *huma* bird canopy from the throne was presented to the king and later used by William IV as a centerpiece at state banquets; and at the new Government House in Calcutta, Wellesley set his own chair on "a musnud [carpet] of crimson and gold, formerly composing part of the ornaments of Tippoo Sultan's throne."[10]

In short, to view Tipu's Tiger—or the train of events that led to its collection—only in terms of chauvinistic cultural messages is to accept at face value what was in fact a carefully constructed and somewhat deceptive front. Asian "otherness" was just one strand in a wider set of representations at least as much concerned with bolstering the Company's image as with besmirching Tipu's. By using objects in this way, Richard Wellesley established a precedent that would be followed by the Company for years to come; by midcentury, the celebrated relics of the "Tiger of Mysore" were joined by the gold throne and other possessions of the vanquished Sikh ruler Ranjit Singh, "Lion of the Punjab." If collecting is about reinvention, then the objects collected in

Mysore let the East India Company show off its new ruling profile. Its features were stately and rather Roman, many liked to think: proud, martial, noble, and, crucially, triumphant. (Wellesley was less successful at reinventing himself. The "Emperor of Seringapatam," as a friend jestingly called him, had hoped to be rewarded with an English peerage and a seat in the House of Lords. But he learned that he had received the coveted rank of Marquess, only to discover that the title was, again, Irish! "My double-gilt potato," he sneered, and took to his bed for ten days in a bad fit of the hives.)[11] Just as the capture of Seringapatam signaled the Company's coming of age as an imperial conqueror, so its trophies made a bold statement about the Company as an imperial collector. From now on, the Company was king in India—or at least, so it began to show and see itself.

The public, official exhibition of trophies was just one part of a far wider circulation of Seringapatam objects, in the hands of individual soldiers and civilians. It was during that chaotic night of looting, after the fall, that hundreds of ordinary soldiers were able to collect their own private pieces of Seringapatam. The pervasive plundering made Arthur Wellesley, who was responsible for discipline in the city, very nervous. All these objects, he worried, could be dangerous, in the wrong hands. "The prize agents," he wrote to his brother Richard in August 1799,

> have got a large quantity of clothes belonging to, and worn by, the late Sultaun, which, unless prevented, they will sell at public auction, and which will be bought up as relics by the discontented Moormen of this place. This will not only be disgraceful, but may be very unpleasant; and I therefore recommend that the whole may be bought by the Government, and either given to the Princes, or anything done with them that you may think fit.[12]

Arthur Wellesley's concern was not unreasonable. Seven years later, in Vellore, where Tipu's family was then living in British custody, Company sepoys mutinied, using Tipu's name as their rallying cry and one of his banners captured at Seringapatam as an ensign.[13] In the Sufi traditions to which Tipu himself adhered, objects associated with a revered individual could be venerated as repositories of his *barakat*, or charisma. Tipu's personal possessions, and his clothing especially, were invested with a transcendent spiritual power that remains palpable for some Muslims in India today.

Arthur Wellesley did not have to worry for long, however, for his fellow Britons needed no encouragement to acquire Tipu's charismatic objects themselves. In a strange mirroring of the relic-hunting they were afraid might overtake the people of Mysore, the British themselves avidly collected anything and everything associated with Tipu. One of the first to be caught up in "Tipumania" was none other than the governor-general himself, who asked his brother to "try to get Tippoo's small seal or ring for me, and some swords and handsome guns for the Prince of Wales and Duke of York: any sword known to have been used by Tippoo would be curious."[14]

British fascination began with Tipu's body. The corpse was laid out in the palace until its burial at the end of the day on May 5. Lieutenant Benjamin Sydenham, who was with Baird when the body was discovered, made a careful description of it, an inventory of sorts: a cut above the right ear, a bullet embedded in the left cheek, three slashes in the torso and limbs. Medium height, dark skin, on the whole "rather corpulent, had a short neck and high shoulders but his wrists and ancles were small and delicate. He had large full eyes, with small arched eyebrows and very small whiskers." Dressed as was his wont, simply but well, in "fine white linnen" and a crimson cummerbund, Tipu "had lost his turband and there were no weapons of defence about him." All that distinguished him in death was a kind of ineffable refinement about the face: "His appearance denoted him to be above the common stamp and his countenance expressed a mixture of haughtiness and resolution."[15] Throughout the day the British came to see the body of the prince. David Price, the prize agent, was among them. As Price stood on his one good leg, contemplating the dead sultan, the officer next to him leaned over and "asked me if I could lend him my pen-knife; which I accordingly did." Then, quick as a flash, and "before I could recollect myself," said Price, "he had cut off one of the Sultaun's mustachios; which he said he had promised to his friend, Dr. Cruso, of our establishment."[16]

The mustache was the last, most intimate trophy claimed from Tipu's body, but it was by no means alone. Indeed, Tipu died, it was said, defending himself from plunder: shot dead by a soldier who was attempting to snatch his jewel-studded sword belt.[17] To judge from all the objects in collections today that are said to have been found on Tipu's body, the king had staggered into battle swaddled in turbans, padded jackets, helmets, and sashes; slung around with pistols, muskets, daggers, and sabers; and packed up with a baffling assortment of trinkets and bibelots—from a folding wooden telescope to a gold European pocket watch. It hardly needs saying that most of these claims were unsubstantiated. The notable thing is that they were (and are) made at all. A direct connection to Tipu infused objects with a special relic value, in the way people identify locks of Bonnie Prince Charlie's hair or beds where George Washington slept.

Although it is impossible to quantify the extent of collecting by individuals that followed the capture of Seringapatam—just as impossible as it is to gauge exactly how much looting occurred on the night of May 4–5—one thing is clear. Nothing quite like it had happened before. A great dispersal of objects took place at a series of auctions in May and June 1799, held by the prize agents to raise cash for prize payments. No record exists of all the transactions that took place "at the Green Tent at Seringapatam," but surviving receipts indicate that dozens of officers bought "collectibles" such as silver betel boxes, silk carpets, or ornamental weapons.[18] This kind of self-conscious collecting by soldiers was unusual in itself. But still more remarkable was the degree to which Seringapatam objects were acquired by British civilians, many of whom had no direct connection to India at all.

Fragments from Seringapatam could soon be found scattered through the salons of Britain's elite. The aesthete, author, and eccentric William Beckford (who also owned some of Antoine Polier's albums of paintings) added Tipu's jade hookah to the extravagant clutter of his Gothic fantasy palace, Fonthill Abbey. Sir John Soane, the noted architect and connoisseur, furnished a sitting room of his house in Lincoln's Inn with Tipu's ivory table and chairs, where they can still be seen today. The novelist Sir Walter Scott proudly placed one of Tipu's sabers in his substantial armory at Abbottsford. Another collector ingeniously adapted a gold tiger's foot from the base of Tipu's throne into a snuffbox; and the tenth Earl of Lindsey enjoyed the singular privilege of being baptized in one of Tipu's Sèvres porcelain tureens, a gift from Louis XVI.[19]

What sort of Tipu did these objects tell of? In marked contrast to Tipu's Tiger, on public display, these were rich, princely possessions; they spoke of wealth, cultivation, and rank. Even Tipu's weapons were (and still are) admired by collectors for their technical sophistication, workmanship, and precious materials. The ready assimilation of Seringapatam objects into British drawing rooms also suggests how consumer taste can transcend apparently wide cultural differences. A parallel to Tipumania would occur in 1860, in the wake of the second Opium War in China, when in a "solemn act of retribution" for the killing of some British emissaries, Britain's high commissioner ordered that the Chinese emperor's Summer Palace be sacked and burned to the ground. The scale of looting was enormous; as was the dispersal of objects across Britain (and France, which had also taken part). In both cases, Britain's imperial enemy had been specifically demonized for Asiatic cruelty, while the emperor's possessions were eagerly collected by European civilians, both for their aesthetic appeal and for their novelty value. Princely objects brought British and Asian cultures of consumption together across the continental divide.[20]

A "savage" some Britons may have thought him, but Tipu Sultan was also—like his British peers Beckford, Soane, and Scott—a connoisseur. His collection, neatly labeled and housed in a wing of the palace, was his refuge. It was said that he "passed the greatest part of his leisure hours in reviewing this various and splendid assemblage of his riches."[21] Tipu participated in the same tradition of royal collecting as his contemporary, Asaf ud-Daula, in a culture in which objects might be regarded as repositories and symbols of power.[22] Asaf ud-Daula had used collecting to bolster his authority in the face of several challenges: pressed between Mughal and Company rule, he also governed Awadh as a minority Persian Shiite, and a member of a relatively new dynasty. Tipu Sultan had at least as great a reason to assert his legitimacy. The British had often branded Haidar Ali and Tipu as "usurpers"—unfairly, to be sure, since the "legitimate" Hindu Wodeyar dynasty was not really long established. Nevertheless, Haidar and Tipu were new rulers on the throne—outsiders and Muslims in an overwhelmingly Hindu region, and threatened on all sides by war.

Because Tipu Sultan was not born a prince, he had to make himself one. He expressed his power in imaginative and wide-ranging ways, by synthesizing Indo-Persian and local Hindu traditions, and by inventing entirely new symbols and systems, such as a unique Mysore calendar (another point of commonality with his French revolutionary friends). But as his collection showed, he continued to draw on Mughal princely idioms of power, and to splendid effect. On seeing his collection, even the British were impressed, and surprised, to discover how far his reach extended: "There was every thing that power could command, or money could purchase, in this stupendous collection: telescopes, and optical glasses of every size and sight, with looking-glasses, and pictures in unbounded profusion; while of china and glass ware, there was sufficient to form a large mercantile magazine."[23] As a collector, he was able to exhibit his mastery over far-flung domains, to tie himself in to indigenous traditions, and to advertise his modernity, all at the same time.

If Tipu's collection stood at some odds with the British image of him as a warmongering barbarian, still more shocking to the captors of Seringapatam was discovering his library. It consisted of more than two thousand volumes in several languages, which there is every reason to think that Tipu may have read. "After all," one officer conceded, "this horrid ferocious being, this harpy tyger is reported to be a man of some learning." All the manuscripts were in good condition; many were "very richly adorned and illuminated in the style of the old Roman Catholick Missals found in Monastries."[24] They covered a range of subjects, from copies of the Koran and the Prophet's sayings (*hadith*) to classic Mughal histories; from Sufism and cosmology, to medicine, cooking, and etiquette. This was a library to do a Mughal prince proud. It was also a library that East India Company Orientalists were eager to ship to Britain, where it would be "the most curious and valuable collection of Oriental learning and history, that has yet been introduced into Europe."[25] The prize agent David Price, himself a collector and student of Persian manuscripts, and his colleague and fellow manuscript collector Samuel Ogg, were deputed to value Tipu's library and to select titles for the Company. As they set about their task, unpacking the volumes from the chests in which they were kept, they noticed one of Tipu's sons watching them. The young prince "was overheard, in rather an audible whisper, to observe to his attendants—'Only see how these hogs are allowed to contaminate my father's books.' "[26] In the event, only about three hundred volumes were sent to London, where they form the core of the British Library's Oriental manuscript collections.[27] The rest of Tipu's splendid manuscripts, perhaps as many as 3,500, have been lost.

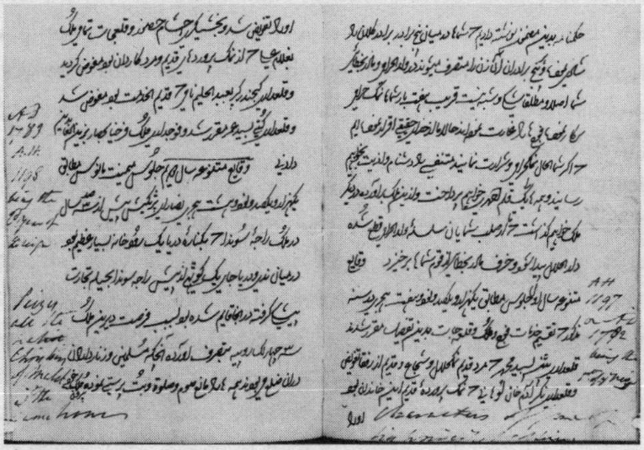

A page from Tipu Sultan's memoirs, "written by himself," with marginal annotations by William Kirkpatrick.

As the prince's remark implied, cross-cultural collecting did not necessarily equal cross-cultural rapprochement. But the variety and circulation of Seringapatam objects in Britain demonstrated both how tangible and in what diverse forms East and West might encounter each other. In much the way that Seringapatam trophies provided visual support to the Company's persona as a collector of territory, so looted objects gave the idea of Indian empire a material reality for hundreds of individual Britons. How this happened in practice can be understood in intimate detail by looking closely at perhaps the most avid Seringapatam collectors of all: Henrietta Clive and her husband, Edward, Robert Clive's eldest son. Their story, the continuing story of the

Clives of India, opens a window onto how empire touched individual lives during this period of transition.

## II. A Tropical Grand Tour

The governor's wife had "a most indescribable wish" to see Seringapatam, and that was enough. Thus, at the beginning of March 1800, Lady Henrietta Clive, wife of Edward, Lord Clive, governor of Madras, set out from Madras for Tipu's capital. She took her two daughters, Henrietta and Charlotte, with her, age fourteen and thirteen, respectively, and their Italian governess, Anna Tonelli, a temperamental woman with a talent for painting.[28] Edward could not join them on the excursion, but the women were not lacking for company: their retinue of elephants, bullocks, camels, palanquins, guards, grooms, washermen, cooks, Lady Clive's *munshi*, bearers, bearers for the bearers, and for the girls' pianoforte, snaked on to seven hundred fifty people all told—"which is not in India a very great number, and it is not to be wondered at when all is considered," observed Charlotte, "for travelling in India is not like travelling in Europe."[29]

Charlotte Clive kept a journal of the trip, which survives in a mid-nineteenth-century manuscript version with Anna Tonelli's watercolors copied in. It is a winning, wide-eyed record, and a very unusual one—probably the only diary of a child in pre-Victorian India to have found its way into a major archive. Together with her letters to her father, and those of her mother and sister, Charlotte's account of the trip provides a rare glimpse into British family life in late-eighteenth-century India. The Clives' tour was remarkable not least because they managed to spend a full seven months on the 1,153.5-mile circuit (Charlotte's calculation) from Madras southwest to Tanjore, via Bangalore and Mysore, then back up the coast—longer than their five-month crossing from Portsmouth to Madras in 1798, or the six months that it would take them to sail back to Britain in 1801. The trip was remarkable simply for their making it in the first place. The Clives were straightforwardly tourists—and women tourists to boot—at a time when few Europeans traveled in India purely for the sake of sightseeing. Traveling in India may not have been like traveling in Europe. Nevertheless, the Clives' stately progress through South India was effectively a tropical Grand Tour: an aristocratic ramble in pursuit of pleasure and self-improvement.

The focus of their journey—their Rome, so to speak—was Seringapatam. They were the first European tourists ever to visit it, and they journeyed there through a country still overcast with Tipu's presence. In Vellore, they met Tipu's elder sons (who had been in Company custody since Tipu's defeat in 1792) and inspected the quarters being prepared by the Company for Tipu's female relations. In Bangalore they admired the late ruler's "very magnificent" palace. They reached Seringapatam in August, the midpoint of their journey, and decamped in the zenana of the Daria Daulat Bagh palace, which Arthur Wellesley had now taken over as his residence. During their short stay on the island, they met the rest of Tipu's sons and some of his wives. In what must have been a poignant scene—as the family of the vanquished encountered that of the vanquisher—Tipu's wives "gave Mamma a great many petitions one or two of them were written in English, the direction of one was Lord Clives Lady Esq." Charlotte especially admired the countryside, "like Shropshire . . . by far the prettiest place we have seen yet."[30] Edward Clive's daughter was neither the first nor the last Briton to see hints of home in the Mysore countryside. But the Clive ladies were the first to try systematically to take it back with them.[31] For like a Grand Tour, their trip was consecrated to collecting.

All four women collected obsessively, stones and plants most of all. Encouraged and guided by "Signora Anna," the girls picked up samples and specimens wherever they went: "We cannot help collecting and loading our Imps, with them," said young Henrietta.[32] Lady Clive was a superb model for her daughters, because like many British noblewomen of her time, she was an enthusiastic collector of natural history specimens. It was no accident that this widely practiced "womanly" pursuit was considered distinctly marginal both to the collecting world and to the scientific world of eighteenth-century Britain. ("To have rambled in search of shells and flowers had but ill-suited with the capacity of Newton," sniffed Samuel Johnson.)[33] So much was natural science considered the province of women and amateurs that when the celebrated naturalist and president of the Royal Society, Sir Joseph Banks, began his own study of botany in the 1760s (inspired by an herbal he found in his mother's bedroom), the only teachers he could find were the local women who collected wild plants for apothecaries.[34] Banks played a decisive role in raising the status of natural science in Britain, but the Duchess of Portland owned Britain's second-largest collection of natural specimens after Banks, and Kew Gardens greatly benefited from the patronage of Queen Charlotte, a student of botany.[35]

Lady Clive would leave India with an extensive collection of shells, rocks, plants, stuffed birds, and live animals, many of which she acquired on her South Indian journey. (Transporting them to Britain from India proved to be easier than getting them from the ship to her home. Thanks to bureaucratic difficulties with the Treasury, her cases were held up at India House, where

"The Birds Shells etc.," she reported bitterly to Edward, "are . . . to be put up to the Public Sale for the valuation. The Jews that come there usually steal the best of each it is really provoking.")[36] "All my Shells are safe and all the other treasures I am beginning to unpack and it delights me," she wrote to Edward from their Shropshire estate in 1802. She planted her Indian seeds in the hothouse, grazed her Tanjore bull on the estate's grounds, set up her stuffed birds of paradise in her sitting rooms. It made her feel "as great as any Eastern Princess in the midst of my treasures."[37] She had good reason to gloat: her personal collection of Indian specimens was started earlier, and may have been larger, than that of the East India Company itself.[38]

A vignette of traveling in India, from Charlotte Clive's diary.

Then there were the animals! The Clives had started from Madras with only their beloved bird "Cocakatoo" for company. (They left their dog Tippoo at home.) But now, everywhere they went, people pressed them to accept pet animals as gifts. The girls were delighted, though their mother sometimes balked. She made Henrietta reject a puppy "as she says the House will be like Noah's Ark"; and Charlotte's long-desired monkey ("detestable monsters," her mother thought them) was consigned to the care of a servant. But on the whole, Lady Clive was quite willing to accept these new companions into the family fold. "Our collection of animals increases very much," Henrietta reported to her father in October. By then they had been given a spotted deer, two antelopes, a green parrot, a lark, two lories ("the plague of poor Cockatoo's life"), a mongoose for Lady Clive, and, for Charlotte, a small gazelle so tame that it rode in her palanquin, slept by her bed, and followed her everywhere just "like a dog"—until one morning, after their return to Madras, it wandered off the roof of their house and fell to its death. "It was a sad grief," wrote Charlotte.[39] Equally sad, as they left India, was watching her mother turn down the present of a "beautiful little sucking elephant. . . . We longed to keep it, it was so young and small, and covered with a handsome cloth and long tassels, but it was thought it would require so much water to drink, it would not be right to take it."[40]

A nice mental image takes shape of this menagerie, traipsing with its new owners slowly past the lush cane fields and rocky rises of southeastern India. Charlotte must have thought all the people they met very kind and generous—as perhaps they were. But like any gifts in the symbolic economy of India at that time, all these animals were also the bearers of their givers' hopes and reputations. Presents to well-connected private individuals like the Clives were especially forthcoming because East India Company servants were prohibited from accepting personal gifts. The Clive women, therefore, would have been seen as conduits to Company officials. Two years later, when the young aristocrat Viscount Valentia took his own unconventional Grand Tour in India, he was so burdened with gifts from people who treated him (correctly) as the back door to Richard Wellesley that he decided not to accept them. (His decision was considered "highly honorable to the British Character"; though it also meant, crucially for his budget, that the Company assumed the cost of providing the ceremonial gifts Valentia was expected to make in return.)[41] The striking thing about the gifts made to the Clive women is that they reveal a gendered side to this ceremonial culture. Valentia, like all men, European and Indian alike, gave and received khelats, weapons, and sometimes jewels.[42] But the Clives got animals in place of swords—and especially sweet and feminine animals at that. What they bestowed in return is unknown, but it is unlikely to have been the ornate European pistols most British officials gave to Indian rulers.

The specimens and the animals attest to two distinct aspects of Lady Clive's collection in particular, and to the collecting culture of the period more generally. She collected botanical and mineral specimens with something of the same instinct that a man of her rank, on his Grand Tour, might have applied to Greek vases or Old Master paintings. Collecting natural history was part of a gentlewoman's accomplishments, and Lady Clive raised her daughters to pursue it in exactly the same way that she did. At the same time, as the wife of an important man ("Lord Clives Lady Esq."), Lady Clive accepted the gift animals almost as a diplomatic obligation. She and her entourage constituted an embassy of sorts—a precursor to the quasi-royal governors' and viceroys' tours that would lumber through the princely states of Victorian India in gold-tasseled howdahs. (An early example would be Emily Eden's journey through northern India with her brother, the governor-general Lord Auckland, in the late 1830s.) Their splendid progress was a further step toward the creation of the proconsular, aristocratic imperial government that Richard Wellesley aimed to build.

A third aspect of Lady Clive's collection stands out most of all: her collection of Indian artifacts. Although she liked the animals, she wanted the weapons, too—especially if they were connected to Tipu Sultan. Tipu exerted a magnetic fascination over Lady Clive, and she took every advantage of her situation, geographical and social, to indulge it. "As the character of Tippoo Sultaun has been much talked of," she wrote in Madras, "and that I am now in the way of hearing a good deal about him," she even started to keep a journal of anecdotes about Tipu "for the amusement of others and myself in England."[43] Lady Clive's enthusiastic acquisition of Tipu relics made her not only one of the first and most significant collectors of Seringapatam objects, but also one of the only British women of the period to collect Indian artifacts.[44] The Clives' extensive collection of Tipu-iana attested to an aristocratic brotherhood of taste that spanned cultures.

Weapons were the most widely collected items from Seringapatam, and the Clives had three of Tipu's swords and one of his guns.[45] (These very nearly ended up in the wrong hands, when a "crate of toys sent for Thackeray's children [cousins of the novelist]" by James Kirkpatrick "got swapped for one containing Lord Clive's collection of arms and armour, to the latter's amazement when he opened it and found playthings instead.")[46] All the pieces are elegantly chased, inscribed with Arabic calligraphy, and covered in tiger motifs. Part of the attraction was clearly aesthetic; but part was anecdotal, for one of the swords was said to have been used by the dead king himself. A similar sort of charismatic association explained the rather more unlikely appearance in the Clive collection of the Sultan's curly-toed slippers, of a traveling "bed made for Tipu," and of a capacious, elaborate chintz tent, in which, it was presumed, he had kept his headquarters while on campaign. Like so many Seringapatam objects, the actual connection of some of these items to Tipu is unverifiable. But it was the idea that counted. Owning the possessions of the king was like brushing cheeks with history.

And it was a history in which the Clives themselves could be proud of having played a part. For like so many imperial collections, this one held a mirror up to its collectors. Both Edward Clive and Tipu Sultan (like their peers,

Wellesley and Napoleon) were newly minted aristocrats and connoisseurs; both were second-generation rulers and heirs of self-made fathers. The Clives' most valuable artifact from Tipu's court was a jeweled tiger-head finial from his throne, which embodied the ruler's kingly charisma. Owning it put the Clives in the select company of collectors, King George III among them, to have a piece of the throne. But the most evocative item in the Clive collection was less ostentatious: a dozen Sèvres coffee cups from the dinner service presented to Tipu by Louis XVI. This delicate porcelain had survived travel across immense physical distances: from France to India through the Persian Gulf; then back again from India, around the Cape, to Britain. The historical distance it traversed was still greater. From kilns fired on the eve of the French Revolution, through the tumultous sack of Seringapatam, the cups survived cataclysms that their givers and owners had not. Today the cups remain in peaceful retirement at Powis Castle on the Welsh border, wonderful testament to the ability of objects to cross cultural, geographical, and temporal divides, while remaining in the hands of elite consumers.

Tipu Sultan's Sèvres porcelain teacups,
now in the Clive collection at Powis Castle.

How specifically the Clives acquired many of their objects is unknown. Though some were picked up by Lady Clive on her travels, more were probably purchased for her and her husband by friends at the Seringapatam prize sales.[47] Nor is the root cause of her "most indescribable" obsession with Tipu much clearer now than it evidently was to her. But a suggestive glimpse into Lady Clive's collecting habits was given a dozen years later by another gentlewoman to travel to Seringapatam: Lady Maria Hood, eldest daughter of the Earl of Seaforth, whose husband had been appointed commander in chief of the navy in the East Indies.

Lady Hood toured the region for seven weeks in 1812, without her husband, but with her sketching equipment and her observant eye. Her visit—like the Clives', undertaken for recreation—showed how Seringapatam was entering the Romantic tourist imagination, in something of the way that the battlefield of Waterloo later would.[48] As the evening cool settled in on July 23, she "got the first sight of this celebrated City, from a hill five miles before we reached it, and I could not but feel, tho' I had taken a long journey for the purpose, a <u>kind</u> of <u>surprize</u>, at finding myself actually in view of a place so famous." She stayed in the Daria Daulat Bagh, and spent several days "walking over these deserted mansions of the Sceptered dead," preoccupied by "an awful instance of human vicissitudes. These so lately the scenes of the pleasures and the magnificence, of a great Prince, have now passed into the hands of a Company of Merchants, in a remote Island whose very existance is hardly understood by the Natives of India, and whose power he and his Father threatened with destruction for ½ a Century."[49]

Lady Hood was traveling very much in the Clives' footsteps, and she knew it. It was on her visit to Tipu Sultan's tomb that she felt the shade of her predecessors most immediately:

> The Mufti or Chief Priest at the Tomb told us of an English *Burra Bibi* or great Lady who was very anxious to have one of their Copies of the Koran, which he was not able to give her. She seemed to have impressed this old mufti with a high degree of respect, but he could not remember her name. I thought it must be *Lady Powis* and mentioned the name of *Clive* which he immediately respected with the greatest eulogiums. Ly Powis seems to be the only European Traveller, who inspired any idea of *innate* superiority in these parts.[50]

"*Innate* superiority": it is a curious phrase, and a revealing one. (Lady Hood knew about innate superiority: she became chieftainess of Clan Mackenzie on her father's death in 1815, and was described by Sir Walter Scott as having "the spirit of a chieftainess in every drop of her blood.")[51] Granted, the Countess of Powis, as Lady Clive had by then become, was a peeress—and to some, perhaps, this alone rendered her "superior." But she was more than just any peeress. She was a Clive, and proud of it.

To be a Clive meant something in those parts, for Indians and Europeans alike. Charlotte Clive (who was born well after her grandfather Robert's death) happily wrote of "a visit from a man who had been an orderly of Grandpapa's," some fifty years before. "He was not a little pleased to see us," she continued, "and proved his knowledge of Lord Clive by saying, 'when

Lordship think, always put handkerchief in his mouth,' this habit was well known to his family."[52] One month to the day after Seringapatam fell, Edward and Henrietta Clive presided over a day of victory celebrations in Madras. The festivities began at four o'clock in the morning with the hoisting of Tipu's captured standards over Fort St. George, and continued with a victory ball well into the night. "It was one of the most pleasurable and fatiguing days I ever had in my life," Lady Clive wrote to her brother. The high point, she reported fulsomely, came at dinner, when "Lord Mornington [Richard Wellesley] said something that pleased *me much*. It was that it seemed impossible that there shou'd be a great victory in this Country without a Clive being concerned in it."[53]

In short, it was as a Clive that Henrietta was most a Seringapatam collector. She collected as a peeress, with the training and outlook of her class, by acquiring rocks and plants. As the governor's wife, she also filled a social and semipolitical role, and participated in the gift-giving rituals that accompanied her position. But Henrietta was a Clive and conscious of it, and as she collected objects associated with Seringapatam and Tipu Sultan, she was laying a more particular claim to India. These artifacts belonged to a place, a history, and a social rank with which her family had deep connections. They were ties that both she and her husband were keen to tighten.

And it was as a collector and an aristocrat that Edward was most a Clive. Edward carried the social ascent begun by Robert to glorious, and methodical, completion. In 1774, he inherited his father's fortune, estates, and title. In 1784, he married Henrietta, whose father, the Earl of Powis, had become close to Robert Clive through neighboring estates and allied political interests. Judging by Edward and Henrietta's letters, they enjoyed a happy marriage, cemented by a mutual passion for collecting, gardening, and home improvement. In 1794, essentially in belated recognition of Robert Clive's achievements and fortune, Edward was awarded the British peerage that his father had so coveted. And in 1804, three years after the death of Henrietta's only brother, Edward was made Earl of Powis himself.

Robert Clive was a self-made man who had invested immense quantities of time and money in acquiring the trappings of gentility. But Edward, albeit not quite to the manor born, was bred to it. He received a gentleman's education at Eton, rounded off by four years of study in Switzerland and a Grand Tour, from 1773 to 1777. Art appreciation and collecting of course formed a core part of this aristocratic upbringing. A list of cases sent home from a trip Edward and his family took to Italy in 1788 gives some indication of the range of their artistic tastes.[54] Two chests of paintings included family portraits done in Rome by the Irish painter Hugh Douglas Hamilton and by Angelica Kauffman, and numerous pictures of the sort most prized by contemporary standards: "Four Landscapes by Tempestia. A descent from the Cross by Alberto Durer. Two Landscapes by Salvator Rosa. A Landscape by Memper. Hamilton's sketch of his Apollo washing his hair. A Holy family by Schidein. Two battles by Gie.mo Borgognone and a picture by Rosa di Tivoli." The Clives also bought prints of Titian, Veronese, Rosa, and of the frescoes in the Brancacci Chapel in Florence; Piranesi's *Vedute di Roma*; "five boxes of Drawings for Lady Clive"; and three antique vases, along with "a small box marked I.P. in which Lady Clive's Etruscan Vase"—a gift from Sir William Hamilton—"is packed up in."

Everything on this list could equally have been found in the luggage of any number of Georgian gentlemen returning from the Continent. The artworks were choice but not arcane, educated but not scholarly, personal but not perverse. More to the point, they were precisely the kinds of things that would have supplemented Edward's inheritance from his father: the collection of Old Masters and European artifacts that Robert had bought, largely with the help of outside advisers, in that whirl of acquisition during the last years of his life. As the aristocrat that Robert had so wanted to be, Edward was very much his father's son.

The irony was that, as an empire builder, Edward emphatically was not like his father. With virtually no experience of administration or Indian affairs, Edward Clive was appointed governor of Madras in 1798, mostly on the strength of his name. There, until 1803, he was Richard Wellesley's direct subordinate during one of the most decisive periods in the history of East India Company rule. But his career was distinguished chiefly by its insignificance. The East India Company might no longer have been the adventurer's hunting ground his father had known. Yet even in the Company of Richard Wellesley—so devoted to the promotion of order and aristocratic privilege—Edward Clive seemed conspicuously out of place. Arthur Wellesley was distinctly unimpressed by the "mild, moderate . . . remarkably reserved" new governor, who had "a bad delivery, and apparently a heavy understanding. He certainly has been unaccustomed to consider questions of the magnitude now before him, but I doubt whether he is so dull as he appears, or as people here imagine he is."[55] The sad truth is that—at least when it came to matters of state—he actually was. Richard Wellesley promptly went down to Madras himself, where he remained for the duration of the Mysore War. "If I had not arrived here and taken the whole conduct of the army into my own hands," he said, "not a man nor a gun would ever have been in Mysore."[56] Lady Clive, certainly more acute than her husband, resented Wellesley's arrival as "entirely an awkward thing to have a *Supremo* to come over us."[57] But Edward, for his part, was relieved.

In India, as in Britain, Edward passed his time in gentlemanly pursuits. As Richard Wellesley correctly observed, he was "deficient" as a politician "because the whole current of his thoughts has been accustomed to the confined channel of retired and private life."[58] While Wellesley was busy expanding the East India Company's empire, Clive's major concerns while governor were three: to improve the governor's house and its gardens; to collect plants and artifacts; and to go back to Britain as quickly as possible. (His wife and daughters returned in the spring of 1801, and he missed them desperately. He wrote to Henrietta: "[Y]ou know that the luxurys of the East never much prized by us will be amply compensated for by any reunion with my Wife and Family.")[59] If he had been asked what his greatest achievements as governor were, one of his answers would surely have been the refurbishment of a great council hall in Government House, whose *chunam* ornaments were, he informed his wife, "in a Stile that you would greatly admire."[60] Another would have been the successful grafting of a mango tree, which he then exported to Kew Gardens. "If they should succeed" in thriving in Britain, he told Henrietta, "I might be tempted to construct a [hot] House for that purpose should you have no apprehension of being rated my lady Mango."[61]

And of course, Edward continued to collect. Robert Clive's Indian collection had consisted primarily of souvenirs and keepsakes picked up during the course of an Indian career. Edward and Henrietta, on the other hand, actively sought out Indian artifacts. It is difficult to pin down hard evidence of aesthetic appreciation for Indian art in European collections of the time. But testimony of the Clives' taste is offered by more than twenty bronze statues of Indian gods, mostly of Vishnu, that the Clives acquired, and perhaps commissioned, in Madras.[62] Though many of the things the Clives took away from India were fairly conventional—richly woven textiles, ivory boxes, and so on—it was still extremely unusual for Europeans to collect Hindu images. The few who did (such as Polier, Hastings, Charles Wilkins, and Sir William Jones) invariably had some kind of scholarly or antiquarian interest in Hinduism; the first major private collection of Hindu images would be formed slightly later by an obscure border-crossing major-general, Charles "Hindoo" Stuart. The Clives, by contrast, may be the first documented example of Britons who collected Hindu sculpture without being Orientalists. They collected, instead, as aristocrats and Grand Tourists who genuinely admired the architecture and sculpture they saw in South India. ("I hope you will not think me a Pagan because I presented the God with a Jewel and a Cloth of Gold," Edward joked to his wife after visiting the great temple of Kanchipuram.)[63]

The pages of Charlotte Clive's journal deliver more intimate testimony of her father's interest in Hindu art. In October 1800, the Clive women were nearing Madras, their tour almost complete. Edward had not seen them since they had left, almost seven months before, and he traveled out to meet them in Mahabalipuram, on the coast south of Madras. It is an idyllic spot, developed by the Pallava kings in the seventh and eighth centuries, famous for reliefs and temples hewn into the living rock, and for the elegant Shore Temple, poised on the edge of the foaming sea. The family delighted in the sights. "Papa," wrote Charlotte, "was so pleased with the carvings, he wished to purchase one, of two monkeys very well executed, but the natives would not part with them."[64] Preservationists should be thankful that Clive did not succeed (unlike his contemporary Lord Elgin, whose agents were just about to start cutting the friezes off the Parthenon).

As he packed up his own Indian objects—ivory carvings, a gold *pan* set, weapons, and elaborate textiles—might Edward's thoughts have turned to that chest of Indian objects his father had left him? There are definite similarities between the kinds of objects collected by the father and those collected by the son. Yet there was also one signal difference. Unlike Robert, Edward Clive was secure in his social position: he was a British aristocrat in India, rather than an "Indian" nabob in Britain. Robert, keen to disguise much of his Indian past behind his aristocratic public image, had preserved his Indian objects as personal keepsakes, tucked away from view. But for Edward, there was no shame in a connection to India—in fact, quite the opposite. After Seringapatam, and a full generation after Plassey, being a part of the burgeoning history of British India was something to be celebrated and advertised. For example, Lord and Lady Clive threw garden parties using Tipu's tent as a marquee.[65]

There are no admiring biographies, published papers, or marble monuments for Edward, the forgotten Clive. But he was the Clive that Robert wanted him to be: a successful aristocrat. What was more, there was a place in his aristocratic image for Indian empire, and for his family's special involvement in building it. Whereas Robert Clive had worked hard to be Clive of Claremont and to efface the connection to India, Edward—the English earl his father never was—facilitated the apotheosis of Clive of India by commissioning a monumental biography of his father by Sir John Malcolm. (This was the work reviewed by Macaulay in his "Essay on Clive," which also helped revise Robert Clive's profile.) Edward also worked to ensure that the union of Clive, India, and aristocracy would endure. Edward's son went on to inherit Powis Castle, the Herbert family seat, where the "Clive Museum" of Indian objects is housed today—and where the legacies of Robert, Edward, and Henrietta meet. It encapsulates, across genders as well as generations, a transition in the definition of Britain's empire in India, and in India's role in defining what that empire would be.

## III. From Kaveri to Nile

As visitors filed in by the hundreds to crank up Tipu's Tiger in the India Museum, and as the Clives settled into Powis with their Indian things, Seringapatam objects underscored just how differently British rule in India was received and responded to after 1800 than it had been a generation earlier. Less than fifteen years before, Warren Hastings was spectacularly impeached for his ostensibly rapacious conduct as governor-general; fifteen years before that, Clive and his "Indian" peers were social pariahs. Now Indian objects and Indian money were incorporated, and even to an extent welcomed, in British public arenas. So was a militaristic approach to acquiring Indian territory, bolstered by the patriotic climate of the Napoleonic Wars. As a visitor to Richard Wellesley's new Government House in Calcutta (completed in 1803) might see it, British imperial rule in India was a splendid and glittering thing. Modeled on Kedleston Hall in Derbyshire (built in the early 1760s by the Curzon family, one of whose scions would later become the most famous viceroy of India), Government House was a British stately home transplanted into the aromatic greenery of the tropics: a gleaming white Palladian palace, flanked by cannons and lions, filled with rich polished marble and neoclassical busts of British imperial grandees. Mirrors and girandoles bought from Claude Martin's Lucknow estate were installed in its halls.[66]

By no means, of course, did the Revolutionary-Napoleonic Wars or the wave of conquests in India mean that direct imperial rule was unanimously embraced in Britain. One source of mistrust came from the East India Company directors themselves, who recalled Wellesley in 1805 for his costly campaigns (and costly Government House), to say nothing of his overbearing style. Yet even they would have acknowledged that the nature of Britain's empire in India was changing in fundamental ways. There was the simple fact of its territorial expansion. By 1801, the East India Company had absorbed Mysore, Hyderabad, and Awadh into formal or informal control. Hard-won victories over the Marathas between 1803 and 1805 asserted British power in the face of another mighty "Francophile" indigenous opponent. With the Maratha Wars of 1817–1818, the confederacy was defeated and British dominance extended to the borders of the Punjab. Another sign of change was the way such conquests were received. Where parliamentary challenges to Clive and Hastings had once put East India Company rule itself on trial, now (and partly in consequence of those controversies) the British government was increasingly involved in administering Indian domains. Parliament supervised Company affairs through the Board of Control, and more than twenty thousand Crown troops were stationed in India, alongside the two hundred thousand–strong army of the East India Company.[67] Wellesley's recall was due not so much to British wariness about rule in India as to Company concern over its balance sheets. If anything, Britons with no personal investment in empire were probably more enthusiastic about territorial expansion than Company shareholders.

The capture of Seringapatam and its material impact on British culture made two transitions manifest: the turn to open conquest, and heightened public involvement in it. But the full significance of the event, and its effect on the nature of Britain's Eastern empire, was to be driven home with a final episode in the Seringapatam campaign—and a further act of imperial collecting by the Company state. The full story of Seringapatam would end where it all began: in Egypt.

The Mysore War had been in part a proxy war with France, touched off by Napoleon's invasion of Egypt and by fears of further French encroachments into India. On the Indian front, Britain scored decisive victory: Tipu was killed, Mysore partly annexed, British power on the Indian subcontinent expanded and consolidated. But back in Egypt, the Armée d'Orient remained at large—and if the French invasion had taught British strategists one thing, it was that the French presence there mattered. The security of British India depended in part on the security of Egypt. So it was that in March 1801 (as Henrietta Clive and her daughters sailed away from India with their objects and specimens), the East India Company and the British government prepared to complete their defense of India by moving directly against the French in Egypt. Launching a counterinvasion of Egypt on three separate fronts, Britain aimed to return Egypt to Ottoman control, and to secure the region in a British sphere of influence. Egypt would be the last, largest piece of Britain's own territorial Seringapatam collection.

The British invasion of Egypt in 1801 is a little-known episode in the history of the British Empire, yet unfairly so. In terms of Britain's global war with France, the successful campaign ended a long string of defeats on land that had beset Britain and its allies on the Continent and elsewhere since 1793. It also represented an important shift in both the purpose and the location of Britain's imperial expansion. This was Britain's first imperial intervention in Egypt, a region that would be absorbed into the British Empire with military occupation from 1882, and under protectorate status in 1914. Mad, prophetic George Baldwin experienced a small sign of the changing times firsthand. Whereas his earlier calls for deeper involvement in Egypt had gone largely unheeded, now he was summoned to Malta by British commanders to contribute his knowledge to the counterinvasion effort.[68]

The Egyptian campaign followed on from Seringapatam as part of

Britain's general move toward territorial expansion in the East, also evidenced by other campaigns beyond Indian frontiers, such as Ceylon (1795), Mauritius (1810), and Java (1811). It was related still more intimately to the Mysore War. Where Crown regiments had joined Company soldiers at the walls of Seringapatam, now the East India Company dispatched eight thousand of its men to Egypt, to join British Crown forces there. At the head of the Indian detachment stood none other than General David Baird, the hero of Seringapatam. "A more worthy sequel to the storm of Seringapatam could not be presented to your genius and valour," declared Richard Wellesley, with characteristic pomp. "May the same providential protection which accompanied you to the gates of Tippoo Sultaun's palace conduct you to Cairo; and may you be the happy instrument of completing the exclusion of the French from India; a work so nobly commenced in Mysore."[69]

Much had changed for the French since Napoleon's march into Palestine in the winter of 1798–1799—all for the worse. The Palestinian offensive had failed at the walls of Acre, where the French laid bloody and unsuccessful siege from March to May 1799; losses from combat and a new menace, plague, were high; morale, particularly on the retreat through Sinai in June 1799, was at a dangerous low. In Egypt, in the meantime, the Armée d'Orient faced wide indigenous opposition, both from the French-appointed emir al-Hajji, who was responsible for leading the pilgrimage to Mecca, and from a millenarian movement in the Delta. In Upper Egypt, the Mamelukes continued to battle Desaix and his men, while in the Mediterranean, the British navy kept up a blockade and bombarded Alexandria. It was not an inspiring scene.[70]

Nor would Napoleon involve himself in it for long. On August 23, 1799, Napoleon left Egypt, as he had arrived, at dawn. He slipped out of Aboukir during a short break in the British blockade, and sailed for France. For his abandoned army he left behind only a letter announcing that he was leaving in "the interests of *la patrie*, its glory, [and] obedience."[71] On October 9, Napoleon landed at Fréjus, where Vivant Denon—one of a handful of supporters to accompany him from Egypt—described the "élan sublime" of the crowds that thronged to meet him: "It was *la France* who seemed to rush toward the one who would restore her splendor to her; and who from her frontiers already asked for the Eighteenth Brumaire."[72] Baldly disregarding quarantine restrictions, Napoleon raced straight to Paris, to rejoin Josephine on the Rue de la Victoire, and to join a well-advanced conspiracy to topple the Directory government. On November 9—the Eighteenth Brumaire, on the French revolutionary calendar—one month to the day after his return from Egypt, Napoleon took command of the Paris army and sealed off the city. The next day, with his troops massed in the gardens outside, he walked into a meeting of the Council of Ancients at the Palace of Saint-Cloud and forced it to vote him, and two collaborators, into triumviral power. The Revolution was over; the age of Napoleon had begun.

For Napoleon, Egypt was a stepping-stone to executive power in France, and a personal victory of sorts.[73] But for the Armée d'Orient he left behind, under the command of Jean-Baptiste Kléber, the situation was bleak indeed. Bankrupt, angry, demoralized, and under attack on all sides—from the Ottomans in Palestine, from the British in the Mediterranean, from the Mamelukes in Upper Egypt, and from insurgents in Cairo—the French might well have seen themselves as modern-day victims in the land of ancient plagues. Their troubles continued when Kléber was assassinated by a "Muslim fanatic" in June 1800, and replaced by the universally unpopular Menou (widely known as Abdallah since his conversion to Islam). The British commander General John Hely-Hutchinson, who presided over France's withdrawal in 1801, observed "a prodigious antipathy in the minds of all the French soldiery to every thing that relates to Egypt, and the most rooted aversion to the Country . . ."[74] Even Napoleon's most ardent supporters, the savants, grew disillusioned and depressed. The brilliant young naturalist Geoffroy Saint-Hilaire, who had spent his first year in Egypt gushing over everything from the illustrious company he kept ("I think myself in Paris") to the "Oriental" mustache he grew, now found Egypt "insupportable. . . . I cannot think without sadness of all that I gave up for my current position, I left good and true friends to throw myself into a society . . . which is like that of a small provincial town. I haven't stopped being sick and . . . I fear I may never have the benefit of being able to see my dearest friends and relatives again."[75] "Everybody wants to see France again, from which we don't even receive news," wrote Édouard de Villiers du Terrage, who had arrived in Egypt at the age of seventeen fired with enthusiasm. "Our situation . . . is becoming critical."[76] Paradise had become a purgatory.

This was not the sort of conquest Napoleon had intended; and even he had had few illusions about it. Nevertheless, to Napoleon's British opponents, the French invasion was by no means entirely a failure. As long as a French army remained in Egypt, even a small one, Napoleon preserved a crucial strategic foothold to which he could send reinforcements when the opportunity arose. In the summer of 1800, with Napoleon's personal authority in France assured, his armies advancing across the Continent, and his sights never far from an invasion of Britain, it was a moot point whether or not the French threat to India was imminent. What mattered was that the threat persisted at all. "On our Part, it must be sound policy to exterminate them," a British officer wrote in his diary, capturing the mood of the moment, "and the

Napoleon's savants in better days, measuring the Sphinx.

Height of Folly to wait their arrival on this open, unprotected, and plentiful side of the Peninsula of India."[77]

What, then, was to be done? In the opinion of the commander of Britain's Mediterranean fleet, Sir Sidney Smith, "The absolute eradication of this French Mahometan Colony from *Africa* is only to be effectuated by a general and combined Attack on all sides at once."[78] One side was Palestine, where Britain's Ottoman allies had been fighting the French since late 1798. A British advisory mission traveled to the region to urge the Turks onward, and to help train their troops. But when its leader joined the Ottoman commanders in Jaffa in July 1800, he was appalled by "this chaos of an army," undisciplined, disorganized, and utterly lackluster. "The apathy of the Turks since their last shock" (they had been badly defeated by Kléber at Heliopolis, in March) "is unconquerable," he concluded. "Our hopes now rest entirely upon the speedy arrival of a British Reinforcement."[79]

As these grim reports helped confirm, Britain also had to pursue a second line of attack against the French: a full-scale landing on Egypt's Mediterranean coast. Dangerous, uncertain, and expensive, it was an all-or-nothing operation, a sign of how seriously, and how desperately, Britain rated the possession of Egypt. On March 8, 1801, a 15,000-strong British expeditionary force, commanded by Sir Ralph Abercromby, began to land at Aboukir, under the fire of French guns. Abercromby's army fought the Armée d'Orient westward, between the salty flats of Lake Mareotis and the sea. Two weeks later, after a morning of vicious combat in the dunes east of Alexandria, the British definitively defeated the French and secured control of the city. Among the 1,400 British casualties was Abercromby himself, who died a week later of his wounds. (His body was taken to Malta, which he loved, and buried in Fort St. Elmo, overlooking the sea.) Abercromby's successor, General Hely-Hutchinson, proceeded to fight the French south along the Nile to Cairo. After a two-week siege, Hely-Hutchinson entered Cairo in late June and opened peace negotiations. Menou, making a last stand in Alexandria, was defeated in late August; and on September 2, France signed a treaty of capitulation.

Britain's victory in Egypt played a crucial role in building morale and public confidence in the British army, long considered greatly inferior to the French. It showed how land forces could supplement British sea power to break the deadlock that would otherwise have arisen between the two

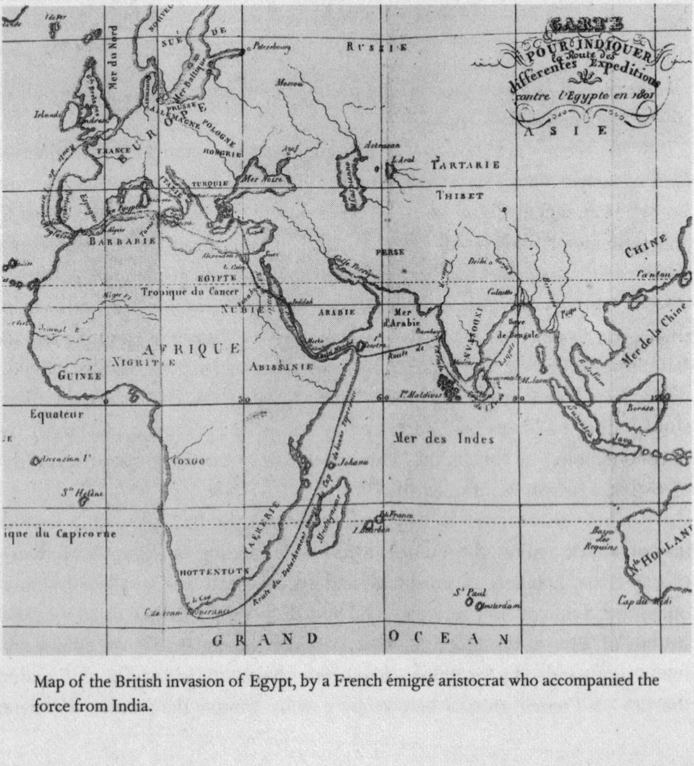


Map of the British invasion of Egypt, by a French émigré aristocrat who accompanied the force from India.

nations—one so strong at sea, the other on land—and anticipated British successes in the long years of war ahead.[80] But through the lens of imperial history, the most enduring consequence of Britain's Egyptian campaign was taking shape on the Red Sea coast. It was there that General Baird and his sepoys—some of them Seringapatam veterans like him—opened a third front against the Armée d'Orient, and a connection between India and Egypt that would endure as long as the British Empire.

Baird and his men arrived at the Red Sea town of Quseir in mid-June 1801.[81] Their orders were to march due west, across the desert, to the Nile, and then to proceed downriver and attack Cairo from the south, while Hely-Hutchinson's men moved in from the north. The plan sounded simple in principle. But in practice it was foolhardy: the desert way was dangerous and hard; water supplies were uncertain and the location of wells for the most part unknown. Captain Charles Hill, of the Sixteenth Grenadiers, described each day's painful march in his diary: "tho' the weather is now so intensely hot, that my pen is splitting as I write, notwithstanding I dip it in water very often, which if I did not, the Ink would soon dry up in it." All day long the wind blew, and the swirling sand chafed the skin off their lips. Blood streamed from their noses in the dry air; and for their thirst, they could drink only stagnant "water which (far from quenching it!!) only adds to it!!!"—and gave them diarrhea to boot. For nearly three weeks they walked into the inferno, into "the very middle of this horrid Desert."[82] Mirages flickered in silver sheets wherever they looked. Once they saw dried human bodies sticking out of the sand.[83]

The Nile, when they reached it, must have seemed like a dream. They came out of the desert at Qena in early July and gulped down the fresh waters of the river like nectar. Yet their arrival was bittersweet. It turned out that while the columns of the Indian army were inching their way across the desert, Hely-Hutchinson had already entered Cairo. General Menou had agreed to evacuate Egypt; peace discussions were under way. Britain had won before the Indian force had even had a chance to fight. At noon on July 9, the troops fired a twenty-one-gun salute to the victory, but pleased as they were, *unlucky* was a word on many lips.[84] As one disaffected subaltern complained, "So here we have come this immense distance without seeing a single shot fired, which is rather hard upon Volunteers who have come so far for that purpose."[85]

The Indian army played no role in the surrender of the French, and its appearance in Egypt has been largely forgotten. But Indian participation in the campaign signaled important characteristics of the nineteenth-century British empire that was beginning to take shape. East India Company and Crown troops had collaborated overseas only once before, in a 1762 expedition against Manila. Now, just as Crown forces were playing a more conspicuous role on the Indian subcontinent, Company troops would increasingly fight beyond South Asia, in Burma, Afghanistan, and China. Similarly, the Egyptian campaign was the first time that Indian sepoys served overseas in such large numbers. For the Hindus among them, this meant overcoming a widely held conviction that one's caste was lost by crossing the ocean, the *kala pani*. For their British officers, it meant preserving an exceptionally high standard of cultural consideration, without which Indian service for the British would have been unthinkable. Nobody understood this better than Baird, who sharply opposed a suggestion that his sepoys be mixed with Crown regulars. "By a long series of attention to their Customs, and prejudices," he said, "we have brought them to their present state of discipline and confidence in us, and have at length, induced them, to embark for foreign service." But, he cautioned Hely-Hutchinson, "if placed under Commanders, and serving with Corps, totally strangers to them, their languages, and their habits, the disgust they must naturally contract, would on their return to India, spread through the service, and lead to our giving up for ever, the Idea of our prevailing on them, to embark again, on any expedition whatever."[86] Sending sepoys overseas became a mainstay of British imperial defense well into the twentieth century—but it came with the risk, and sometimes the reality, of mutiny among the men.

This was the final way in which the campaigns of Seringapatam and Egypt formed a focal moment in the shaping of Britain's Eastern empire. The widening of imperial boundaries brought a widening of what and who was to be contained within those boundaries, and on what terms. India and Egypt were combined into a single geopolitical vision, uniting national security with commerce and creating a union of peoples on the ground. While Britain's invasion of Egypt opened up a new sphere for imperial intervention, and reflected a tightening sense of imperial mission, it also merged British imperial subjects, ambitions, and masters in striking and enduring new ways. A vignette of cultural collision eloquently tells how.

On the opposite bank of the Nile from Qena, where Baird's troops were encamped, rises the yellow stone mass of the Temple of Dendera. This immense temple to Hathor is one of Egypt's most imposing ancient monuments and marvels of preservation, with its looming ceilings and shallow staircases almost perfectly intact, streaks of blue, green, and red paint still visible. Stepping into the temple's cavernous hypostyle hall on Christmas Eve 1798, the French artist Vivant Denon found himself at a loss for words: "I believed myself to be . . . in the sanctuary of the arts and sciences. . . . In the ruins of Dendera the ancient Egyptians seemed to me to be like giants."[87] It is a place where gods and man meet: on the walls, carved with larger-than-life images of kings and deities; on the ceilings, where the willowy goddess Nut curves around astral constellations; and in the stairwells, lined by processions of priests wending their way up to shrines on the temple roof. From the rooftop, etched in the clear, sharp sunlight, the countryside looks like an unfurled map, the Nile like a great green cut in the desert rock. It was there, on Dendera's uppermost walls, that Vivant Denon carved his name, as if laying claim to the very landscape.

Early one July morning in 1801, Captain John Budgen, one of Baird's aides-de-camp, crossed the river with two British friends and "2 Bengal sepoys of the Brahmin caste" to see the ruins. Even though "the inner apartments are almost choked up with rubbish, so much so that nothing could well be distinguished," Budgen and his friends spent hours inspecting the carvings and hieroglyphics, which were still tantalizingly undeciphered. They spotted Greek inscriptions; and "on the ceiling," they "could distinguish several of the signs of the Zodiac; and Sagittarius was represented precisely as it is at this day on our globes." The two Indian soldiers were also busy investigating. On the outside of the temple, Budgen said, "the Sepoys discovered effigies of their God Vishnu, very much mutilated, and they observed they had almost all the figures that were carved on the walls and pillars, in their temples in India."[88] The sepoys' communion with the gods was interrupted by an Egyptian man, probably one of the many who lived in the huts and lean-tos surrounding the temple. The Arab "observed that the temple was not good." The sepoys were outraged at the man's blasphemous talk. "One of the Sepoys remarked, that they were restrained by their orders from quarrelling with the natives, but that if they had been in Bengal, the man should have had a good drubbing for his remark."[89] In a version of the story repeated later in Cairo, it was said that the sepoys "were with difficulty restrained by their officers from assaulting the Arabs, on account of the neglected state in which *his* temple [i.e., Vishnu's], as *they* supposed, was suffered to remain."[90]

Vishnu on the Nile? It seemed an unlikely vision. And yet an understandable one: were Horus, the hawk-headed god, and Anubis, the jackal-headed, so far removed from Ganesh, the Hindu elephant-headed deity, or Hanuman, the monkey? Eighteenth-century antiquarians speculated on connections between ancient India and Egypt, and on parallels between their gods and myths. These sorts of theories smack today of pseudoscience. Yet at such an extraordinary moment as this, when modern Hindus and ancient Egyptians—for the first recorded time—came abruptly face to face, the idea that living cultures might have embraced the dead seems more plausible. The gap between ancient and modern meant little when the gods still lived: to insult their images or let their domain decay was sacrilege of the most immediate kind.

What this fleeting Indian perspective on Egypt so vividly demonstrates is that imperial expansion came with a wide range of human voices and visions. For all that the British Empire in the East was gaining definition—on the ground, in political policy, and in the minds of the British public—empire's expansion palpably also involved new blendings and fusions. Another conspicuous crossing of India, Britain, and Egypt some months later, underscored the multicultural consequences of British imperial expansion. In August of 1801, General Hely-Hutchinson celebrated the preliminaries of peace with a banquet for his officers in Cairo. They dined on Rhoda Island, a cool, leafy retreat in the Nile. Unless a dust storm was brewing, they would have seen the pyramids rising from the desert in the west. To the east, Cairo's skyline of minarets could be traced behind the crescent-shaped sails of the feluccas coasting in the river.

The banquet was a lavish affair, with the officers in full-dress scarlet, white breeches, and festooned with gold braid; and the clink and shine of porcelain and silver on mahogany tables. One of the guests was a young Cambridge mineralogist named Edward Daniel Clarke, who was completing a two-year tour of Europe's peripheries, in Scandinavia, Russia, and the Levant.[91] The company feasted, Clarke fondly recalled, on "English porter, roasted pigs, and other English fare, together with port, claret, and Madeira wines." It was all very familiar in some ways. And yet, in others it was strangely different, for "the dinner," Clarke continued, "was cooked by Indian servants. . . . After dinner the officers smoked the *hooka*. . . . The servants in waiting were principally negroes, dressed in white turbans with muslin jackets, but without stockings or shoes." All told, Clarke decided, the setting "where persons from India and from England were met to banquet together," was "so incongruous with the natural . . . barbarism of the country, upon the border of an interminable desert, and in the midst of . . . the Nile . . . that perhaps no similar result of commerce and of conquest is ever likely to occur again, in any part of the habitable globe."[92]

Of course, Clarke was quite wrong. This kind of coming together—of British imperial officers and British imperial subjects, in an overseas domain foreign to both—this union "of commerce and of conquest" would recur time and again in the century to come, not least in Egypt, which from 1882 was garrisoned by Indian troops. Britain's enemies Napoleon and Tipu Sultan had tapped into other cultures to shore up their power; now Britain's imperial security rested on finding ways of incorporating foreign "others" into a wider British polity. The expansion of British rule in the East would in some ways work to harden and impose cultural boundaries. But it would be a mistake to consider imperial expansion as only an exclusionary process, or as being at odds with the mixing of cultures. As empires grow, they come to include more people, more cultures, more regions, and more exchanges. Combined in a British collecting worldview, India and Egypt, empire and culture, would step into the new century hand in hand.

PART THREE

# EGYPT

1801–1840

CHAPTER SEVEN

# *Rivals*

## 1. Expansion Under Cover

Every year, more than five million pairs of feet skip up its wide stone steps, between the fluted columns and through its heavy doors. Fronted by a glowering pediment sculpted with toga-clad worthies, and anchored inside by Norman Foster's luminous stone Great Court, domed in glass and steel, the British Museum is part Parthenon, part Pantheon, a temple to the classical world. But turn left through the crowds and you enter a quite different ancient realm. Here, ranked along the museum's western wing, stands an army of giants. Hewn from a hunk of polished red granite about nine feet high, the head of the pharaoh Amenhotep III gazes smugly, as it has for some three thousand years, under the cresting double crown of Upper and Lower Egypt. His forearm and clenched fist lie nearby, this one limb alone as large as an adult human. Behind Amenhotep looms the broad-shouldered torso of his later and grander successor, Ramses II, probably the best-known Egyptian pharaoh. Sculpted out of a single two-toned block of stone, and weighing more than seven tons, the block is so massive that the first modern collectors who tried to move it—Napoleon's savants—succeeded only in leaving a large hole bored in its chest. Along the sides of the Egyptian sculpture gallery stand other startling yet strangely accessible figures: statues of scribes and officials, etched with hieroglyphics; a monolithic granite sarcophagus that once nested a mummy between cases of painted papier-mâché; rams, lions, baboons, and giant scarab beetles in polished stone. In an alcove sits one of the most famous Egyptian antiquities anywhere: the Rosetta stone, a slab of black basalt carved with Greek, demotic, and Egyptian hieroglyphics, which proved to be the key by which the unknown Egyptian characters were deciphered in 1822. For many visitors, the British Museum is an *Egyptian* museum, impressed on the mind and memory through these miraculous, mysterious, and remarkably well preserved remnants from a distant past.

Across the Channel, all of the six million or so people who visit the Paris Louvre each year meet Egypt even more directly. With stately Renaissance pavilions laid on the foundations of a medieval fortress, and extended by French rulers through Napoleon and beyond, the Louvre is a palace first and a museum second, a celebration of culture and majesty. But even those tourists who cross the cobblestones planning to head straight for the Louvre's most famous possession, the *Mona Lisa,* cannot avoid a glimpse, however oblique, of Egypt. You enter the museum not through one of the many palace doors, but through its newest addition: I. M. Pei's controversial pyramid, completed in 1989. The pyramid, another collaboration of glass and steel, puts Egypt literally front and center in the Louvre. Positioned a mile or so due east from the obelisk at the Place de la Concorde, this Egyptian reference is deliberate and apt. (One of the Louvre's three wings is named for Vivant Denon, who directed the museum for twelve years after his return from Egypt.) Displayed on three levels, the Louvre presents one of the world's most comprehensive collections of Egyptian antiquities. You can look in the face the almond-eyed pharaoh Akhenaton, instantly recognizable with his sloping cheekbones and full, heart-shaped lips; or match your height against a series of upright stone sarcophagus lids. Creaking across the parquet floors of a string of ornate galleries on one side of the Cour Carrée, you can inspect painted limestone reliefs, papyri written in minute hieroglyphics, gold enameled jewelery, or blue faience *ushabti* figurines placed in tombs as proxy laborers for the dead. This is a museum within a museum: four of its rooms were set aside in 1827 as the Musée Egyptien and decorated with custom-designed murals celebrating France's connection with Egypt.

How was Egypt transposed to the galleries of London and Paris, and why? The answers, at one level, are almost as old as the objects. Already in ancient times, Egyptian antiquities had been prized by imperial rulers. Roman emperors from Augustus onward transported at least a dozen obelisks across the Mediterranean and erected them in their capital. In the late sixteenth century, the ambitious Pope Sixtus V placed one of those obelisks in front of St. Peter's itself; soon obelisks discovered among ancient Roman ruins would reappear throughout papal Rome: at the center of Bernini's opulent Fountain of the Four Rivers in Piazza Navona; on the back of a chuckling elephant in Piazza della Minerva; in the forecourt of San Giovanni in Laterano. In the Hippodrome of Constantinople, the fourth-century Roman emperor Theodosius the Great set up a pink granite obelisk from Karnak; its top still remains there, overshadowed now by the pencil-thin minarets of the Blue Mosque.

The diaspora of Egyptian antiquities in the modern world ranges even farther. Consider obelisks alone: today they rise on the Place de la Concorde, where the guillotine once stood; on the Thames Embankment in London; and in New York's Central Park. So massive was the haul of antiquities removed from Egypt in the nineteenth century that it has been called "the harvest of the gods," or more sensationally, "the rape of Egypt."[1] For Britain and France, as it had been for Rome, collecting in Egypt was bound up with empire. But whereas the Romans had collected antiquities as Egypt's masters, Britain and France would collect in place of imperial rule. In the decades following the French invasion, antiquities would become a substitute for real power, and British and French collectors would fight to acquire them, for the glory of their nations—and themselves.

The competition for Egyptian antiquities unfolded against an imperial landscape significantly altered by twelve more years of Anglo-French war, and by the consequences of the post-Waterloo peace. On September 2, 1801, after holding out in besieged Alexandria for weeks, General Jacques "Abdallah" Menou of the Armée d'Orient signed a treaty of capitulation with the British and Ottoman commanders. Edward Daniel Clarke, the traveler and Cambridge geologist, rode into the city soon after its surrender and described a horrible situation:

> In the desolate scene of sand and ruins which intervenes between the outer gates and the interior fortifications, a party of miserable Turks were endeavouring to crawl towards their camp. They had been liberated that morning from their dungeons. The legs of these poor creatures, swol[le]n to a size that was truly horrible, were covered with large ulcers; and their eyes were terrible from inflammation.

Inside the famine-stricken city, Clarke found "a father, surrounded by his children, weeping at the news that the English were not yet to enter the city. They had lived entirely upon bad rice, of a black colour, and very unfit for food. . . ." For the people of Alexandria, the coming of the British meant food and water—a return, of sorts, to peace.[2] For the French, too, surrender was a relief. More than ten thousand French soldiers who were still in Egypt, and almost seven hundred civilians—including the beleaguered savants—were allowed to go home. Under the terms of the treaty, British forces were also to be evacuated and Egypt restored to full Ottoman control.

The 1801 armistice formed part of ongoing negotiations that would soon bring peace to Europe as a whole. In March 1802, Britain, France, Spain, and the Netherlands signed the Treaty of Amiens, formally ending almost a decade of conflict. The terms were favorable to France, which was allowed to retain—and even in some cases regain—most of its overseas colonies, as well as have a ruling hand in Italy, the Netherlands, and Switzerland. Malta was to return to the Knights of St. John; Egypt to the Ottoman sultan. Despite the treaty's concessions to France, Britons widely rejoiced at the peace. Some, like the radical Whig Charles James Fox, embraced the moment to pay their first visits to Napoleon's France. Artists rushed across the Channel to look at the continental masterpieces that had been hidden from them by war, and to admire all the Italian artwork that Napoleon had triumphantly installed in the Louvre. The painter Joseph Farington told in his diary of six wonderful weeks in Paris, looking at art with his friends and fellow artists Henry Fuseli, Benjamin West, John Flaxman, Robert Smirke, Johann Hoppner, and Joseph Mallord William Turner (a remarkable assemblage of talent); and savoring Parisian society (and cuisine) everywhere, from Madame Récamier's prestigious salon to Napoleon's own dinner table.[3]

Many hoped the Peace of Amiens would return Europe (and indeed the world) to a state of tranquillity. For Benoît de Boigne, for example, a dislocated continental European in Britain, peace was a poignant personal opportunity: a time to go home. But the calm, both in Europe and beyond, was short-lived. Napoleon Bonaparte, who was made First Consul for life in 1802 (and began now to style himself simply Napoleon, in monarchical fashion), exercised his authority to annex Piedmont, to exclude British trade from the Continent, and—especially threatening to British imperial interests—to plot further exploits and campaigns in the Middle East. In light of these French maneuvers, Britain refused to evacuate Malta as the treaty had stipulated. (A crucial Mediterranean base, Malta would remain a British colony until 1964.) This was the provocation both sides had effectively been looking for. In May 1803, Britain and France went back to war—and would remain at war (with one brief interruption, when Napolean was on Elba) until Waterloo, in June 1815.

Just as it had in the past, the renewal of Anglo-French hostilities had sweeping consequences for Britain and the British Empire. (It also had profound effects on the making of another modern empire: on the eve of returning to war with Britain, Napoleon decided to abandon French claims to the Mississippi and sell the Louisiana Territory to the United States.) The first phase of the wars had been marked by bad British losses on land, ineffective coalitions, and sometimes inconsistent leadership. Now Britain's goal (particularly under the last administration of William Pitt, from 1804 to 1806) was straightforwardly to annihilate Napoleon's empire altogether. Given France's overwhelming military power on the European continent, victories overseas (and, as ever, *on* the seas, where British naval strength was paramount) were vital to British success. In the Caribbean, where massive offensives during the 1790s had ended in huge numbers of deaths, Britain now pursued piecemeal campaigns that resulted in the acquisition of numerous French and Dutch colonies and the confirmation of Haitian independence. With the beginning of the Spanish Peninsular War in 1808, Anglo-French rivalry extended into Latin America. Though Britain failed to win new colonies in South America (to the extent it tried to do so), it helped secure the independence—and eventual integration into its informal empire—of a new generation of postcolonial American states. And it was in the East that the imperial scope of the wars was most evident. In India, Richard Wellesley pursued his vision of empire in the Maratha wars; his successor as governor-general, Lord Minto, sustained the principle of offensive expansion with successful campaigns against French Mauritius and Dutch Java. These years also saw a British imperial policy first take shape in the eastern Mediterranean.[4] Indeed the very fact that tiny Malta (with its strategic harbor) was the casus belli that broke the peace of Amiens suggested how important the region had become to Britain's (and France's) sense of international security.

The decades after Waterloo saw British imperial hegemony at its height. No other power could rival Britain in terms of global military, economic, or political and diplomatic strength. Yet for all that Britain appeared to hold sway from the Atlantic to the Pacific, the Middle East—and Egypt in particular—remained a contested region, in some ways off-limits to European expansion. The Ottoman Empire, which stretched from Algeria to Bulgaria to the borders of Persia, had been challenged both within and without, and seemed at times perilously close to collapse. But its survival stood central to the European balance of power, so carefully hammered out around the post-Waterloo conference table in Vienna. Once one portion of the sultan's empire fell into foreign hands, the worry ran, Europe would erupt once more into a dangerous war, competing for the empire's pieces. The so-called Eastern Question—how to protect Ottoman integrity and preserve European peace—would dominate European diplomacy across the nineteenth century.

Egypt occupied a pivotal place in these diplomatic calculations. On the one hand, the events of 1798–1801 had catalyzed British imperial interest in the region and opened another arena of heated Anglo-French competition.

On the other, as both nations recognized, outright conquest of Egypt (even if it were militarily possible) would upset Ottoman authority and threaten to unleash a dangerous chain reaction. In theory, Egypt was to return to the status quo ante bellum, almost as if the French and British invasions had never taken place. But reality would look different. Rather than rest in the hands of a docile Ottoman subordinate, within five years Egypt would be governed by a new pasha, Muhammad Ali, who from 1805 to his death in 1849 transformed the Ottoman province into an autonomous, modern, industrialized state, with imperial ambitions of its own. Rather than withdraw from the region, Britain and France would spend much of the nineteenth century vying with each other for strategic, commercial, and cultural influence in it. Indeed, Egypt would remain formally independent of European control until 1882, when it fell under British occupation; it joined the British Empire only in 1914, when it was made a protectorate.

Egypt's nominal autonomy had two important consequences for the nature of British and French intervention. It meant that the game was never up between Britain and France. Napoleon may have been defeated, but France had not abandoned its desires for or interests in the area. Indeed, for all that Britain's imperial star had ascended in the East, it was France that would become the dominant European power in the Arab world, formally beginning with its invasion of Algeria in 1830. Egypt's independence also meant that Anglo-French rivalry was pushed under cover. No longer able to pursue conquest of Egypt—at least not openly—Britain and France vied instead for a more symbolic form of power. They vied for cultural ascendancy. This new war would be waged for prestige and influence, and its battles would be for antiquities. On its front lines would be three marginal men and collectors: the adoptive Briton Giambattista Belzoni and the consuls of Britain and France, Henry Salt and Bernardino Drovetti. Out of apparent peace—the end of the only open Anglo-French war in the Middle East—a new arena of imperial competition and desire was set to emerge.

## II. War and Piece

If Napoleon's landing at Alexandria in 1798 had opened a new phase in European attempts to colonize Egypt, the retreat of the French forces would mark the beginning of a competition to collect it. The culture wars started in the Treaty of Capitulation itself, in what seemed at first glance to be an innocuous enough point: what was to become of the collections formed by the savants? According to Article XVI of the Treaty of Capitulation, the French savants could "take with them all the artistic and scientific instruments that they brought from France, but the Arabic manuscripts, the statues, and the other collections that were made for the French Republic will be considered as public property, and will be at the disposition of the generals of the combined armies."[5] All the hard-won fruits of the savants' research—all the scholarship that was supposed to make the French conquest different from all other conquests—would pass unceremoniously into the hands of the victorious British; confiscated, in the words of the zoologist Étienne Geoffroy Saint-Hilaire, by "a camp of soldiers that turned itself into a band of customs agents."[6]

This piece of British booty-taking, for such it was, was a more decorous affair than the free-for-all pillaging that followed the capture of Seringapatam. But for the French savants, the sense of despoliation cut painfully deep. "We were disgusted by this article," remembered the young engineer Édouard de Villiers du Terrage, "and pointed out to General Menou, that if he had the power to treat over everything concerning the government and the army, our collections and our manuscripts were private property, and nobody other than us had the right to dispose of it."[7] The collections belonged to them and to them alone. They saw them almost as a form of intellectual property. In the impassioned words of Geoffroy Saint-Hilaire, they had "won" that property:

> fair and square, with the sweat of their brows, in spite of the Arabs, in spite of the perpendicular sun, in spite of the biting sand, in spite of

James Gillray, "L'Insurrection de l'Institut Amphibie," a satire of the French savants.

> our soldiers themselves, who often laughed at this uncompromising ardor. It was theirs, all this—or, indeed, it was France's and the world's; but lost to the world and to France if it was taken away from them, because only they had the key.[8]

If the collections were to go to England, Saint-Hilaire insisted, then he would go with them.

Their protests fell on deaf ears. As far as the prickly Menou was concerned, if the savants wanted to follow their cases to England, good riddance. Indeed, he suggested irritably, "if they wish to have themselves stuffed for the purpose, I shall not prevent them."[9] It must have been with a perverse sense of humor, then, that he let a delegation petition General Hely-Hutchinson directly. Geoffroy Saint-Hilaire, heading the group, pressed the case in graphic style:

> We spent three years conquering these treasures one by one, three years collecting them in every corner of Egypt, from Philae to Rosetta; each of them is associated with a peril surmounted, a monument etched and engraved in our memories. . . . Rather than let this iniquitous, vandalous spoliation take place, we will destroy our property: we will throw it into the Libyan sands, or throw it into the sea. . . .[10]

But Hutchinson, too, was unmoved. He dispatched Edward Daniel Clarke and Clarke's traveling companion, William Richard Hamilton (private secretary to Lord Elgin, the British ambassador in Constantinople), to "discover what national property . . . was in the hands of the French," and threatened to arrest the savants as prisoners of war if they did not hand it over.[11] "No, no, we will not obey!" cried Saint-Hilaire, aflame with "patriotic indignation." "We will burn our riches ourselves. It is fame that you aim at? Well then! Count on the memory of history: you too will have burned a library in Alexandria!"[12] On Clarke and Hamilton, though—both of whom were serious collectors and antiquarians—the savants' appeal finally had an effect. Hamilton persuaded the general to let the browbeaten scholars keep fifty-five cases of specimens and scientific papers. Saint-Hilaire took his collections back to the Muséum d'Histoire Naturelle in Paris, where, studying his stuffed and preserved creatures, he began to formulate theories about the structure of vertebrates for which he is still famous.

But the large antiquities, the trophy pieces most suitable for display, were bound for Britain. The savant and mathematician Jean-Baptiste Fourier, who later wrote the preface to the *Description de l'Égypte*, drew up a list of fifteen major items in French possession in Alexandria.[13] More than half had been brought from distant Thebes and Upper Egypt, among them two small obelisks and fragments of several animal-headed statues. The list also included three massive stone sarcophagi completely covered with hieroglyphics, one of which, found in the Attarine Mosque in Alexandria, was believed by some (including Clarke) to be the "tomb of Alexander" the Great.[14]

The greatest prize, however, was unquestionably "A stone of black granite carved with three bands of hieroglyphic characters, Greek and Egyptian, found at Rosetta": the famous Rosetta stone. At that time, Egyptian hiero-

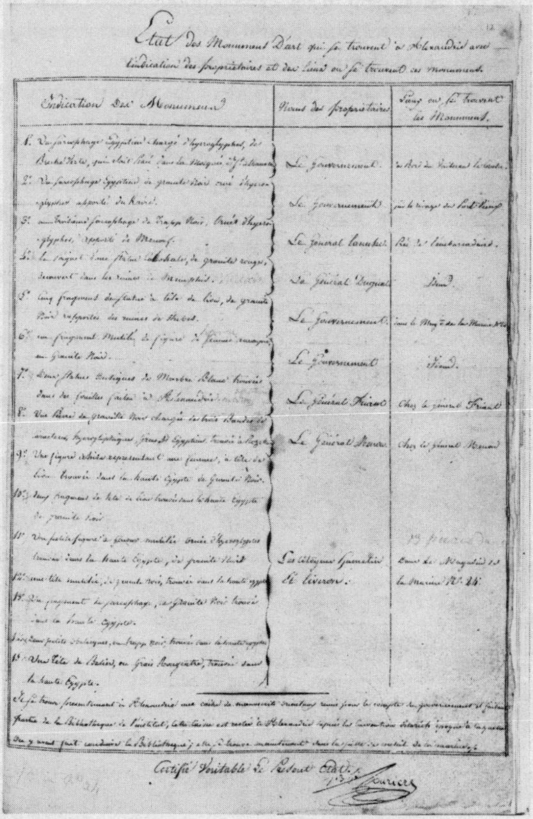

Etat des Monument D'art qui se trouvent à Alexandrie avec l'indication des propriétaires et des lieux où se trouvent ces monuments.

| Indication des Monuments | Noms des propriétaires | Lieux où se trouvent les Monuments. |
|---|---|---|
| 1. [illegible] | Le Gouvernement. | [illegible] |
| 2. [illegible] | Le Gouvernement. | [illegible] |
| 3. [illegible] | Le général [illegible] | [illegible] |
| 4. [illegible] | Le général [illegible] | Idem. |
| 5. [illegible] | Le Gouvernement. | [illegible] |
| 6. [illegible] | Le Gouvernement. | Idem. |
| 7. [illegible] | Le général Friant | Chez le général Friant |
| 8. [illegible] | Le Général Menou | Chez le général Menou |
| 9. [illegible] | | |
| 10. [illegible] | | |
| 11. [illegible] | [illegible] | [illegible] |
| 12. [illegible] | | |
| 13. [illegible] | | |
| 14. [illegible] | | |
| 15. [illegible] | | |

[illegible]

Certifié Véritable le Présent Etat. [illegible]

List of antiquities ceded by the French in 1801. The Rosetta Stone is item 8.

glyphics remained completely opaque: nobody had known how to read them since late antiquity. Because the Rosetta stone presented what were apparently identical texts in Greek, which was legible, alongside Egyptian, which was not, it was widely recognized to be a possible key to the hieroglyphic code. Even General Menou appreciated its value, and claimed the Rosetta stone as his own personal property in order to keep it out of British hands. "When I ask for the Arabic manuscripts, the statues, various collections and antiquities, I am only following the fine example that you have given Europe," Hely-Hutchinson snapped back. "Were you at war against the Apollo Belvedere, the Laocoön, and several fine pieces that you took from Rome?"[15] Clarke and Hamilton seized the Rosetta stone from its hiding place and whisked it off to London "lest the indignation of the French troops should cause its destruction."[16] Thus the stone went to the British Museum, where it remains, possibly the most famous symbol of Britain's victory over France.

In both Britain and France, the seizure of the savants' antiquities set the stage for the dramatic history of Egyptian collecting in the decades ahead. The invasions of 1798–1801 fundamentally transformed European attitudes toward, and knowledge of, ancient Egypt. Before then, European acquaintance with ancient Egypt was mostly confined to the Greek and Roman periods—the age, for instance, of Antony and Cleopatra—familiar from classical authors. Virtually nothing was known of preclassical, pharaonic Egypt, beyond what information was provided by a few key sources, notably Herodotus's *Histories* and the Old Testament of the Bible. European knowledge of Egyptian topography was similarly biased. Alexandria, the capital of Alexander the Great, faced Europe on the Mediterranean coast, but the great monuments of the pharaohs lay in the Nile Valley far to the south, in Middle and Upper Egypt. These sites had been described and drawn by only a daring handful of Europeans who ventured below Cairo before 1798, such as the enthusiastic Anglican bishop Richard Pococke, and Frederick Norden, a Danish naval officer, both of whom

The Sphinx as Richard Pococke wrongly depicted it in 1743, with its nose intact.

visited Egypt in 1737. Another glimpse at the monuments of pharaonic Egypt was provided by the popular travel narrative of the Scottish laird James Bruce, who passed briefly through the region on his way to Abyssinia in 1768. But neither of the most popular travel writers who visited Egypt before Napoleon's invasion, the French philosophes Constantin Volney and Étienne Savary, had journeyed into Upper Egypt. Nor was the available information on pharaonic Egypt always reliable: Norden was the first person to depict the Sphinx correctly, without its nose.[17]

The general lack of European familiarity with pharaonic Egypt was also evident in collections. A respectable early modern cabinet of curiosities would generally contain small Egyptian items, such as amulets, scarabs, wooden and bronze figures. Mummies were especially popular collectibles thanks to a belief, widespread in the sixteenth and seventeenth centuries, that they possessed extraordinary medicinal properties—when eaten. (European apothecaries did good business in "mummy" extracts; as did the grave robbers and dealers who gruesomely faked them from the corpses of executed convicts.)[18] But the monumental stone sculptures, carved panels, sarcophagi, paintings, and burial objects associated with ancient Egyptian daily life—all the things that spell out Egypt to museumgoers today—were almost wholly unknown in Europe before 1798.

So when Vivant Denon published his well-illustrated account of the Egyptian campaign, *Voyage dans la basse et la haute Égypte*, in 1802, the book was a revelation to readers across Europe. Here for the first time were detailed and reasonably accurate images of the stunning temples of Upper Egypt, accompanied by soaring, evocative descriptions. The book was an instant hit, promptly translated into English and German, and is credited with kicking off "Egyptomania," the European fad for all things Egyptian that infected the design of such diverse things as clocks, candlesticks, inkpots, wallpaper, and furniture legs. Denon personally encouraged the Sèvres porcelain manufactory to produce an elaborate "Egyptian" table service, eventually presented to Tsar Alexander I. Napoleon ordered a second service for his empress Josephine, as a sort of parting gift at the time of their divorce; but the ex-empress (who was otherwise a great enthusiast for things Egyptian) found the final product "too severe" and sent it back. In an apt twist, it was later presented to the Duke of Wellington by Louis XVIII.[19] This popular enthusiasm for ancient Egypt significantly raised the profile of modern, contemporary Egypt in Britain and France. At the same time, it deepened a division between ancient Egypt, which was increasingly embraced as part of the Western tradition, and the modern land, which European powers approached as a site of political and imperial intervention.

For the French, losing the antiquities in 1801—to say nothing of losing Egypt itself—meant confronting the uncomfortable (and at that point relatively unfamiliar) reality of defeat. Back in Paris, the savants turned to their fifty-five salvaged cases of notes and papers to overcome their loss. From February 1802, they began to work on a massive compendium of their Egyptian research, designed to cover every field from antiquities to zoology, and to encompass the ancient, modern, and natural worlds. The result, the *Description de l'Égypte*, appeared in twenty-three folio volumes between 1809 and 1828. Simply in terms of money, man-hours, paper, and ink expended, it counts as one of the greatest publishing ventures of the nineteenth century. Even today, some celebrate the *Description* and the savants' labors as a validation of sorts of the French invasion.[20] Certainly Napoleon and his successors, who financed and sponsored the publication, actively supported the idea that an intellectual victory might compensate for a military defeat.[21] To this extent, the *Description* was a political, imperial, and Orientalist undertaking through and through.

Yet the driving preoccupation of the text—made especially evident in the bombastic historical preface by Jean-Baptiste Fourier—was not so much to subordinate Orient to Occident in general, as it was to glorify France, and Napoleon, in particular.[22] Furthermore, the *Description* actually had rather little to do with modern, "Oriental" Egypt: up against nine volumes of text and images devoted to ancient Egypt are just four concerning modern Egypt; the remaining ten treat natural history.[23] The compendium was particularly concerned to cultivate a connection between France and *ancient* Egypt. Nothing illustrates the point better than the publication's frontispiece. In the foreground of the picture, easily recognizable, lie all the savants' confiscated antiquities, including the Rosetta stone. The entire image is framed by a heavy border, studded with patriotic symbols: medallions with the names of the Armée d'Orient's victories, a crowned *N*, and cartouches containing a star and a bee, Napoleon's personal emblems. This is not just Orientalism. It is Bonapartism, French national and imperial ambition rolled into one. Considered as a whole, the *Description* is a monumental attempt to compensate for loss—a vicarious collection and an intellectual one.

While Napoleon and the savants were busily transforming their defeat into a propaganda victory, on the other side of the Channel, the arrival of the Egyptian objects had equally far-reaching consequences. In much the way that spoils from Seringapatam had turned the East India Company's museum into a showcase of imperial power, the Egyptian booty would help transform the British Museum into a genuinely public, national, and indeed imperial, institution. When the crates of antiquities arrived in London in 1802, the

British Museum still very much resembled the cabinet of curiosities it had started its life as, in 1753.[24] The museum owed its origin to the massive private collection formed by the surgeon and naturalist Sir Hans Sloane. (Sloane was even an imperial collector of sorts, having spent a year in Jamaica gathering plant specimens.) In his will, Sloane bequeathed his cabinet—by then, some seventy thousand "curiosities" strong—to the British nation. Significantly, the British Museum was not a royal institution but a national one. Yet, housed in what was effectively an aristocratic residence, Montagu House, and accessible only to select visitors approved, upon application, by the principal librarian, the museum was in practice more like a stately home than the public museum it is today.

The 1801 booty transformed the British Museum's collections in two major respects. Like many eighteenth-century collectors, Hans Sloane had picked up several Egyptian objects in the course of his career, but they were all small items—bronzes, terra-cotta figures, and amulets—dating mostly from the Greco-Roman period. The British Museum also owned four mummies, which it displayed, in keeping with the usual organizing practices of cabinets

Frontispiece to the *Description de l'Égypte.*

of curiosities, alongside other natural history specimens.[25] The arrival of the French spoils marked the first time that monumental Egyptian sculptures had been seen in Britain. Not only were they on an entirely different scale from most other Egyptian objects in Europe—as well as far older—they also looked completely different from the Greco-Roman pieces familiar to (and appreciated by) European viewers. They would have made a radical aesthetic impact on contemporary visitors and potential future collectors.

The booty signaled a new direction for the British Museum's collections more generally. With the exception of artifacts collected in the Pacific during Captain Cook's voyages, all the museum's acquisitions before 1801 had come from private individuals. The Egyptian antiquities were effectively the first public collection to arrive at the British Museum, acquired by the nation, for the nation. Ten years later, this new sense of the museum as a repository of "national" collections would seize the limelight in the notorious case of the Elgin Marbles. While serving as ambassador in Constantinople, the Earl of Elgin had gotten a *firman* (decree) from the Ottoman sultan authorizing him to remove the friezes from the Parthenon in Athens. (Greece was then a province of the Ottoman Empire.) In 1811, Elgin approached the British government hoping to sell the sculptures. Using language that would have been unlikely a generation earlier, Elgin argued that his collection, assembled in his public capacity as ambassador, had been formed on behalf of the British nation, and thus belonged in the British Museum by right. This was a controversial argument and acquisition at the time, and remains very much so today, presenting a potent challenge to the limits and definition of "national" collections.[26] It is worth noting that the Egyptian booty, the British Museum's first national collection, helped establish the terms of the ongoing Elgin Marbles debate.

But transformations rarely happen overnight—at least not in large institutions. When the Egyptian antiquities arrived in London in the summer of 1802, the museum had nowhere to put them. "They were placed in the open court of the British Museum, and considered as curious but unimportant monuments of Egyptian art, glorious to the nation as trophies of its valour, but whose dark and mystic legends, impervious to modern inquiry, excited despair rather than hope of explanation." Thus lamented Edward Daniel Clarke, who pointed out that if a piece such as Alexander the Great's (supposed) sarcophagus had "been conveyed to the metropolis of France" instead, "a prodigious temple would have been erected in the midst of Paris; where, to complete the mockery of Buonaparte's imitation of the son of Philip, that same Tomb that had once inclosed the body of that hero would have been reserved for the bones of his mimic."[27] Sarcasm aside, Clarke was certainly right: Egyptian antiquities were more welcome in France than in Britain, where their alien aesthetic qualities alone kept them well outside the connoisseurial mainstream. Even Clarke's defense of the Egyptian sculptures rested on their historical and monumental significance, not on their artistic appeal. For generations of viewers conditioned to view Greek and Roman sculpture as an artistic ideal, these were at best odd if impressive curiosities. Egyptian antiquities would remain marginal to the British antiquarian establishment for decades to come.

Nevertheless, it was to accommodate these pieces that the British Museum undertook in 1803 to construct its first-ever purpose-built wing, the Townley Gallery, named for the celebrated antiquarian Charles Townley, who had sold his collection to the museum. Hitherto the British Museum had been a gentleman's townhouse; now it became a genuine museum, building in response to its collections. The Townley Gallery was opened to the public in June 1808, with the Egyptian pieces dominating its central hall. In this, the same year that Tipu's Tiger went on display in India House, it was surely not lost on visitors that the Townley Gallery's most prominent contents were also trophies of war—and war in the East, against France, at that.

Egyptian antiquities in the Townley Gallery, c. 1819. Note the two "Oriental" visitors.

The 1801 Treaty of Capitulation, then, framed a relationship between Egypt, ancient and modern, and the West that would mature across the nineteenth century. For France, losing the objects in 1801, like losing Egypt itself, in no way ended French ambitions in the region. It rearticulated them. In the *Description de l'Égypte*, France asserted a stridently nationalist claim to Egypt, anchored in the ancient past, to help compensate for its failure to conquer the modern land. Greece and Rome had long been familiar, investigated, emulated, critiqued, collected. In Egypt, the *Description* seemed to be saying, France presented the West with another part of its heritage, another ancient civilization to study and collect. Egyptian symbols also helped tie Napoleon's empire to the French Revolution, with its Masonic imagery and festival sets of obelisks and pyramids. At the same time, by staking a claim to *ancient* Egypt in particular, France defined the fault line between ancient and modern, classical and Oriental, that remains active and fraught today.

In Britain, gaining the prize objects, like gaining an informal presence in Egypt, widened and helped reshape a public imperial image. In much the way that the French invasion of 1798 had put Egypt on Britain's imperial map, so the 1801 booty fixed Egypt in Britain's world of objects, both for connoisseurs and for a larger viewing public. The objects brought a new Egypt to Britain: an Egypt of pharaohs, monoliths, and hieroglyphics, far older than Greece or Rome. With their arrival, too, the old cabinet of curiosities–style British Museum was shaken up and slowly redefined to become a public institution, more accommodating to different objects and visitors than before. This shift in the museum's function paralleled the redefinition of empire as something more heterogeneous, inclusive, and shaping of British identity than ever before.

But what of Egypt itself? It was there, of course, that the effects of 1801 were most palpable. Despite what the British and French had hoped, three years of war and French occupation had made it impossible for the region simply to revert to the way it was before. Egypt's place within the Ottoman Empire, and the world, would be transformed as its new pasha, Muhammad Ali, consolidated his power and turned Egypt into a virtually self-governing and expansionist state. And the place of France and Britain within Egypt was also set to change, as their diplomatic representatives Bernardino Drovetti and Henry Salt were about to discover.

## III. Personal and Political

In May 1803, the very month that Britain and France went back to war after the brief peace of Amiens, a pair of young Frenchmen disembarked at Alexandria to assume the posts of consul and vice-consul in Egypt. Even the elder of the two, Mathieu de Lesseps, was not yet thirty; as consul, he would be based in

Cairo and attempt to advance French political interests in what was still a country scarred by war. Lesseps's name would later be enduringly linked with Egypt thanks to his son, Ferdinand, who would follow him into diplomatic service in Egypt and take the leading role in the construction of the Suez Canal. But the younger of the new arrivals that day, Bernardino Drovetti, would achieve his own immortality. Staying on in Egypt for almost thirty years, Drovetti would come to personify France there, and to secure a place for France in the favor of his close friend Muhammad Ali Pasha. He would also guarantee French dominance over ancient Egypt by forming the first major collections of antiquities from the Nile Valley.[28]

As his name suggests, Drovetti was not French by birth. Born in 1776 in a Piedmontese village north of Turin, he was (like Benoît de Boigne) a subject of the House of Savoy, and his native language was Italian. At the age of eighteen he took a degree from the University of Turin, and prepared to follow his father and brother into the legal profession. But the future for Drovetti, for Piedmont, and for Europe as a whole was about to change dramatically. Early in 1796, Napoleon swept down through the mountains with his Armée d'Italie, quickly conquering Piedmont and unseating the tottering king of Savoy. Drovetti enlisted in the French army. He received an officer's commission the following year, and was soon appointed to the general staff. When France annexed Piedmont in 1799, Drovetti and his compatriots became French citizens overnight. Within two weeks, "the proofs given by you of your firm patriotism"—to France—won Drovetti a small post in the French provisional government. An able and competent administrator, he rose steadily through the bureaucratic ranks, and in 1802 he was offered a promotion into the foreign service. Only after he accepted the job did he learn his destination: Egypt.

Some people later assumed that Drovetti first went to Egypt as an officer in the Armée d'Orient. This is not the case, but he did go very much as Napoleon's man. His adult career had been spent in the service of the French government in Piedmont. His family was pro-French, and he was a French citizen and proud of it. It is sometimes hard to recapture the enormous enthusiasm that attracted a generation of young men into the cult of Napoleon. Like the hero of Stendhal's novel *The Charterhouse of Parma*, Drovetti was presumably drawn to the young soldier who managed at once to be a revolutionary idealist and a disciplined and effective leader. Drovetti's smooth progress up the ranks epitomized the Napoleonic paradigm of the "career open to talent," of a world of opportunity unshackled by hereditary privilege, waiting for the able men who would run it.

Drovetti and Lesseps arrived at what turned out to be an eventful time.

Bernardino Drovetti.

Just two months earlier, the last of the British forces had withdrawn, leaving behind just one officer, Colonel Ernest Missett, as Britain's man on the spot. With the evacuations complete, it may have looked to British and French officials as if all traces of the French invasion were gone. But years of war and occupation had left Egypt's government, to say nothing of its economy and society, in disarray. Rival factions of Mamelukes competed with one another for power, while the Ottomans sought to assert the authority of the sultan's appointed pasha (governor). A ten-thousand-man-strong Ottoman army remained in Egypt, pushing the resources of the war-torn country to the breaking point.

The Ottoman troops were headed by Muhammad Ali, an officer of Albanian origin who had first arrived in Egypt in 1801 with the Anglo-Ottoman expeditionary force. Muhammad Ali was born, he later liked to say, in 1769, the same year as Napoleon and the Duke of Wellington. This was a piece of poetic license, but Muhammad Ali's fancied resemblance to the two great European commanders of the age was not unjustified. Acutely intelligent, talented, and ambitious, he quickly sized up the power vacuum in Egypt and maneuvered to fill it himself. In just two years, he rose to the command of the Ottoman forces in Egypt, and forged important alliances within the fragmented Mameluke camps. Through a series of partnerships, confrontations, betrayals—and even suspected poisonings—Muhammad Ali successfully eliminated his chief rivals for power. In 1805, he was appointed pasha of Egypt by a *firman* from the Ottoman sultan.[29]

From his perch in Alexandria, Drovetti watched these events unfold and reported them in perceptive dispatches back to the Ministry of Foreign Affairs in Paris. He firmly believed that Muhammad Ali was the only man who could maintain authority in Egypt; and despite instructions from Paris not to meddle in local politics, he worked to bolster the new governor's position as much as possible. In Drovetti's opinion, the future of Egypt, and the interests of France, clearly lay with Muhammad Ali. But Consul Missett and the British thought otherwise.

Though it had now been five years since Britain and France signed their armistice in Egypt, the Anglo-French contest for ascendancy was far from over. Indeed, the traveler Viscount Valentia reported, when he visited Egypt on his way back from India in the spring of 1806, "the rivalry between their countries rages with full force at Alexandria."[30] While the French openly encouraged Muhammad Ali, Britain supported the cause of his inveterate opponent, the Mameluke warlord Alfi Bey. Alfi had even traveled to Britain in 1803 with the last of the occupying forces, and spent several months there trying to garner support. ("He is a very fine man, speaks *Italian*," recorded the painter Joseph Farington in his diary.)[31] Missett was convinced, not unjustifiably, that Napoleon would invade Egypt again given half a chance; with Muhammad Ali now ensconced as pasha, "totally under the influence of France," it was almost as if an invitation had been issued. The only way to prevent another French invasion, Missett argued, was for Britain to step in and replace Muhammad Ali with Alfi Bey. (Or, later, with his supporters, since Alfi died in January 1807.) "Besides these advantages," Missett added, "the popularity which would attach to the British name from my becoming instrumental to the restoration of tranquillity in this desolate province, could not but be favorable to the future views of His Majesty's government upon Egypt."[32]

Missett got his mission. In March 1807, a rarely recounted episode in British military and imperial history unfolded when a moderate force of 6,600 men landed in Alexandria, commanded by the Scottish general Alexander Mackenzie Fraser. The city immediately surrendered; Drovetti made a dramatic escape from Alexandria the same night. "We have thus with little trouble master'd ourselves of Alexandria," boasted the Highland officer Lieutenant-Colonel Patrick MacLeod, "and have every reason to conclude that the people are well inclined to the charge and that the Mamalukes b[ein]g very hostile to the Turks will join their cause to ours and that our influence will speedily predominate over the whole country."[33] It looked as if Egypt would soon and suddenly fall into line with British desires.

But in a month, MacLeod was dead. General Fraser tried to advance on Rosetta, twice, and was bloodily repulsed by the Egyptians both times. At "the disastrous affair at El Hamed," on April 21, 1807, the army "was completely cut up": MacLeod and three hundred fifty British soldiers were killed, and more than four hundred others taken as captives to Cairo.[34] It was Drovetti, of all people, who apparently saved the lives of these British prisoners, by suggesting to his friend the pasha that "it would be more humane, as well as prudent, to offer to his [the pasha's] soldiers, for a live man, double the sum that formerly was given for a [severed] head."[35] Drovetti loaned money from his own pocket to help ransom British soldiers "sold as slaves."[36] In brief, the British expedition was a disaster. In October, the British evacuated Alexandria and sailed quietly off, taking Missett to Sicily, where he lived for the next four years, in exile from his post.

This misbegotten British invasion of Egypt figures little in imperial history books: for obvious reasons, the chroniclers of Britain's empire did not wish to dwell on such embarrassments, and for the most part they had plenty of victories to laud instead. Yet such episodes (another would be the attempted British invasion of Buenos Aires, two years later) testify both to the global range of British imperial ambitions and to the ever-present prospect of defeat. Failures also had significant consequences. The effects of the 1807 campaign would be felt by British and French agents in Egypt for decades to come.

As Muhammad Ali emerged victorious from the events of 1807, France—and Drovetti in particular—won along with him. Drovetti's advice, intelligence, and support had crucially helped Muhammad Ali in the uncertain early days of the British invasion; without Drovetti's help, arguably, the pasha might have fallen. "The Pasha," it was said, "never forgot his services. He consulted him on the form of administration he wanted to introduce in the region and it was by his [Drovetti's] advice that he put everything in place."[37] Personal relationships of this kind sometimes get lost in the annals of history, yet they could have profound and unpredictable effects on politics and international affairs. Between the pasha and the diplomat—between Egypt and France—the bonds were intimate, strong, and enduring. It was a connection that Britain and its representatives would never be able to duplicate.

Drovetti had arrived in Egypt a stranger to the region and a novice at international diplomacy. Four years later, he was now an intimate of the pasha, a practiced political operator, and—from 1806, when Lesseps relocated to Livorno for his health—France's sole representative in Egypt. Drovetti had also begun to push personal roots into Egypt in two further ways that would have ramifications both for his own career and for the affairs of his adopted nation. He acquired a family, and a passion for antiquities.

It may have been within a few months of his arrival in Egypt that Drovetti fell for a married Frenchwoman named Rosine Rey Balthalon. Rosine had been raised (and quite possibly born) in Egypt, where her father had worked as the baker for Cairo's French community since at least 1775.[38] When Drovetti settled in Alexandria, Rosine had been married for about ten years to a violent and abusive Marseillais merchant called Joseph Balthalon. The romantic drama began in early 1804, when Rosine told her husband that she was pregnant, an announcement that seemed to come as a most unwelcome surprise. Balthalon flew into a rage, accused Drovetti of being the father, and attacked his wife so brutally she suffered a miscarriage. Rosine snatched up her money and jewels and fled to the consular mansion—that is, to Drovetti's house—for protection. Reports of the scandal in Alexandria soon flooded into the Paris Ministry of Foreign Affairs. Balthalon wrote bullish letters accusing Drovetti of having "debauched my wife, . . . become my persecutor" and "depriv[ed] me of the greatest part of my fortune."[39] Drovetti insisted he was giving Rosine the security to which she was entitled, and Mathieu de Lesseps wholeheartedly vouched for him. The consulate's two disgruntled dragomans, in the meantime, freely libeled both Drovetti and Lesseps. It was an ugly business, and it may well explain why Drovetti was never formally promoted from vice-consul to consul after Lesseps's departure.[40]

Joseph Balthalon was obviously a monster, but Drovetti was hardly an innocent. The Balthalons were formally separated toward the end of 1804, and Drovetti and Rosine began living together openly. General Fraser referred to her in 1807 as "Madame Drovetti," but in reality, since Balthalon refused to grant a divorce until 1817, it was only on April 12, 1818—some fifteen years after their affair began—that Bernardino and Rosine were married, in the chancellery of the Alexandria consulate.[41] The late date of this event meant that if Drovetti had wanted to return to Europe before 1818, he would either have had to abandon his family or arrive with a mistress and an illegitimate son in tow (Giorgio, born in 1812). Diplomats' personal lives are rarely factored into the history of foreign affairs, but this shadowy family story must have played a major part in Drovetti's commitment to his job, and to living in Egypt. It also helped that Rosine was a woman of property there: she owned the lease on the consular mansion in Alexandria, and in later years the Drovettis would have the pleasure of leasing the house to the French government at exorbitant prices.[42]

A nice profile of Drovetti at about this time—a man embedded in a transnational, expatriate life—was sketched by the Romantic writer, traveler, and aristocrat François-René de Chateaubriand, who stayed with Drovetti toward the end of 1806.[43] Chateaubriand greatly admired the soldier-diplomat, and the two men spent long hours on the roof of Drovetti's house, among the cages of quails and partridges Drovetti kept there, talking about

France, "notre patrie." "The conclusion of all our conversations," said Chateaubriand, was Drovetti's dream of finding "some small retreat" to retire to in France, the country he clearly considered his own. Chateaubriand also made mention of another of the vice-consul's interests, and probably then a fairly recent one: Drovetti had begun to collect antiquities. Chateaubriand saw the collection of small pieces, which Drovetti had most likely bought from Egyptian fellahin, who gathered artifacts at local sites to sell to Europeans.[44] This unstructured antiquities trade was increasingly conspicuous after the French invasion: earlier in 1806, for instance, Viscount Valentia had bought many antiquities from "Bedowee Arabs" at Giza and in the Delta.[45]

Already deeply invested in Egypt both politically and personally, Drovetti would soon bind himself to Egypt most tightly of all through his passion for antiquities. It was in the autumn of 1811 that Bernardino Drovetti truly discovered ancient Egypt. His epiphany was occasioned by the visit of Colonel Vincent Boutin, a spy sent by Napoleon to scout out the possibilities for another French invasion. On the double pretext of "procur[ing] supplies of wheat for Corfu" and of satisfying archaeological curiosity, Boutin and Drovetti traveled to Upper Egypt.[46] This was no simple sightseeing trip for Boutin—who secretly made notes on the military capabilities of the Mamelukes and Muhammad Ali Pasha—but for Drovetti, the seasoned local diplomat, it was. For two months the men journeyed south along the Nile, as far as Aswan; Boutin's expansive signature can still be seen on the walls of the Luxor Temple, a frozen record of the men's progress. One can only imagine what a revelation the journey must have been for Drovetti. He had lived in Egypt for eight years, and had even been collecting antiquities there for at least five. But the staggering pharaonic sites of Upper Egypt belonged to a different world from Alexandria and Cairo. The magnificent temples of Dendera and Philae, the sprawling ruins of Karnak, the tombs of ancient Thebes: this was an Egypt he had never seen, perhaps never dreamed of. And it was a sight he would never forget.[47]

For it was as if in the tombs and temples of Upper Egypt, Drovetti experienced the same visions of glory that had tempted the savants before him: to possess all this was to lay claim to history, civilization, to empire past and present. This was still the reign of Napoleon; the prestige attached to Egyptian antiquities back in France was tremendous. And there were personal rewards in them, too—possible career advancement, social dividends, and, perhaps, money—all of which held obvious appeal to the self-made, self-promoting Piedmontese. For any or all of these reasons, the trip to Upper Egypt inspired Drovetti to collect seriously, not just buying here and there, as he had done before, but to dig up Egyptian treasures for himself.

Chateaubriand was the first person to take note of Drovetti's collection, but he was by no means the last.[48] Within a decade, Drovetti's newfound enthusiasm would yield massive collections of antiquities for Europe's major museums. It would bring him considerable fortune and fame. And it would bring him an enemy and competitor in his British counterpart, Henry Salt.

## IV. An Amateur Abroad

The same year that Chateaubriand visited Egypt and chatted so congenially with Drovetti amid the birdcages, another European aristocrat passed through Egypt on a leisure tour. George Annesley, Viscount Valentia—eldest son of the newly minted Irish peer the Earl of Mountnorris—was finishing up a three-year pleasure trip around India and the Red Sea. Valentia has skipped through these pages already, because he was one of relatively few travelers to visit and write about these regions at the turn of the eighteenth century. In India, he had spent a gratifying year traveling across the subcontinent, where he enjoyed the patronage of Richard Wellesley, whom he greatly admired, and the attentions of various Indian rulers, such as Asaf ud-Daula's successor Saadat Ali Khan. Now in Egypt, Valentia received a warm welcome from Muhammad Ali Pasha. Consul Ernest Missett proudly reported in a dispatch that "no European, not in the command of an army, ever received, in this country, such marked attentions, or such complimentary honors, as have been paid to that nobleman. My sole motive for mentioning this circumstance," he added, "is to give . . . a proof, that my efforts to detach the Viceroy of Egypt from the interest of France, have, at length, proved of some efficacy."[49]

Accompanying Valentia, as draftsman and amanuensis, was a young man called Henry Salt. It is not clear whether Salt and Drovetti met in 1806, but later they would have ample chance to make up for any missed opportunity. Though he would have been astonished to imagine it then, Salt would return to Egypt ten years later as Britain's consul, launching himself into a career in politics and collecting—and a rivalry with Drovetti in both.

To look at them, the rivals were plainly quite different characters. Drovetti had a distinctly roguish air, with springing dark curls and a twirling mustache, a cleft chin, flared nostrils, and a devilish gleam in his eye. His right hand was permanently damaged—from a saber wound, it was said, sustained on the battlefield of Marengo. Salt cut a more elegant figure. Tall, thin, and languid (he had been sickly since his youth and suffered frequent bouts of ill health), he had a prettily oval face, full lips, and wide round eyes. Appearances were not wholly deceiving. But the two men shared one defining trait: both

Henry Salt.

were self-consciously marginal figures keen to reinvent themselves, and both discovered collecting as a prime way to do this. For Henry Salt, collecting antiquities was to be a way of attaining social prominence in Britain; for Drovetti, it was a means to money, power, and influence in a France he had never seen.

While Drovetti's career was a textbook case of Napoleonic meritocracy in action, Salt's journey from a middle-class background in the provinces to the post of consul-general in Egypt demonstrated how far one could get in early-nineteenth-century Britain on the strength of connections and patronage. The youngest of eight children, Salt was born in Lichfield in 1780, to a successful doctor. Dr. Salt provided well for his family: when he died in 1817 he was able to leave Henry £5,000, a very handsome legacy for a youngest son. But much to his chagrin, Henry Salt was not a gentleman, he was not rich, he did not go to university, and—worst of all—he would have to earn his own living.

Forced to find a career for himself, young Henry decided to become an artist, fantasizing that he might become a fashionable society portraitist. (Salt's father supported his son's choice, with the rather more realistic view, it later emerged, that his son would be a drawing master.) Salt went to London in 1797, where he studied with Joseph Farington and then with the portrait painter Johann Hoppner. His performance was mediocre at best. In the frank assessment of his friend, biographer, and fellow painter John James Halls, Salt was neither talented, virtuous ("he was continually falling prey to indiscretions"), nor diligent: "Like the wild Indian, he slumbered away existence until the calls of necessity, or ambition, awoke him from his trance. . . ."[50] He was, however, acutely ambitious. In London the young man gazed upon a world of wealth, luxury, fashion, and style that he craved to join. "It was not very difficult for his intimates to discover . . . the thirst for fame, and the deep-seated ambition that formed the master-spring of his actions," Halls recalled:

> In the gratification of his love of distinction he neglected nothing which seemed likely to ensure his final triumph, and no honourable means of obtaining it appeared too insignificant for his notice. . . . [I]n his serious moments, he frequently observed to me, it should go hard with him, if before the close of his life he did not obtain some respectable niche in the temple of Fame.[51]

Salt had no doubt he was destined for greatness. The trick was figuring out how to achieve it.

A chance encounter, one June day in 1799, gave Salt his big break. While visiting the gallery of the Swiss-born painter Henry Fuseli, he happened to run into an uncle, who was there with his employer's son, Lord Valentia. Salt immediately cultivated a friendship with the viscount, who was ten years his senior. When he learned that Valentia was planning a major expedition to the East, Salt begged to be able to go with him as artist and all-purpose acolyte. Amazingly, the viscount engaged him. Suddenly Salt "saw the path to fame opened before him"; the voyage would alter the course of his life.[52] Valentia and his party arrived in Calcutta in January 1803, and for the next three years meandered through South Asia, the Arabian and African coasts of the Red Sea, and finally Egypt. Throughout their travels Valentia kept a journal, while Salt labored hard to document the voyage visually. After returning to Britain in 1806, Valentia published his notes in a lavish three-volume narrative, *Voyages and Travels in India, Ceylon, the Red Sea, Abyssinia and Egypt* . . . (1809), accompanied by a separate folio of twenty-four colored plates by Salt. Salt's work, while not inspired, was competent and well received, and earned him a modest degree of recognition.

At a time when tourism rarely took Europeans overseas, Valentia's extended trip around the Indian Ocean was highly unusual, to say the least. It has been likened to a Grand Tour, displaced to the East because the Continent was closed off by war. But it would be more accurate to consider Valentia as one of the first British *imperial* tourists. (He had already visited continental Europe at least once, in 1793.) For one thing, his circuit testified to the imperial geography that was coming to link such disparate locations in the first place.

And Valentia envisioned his travels in distinctly imperial terms. He portrayed himself as a gentleman explorer and unofficial diplomat, donating his wealth and free time to the nation's service. His pet project was to encourage British commerce in Arabia and Abyssinia. To this end, he undertook to map the shores of the Red Sea; though the charts were never finished, Annesley Bay, near Massawa, on the Eritrean coast, offers enduring tribute to the viscount's vanity. He also sought to open relations with the regional rulers of Ethiopia, the most powerful of whom—the Ras of Tigray—invited Valentia to come and visit. Considering himself to be "of too much importance to have his own life risqued," Valentia sent Salt into Abyssinia instead, a man "comparatively of no consequence." It was Salt's first diplomatic mission, and it was to help launch him on his future career.[53]

Valentia's accounts of his travels have been widely cited as an example of the patriotic and morally self-righteous British imperial attitudes emerging in the early nineteenth century. Obsessed with racial purity and social hierarchy, convinced of the superiority of whites to non-whites, Christians to heathens, and Britons to everyone else, the Valentia who comes through in the *Voyages and Travels* . . . is an obvious precursor to the "white man's burden" school of late Victorian imperialism. Much of his outlook can be discerned in his character assassination of Claude Martin alone, penned when visiting Lucknow in 1803, which manages to attack France, the nouveau riche, cultural mixing, and loose sexual habits all at the same time. In these attitudes, Valentia took after his idol, Richard Wellesley, and resembled the "Anglicist" imperial administrators of 1820s India, who were committed to imposing Western civilization over "barbaric" Indian practices such as sati, the Hindu custom in which a widow burns herself on her husband's funeral pyre.

But there was more to the moralizing viscount than met the eye. In 1796, not long before Salt met him, Valentia had brought a suit of "criminal conversation"—i.e., adultery—against his wife, Anne, to whom he had been married six years. Such suits were inevitably scandalous, and this one was particularly nasty. Valentia claimed that his wife had had an affair with one of his carousing companions, a well-known rake named John Bellenden Gawler. Anne claimed her husband had done still worse. The noble viscount, her lawyers protested, had "a great aversion" to his wife and a "great intimacy," instead, with his footman George. "They were frequently playing and toying together with each other," deposed Lady Valentia, who "observed said Viscount to pinch said George, and to make use of most indecent familiarities with and toward said George."[54] Since, in the meantime, Valentia "had repeatedly declared he wished for heirs . . . and, so as he had them, he cared not who got them," he had invited Gawler to do the honors. In short, according to the defense, the lord was homosexual, the lady prostituted, the heir illegitimate.

Was it true? The court decided not, and awarded Valentia damages of £2,000. But this was pretty shocking stuff. A full fifteen years after the divorce trial, the poet Lord Byron—hardly a model of propriety himself—found with some embarrassment that "as everybody speaks to him [Valentia], one can't very well avoid it."[55] Certainly the scandal offered ample incentive for the viscount to disappear to the East. It may also explain why there is no entry for him in the compendious *Dictionary of National Biography* (though there is one for Salt).[56] Dredging up Valentia's disgraceful past puts his "imperial" attitudes in a new light: given his notorious background, he had strong personal reasons to insist loudly and publicly on his moral rectitude, and to decry its absence in others.

How much Henry Salt knew about his patron's past is unclear, but he certainly knew how to make the most of his connections. Salt returned from his tour with Valentia bursting with ambitions and dreams. He began to build a patronage network among London's great and good, including the influential Sir Joseph Banks, who was the president of the Royal Society, president of the African Association (founded in 1788 to sponsor African exploration), trustee of the British Museum, and all-purpose nerve center of the British scientific and natural collecting worlds. Thanks to Valentia's urgings at the Foreign Office, and the financial backing of the African Association, Salt received a commission in 1809 to return to Abyssinia, again in pursuit of Valentia's chimerical scheme for Red Sea trade. This was to be another mission of little consequence, but it served Salt well. (Abyssinia was known to contemporary Britons chiefly through the writings of the widely, if unfairly, discredited Scottish traveler James Bruce.) Capitalizing on the exotic allure of his journeys, Salt was elected to the African Association and the Royal Society, and published a short book about his adventures.

These successes earned Salt recognition in the social circles he longed to join. But high society was expensive: he had to borrow from his father to make ends meet, and he still needed a paying job. So when he heard in early April 1815 that Missett had resigned the consul-generalship of Egypt, Salt jumped at the news. This was exactly the sort of position that appealed to him: it offered rank, prestige, importance, and, crucially, a decent income. He immediately mobilized his contacts to lobby for the post. Sir Joseph Banks wrote to the foreign minister Lord Castlereagh earnestly recommending "my friend Mr. Salt . . . who has done himself so much credit and the Public so much service in the Abyssinian journeys."[57] Within three weeks the position was his—and with it, an annual salary of £1,700 (though this also had to cover the running expenses of the consulate, which Salt later estimated to be a crippling £1,950), and the strong probability of a pension for life.[58]

From the margins of the art world, to the margins of London's elite, to the margins of diplomacy, Henry Salt's early career offers a nice glimpse of Regency high society from below. Clearly, he was not lacking in talent or personal charm, but to all intents and purposes, Salt was a professional amateur, with few qualifications for any occupation in particular. His success at winning the Egyptian consulship points to the reach and power of informal patronage networks in Britain at the time. It also underscores the continuing ad hoc nature of Britain's consular service, which had none of the formal structure to be found in the bureaucracies across the Channel.[59]

Egypt was no longer marginal to British policy in the way it had been during the days of George Baldwin, before 1798. Sir Joseph Banks, for instance, recognized the post of consul in Egypt to be "an office of . . . much Public importance in a Country so highly interesting to the Politics of Europe as Egypt has become since the French invasion."[60] What had until quite recently been, in British eyes, an obscure and little-known corner of the eastern Mediterranean—whose commerce Britain was more or less content to see dominated by France and other Mediterranean nations—was now understood to be vital to British commercial and strategic interests.

There was another way in which Egypt's stature had shot up in Britain since 1798. Egyptian antiquities, now proudly on display in the British Museum's Townley Gallery, had earned a place in the public eye. Shortly before he left for Egypt, Salt had a meeting with Sir Joseph Banks. Acting in his capacity as trustee of the British Museum, Banks encouraged Salt to collect antiquities for the museum.[61] (The exact details of their discussion were not recorded, though; a mistake that would haunt Salt's later career.) Salt also received from the Foreign Office, on the heels of his diplomatic instructions, a request from the Society of Antiquaries, asking him to look for "the remaining fragments of the Stone of Rosetta supposed to have been left in the ruins of Fort St. Julian." "The expence of the undertaking," Salt was told, "whether successfull or otherwise, . . . would be most cheerfully supported by an enlighten'd nation, eager to anticipate its Rivals in the prosecution of the best interests of literature and science."[62]

Salt made rapid preparations for departure. In July 1815, he went up to Birmingham (where he was unsuccessfully wooing a "Miss T") and spent £150 from the Foreign Office on diplomatic gifts for Egyptian officials: "2 Pair Turkey Pistols," assorted gems, "Silver Coffee Pot No. 4161," and a silver-plated breadbasket.[63] He then moved on to Staffordshire to say good-bye to Lord Valentia, who had crossed over from Ireland expressly to see him off. "Consider how long we may be separated and the possibility not to say probability that we may never again meet in this world," Valentia had written plaintively. "After so many years that we have been friends I cannot suppose that you will go without coming to me. . . ."[64] The meeting also gave Salt a chance to learn all Valentia's "wishes, respecting the antiques etc. etc. that you are desirous of my procuring for you in Egypt."[65] "If you have anything Abyssinian which you do not now wish to keep," Valentia added, "I shall consider them as a valuable addition to my family museum," in his house at Arley Hall.[66]

Thus Henry Salt sailed from Brighton in August 1815, armed with a double mandate. As consul he was to pursue British political interests in Egypt against any continuing intrigues by the French. He also had a commission to collect antiquities, both to enrich the British Museum's national collections and on behalf of his personal patrons, rich patricians trained to appreciate such things. This gray zone between official and private, between political and cultural, had been occupied by Lord Elgin before him; and, like Elgin, Salt would fall afoul of the ambiguity. He would also discover that his cultural mandate brought him into even more vicious conflict with Drovetti and the French than his political role as consul.

But for now, he basked in his new office. It was no small irony that Salt traveled to Egypt via France, just in time to witness a reprise of sorts of Article XVI of the 1801 Anglo-French treaty of capitulation: another confiscation of French plunder, this time on a grander scale. It was just three months after the Battle of Waterloo, and the British were proudly and conspicuously in evidence in the land of their worst enemy. What a wonderful time, glowed Salt, to be British, to be important, and to be in France! Thanks partly to his new rank, he was able to rub shoulders with dignitaries such as Admiral Sir Sidney Smith and even, briefly, with the Duke of Wellington himself. But perhaps the most memorable moment of his brief stay in Paris was his visit to the Louvre.

Many of Salt's friends and teachers in the art world had flocked to Paris in 1802 to see the continental artworks seized by Napoleon. Now, under the terms of the peace laid down on France by Britain and its allies, all were to be returned to their countries of origin. In a letter to Valentia, Salt gloated,

> Nothing has produced so strong a sensation among the French as the taking away of the pictures and statues from the Louvre. This very sensible and politic measure has rendered the malignant part of the populace perfectly furious, as it at once lowers their pride in the face of the world, and will serve as an everlasting testimony of their having been conquered.

The Apollo Belvedere, the Laocoön, the Venus de Medici, Flemish paintings, hundreds of artworks from Prussia and Vienna, the horses of San Marco—

"which it really was a mercy to take from the execrable triumphal arch on which they had been placed"—all were being returned to their original owners.[67] It was, in effect, the antithesis of collecting an empire: the breaking up of Napoleon's empire was underscored by the dissolution of the Louvre collection, in much the way that artworks plundered by the Nazis would be repatriated after World War II. "The work of devastation had been nearly completed when I left Paris," Salt concluded, but "fortunately for France (as well as England), as I mentioned rather maliciously to one of the French painters, they will still have the *superb* works of David to console them for their losses."[68]

As a onetime artist, Salt of course had particular interest in the fate of these pieces. But what he could not possibly have guessed was how intimately the emptying of the Louvre was to touch his own life. For it was partly to fill these void galleries that France would turn, once again, to Egypt—to collections of antiquities that would bring it honor and acclaim as a nation resurgent. Within a matter of weeks, Henry Salt would find himself at war with Bernardino Drovetti over which nation would possess the better collection, and which man would provide it.

CHAPTER EIGHT

# *Removals*

## 1. The Partisans

Henry Salt reached Alexandria in March 1816. His arrival was a genuine relief for the long-suffering Colonel Missett, whose "health has been so materially injured" by his long service in inhospitable climates "that I have lost the use of my limbs."[1] Almost entirely paralyzed, the outgoing consul was confined to a wheelchair, and suffered terrible pain. The incoming consul, Salt, in the meantime, energetically proceeded down to Cairo, and paid his first official visit to Muhammad Ali in early June. Salt had last seen the pasha during the unsteady days of 1806, when civil war raged in Egypt, and Britain and France each suspected the other of planning an invasion. The two men met again now in a changed world.

From an initially precarious position, challenged by strong Mameluke factions (such as that headed by Alfi Bey), Muhammad Ali Pasha now ruled supreme in Egypt. He had cemented his power in 1811 with a single stroke, as decisive as it was dastardly: In an apparent gesture of goodwill, he invited all the leading Mamelukes—his rivals for power, and sometimes open enemies—up to the Cairo Citadel to attend a ceremony for one of his sons. The Citadel, like most great fortresses, commands a secure hilltop location, with only a few easily closed-off entrances—and exits. After the ceremony, as the beys and *kashifs* (provincial administrators) began to wind their way out of the Citadel, the pasha blocked off the exit gates, trapping them inside the compound. His troops then encircled them and slaughtered every single one. (Drovetti, among others, was shocked by the treachery; but the sultan Mahmud II, who had faced down opposition from the powerful Janissary corps, congratulated Muhammad Ali on this bold and definitive response to internal resistance.)[2]

With his opponents within Egypt thus eliminated, Muhammad Ali began to extend his reach abroad. His first overseas adventure was in the Hijaz province of Ottoman-ruled Arabia. By 1803, followers of the "puritanical" Muslim cleric Muhammad ibn 'abd al-Wahhab had occupied the holy cities of Mecca and Medina, expelling the Ottoman authorities and establishing their own régime and brand of "fundamentalist" religious interpretation. (Wahhabism was revived in the region a century later, and is the established doctrine of present-day Saudi Arabia.) The sultan ordered Muhammad Ali Pasha, as his vassal, to put down the rebellious Wahhabis and reclaim the holy cities for the caliphate. At first Muhammad Ali demurred, but then he embraced the prospect as a chance to increase his power. The invasion of the Hijaz was the first of many campaigns Muhammad Ali and his sons would undertake in various parts of the Middle East. Though initially he ostensibly fought on the sultan's behalf, in practice, Muhammad Ali sought to build an empire within an empire, chiefly at Ottoman expense. In 1831 his son Ibrahim triumphantly invaded Syria and marched onward through Anatolia, almost to the outskirts of Constantinople itself. From 1822, Muhammad Ali occupied the Sudan, and briefly tried to form an army of black Sudanese askaris along the lines of the East India Company's sepoy force. He also hoped to open his own Red Sea trade with India, a subject he raised during his first official meeting with Consul Salt.[3]

By the time Salt returned to Egypt in 1816, Muhammad Ali had also begun a series of internal projects to "modernize" Egypt along European lines. He worked actively to develop Egypt's agricultural potential, industrial production, and educational, medical, and military institutions. Major undertakings included the building of the Mahmudiyya Canal, linking the Mediterranean and the Nile; the founding of numerous schools, hospitals, and the first Arabic newspaper; and the introduction (in 1820) and widespread cultivation of long-fibered Jumel cotton to Egypt, which by 1823 was yielding more than 16 million pounds per year.[4] To achieve these ends, the pasha sought European, and especially French, advisers of all kinds. (Though he had a decided preference for Italian doctors.) As Salt reported in 1816, "Fresh European adventurers are daily flocking into this country."[5] Like Asaf ud-Daula's Awadh a generation earlier, Egypt under Muhammad Ali was a magnet for Europeans looking for work and new lives.

In these three ways—by winning supreme authority and autonomy in

Egypt, by fighting for an Egyptian empire in the Middle East, and by "modernizing" Egypt and its army—Muhammad Ali Pasha easily ranks among the most innovative and powerful leaders of his day. Soon after re-meeting him in 1816, Salt loftily judged the pasha to be "a sensible, and, for a Turk, an extraordinary man, and were he not hampered by the prejudices of those around him, we should soon see a different state of things in Egypt."[6] At one level the remark was a classic piece of Orientalist condescension; but at another, it showed how Salt, like many Europeans, admired Muhammad Ali and acknowledged him to be a remarkably *un*stereotypical ruler, almost *not* Oriental. The pasha was not some lowly foreign nonentity that European governments or their representatives could expect to patronize. He was (at least at this point) a figure to cultivate and to defer to. Furthermore, as a rising, expanding, and near-autonomous state within the rather less resilient Ottoman Empire, Egypt would come to worry European diplomats concerned that its strength might destabilize the empire. European diplomats constantly had to juggle the desire to bolster Egypt and its Westernizing ruler with the goal of protecting Ottoman integrity. In 1840, Muhammad Ali would fall victim to his own success, when Britain and other European powers, acting to preserve the Ottoman Empire, stripped him of most of his conquests and curtailed the size of his military. But for now, he was the beneficiary of European attentions—and those of Britain and France in particular, both keen to support his modernizing program and win him as an ally in the post-Waterloo world.

Since Salt's first visit to Egypt, in 1806, the relative positions of Britain and France there had also changed. Though French influence had once plainly been in the ascendant (particularly after the British defeat of 1807), Salt was now delighted to report that "The French influence is at a low ebb, and the English proudly predominant."[7] To be sure, at the time Salt wrote this, his words might have been applicable just about anywhere in the world. Six weeks after Waterloo, Napoleon sailed toward exile on the East India Company colony of St. Helena. In France, the Bourbon dynasty was restored, and King Louis XVIII (a younger brother of the beheaded Louis XVI) was placed on the throne. Internationally, the specter of a pan-European, if not global, French empire that had seemed so palpable just a few years earlier had now vanished. So, of course, had the prospect of an imminent French invasion of Egypt. Drovetti and the French community dutifully marked the Bourbon Restoration by swapping the revolutionary tricolor for the white Bourbon flag, which was now to be the national emblem. But in their heart of hearts (according to Colonel Missett) they "regret[ted] an event which destroys the hopes they had fondly cherished of seeing this country pass under the dominion of France."[8]

Napoleon's defeat had particular personal consequences for Bernardino Drovetti. Like any régime change, the Bourbon Restoration involved major shifts in administrative personnel. Throughout the government, including in the consular service, Bonapartists were weeded out and replaced by those sympathetic to (or at least willing to tolerate) the new king. Drovetti, who had built his entire career in the Napoleonic bureaucracy, was promptly sacked and ordered to come to Paris. He accepted his dismissal with gritted teeth, promising: "I will acquit myself of my last duties . . . with the same zeal and devotion that I flatter myself always to have shown in the service of the French nation. . . ."[9] He stayed at work until the arrival of his replacements—Roussel and Thédenat, both career foreign service officers—and, as instructed, handed over the administration of the consulate.[10] But Drovetti refused to leave Egypt as he had been ordered to do, and Henry Salt would quickly learn to what effect.

The new French consuls lived in Alexandria, "which leaves me at Cairo," Salt bragged, "undisputed master of the field."[11] That may have been so in terms of winning British influence with the pasha, the first part of Salt's mandate. (Muhammad Ali was in Cairo, where Salt had ready access to him.) But when it came to the second part of his commission, to collect antiquities, Salt soon discovered that the balance was skewed entirely the other way. He began looking for antiquities almost as soon as he arrived, but found the pickings surprisingly slim. It turned out that "Monsieur Drovetti, the quondam French Consul, was in Upper Egypt, buying up everything there to complete a collection upon which he has been engaged some years." When it came to antiquities, the undisputed master of the field was Bernardino Drovetti.

Ever since his first momentous visit to Upper Egypt, with Boutin in 1811, Drovetti had been making annual trips up the Nile, and employing European agents to excavate on his behalf. He was the first person consistently to dig there, and though Egyptian excavations were still far from "scientific" undertakings, the discoveries in themselves were astounding. Drovetti's finds were brought to Cairo, where, by the time Salt arrived in 1816, he already had a massive collection. He never said anything explicit about why he began to dig and collect, but two motives can be adduced. He would certainly have known—and, as a Bonapartist, probably have especially appreciated—the cultural and social value of Egyptian antiquities in the post-1798 world. Antiquities could win him prestige and possibly career advancement. Collecting on behalf of France, furthermore, might have offered him—a Piedmontese and thus outsider to France—a way to underline his loyalty to the French state. A second incentive was surely mercenary. Books such as the *Description de l'Égypte* and Denon's *Voyage*, Egyptian antiquities in the British Museum, and Egyptomaniac motifs in the decorative arts and beyond had transmitted interest in Egyptian antiquities across Europe (and to some extent the United States, although serious American collecting would take off only in the 1840s). Museums and private collectors were increasingly eager to acquire such items, which meant that collecting could be an excellent source of cash.

As long as Drovetti had served as consul, collecting could consume only part of his attention. Now that he was unemployed, it became his raison d'être. For more than a dozen years he had made his life in Egypt, together with Rosine and their son. Sometimes he said he would pack up his collection and move to France; but he invariably changed his mind. Drovetti clearly mistrusted the France of the Bourbons, the France that had fired him. But "he did not doubt the friendship of the Pasha," with whom he had now long been intimate. Drovetti also enjoyed the steadfast support of Muhammad Ali's closest adviser, Boghos Bey, who apparently owed his career to Drovetti for having first introduced him to the pasha. "Nobody knows Egypt better," observed Drovetti's successor, Roussel (who was on the whole rather wary of Drovetti, certainly the most influential "Frenchman" in Egypt): "he is a walking dictionary of the country . . ."[12]

Toward the end of 1816, Salt went to inspect Drovetti's collection in

Drovetti and his assistants.

Cairo. It "contains a great variety of curious articles and some of extraordinary value," he found. "The whole is intended for sale . . . [and] I imagine, will not be sold for less than three or four thousand pounds."[13] (Based on the inflation rate of retail goods, this would amount to some £200,000 today.) Expensive though it was, the collection appealed strongly to Salt. Eager to fulfill the wishes of Sir Joseph Banks and acquire antiquities for Britain, Salt "tried to persuade [Drovetti] to send proposals to the British Museum." (Though he did "not know whether" the museum was "rich enough to buy it.")[14] If Drovetti's antiquities went to London, they would make the British Museum's Egyptian collection far and away the greatest in Europe. Of course, it would have been the ultimate piece of *arrivisme*: Britain, which had hardly paid any mind to Egypt and its antiquities before 1801, would acquire in one fell swoop what French agents had invested years in building up (in much the way it had confiscated the savants' antiquities before). But it could also have been the perfect arrangement for Drovetti and Salt personally: Salt would have accomplished his social and cultural mission, and Drovetti would have received his money.

And for one brief moment, it looked as if there might be a meeting of the minds between the two men, and between the rival nations whose interests they sought to serve. But that was the rub. This was not just about money; it was about personal and national prestige. Drovetti had no interest in seeing his antiquities go to the British Museum, as the Rosetta stone had previously done. According to the Comte de Forbin, a director of the Louvre who visited Egypt in 1817, Drovetti's "dearest wish . . . would be to embellish the museum of Paris" with his collection. It was "in this hope that he has ceaselessly refused to sell it, despite the brilliant offers that have been made to him."[15] Drovetti categorically rejected Salt's offers to sell his collection to Britain. If Britain wanted Egyptian antiquities, then Salt would have to dig them up himself.

So it was that within just months of Salt's arrival in Egypt the stage was set for what was to be a decade-long contest between the two men. It seemed so strange, at one level, that Salt and Drovetti should find themselves at odds. After all, as Consul Roussel observed, Drovetti's "taste for antiquity might have seemed to bring him together with Mr. Salt . . . , who having the same inclinations, had full power from the antiquaries of London to make whatever expenditures he thought fit to acquire Egyptian monuments." But rather than come together over antiquities, he noted, with evident surprise, "Mr. Drovetti has wanted to fight against him. The result has been rivalry and hatred."[16] How Drovetti could even afford to pursue the "ruinous struggle for antiquities with Mr. Salt" was a mystery to Roussel.[17]

Yet it must have been that very congruence between them that made their struggle so intense. For like so many imperial collectors, Salt and Drovetti were both marginal men on the make. Their dedicated pursuit of emergent national interests played out the quest for self-advancement on a wider field. Drovetti was not, by birth, French; he was also now a political outsider thanks to the Bourbon Restoration. If he wanted to make his way back into a government job, to say nothing of acquiring further honors and a higher status, he had to find some way of ingratiating himself with the new régime. Salt, for his part, had been scrabbling his way up from the undistinguished ranks of the provincial bourgeoisie ever since he first went to London as a teenager, and he ached to join the glamorous world of aristocrats and connoisseurs. With the consulship, he had attained his highest point yet, and he fully intended to use his new position to continue clambering to the top. Even as the European continent relaxed into peace, in Egypt the elements for another sort of Anglo-French war converged: a competition between Britain and France for informal empire in an up-and-coming Eastern power, and a competition between two marginal men for status, recognition, and money.

And things were about to get a lot more intense. In the summer of 1816, a new agent stepped into the vortex of national and personal ambitions. His name was Giambattista Belzoni, and he was another marginal figure out to reinvent himself. Belzoni would bring the business of excavating and exporting Egyptian antiquities to a new level. He would also spark the tension between Britain and France into open, unabashed conflict.

## II. The Patriot

So small it barely figures on maps of Europe, the island of Malta seems a secret and secluded place, its fantastic natural harbor at Valletta shut away from the sea by high stone walls. But the island is a natural crossroads, too, as even the Maltese language, a form of Arabic with heavy Italian influence, attests. Poised between North Africa and Europe, this is a way station, a place for strangers and birds of passage. Among the drifters wandering the streets of Valletta in the late autumn of 1814 was the thirty-six-year-old Paduan-born Giambattista Belzoni. He was not sure what to do.[18]

Belzoni would have been easy to pick out of the crowd, for he had one defining characteristic: he was a giant. At some six foot eight, he was exceptionally tall, even by today's standards, and was to boot full-chested, burly, and strong enough to lift ten men. It must have been Belzoni's sheer bulk that first caught the eye of the Egyptian admiral Ismael Gibraltar. Ismael had come to Malta to recruit skilled Europeans to work for Muhammad Ali Pasha. Belzoni, rootless and jobless, was only too happy to be enlisted. He told Ismael that he was experienced in hydraulics, and could design a waterwheel for the pasha that would improve agricultural irrigation. Ismael duly promised Belzoni work, and in May of 1815 (just as Henry Salt was lobbying for the consulship), Belzoni and his wife sailed toward Alexandria.[19]

"Hydraulic engineer," as Belzoni represented himself, was a fanciful characterization at best. In fact, Belzoni—the son of a barber—had been odd-jobbing his way around Europe ever since he was eighteen. After the French invaded his native Italy in 1796 he spent seven years roaming the Continent, before crossing to Britain during the Peace of Amiens in 1803. There, thanks to his enormous physical stature, he tried out another new occupation: pantomime actor and itinerant fairground performer. Known as "the Patagonian Sampson," Belzoni performed various feats of strength such as walking up and down the stage carrying eleven men in a specially constructed iron harness.[20] He traveled around much of Britain with fairground troupes, and also acted regularly at the Sadler's Wells Theatre in London. It was there that he gained what experience of "hydraulic engineering" he possessed, by helping the theater's management create the effect of "real water" onstage, for a reenactment of the great Spanish siege of Gibraltar during the American Revolution.

Giambattista Belzoni, in Oriental dress.

Belzoni's early career offers a rare glimpse into a largely anonymous population in wartime Europe: the many civilians who crossed borders looking for work and fleeing from war. Shifting to Britain had a defining effect on Belzoni's future travels and identity. From then on, he circulated primarily in what might be considered a British sphere of influence, accompanied by an English wife, Sarah.[21] (They had no children, "nor would want to have any," Belzoni later wrote, "as they would be a complete hindrance to my travels"—though from 1810 an "Irish lad" named James Curtin traveled with them as a kind of all-purpose servant.)[22] In 1812, Belzoni went to Portugal, Britain's ally; 1813 saw the Belzonis in Madrid, just liberated by the British; and when they arrived in Malta in 1814, they were entering a British colony whose status had just been formalized by the Treaty of Paris. But it was in Egypt, ultimately, that Belzoni would explicitly affiliate himself with his adopted land.

The Belzonis reached Egypt during the plague season of 1815, and waited out the disease in the French compound (*okel*) before traveling on to Cairo, where Boghos Bey arranged lodging for them in a rickety wooden house in Bulaq. It took a full year before Belzoni got a chance to demonstrate his ox-powered waterwheel for Muhammad Ali Pasha. The design appeared to be successful, but the demonstration, alas, was not. "[B]y way of a frolic," the pasha asked to see the wheel turned by men instead of oxen; in the attempt, young James Curtin was thrown to the ground and broke his hip. Thus was Belzoni's foray into hydraulic engineering cursed, and "all that was due to me from the Bashaw was consigned to oblivion. . . ."[23] Suddenly, if not for the first time, Belzoni found himself penniless and unemployed in a foreign country. He would emerge from his predicament in a new incarnation entirely: adventurer in the name of Britain.

In the event, it was another adoptive Briton, the Swiss-born explorer Jean-Louis (or "John Lewis") Burckhardt, who extended the disappointed Belzoni a helping hand. Though he was only thirty-one, Burckhardt was already well on his way into the pantheon of intrepid Eastern travelers. Disguised as a Muslim named "Sheikh Ibrahim," he was the first European to encounter the ancient city of Petra in what is now southern Jordan, which emerges like a magic kingdom at the end of a narrow canyon of pink rock. That June of 1816, Burckhardt had just returned to Cairo after an excursion of more than two years, south into Nubia, where he had discovered the Temple of Abu Simbel; and then across the Red Sea to Arabia, where he had successfully performed the pilgrimage to Mecca. On his journey up the Nile, Burckhardt had been captivated by a massive monolithic bust he saw lying in the sand at the Ramesseum (the mortuary temple of Ramses II), in Luxor. The sculpture was called "the Young Memnon," and had also been much admired by the French savants, who tried to remove it—and failed, leaving a large hole in its chest. How splendid it would be, Burckhardt thought, if Britain could claim the sculpture instead! Virtually a monolith himself, boundlessly energetic, and apparently resourceful, Belzoni struck him as just the right man to attempt the job.[24]

Henry Salt arrived in Cairo just as Burckhardt and Belzoni were concocting a plan. Burckhardt and Salt knew each other from London, where they were fellow members of the African Association and had many mutual friends. (Salt was in fact rather jealous of "Sheikh Ibrahim," four years his junior, more famous, and universally adored.) Burckhardt suggested that they pool their resources to hire Belzoni to move the Young Memnon, and present the bust to the British Museum. Salt instantly agreed. "This is a godsend indeed!" he exclaimed when Burckhardt introduced him to Belzoni. On June 28, 1816, the two men gave Belzoni a set of written instructions to remove the head.[25] Salt also gave him "some thousand piasters [about £25] to enable him to excavate and buy antiquities, solely on his (Mr. Salt's) account."[26]

The agreement launched both men's careers in Egyptian collecting. Salt secured a prized piece for the British Museum, and an agent to dig and purchase on his behalf. Belzoni got a much-needed job, and he also got something more. To Belzoni, the agreement with Salt signaled the beginning of a patriotic and personal mission. "I was making researches for antiquities, which were to be placed in the British Museum," he said proudly.[27] What neither man could know was that their apparently harmonious business relationship would end in acrimony and public recriminations.

For the next three years, Belzoni would later write, "my constant occupation was searching for antiquities." He was fascinated by them, with an "enthusiasm . . . which I can trace from my younger days while in Rome."[28] He was also remarkably lucky at finding and moving them. Burckhardt had not been wrong in his estimation of Belzoni's talents. Between 1816 and 1819, Belzoni successfully managed to open the sand-choked Temple of Abu Simbel; to discover the magnificently decorated tomb of the pharaoh Seti I in the Valley of the Kings; and to locate the entrance to the Second Pyramid at Giza. In addition to shipping the Young Memnon to London, Belzoni was also responsible for moving and exporting some of the biggest and best-known Egyptian antiquities in Britain today, including the alabaster sarcophagus of Seti I, which now sits in the basement of the Sir John Soane Museum in London, and the massive red granite head and arm of Amenhotep III, joining the Young Memnon in the British Museum.

Belzoni described his adventures in a best-selling book, *Narrative of the*

*Operations and Recent Discoveries in the Pyramids, Temples, Tombs, and Excavations, in Egypt and Nubia* . . . (1820), which ran to three editions in as many years. His exploits make as gripping reading now as they did when first published, a time when stories of adventure and exploration were massively popular with the British public. But the tale of collecting in Egypt, as Belzoni told it, was more than just another exotic travel narrative. This was a chronicle of war: war with Drovetti and with France.

From his first days traveling up the Nile in 1816—when he was darkly advised "not to meddle in this business, for I should meet with many disagreeable things, and have many obstacles to encounter"—to his last weeks in Egypt in 1819, spent in a fruitless legal proceeding against two of Drovetti's henchmen, Belzoni felt the dark forces of France militating against him at every turn. In the field, French agents tried to deprive him of the best excavation sites, to interfere with his supplies and transport, and even to damage his discoveries, if not his person. Egyptian government officials, bribed by French agents, denied him permissions; and local Egyptians, bullied into submission by partisans of France, refused to work for him. The kingpin of this dastardly ring was Bernardino Drovetti, to whom Belzoni had applied for patronage in his first months in Egypt, but whom he would leave Egypt cursing, four years later.[29] Indeed, so obsessive is Belzoni's anti-French tone throughout the book that one has to wonder whether he was moved by patriotism or paranoia. How much he consciously tailored his narrative of "French" villainy to appeal to his British readership is also an open question.[30] But the message itself was clear enough. Each antiquity he collected was a trophy of victory: over time, over the sun and the sand, over the Egyptians, and, especially, over France.

The Young Memnon was a case in point. Belzoni found the bust just as Burckhardt had described it, in the ruins of the Ramesseum, pitched into the sand near the broken "remains of its body and chair, with its face upwards, and apparently smiling on me, at the thought of being taken to England."[31] The granite head stands some nine feet high and weighs eleven tons, so figuring out how to move it was no mean feat. Belzoni successfully levered the monolith onto a rolling platform, and had it tugged toward the river a few hundred painful yards per day by a team of laborers. By October 1816, just in time to take advantage of the Nile's seasonal fluctuations, the bust was sitting on the riverbank ready to be embarked for Cairo. Belzoni congratulated himself on a job swiftly and speedily done.

But "two French agents of Mr. D[rovetti]"—the Marseillais Jean-Jacques Rifaud, who was Drovetti's principal agent, and a mineralogist named Frédéric Cailliaud—were less than pleased. "On seeing the head," Belzoni

Moving the "Young Memnon."

claimed, "they positively declared . . . that the French invaders did not take it away, because they thought it not worth the taking!" Their Niçois dragoman Joseph Rossignana, whom Belzoni described as "a renegado Frenchman, observed to me, that, if I persevered in my researches, I should have my throat cut. . . ." The Frenchmen apparently went on to tell the villagers "that, if they sold any article of antiquity to the English party, they would have them well beaten" by the *kashif* (the regional administrator).[32] Their intrigues notwithstanding, Belzoni obtained the *kashif*'s permission to embark the bust in mid-November, sealing his bargain with a gift of "two small bottles of anchovies and two of olives."[33]

The Young Memnon reached Cairo with the Belzonis a month later, where the historian al-Jabarti went with Burckhardt ("Sidi Ibrahim al-Mahdi al-Inklizi") to see it at Salt's house. Belzoni then accompanied it on to Alexandria, from whence it would be shipped off to Britain.[34] "The English in Egypt place a lot of importance . . . on the transport of this head from Luxor to Alexandria," grumbled the French consul Roussel. "What the French army, they say, could not execute, one man alone, funded by us [the boasting British], has achieved."[35] The leading British merchant in Alexandria, Samuel Briggs, "felt the pleasure of a true Englishman, in seeing one of the most finished monuments of Egyptian art ready to be embarked for his native country."[36] Salt was equally delighted. Belzoni's "great talents and uncommon genius for mechanics," he wrote, "have enabled him, with singular success, both at Thebes and other places, to discover objects of the rarest value in antiquity . . . and with trifling means to remove colossal fragments, which appeared, by their own declaration, to have defied the efforts of the able engineers which accompanied the French army."[37] The Young Memnon was shipped in late 1817, and by the following year it was on display in the British Museum.[38]

In every way it was a triumph—and just the first of many such victories Belzoni scored against the French while on the trail of antiquities. Salt was so pleased by Belzoni's success that "seeing the necessity of 'striking while the iron was hot' (to use a vulgar phrase), all the world having begun to look after antiquities, and Drovetti having employed half a dozen agents, I succeeded in engaging Belzoni to stay another year."[39] Belzoni set off for Luxor again in the winter of 1817. As ever, the French were on his tail, "making a forced march to Thebes . . . to arrive there before us, and purchase all that had been accumulated by the Arabs in the preceding season; so that we should have had no chance of buying anything on our arrival."[40] Like claimants in a gold rush, the two sides dashed into the ruins of Karnak and Luxor to stake out the patches most "evidently pregnant with objects worthy the risk of excavation." The contest for space was so bitter that in later seasons the French and British would prearrange their turf, "so all was well understood" about who could excavate where.[41]

This was to be Belzoni's greatest season for feats and finds. On October 16, 1817, "one of the best [days] perhaps of my life," he discovered the entrance to the tomb of Seti I in the Valley of the Kings. The brilliantly painted tomb, though three thousand years old, seemed "as if just finished on the day we entered it." Belzoni thrilled with "the pleasure of discovering what has long been sought in vain, and of presenting the world with a new and perfect monument of Egyptian antiquity. . . ." Deep inside they found a sarcophagus made of creamy, translucent alabaster, "not having its equal in the world, and being such as we had no idea could exist. . . . I cannot give an idea of this beautiful and invaluable piece of antiquity, and can only say, that nothing has been brought into Europe from Egypt that can be compared with it."[42] The tomb is still referred to as "Belzoni's Tomb," and discovering it has placed Belzoni with some justice among those early antiquities-hunters who might also in some sense be considered Egyptologists. (The same has been said of Drovetti's agent Rifaud, who spent twelve years excavating, and making detailed drawings and notes.)[43]

It was a good time for British digging in general. Salt had been "working to obtain from the Pasha the exclusive right to acquire and export ancient statues," and by the end of 1817 had gotten the pasha's "*carte blanche*" to excavate.[44] With "lots of money, and lots of presents," the British had won "the affection of the Arabs." (Salt also kept Muhammad Ali well supplied with what some said was his favorite European product of all, Bordeaux wine.)[45] But conflict was never far off, for "M. Drovetti in the meantime struggles with perseverance against these new masters of Egypt," observed the Louvre director Forbin—and Belzoni would soon feel the consequences.[46]

In the summer of 1816, Belzoni had traveled as far south as the Nile's first cataract, to the lovely Ptolemaic temple of Philae, on a small island near Aswan. While there, he "took possession" of sixteen stone blocks with reliefs and a twenty-two-foot-long granite obelisk, "in the name of his Britannic Majesty's consul-general in Cairo." He paid the Aga of Aswan to post a guard on the antiquities until he could come back with a boat large enough to carry them away. The following spring, Belzoni duly returned to Philae to take away the stones. But a nasty shock awaited him. The carvings had been "mutilated, and written upon in the French language, '*opération manquée*.' " There was no mistaking the hand behind this: Belzoni blamed the vandalism on the same unholy French trio who had stood in his way when he was moving the Young Memnon.[47]

Worse was to come. Salt had promised the Philae obelisk to William John Bankes, a gentleman traveler from Dorset, who asked Belzoni to move it up to Alexandria for him. Belzoni "gladly accepted" the job, "as I was pleased to have the opportunity of seeing another piece of antiquity on its way to England . . . ," and returned to Philae for a third and final time, in November 1818, to fetch the obelisk. As soon as he arrived, however, an old man accosted him and thrust a piece of paper in his face. It was an officious note written by another of Drovetti's agents, Lebolo, announcing that the obelisk belonged to the French and was on no account to be removed. Lebolo, it seemed, had "adopted the method of a trick" to persuade the locals that the piece belonged to him: "he pretended he could read the hieroglyphics on the obelisk, and said it was written, that the obelisk belonged to Mr. Drovetti's ancestors; consequently he had a right to it." Then he bribed the local judge to issue a decree to that effect.[48] Fortunately, Belzoni had "gifts" in hand, too: a gold watch for the Aga of Aswan, who supported Belzoni's claim. Disregarding the objections of the Drovetti camp, Belzoni loaded the obelisk onto a boat and sailed it back up to Luxor, where he tied it up near his ongoing excavations, right "under the nose" of the French.[49]

On Boxing Day 1818, Belzoni returned to his dig at Karnak, riding into the temple on an ass. "Our opponents, with their commander, Mr. Drovetti, were lodged in some mud houses among the ruins of Karnak," Belzoni said; on several patches of ground he had marked out for himself, he found "the labourers of Mr. Drovetti" working instead. Belzoni sensed something was afoot, but rode quietly on through the ruins. Suddenly, Lebolo and Rossignana came running toward him, followed by thirty or so Egyptians. Grabbing the reins of Belzoni's donkey and brandishing a large stick, Lebolo demanded to know why Belzoni had taken the Philae obelisk. Belzoni's servant was knocked to the ground and beaten; and "the renegado Rossignano reached within four yards of me, and with all the rage of a ruffian, levelled a double-barrelled gun at my breast, loading me with all the imprecations that a villain could invent. . . . Rossignano still keeping the gun pointed at my breast, said, that it was time that I should pay for all I had done to them." In the midst of this, another band of Egyptians appeared, led by Drovetti himself, who "demanded in a tone not inferior to that of his disciples, what reason or authority I had to stop his people from working. . . ." With his servant lying beaten on the ground, dozens of hostile men surrounding him, and a gun aimed at his chest, even the giant Belzoni trembled.[50]

In the end, Belzoni escaped the melée unscathed. He was saved—"would anyone suppose it!"—by the Egyptians of Karnak: "Those wild Arabs, as we call them, were disgusted at the conduct of Europeans and interfered in my behalf. They surrounded the renegado Rossignano, whose conduct they thought most outrageous and base, not for an European, but even for the worst of Arabs." But the incident had killed something in Belzoni. Antiquities, he decided, were no longer worth the fight. He gathered up his most recent discoveries and headed downriver with the steadfast Sarah, the offending obelisk, and fresh scores to settle. In Alexandria, he pursued a case against Lebolo and Rossignana, but "the French consul put an end to it . . . by only saying, that the two persons accused were not French subjects, but Piedmontese; and that if we wanted redress, we must go to Turin for it."[51] It was the crowning insult.

So it was that Giambattista Belzoni left Egypt in 1819, thanking God, "not that I disliked the country I was in, for, on the contrary, I have reason to be grateful; nor do I complain of the Turks or Arabs in general, but of some Europeans who are in that country, whose conduct and mode of thinking are a disgrace to human nature."[52] Two years later, he still remembered the attack as if it were fresh. "Nonistanding the Two yars [*sic*] which had elapsed since the atempt was met on my life," he wrote to a friend in Egypt (in a rare sample of his unedited English),

> I can not look back on these scines without horor and contempt for those whom have been the cause of it, Mr. Drovettis persecution against me did not end in Egypt, [h]is [defenders] med an atempt even in Paris, but with that suceses it deserve, and he found that the rights of law and justice, was not so easly thretned away in Paris as it was in Alexandria.[53]

Of course, the French consul's insistence that Lebolo and Rossignana were "not French subjects" underscores the central paradox in all this melodrama. Neither Belzoni nor Drovetti had a drop of British or French blood in his veins. As Belzoni announced on the very first page of his book, "I am not an Englishman"; and he never severed his ties with his Paduan family and home. Yet it was in the name of Britain that he proudly collected, and it was to Britain that he returned in 1819 with his antiquities. His hostility to France was everywhere evident, cemented by personal animosity toward Drovetti and his agents. But Belzoni's sworn attachment to Britain also brought him into conflict with an enemy in an unexpected quarter. For there was another rival in Belzoni's life, and that was none other than Henry Salt.

## III. A Clash of Reinventions

Without a doubt, Henry Salt had started putting on airs. As His Britannic Majesty's Consul in Egypt, Salt had become a man of title and rank. In the spring of 1817, he inherited £5,000 from his father—the equivalent of several hundred thousand pounds today—which made him a man of means as well. What better way to show off his newfound affluence, and his prestigious position, than to collect antiquities? Two prominent models of gentlemen collec-

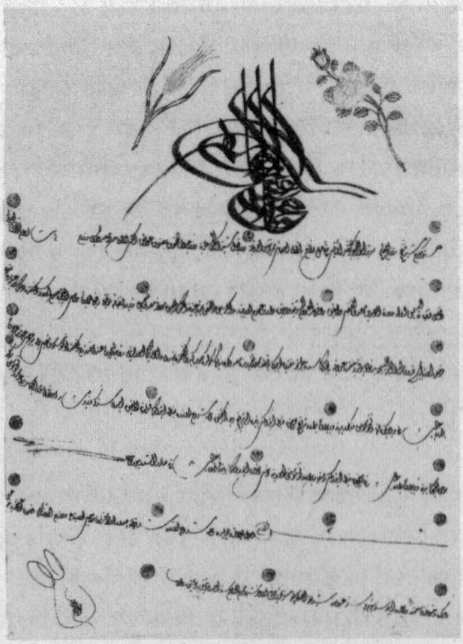

Henry Salt's *firman* granting him permission to excavate and collect antiquities.

tors in diplomatic office might instantly have presented themselves: Sir William Hamilton, who as British envoy in Naples avidly collected (and dealt in) Etruscan vases and other antiquities; and of course the notorious Lord Elgin, who had used his diplomatic negotiating power with the Ottoman authorities to win the *firman* to remove the friezes from the Parthenon, the "Elgin Marbles."

By the end of 1816, Salt had "been very successful" in acquiring antiquities for Lord Valentia, "so that I shall in spring have to send you a cargo of such things as I believe you have not before seen." (Valentia had recently inherited his father's title, the Earl of Mountnorris, and was henceforth known as Mountnorris.) But, Salt continued,

> I must however inform you, that I am so bit with the prospect of what may still be done in Upper Egypt, as to feel unable to abstain from forming a collection myself; you may however depend on coming in for a good share, and though my collection may prevent yours from being unique, yet you may rely on the refusal of it, should I ever part with it, and upon my leaving it to you should I die.[54]

It was a breezy announcement, and indeed a breezy enough sentiment: Salt was in Egypt, with money, with access to antiquities, and with social ambition aplenty. Though he had arrived in Egypt intending to collect for his nation and his patrons, now he was in it for himself, too.

But this casual statement evidently struck the Earl of Mountnorris hard, as a letter from Salt implies. "You say in your letter that you are sorry I did not when we talked on the subject give you notice that I meant to collect as it has proved a great disappointment," Salt blurted out defensively, "but the fact was I had no intention of the kind. Circumstances which occurred after I arrived led me to think much might be done and I was therefore tempted to make a bold push—before Drovettis eyes were opened." "My ideas of collecting," he added in a postscript, "have been brought on by finding it the only solace of existance in this place for as to the society it is most wretched." Furthermore, Salt had been told "that no Pensions are ever allowed to Consuls," and he hoped "to collect a few things of such value that if ever I should be obliged to quit Egypt from ill health or an inclination to return it might furnish . . . the means of living in some nook or corner in Europe. . . ." "If I should be lucky in this way [collecting]," he concluded, "you will own that it is more reasonable that I should reap the advantage than even my best friend."[55]

Apparently Mountnorris did not. Months after their first hostile exchange, Salt was still justifying his actions: "I have been hurt by the content of your letter as I never made any promise (to my recollection) to collect exclusively for you but merely offering to do so as a means of obliging you."[56] Indeed, he insisted, he sent the best of everything to Mountnorris, keeping for himself only lesser objects:

> which I think of sufficient value to cover all my expences of that year. And this I considered myself fully entitled to do as indeed you fully admit in one of your last letters . . . [I] trust you will then renounce your opinion "that you believe you have received the tracts [dregs?] and that what was worth keeping has found its way into my collection" otherwise "we must measure swords and part."[57]

Why was Mountnorris so bitterly disturbed at the idea of Salt collecting for himself? Part of the answer may simply have been greed. Salt's glowing reports of his (or rather, his agents') great discoveries at Thebes rankled with the earl, who wanted his own collection to be unique and unrivaled in Britain. Part, surely, stemmed from snobbery. It was looking to Mountnorris alarmingly as if Salt, his junior and his obvious social inferior, might out-collect him, surpassing him on an important cultural playing field. This upstart, his former protégé no less, was aiming to join the ranks of gentlemen.

Mountnorris was not the only one to criticize Salt for entertaining ideas above his station. A piece of doggerel penned in 1820 by the Naples-based Sir William Gell—a sometime diplomat and courtier, and a noted antiquarian—cleverly, if cruelly, satirizes Salt's social affectations. Gell entitled his poem "Saline Verses":

*If you travel in Egypt tis reckon'd a fault*
*To be seen on the Nile without letters for Salt.*
*But be sure, when you shew your credentials to say*
*What dropp'd from Your intimate friend Castlereagh*
*Whom you met at the travellers club t'other day.*
*Who seem'd quite consoled when he thought that at Cairo*
*That good fellow Salt rul'd instead of old Pharaoh . . .*
*Not a word of Mountnorris—that interest is past*
*Sense of favours conferr'd is not likely to last.*
*And hint not oh hint not one word about painting*
*Unless you would set the Great Consul a fainting*
*But lock up your papers and hide all your drawing*
*If you wish to be safe from his pilfering and clawing*
*And whatever you do hold your head up in Alt*
*Or you're likely to profit but little by Salt.*[58]

Gell's caustic rhymes show how Salt was seen in exactly those genteel British diplomatic and scholarly circles he fancied himself a part of—and that is, snidely. Gell himself never went to Egypt (he knew and corresponded with Salt, however), but he passed his derision along to a number of young British gentlemen travelers who did visit Egypt in the 1820s, and thus arrived primed to scoff at the consul. (One of the more prominent of these men, James Burton, copied "Saline Verses" into his notebook.)

Mountnorris, Gell, and others sniffed at Salt from above, clearly made uneasy by his penetration of the elite collecting world (especially because they themselves were nearer its margins than its center). But none had greater cause to complain of Salt's pretensions than his own social inferior, Giambattista Belzoni. The problems between the two men began in 1817, when Salt made his first visit to the storied temples of the south, in the company of an aristocrat, Somerset Lowry-Corry, Earl of Belmore. (Like Mountnorris, Belmore was an Irish peer, a marginal aristocrat.) The earl was traveling around the eastern Mediterranean accompanied by his countess, his half-brother, his children (both legitimate and illegitimate), his chaplain, and his personal physician, the pompous Dr. Robert Richardson, who came to treat the earl's gout—the relief of which was the ostensible purpose of the journey.[59] This was the first time that a British family had come to Egypt simply as tourists, let alone a party of such high rank. Looking after them gave Salt a splendid chance to show off his talents as diplomat and gentleman connoisseur. After a stay in Cairo (where Salt introduced Belmore to Muhammad Ali, and took the family on a camping trip to the pyramids), the consul accompanied the Belmores on a luxurious tour into Upper Egypt.[60]

Their flotilla of five boats tied up at Thebes in mid-November, where Salt found Belzoni hard at work in the tomb of Seti I, discovered just one month before. Everybody who saw the tomb was overwhelmed by it: Drovetti, apparently, was so lavish with his expressions of praise "that when he came to something that really called for epithets of applause and admiration, his magazine of stuff was expended, and he stood in speechless astonishment. . . ."[61] Salt, for his part, was over the moon with delight at the discovery—made, as he put it, "under my auspices." "In the new tomb I have found a sarcophagus of white alabaster, covered with hieroglyphics," he proudly wrote to Mountnorris (note the pronoun "I") and listed off the other finds "he" had made.[62] Indeed, "so enraptured" was he by all that he saw that he stayed on in Thebes for four months to superintend excavations himself.[63]

But Salt's proprietary attitude toward the discoveries at Thebes sat very poorly indeed with Belzoni, who was deeply insulted by Salt's treatment of him as little better than a glorified manservant. Belzoni was not digging for this pale, pretentious functionary; he was digging for Britain! Righteous outrage welled up within him. One day, soon after the Belmores left Luxor, Belzoni overheard Salt telling another group of English visitors how long the Paduan had been "in my employ." That was it. Belzoni snapped. "Suddenly" he "broke out in the most violent terms." He "declared, to my great astonishment," Salt later recounted, "that 'he had never been employed by me, that he had been working for the British Nation, (being the first time he had ever started such a notion,) and . . . that he was an independent man,' &c." Salt was completely taken aback. From that moment on, he said, "the conduct of Mr. Belzoni became strangely changed: repeated and very unpleasant altercations took place, in which he unfolded pretensions to which I informed him I could never accede, while throughout he exhibited an unfounded jealousy of my assuming all the merit of these discoveries."[64]

Belzoni's outburst was dramatic, certainly; but were his fears as "unfounded" as Salt believed?[65] "I have uniformly done justice to his talents and to his discoveries . . . ," Salt insisted. "In fine, I found him in difficulty and almost in despair, and afforded him the means of distinguishing himself; through me, his situation in life was entirely changed, and he has become, on account of his discoveries, the object of public admiration." Yet as even this rather patronizing explanation makes clear, there was no doubt that Salt, the self-declared gentleman collector, considered Belzoni his lackey: "I looked upon myself, with regard to him, in no other light than as a gentleman might consider himself relatively to an architect whom he had employed to build a house," he said.[66] And nothing could offend Belzoni more. He had waged his entire competition against Drovetti and "the French" to collect antiquities for *Britain*, not for Henry Salt. Belzoni would later take pains to point out that "it has been erroneously stated, that I was regularly employed by Mr. Salt. . . . I positively deny that I was ever engaged by him in any shape whatever, either by words or by writing." In Belzoni's mind, he served no master but Britain and the British Museum, "and . . . would not have made these excursions [into Upper Egypt], had I been previously aware, that all I found was for the benefit of a gentleman, whom I had never had the pleasure to see before in my life."[67]

Like so many others on the edges of empire, Salt and Belzoni turned to collecting as a form of reinvention, in search of social status and wealth. The problem was that their reinventions were mutually exclusive. For his whole life, Salt had yearned to be a gentleman. Collecting in Egypt gave him his best chance: now he could possess the same kinds of objects coveted and valued by his aristocratic friends; he could dispense patronage to underlings such as Belzoni. Belzoni, for his part, sought fame and security of a more public kind. His insistence on collecting for the British Museum, and for the British people more generally, suggested a hunger for popular success, acclaim, and for acceptance into his adopted national community. Each man depended on the other to pull off his self-fashioning: Salt needed to have his hirelings and minions, while Belzoni needed the British consul's stamp of approval. Yet each man's ambitions also stood in the way of the other's. It was a clash of imagined identities.

The two men eventually resolved their dispute in April 1818, with a written agreement arranging pay and allocating the antiquities between them. Belzoni conceded that he had held "some erroneous ideas . . . with respect to the objects collected under the auspices and at the expense of Henry Salt, Esq. in Upper Egypt, as being intended for the British Museum; and . . . that such ideas were altogether founded on a mistake." Salt, in turn, paid Belzoni £500 for the excavations he had performed up to that point, and gave him a large portion of the finds. The only piece they continued to hold jointly was the alabaster sarcophagus of Seti I, which Salt promised to offer for sale to the British Museum within three years, giving Belzoni a share in the profits.

In the end, they parted amiably—"I hope we shall continue the best friends," Belzoni said when they signed the papers—and each man returned to his digs on his own terms.[68] Belzoni wrote (via Salt) to Sir Joseph Banks, offering to "enter into an arrangement with the Trustees of the British Museum to employ myself in excavating and collecting antiquity in Egypt," for a period of two years, with a budget of £1,500 plus "whatever recompenses they may think proper for my own exertions on these occasions."[69] Salt, for his part, continued to collect from his own funds, and in his own interests, like the entrepreneur he had become. Thus the two men took their separate roads back into the field of antiquities collecting: Belzoni aiming at public acceptance and profitable work; Salt at private social advancement within a select gentlemanly community. How well would they fare?

## IV. Gentlemen and Capitalists

Ramses II, the pharaoh who ruled Egypt at the height of its imperial power in the thirteenth century B.C., understood that erecting stupendous monuments was a fine way to seek immortality. Among his many constructions still standing three thousand years later is the Ramesseum, at the pharaohs' burial site of Thebes. This funerary temple was supposed to be his most enduring and sacred building, a site where for centuries after his death he would be worshipped and ritually reborn. Like so many of his edifices, it was a celebration of himself. Scenes of his military triumphs decked the walls. The first pylon was lined with giant images of him in the guise of the god Osiris, wrapped tightly in a burial shroud, arms folded over his chest. A colossal statue of Ramses bestrode the temple's front like a warning and a challenge to all who entered. This was meant to last.

But the temple was built too close to the Nile, and already in ancient times the river's floods crashed into it. Today, the Ramesseum is a vacant and rather sad place. The heads have been struck off the Osirian pillars. Fallen stones and broken sculptures lie scattered like the cast-off playthings of a young giant. It was here that Giambattista Belzoni found the head of the Young Memnon, smirking out from the sand. A second, yet larger head and shoulders, from the statue of Ramses that once guarded the temple's gate, still lies there. Its face is turned up to the sky, washed featureless by water, wind, and sand. "Memnon" was one name for Ramses II. Another was "Ozymandias," and it was by this name that the Romantic poet Percy Bysshe Shelley referred to one of these damaged statues, in his sonnet of that title.[70] Shelley describes a stone colossus, put up by a mighty ancient emperor in a bid for posterity:

*And on the pedestal these words appear:*
*"My name is Ozymandias, king of kings,*
*Look on my works, ye Mighty, and despair!"*
*Nothing beside remains. Round the decay*
*Of that colossal wreck, boundless and bare,*
*The lone and level sands stretch far away.*

An arrogant boast from a vanished kingdom, the words of Shelley's broken colossus speak of the fragility and impermanence of empires and other man-made things.

Written in 1818, when Britain's global hegemony was greater than ever before, "Ozymandias" expressed a timely and moving indictment of empire. The Napoleonic Wars had left Britain triumphant. But they had also left it with massive debts, widespread unemployment, huge numbers of demobilized soldiers, industrial discontent, and a visibly unrepresentative Parliament in need of reform. The "Peterloo massacre" of 1819, at which soldiers opened fire on an apparently peaceful workers' rally at St. Peter's Fields in Manchester, pointed to the uglier possibilities of the peace. It looked to some as if authoritarian, militaristic, antiliberal government—just the things that Napoleon had represented—might be visited on Britain, too. Invoking ancient Egypt at a time like this was thus particularly meaningful. "Ozymandias" held a mirror up to Britain that reflected a frightening image back: the autocratic empire of the pharaohs, whose ruthless tyranny was embodied in these very monuments, built on the backs of thousands of slave laborers. Such an empire could not last.

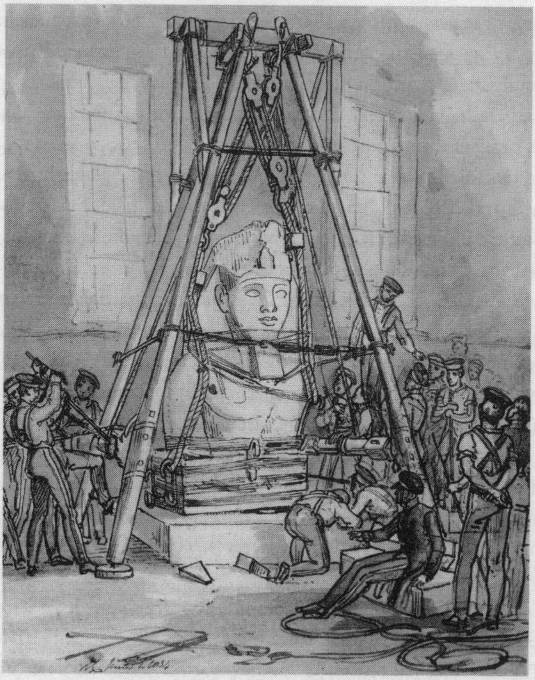

Installing the "Young Memnon" in the Townley Gallery at the British Museum.

The Young Memnon arrived in the British Museum the same year that "Ozymandias" was written. This was the first major Egyptian antiquity to come to Britain after the 1801 booty; and for Belzoni and Salt, at least, it too was a trophy of sorts, of British victory over France. Yet, as Shelley's sonnet alone suggests, such acquisitions were by no means greeted with unanimous patriotism. The museum had just emerged from a vituperative fight over the purchase of the Elgin Marbles, in 1816. That acquisition was violently opposed by Philhellenes—those who supported the nascent call for Greek independence from the Ottoman Empire—who viewed Elgin's "collection" as nothing short of theft. Prominent among them was Shelley's friend Lord Byron, who cruelly quipped of the unfortunate earl, whose nose had been eaten away, it was said, by syphilis: "Noseless himself, he brings here noseless blocks / To show what time has wrought and what the pox."[71] The Philhellenes' objection sounds entirely familiar to modern ears: as long as the Elgin Marbles have been in the British Museum there has been debate over where they belong. A less well known objection to the purchase at the time, however, was levied by some of the very people one might have expected to support it most enthusiastically: antiquarians and connoisseurs. Schooled to appreciate Roman and Hellenistic Greek art, many antiquarians at the time found these much older Hellenic sculptures primitive and difficult to appreciate. The influential connoisseur Richard Payne Knight, for instance, thought the Marbles were vulgar and ugly, and almost put an end to the sale.

If even the Elgin Marbles did not conform to the refined tastes of the connoisseurs, then where did Egyptian antiquities fit in? How, if at all, did they conform to a widening British public investment and participation in empire, or in the greater Eastern world? These were the questions awaiting Salt and Belzoni when they sought to bring their collections into Britain. While Salt would encounter unexpected failure in the established bastions of British collecting culture, Belzoni would discover tremendous success in new venues.

When he parted ways with Belzoni in 1818, Henry Salt had hoped to find his social and financial investment in collecting quickly and amply rewarded. He had sunk more than £2,000 in excavations, "yet having been successful beyond my hopes," he said, "I have no fear of being ultimately repaid."[72] He wrote to his old acquaintance and onetime Foreign Office boss William Richard Hamilton (the same man who had accompanied Edward Daniel Clarke to claim the Rosetta stone from the French savants), with a description and catalogue of the collection. It featured the monumental head and arm of Amenhotep III in polished red granite; "the celebrated French stone," a sculpted panel that had been described in the *Description de l'Égypte;* several excellent statues of the lion-headed goddess Sekhmet; a seated figure in black basalt "as large as life in the attitude of Memnons Statue a Style unique for excellence fine polish"; and "some very fine specimens (unique, I believe) of their sculpture in wood." The greatest treasure of all was clearly the sarcophagus of Seti I, "*unrivalled* in its delicate workmanship," and whose value was quite "impossible for one to estimate."

In a rare, early instance of Egyptian antiquities being explicitly classified as "art," Salt placed an *X* in the margin of his catalogue next to ten of the twenty-three items. "The Statues marked thus are valuable as specimens of art that would do honour to the Royal Academy to possess," he explained. "The rest matters of curiosity for a museum."[73] "Now," Salt went on to tell Hamilton,

> if the Government would take these . . . at a fair valuation, I shall be glad to put them at their disposition at Alexandria. . . . As to the *value*, I would most willingly leave *that* to yourself. . . . The Conte de Forbin [the director of the Louvre, who visited Egypt in

> 1817–1818], when here, pressed me much to let him have a portion for the King of France, and I know that they would be disposed to pay a handsome price; but I should be sorry to see such articles out of England.[74]

Salt's dig about the French was hardly subtle. Still less subtle was he about one further particular. Why bother waiting for British antiquarians to consult and decide on a price for his collection when he could so easily put values on the pieces himself? Next to each one, Salt penned in a suggested price: £3,500 for the sarcophagus, £400 for the seated Ramses, £500 for the head of Amenhotep III, and so on. The total came to £8,210, excluding transportation costs to Britain—twice the amount he later figured it had cost him to assemble the collection.

It seemed so straightforward, so businesslike. And yet by writing down the numbers in his letter to Hamilton, Salt could not have committed a more egregious faux pas. The price list offended the cardinal rule of transactions between gentlemen: *never* mention money. It was one thing to speak of the value of antiquities in general terms with Mountnorris, for instance, who had effectively hired Salt as his agent to handle the measurable expenses of labor and transport. It was also acceptable for Salt to talk numbers with Belzoni, his sometime employee and collaborator. But to approach the antiquarian establishment of London—to say nothing of the British government itself—as if they were a bunch of customers at a butcher shop? The thing was preposterous. Gentlemen could not deal on such terms.

Salt's list met with universal outrage among Hamilton and his friends. The consul was immediately branded "a dealer, a Jew, a *second Lord Elgin.*" This last was a particularly apposite slur, since Elgin had just been denied adequate recompense, and had been dragged through the mud (in the words of Salt's friend, fellow artist, and biographer, J. J. Halls) "as a sacrilegious despoiler of the sacred territory of Greece."[75] It was left to Sir Joseph Banks, who had encouraged Salt to collect in the first place, to compose a "cool and rather sarcastic" reply to the consul's indecent proposal. "Though in truth we are here much satisfied with the Memnon," he pronounced,

> and consider it as a *chef-d'œuvre* of Egyptian sculpture; yet we have not placed that statue among the works of *Fine Art*. It stands in the Egyptian Rooms. Whether any statue that has been found in Egypt can be brought into competition with the grand works of the Townley Gallery remains to be proved; unless however they really are so, the prices you have set upon your acquisitions are unlikely to be realized in Europe.[76]

To be sure, Banks himself was hardly an expert on "fine art": though the naturalist had traveled to the South Pacific on Captain Cook's first voyage, he had never visited the Continent, and he collected seeds and leaves in preference to paintings and sculpture. Nevertheless, as president of the Royal Society, trustee of the British Museum, and linchpin of the British scientific community, Banks acted as an opinion maker, trendsetter, and arbiter of taste. Quite aside from the sheer impropriety of suggesting prices in the first place, Salt was asking far too much. William Richard Hamilton, a better judge of antiquities than Banks, forwarded Banks's letter to Salt with an added caution: "I can only unite with Sir Joseph in recommending to you not to dip too deep in search of the hidden treasures of Egyptian sculpture, for in these economical times, John Bull may be easily induced to withhold his purse-strings, even at the risk of losing the unique monuments which you have discovered."[77]

Poor Salt was devastated. He replied to Banks by return post: "I feel most exceedingly hurt and distressed at my meaning . . . having been so completely misunderstood." He immediately withdrew his "foolish list," and offered "my *whole* Collection to the British Museum . . . without any condition whatever, and shall feel a great pride hereafter in rendering it complete."[78] He also wrote long letters of apology to all his patrons and benefactors in London. But it was to Mountnorris that he gave vent to his most desperate feelings:

> I am neither dealer nor Jew as you will ultimately find. If friends thus traduce me what must I expect from enemies. . . . I will sacrifice anything if you will but let me only live in quiet—and if I cannot obtain what I seek in any other way, I will close my commerce with mankind, by giving up, at once, all, but my official correspondence.[79]

His apologies worked. "Salt's Explanation is very satisfactory," Hamilton wrote to Mountnorris, "and I have no doubt when we meet in Town we may do something for him."[80] The British Museum agreed to take Salt's collection (with the exception of the sarcophagus of Seti I, which its co-owner Belzoni insisted be valued and sold separately) and pay for its transport from Alexandria. After all, there was also the national honor to consider. In the words of one of Salt's advocates, writing to Sir Joseph Banks, "It would be an indelible disgrace if such articles as these were . . . permitted to find their way to any foreign museum. . . . Surely this can never be; and, even should the House of Commons prove so tasteless and supine, I trust the Prince Regent will never suffer so great a blemish to fall on the national honour."[81] Sir Joseph Banks (like the old, mad King George III) died soon after the incident, in 1820, and Salt's unwholesome list was duly forgotten.

But though his honor was restored, Salt's recompense came slowly and sparingly. He transported his antiquities to Alexandria, as he had been told to do, and awaited "the vessel promised by Government. . . . [B]ut I have had no answer whatever direct from the Museum or from Sir Joseph—really one would think that I was asking instead of conferring an obligation."[82] His hundred-odd cases of antiquities sat in Alexandria for a year before being taken to Britain on a naval transport; and another year went by before serious discussions began about how much the British Museum would actually pay for them. "Pray do all you can towards bringing my affair with the museum to a conclusion," Salt wrote plaintively to Mountnorris in May of 1822. "It is the only hope I have of some time or other getting away from Egypt."[83] In 1823, after protracted negotiations through Salt's agent Bingham Richards, the museum finally offered Salt the rather insufficient sum of £2,000 for his pieces, about half what he had spent to gather them. Yet another year passed before Salt and Belzoni sold the jointly owned sarcophagus of Seti I, for another £2,000, to the architect and collector Sir John Soane.[84]

It had taken six years, from start to finish, for Salt to sell his antiquities. "I might have expected some small thanks for my exertions, advance of all I had in the world, risk and loss of interest to which I have been exposed," he complained to Bingham Richards in the middle of it all. "But they do these things differently in England from other countries, and it is always useless to complain."[85] He had begun filled with such enthusiasm, keen to represent his country in Egypt; and to represent Egypt to his country, through its antiquities. Now Henry Salt was sick of Egypt, sick of the British Museum, and sick of the British government. But he was not yet sick of collecting—and in time, he would try again to make it pay.

While Salt's antiquities languished on the quaysides of Alexandria, *The Times* noted the return to London, in March 1820, of "the celebrated traveller Mr. Belzoni," fresh from his feats in Giza, Thebes, and beyond—and bearing his own Egyptian spoils. He had left Britain in complete obscurity, a foreign itinerant actor; he returned the talk of the town. "Belzoni *is* a great traveller, and his English is very prettily broken," said Lord Byron.[86] Countesses had him to dinner; Sir Walter Scott spoke glowingly about meeting "the great lion—great in every sense . . . the handsomest man (for a giant) I ever saw"; he was inducted into a select Masonic lodge. The publisher John Murray, whose clients ranged from Romantic poets to outlandish travelers, promptly signed Belzoni up to write a book about his adventures. Belzoni's *Narrative of the Operations and Recent Discoveries* appeared before the year

1820 was out, and was an instant hit: the initial print run of one thousand was quickly followed by two more editions by 1822, and by French and Italian translations.[87]

With a book on the way, and the Young Memnon comfortably ensconced in the British Museum, Belzoni enjoyed a definite buzz of publicity. The veteran showman now put his theatrical experience back to work. He had hatched a scheme while still in Egypt. Since so few Britons could visit Egypt themselves, why not make a replica of Egypt they could see in London? Belzoni planned to build a copy of Seti I's tomb, and to exhibit inside it all the antiquities he had discovered. His chosen venue, the Egyptian Hall in Piccadilly, could not have been more apt. Built in 1812 under the influence of drawings in the *Description de l'Égypte* and Denon's *Voyage*, the hall was a marvelous specimen of "Egyptomaniac" architecture, complete with lotus-patterned columns, vaulted gateways, and massive figures of Isis and Osiris flanking the façade.

It had been constructed by the showman William Bullock, who used it to house his "natural history museum" and assorted curiosities, and to put on special exhibitions such as a tremendously successful show of items associated with Napoleon, featuring the emperor's coach from Waterloo. Drawing a wide public audience and hosting "popular" exhibitions, the Egyptian Hall was a far cry indeed from the British Museum, with its stuffy admissions procedures and dusty collections. In 1820, Belzoni rented the hall from Bullock

The Egyptian Hall, Piccadilly.

and got to work re-creating his patch of Egypt in the heart of London.[88] For months, he and Sarah had worked long, hot days in the Valley of the Kings, copying down the images in Seti I's tomb and taking wax impressions of its reliefs. Using those casts and drawings, Belzoni carefully reconstructed two rooms of the great tomb full-size, and made a scale model of the rest. In the brilliantly painted chambers he set out his antiquities: amulets, jewelry, statuettes, and, of course, mummies—one of which, with the flair of a natural performer, Belzoni publicly unwrapped some days before the grand opening. On the first day alone, in May 1821, almost two thousand people paid a half-crown each (analogous to the ticket price of a major tourist attraction today) to visit the show.[89]

The great popular success of Belzoni's Egyptian exhibition, at precisely the time that the British Museum was hemming and hawing over the acquisition of Salt's collection, points up a split in the way ancient Egypt was perceived and presented in Britain. Salt, as a would-be gentleman collector, aimed to incorporate ancient Egypt into the connoisseur's world: a world based in the British Museum and the Royal Academy, and governed by collectors, aristocrats, antiquarians, and artists. That proved to be impossible. To them, Egypt could never be more than the poor country cousin of Greece and Rome; certainly not something Britain's social elite would pay good money for. Belzoni pitched Egypt to an entirely different audience. What visitors came to see in the Egyptian Hall was not a didactic presentation of fine art, like the British Museum put on offer. They came for sheer *spectacle:* the scale, the novelty, the mystery, and the tremendous antiquity of this distant culture. Here, in Belzoni's simulated Egypt, they got a glimpse of how ancient Egypt looked and felt, how its people lived and died. Belzoni's patrons came for exactly the reasons that continue to draw record-breaking crowds to Egyptian exhibitions around the world today. And this was the secret of Belzoni's success. He saw—as Salt did not—that Egypt *outside* the museum was more vibrant, animated, and popular than Egypt could ever be within it, when pressed into the aesthetic categories of connoisseurs.

Salt's offer to the British Museum had almost destroyed the gentlemanly reputation that he had worked so hard to construct. Belzoni's tremendously popular show, on the other hand, helped confirm his reinvention as a celebrity and public figure accepted and fêted in Britain. His patriotic dream of collecting for the British Museum may have been only partly fulfilled, but he received all the acclaim that he could have desired.

Yet performances are ephemeral things. By 1822, there were signs that Belzoni's show was getting old. Social invitations were less forthcoming, and on several occasions, he burst into a rage at perceived slights and allusions to his undistinguished past. If Belzoni wanted to retain his newfound fame, he was going to have to change his act. Thus, in June 1822, almost exactly a year after his exhibition had opened, Belzoni sold it. Everything, from the massive panels of the mock tomb to the display cases themselves, was auctioned off. Judging by the relative dearth of Egyptian antiquities that passed through Christie's auction house at this time (another sign of their marginal status in elite collecting culture), Belzoni's must have been the biggest Egyptian sale yet held in Britain. Surviving records of some of the prices his items fetched suggest that it was a very lucrative affair: the facsimile of the tomb's two main rooms sold for £490, for instance. Two somewhat damaged statues of Sekhmet, which the auction catalogue boasted were "of the Best Egyptian Workmanship" and like two "found by Mr. Belzoni, . . . now in the British Museum," earned £380 (a price entirely in keeping, it might be noted, with the £400 that Salt had set on the similar pair in his infamous list).[90] All told, the sale must have netted Belzoni more than £2,000—the amount Salt would eventually get from the British Museum at much greater cost of time and pain.

Money in hand, Belzoni prepared to set off on another adventure. He had concocted a plan as a tribute of sorts to his great friend and benefactor, John Lewis Burckhardt, who had died in Cairo in 1818 at the cruelly premature age of thirty-three. Burckhardt's death was shattering for Belzoni, Salt, and many others who had not only liked and deeply admired him, but looked to him for further revelations like those he had made at Mecca, Petra, and Abu Simbel. Before he died, Burckhardt had been planning to travel into central Africa with the Arab caravans, in the hopes of visiting the marvelous city of Timbuktu. Now Belzoni took up the challenge instead.

No European had ever traveled to the African city—which legend held was made of gold—and lived to tell the tale. The African Association had already sponsored several expeditions into West Africa, with the goal of navigating the Niger River and locating Timbuktu. Their most successful explorer was the Scottish surgeon Mungo Park, who ventured far up the Niger in 1796 and 1797, but vanished in 1806 on a second expedition, sponsored by the Colonial Office. In 1815, Belzoni's publisher, John Murray, issued the journal of Park's ill-fated second voyage. The following year, Murray published another Timbuktu narrative by one Robert Adams, a young American sailor who had been shipwrecked on the Mauritanian coast in 1810, captured by "blacks," and carried off to a city that his captors told him was Timbuktu. According to Adams, the celebrated city was built of mud, not of gold. Adams's narrative was widely discredited in Britain, but Belzoni certainly read it (maybe Murray even introduced him to Adams) and was persuaded to set off to Morocco and reach Timbuktu by traveling south, with the Saharan caravans.[91]

Sarah Belzoni gamely accompanied her husband as far as Fez, in the spring of 1823, and described their progress in a rare surviving letter, addressed to her friend Jane Porter, a novelist:

> Back to Paris fly from there to Marseilles embark for gibraltar and there for Tangiers depart for fas [Fez] the metropolis of the north of Merocco Pass through A garden of flowers arrive there our habitation an enchanting Paridise the air scented with the odours from orange groves a Mirtle Bower and many other oderefers [oderiferous] Plants filled with the sweet mellody of the feathered Race.[92]

But Belzoni found the desert route south from Morocco blocked. Returning to Gibraltar (from whence Sarah went back to London), he made his way instead to the Canary Islands and caught a British naval transport to the West African coast. Sarah wrote to him from London: "My dear jovanni, I arrived here on thursday night 24th july . . . much troubled in mind on your account the manner we parted in so unexpected neither saying farewell. . . . [D]o not be too venturesome recollect poor Mungo Park. . . . May God Bless and Protect you trust in him my dear jovanni and happy return to England."[93]

It is unlikely that "Jovanni" ever received her letter. He arrived at a British fort on the Ghanaian coast in mid-October 1823, and proceeded to a British factory on the Benin River. From there, he traveled inland to Benin City, an imposing capital whose palace was ringed by elaborate bronze reliefs. (In 1897, the friezes would be carried off by marauding British troops and would end up at the British Museum, where they still are.)[94] But Giambattista Belzoni was to travel no farther. Falling ill with dysentery, he felt his fabled strength and willpower ebb out of him. On December 3, 1823, he died in the town of Gato, Benin. His British companions buried him under a huge spreading tree and put up a tablet to "the celebrated and intrepid traveller" who lay beneath.[95]

In the end, maybe it was the pressure of reinvention that killed Belzoni: the need to bolster his newfound public stature as an acclaimed adventurer, and to refill his purse in the process. Timbuktu was a journey too far. "I die at last a beggar," Belzoni wrote in those last days in Africa. His widow, Sarah, was left with nothing but her husband's reputation for discoveries. She briefly tried to revive an Egyptian exhibition, though with little success, and she devoted herself instead to tending his memory. Sarah's poverty became something of a cause célèbre: charitable appeals were made on her behalf in newspapers on both sides of the Atlantic; from 1851 to her death in 1870, she drew an annual pension of £100 from the Civil List.[96] But Belzoni did achieve a kind of apotheosis. This was graphically illustrated in an engraving Sarah commissioned shortly after his death. It shows a very different Belzoni from the man depicted in the frontispiece of his *Narrative*, where he sports full Oriental regalia and a long, silky beard curling down over his chest. Here Belzoni appears rather Byronic, in a high-collared coat, stylish white cravat, and fashionably curled mustache. His image is suspended in the clouds, which part around him to form a sort of halo. On the ground below, easily identifiable, are the major antiquities he brought to Britain.

Perhaps the most enduring celebration of Belzoni, however, appeared in the unlikely form of a children's book. At the height of Belzoni's success in Britain, an author writing under the name of Sarah Atkins published an adaptation of his *Narrative* called *Fruits of Enterprize Exhibited in the Travels of Belzoni in Egypt and Nubia, interspersed with the observations of a mother to her children.* The children's book rewrites the paranoid and defensive Belzoni of the *Narrative* into a model of perseverance, energy, self-motivation, and purpose. "Patience conquers difficulties, and crowns all our efforts with success," pronounces one of the children when Belzoni's uplifting tale is done.[97] This Belzoni embodies the pluck and virtue of a new type of British self-made hero—so well that *Fruits of Enterprize* was still in print, in its ninth edition, twenty years after his death. And while the juvenile audience of *Fruits of Enterprize* was urged to emulate Belzoni's patience and dedication, older readers could take lessons from the Belzoni described in *Biography of Self-Taught Men* (1832), wherein the traveler is profiled alongside Eli Whitney, Humphry Davy, and Henry Clay.[98] Self-directed, entrepreneurial, and financially successful, Belzoni turned out to be a figure well suited to the values of Victorian Britain and America, where his travels were widely read. (Ralph Waldo Emerson, for instance, refers to Belzoni in several essays; and in 1832, a rich Mississippi planter named Alvarez Fisk was so impressed by the explorer that he named his plantation Belzoni. Today, the name survives in the little town of Belzoni, Mississippi, "heart of the Delta," "catfish capital of the world.")[99]

Another and less benign way in which *Fruits of Enterprize* looked ahead to later Victorian values, however, lay in its portrayal of Egypt. While Belzoni himself had set Anglo-French conflict at the heart of his narrative, *Fruits of Enterprize* transforms his story into a battle with Egypt itself. Many of Belzoni's specific gripes against the French are left out; the reviled Salt gets mention only in connection with the moving of the Young Memnon. Instead, "Orientalist" stereotypes are cruder and more pervasive than in Belzoni's book. Readers learn that "Effeminate indolence is born with the Egyptian, grows as he grows, and descends with him to the grave"; that "the Turks are famed for their indolence"; that "nothing has so much influence on the mind of an Arab as reasoning with him about his own interest," and so on.[100] A further telling touch of European propriety is that all the illustrations depict Belzoni without his Orientalizing beard. From a conflict between Britain and France—as Belzoni presented it—his story becomes one of Europe versus the Orient. This was to be the most important rewriting of all.

The persisting rivalry in Egypt between Britain and France would endure and indeed intensify in the years to come. But, as the reception of Egyptian antiquities and collectors in Europe suggested, by the 1820s another narrative that would long dominate European responses to Egypt was becoming established. Modern Egypt was presented as a place of decadence, corruption, and stagnation. Ancient Egypt, by contrast, was a land of marvels, mysteries, and classical (to say nothing of Biblical) associations—and it needed Europeans to come to its rescue.

Salt and Belzoni's graffiti on the wall of the Ramesseum, Thebes.

As for the personal rivalry between Salt and Belzoni, one poignant vestige can be seen in the Ramesseum today. On the wall of one of the hypostyle courts, small, shallow letters spell out the name "Salt." It is a discreet mark, as grafitti go, the gentlest wink at posterity. But emblazoned above it, cut deep into the stone in strong, clear characters, is the name "BELZONI." Nothing modest about this: Belzoni was there, too, and wanted to be sure future visitors knew it. There is something especially apt about finding his declaration here. The Young Memnon, whose removal from this very temple Belzoni had masterminded, still sits in the British Museum with only the names of its donors, Henry Salt and John Lewis Burckhardt, on the label. Thus Salt earned his immortality in the British Museum, just as he had wished. And though Belzoni's reinvention as an acclaimed "British" adventurer may have led him to his death, here, in the place where he made his name, it remains legible still.

CHAPTER NINE

# *Recoveries*

## 1. The Two Egypts

Lightning struck on a mid-September morning in Paris, in 1822. The thirty-two-year-old scholar Jean-François Champollion had been sitting in his third-floor study poring over the cartouches in a hieroglyphic inscription, with his notes by his side. Painstakingly he worked to spell out the sounds he conjectured that the characters represented. From the opaque images before him, syllables emerged, then names: Ramses, beloved of Amon; Thutmoses. He had worked toward this moment for years. Now, in the flash of one morning, Champollion was able to confirm the phonetic theory he had devised for how to translate the "writing of the speech of the gods," as the Rosetta stone called Egyptian hieroglyphics, into Greek, "the writing of the books." For the first time in more than a millennium, the lost language of the Egyptians was legible again. He rushed across the street to tell his brother, and then collapsed into a speechless stupor that lasted five days.[1]

In later years, Champollion's achievement would be seen as his destiny. At the age of nine, it was said, this boy-genius had read about the discovery of the Rosetta stone in an issue of the *Courrier de l'Égypte*. Some years later, as a precocious schoolboy in Grenoble, he had learned about Egypt directly at the knee of a savant, Jean-Baptiste Joseph Fourier, author of the historical preface of the *Description de l'Égypte*, who entranced the lad with papyri and inscrip-

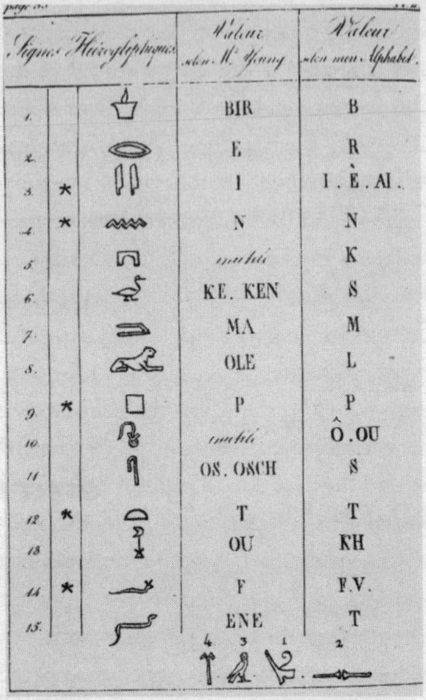

| | | Signes Hiéroglyphiques | Valeur selon Mr. Young | Valeur selon mon Alphabet |
|---|---|---|---|---|
| 1. | | | BIR | B |
| 2. | | | E | R |
| 3. | * | | I | I . È . AI . |
| 4. | * | | N | N |
| 5. | | | nulle | K |
| 6. | | | KE. KEN | S |
| 7. | | | MA | M |
| 8. | | | OLE | L |
| 9. | * | | P | P |
| 10. | | | nulle | Ô . OU |
| 11. | | | OS. OSCH | S |
| 12. | * | | T | T |
| 13. | | | OU | KH |
| 14. | * | | F | F.V. |
| 15. | | | ENE | T |

A table of hieroglyphics in Champollion's breakthrough *Précis du système hiéroglyphique* . . . , showing his conclusions next to the hypotheses of his British rival, Thomas Young.

tions. And if the decipherment seemed to be Champollion's personal destiny, many also saw it as a kind of national destiny for France, "an eternal honor to French letters."[2] The French had opened Egypt to the West in 1798; now it was the French who would expose ancient Egyptian culture to modern eyes. As Champollion himself would put it: "A conquering France [*la France guerrière*] let modern Egypt be known in depth. . . . It is also for France . . . to gather the souvenirs engraved on these [ancient] monuments, witnesses of primitive civilization . . ."[3] Or in the revealing words of another contemporary:

> Egyptian archeology is, for France, a kind of copyright, as Indian archeology is for England: these two important branches of human learning have been naturalized [as citizens] in the two kingdoms by the undertakings of their travellers, the zeal of their scholars, and the protection of their governments.[4]

The parallel with British rule in India was striking, given that France had no formal role in Egypt at all. Territorial conquest might have failed, but in the realm of culture and history, it was as if Egypt belonged to France by right, and France had responsibilities toward it in turn.

The decipherment of hieroglyphics signaled one of two major ways in which the relationship between Egypt and the West—and between collecting and empire—would be refigured in the 1820s and 1830s, anticipating trends that would continue into the later nineteenth century and beyond. The decipherment opened the way for the development of formal Egyptology and scholarship on ancient Egypt. (The word *Egyptology* became widespread only in the 1870s, but the foundations of the field were laid earlier.)[5] By reiterating France's intellectual claims, Champollion's discovery also infused new life into the Anglo-French competition for antiquities, and influence, on the ground in Egypt. This rivalry would be colored by a second transforming event. The outbreak of war in Greece, which sought to win independence from the Ottoman Empire, had unexpected consequences for the relationship between Europe and Egypt. While Britain and France threw their support behind the Greeks, the sultan called on his vassal Muhammad Ali of Egypt to bolster Turkish power. In a paradoxical twist, Britain and France found themselves joining forces to contain Muhammad Ali outside Egypt, while each was working to strengthen its own position—along with the pasha's—within Egypt. Together, the decipherment of hieroglyphics and the Greek War of Independence helped deepen that perceptual divide between ancient Egypt, now legible to the West and collected with new vigor; and modern Egypt, increasingly bound up in European politics and the interventionist designs of Britain and France. The division would have enduring effects on relations between Egypt and the West, on Egypt's relationship to its own ancient past, and on Anglo-French control over Egypt both ancient and modern.

Salt and Drovetti had acted in the name of their respective nations, but little had distinguished their methods of collecting. From the 1820s, however, British and French approaches to collecting began to diverge more conspicuously. While Salt and Belzoni were bringing Egypt to the people of London as individual entrepreneurs, in France, the study of Egypt continued to be supported by the state, despite the changed political and cultural climate of the Restoration. Indeed it was Napoleon's Bourbon replacement, King Louis XVIII, who supported much of the massive publication costs of the *Description de l'Égypte*. At roughly the same time that the British Museum grudgingly produced £2,000 for Henry Salt's collection, the directors of the Bibliothèque Royale and the Louvre pooled their resources to pay three times that (150,000 francs, or roughly £6,000) for the huge stone zodiac from the Temple of Dendera, which had been hacked off by two Frenchmen in 1821.[6]

But France's collections of antiquities lagged behind those of other nations, despite Bernardino Drovetti's best efforts to the contrary. In 1819, Drovetti shipped his huge collection to Europe and offered it for sale to the French government. His asking price of 400,000 francs, however—eight times more than Salt received for his antiquities—gave the authorities pause.[7] In 1821, Drovetti sold his collection instead to the king of Sardinia (who ruled Drovetti's native Piedmont), in exchange for a cash payment, an annual pension, land worth 450,000 francs, and even a chivalric decoration thrown in for good measure.[8] By 1824—the year that Champollion published his definitive work on hieroglyphics—both London and Turin possessed better collections of Egyptian antiquities than Paris. Given "the crowd of foreigners attracted to Paris by the renown of the French expedition" and the prominence of French scholarship on Egypt, grumbled the editor of the *Description de l'Égypte* Edmé-François Jomard, it was an acutely embarrassing turn of events.[9]

Louis XVIII died in 1824 and was succeeded by his reactionary younger brother, Charles X. Charles's accession was widely greeted with nervousness, distaste, and resentment. But for Egyptophiles, the new king proved to be a remarkable patron. In 1826, he was prevailed upon to open a major Egyptian gallery in the Louvre, the Musée Charles-X. Champollion was named its director and was given state funds to purchase antiquities. The Egyptian galleries stretched along the Cour Carrée of the Louvre, as they still do today, and were decorated with a cycle of murals (still partly intact) celebrating the association of ancient Egypt and Bourbon France.[10] That the famously conservative Charles X should have embraced the symbols popularized by his hated revolutionary and Bonapartist predecessors was just further compelling testament to the way that Egypt had become part of France's national identity. Welcoming Egypt into the royal collections was like a political amnesty of sorts, a tacit acceptance of Napoleon's legacy.[11]

The new surge of French interest in Egyptian collecting intensified competition with Britain in the Nile Valley, in ways Champollion would later experience firsthand. So it was all the more surprising that the source of the Louvre's founding Egyptian collection was to be none other than Henry Salt. Salt had sustained a major loss on his first collection, and found himself caught in a frustrating bind. With his inheritance spent and no certainty of a government pension to look forward to, he was more dependent on profits from antiquities than ever before. At one level he wanted nothing more than to leave Egypt. He felt depressed and exiled there, shut out from his beloved London society. "To stagnate thus at a distance from all science, literature, arts, knowledge, delicacy or taste," he wrote plaintively to Mountnorris, "is a punishment almost sufficient to drive one mad."[12] At the same time, he was trapped there in part by his own ambitions. Only in Egypt, where he held the rank, status, and privileges of consul-general, could Salt afford to support himself in style. Only in Egypt, moreover, could he possibly hope to make enough money—by collecting antiquities—to return to Britain with a gentleman's means. In much the way that Claude Martin had needed to stay in Lucknow in order to sustain his life as a gentleman connoisseur, so Henry Salt was locked in parasitic dependency on the Eastern land that had made him a man of substance.

Not that being in Egypt was always so terrible, all the time. Just months after the agonizing affair of the price list, Salt enjoyed an unexpected stroke of fortune. "You will not be a little surprised, I dare say, to hear that I am on the point of being *married* to a young and very amiable lady," he gushed to a friend in September 1819.[13] The "lady" was a girl of just sixteen, the daughter of a Tuscan merchant named Pensa, who had apparently brought her to Egypt expecting to marry her off to an Austrian acquaintance. Little is known about Mrs. Salt, not even her first name—which is ironic, considering that the record does preserve the name of a slave girl, Makhbub, with whom Salt had a son probably no more than a year before.[14]

Salt, at thirty-eight, was more than twice as old as his bride. He was also desperately ill. "A slight bowel complaint on the day of my marriage" quickly worsened, bringing him to death's door.[15] From then on, he suffered from a constant cycle of recovery and relapse into "my old complaint in the bowels, a continual looseness and discharge of blood"—what turned out, in fact, to be the prostate disease that eventually killed him.[16] Yet he found with his wife a kind of comfort he had never known before: "These sad attacks have been very trying as you may well believe to my young wife, but thank god it has only served to confirm me in the good opinion I had formed of her character. She is indeed I may say with pride a very amiable good girl and renders me very happy."[17] Unlikely as the match may have seemed, people who knew the Salts said "there never existed a happier marriage, or a more devotedly attached couple."[18] They had a daughter in 1821, and named her Georgina Henrietta Annesley, after Salt's great friend and patron Lord Mountnorris. In April 1824, Mrs. Salt gave birth again (a second daughter, Julia, had been born prematurely and died after just two weeks), and Salt delighted in the arrival of another baby girl.

But then, as suddenly as his family had come together, it broke apart. Five days later, while bubonic plague raged through Alexandria, Salt's child bride died of puerperal fever. Their baby died a few weeks later. Salt was raw with grief. His howls could be heard even in his letter to the Foreign Office: "It has pleased God to afflict me with the greatest of all calamities."[19] He decided to send little Georgina and her Italian grandmother back to Tuscany, where at least they would be safe from the Egyptian plagues that seemed to have descended so heavily on the consul's house. Georgina and old Signora Pensa sailed from Alexandria in July 1824. Salt never saw his daughter again.

After they left, he buried himself in the consular mansion and tried to find solace. He devoted himself to a long verse composition, "Egypt, A Descriptive Poem." The lyrics are agonizingly clumsy, and down in Luxor, a young gentleman traveler called Robert Hay sent his friends into fits of laughter by reading aloud "quotations from that *beautiful* poem from the pen of Mr. Salt on the Nile and its wonders."[20] But for Salt, every last line was written in deadly earnest, "with a view to divert the Author's attention whilst suffering under severe affliction."[21] He also worked hard on deciphering hieroglyphics, and wrote a long treatise on the subject—only to learn that Champollion had anticipated him on many points some time before.[22]

A year after his tragedies began, Salt made his second collection available for sale. The collection, like his little daughter, was in Livorno, in the custody of his wife's brother-in-law Pietro Santoni, a banker. The antiquities "would make the collection at the [British] Museum *the choicest in the world*, as an Egyptian collection," Salt said, and he was happy to give it to them in exchange for an annual pension of £600.[23] This time, though, he had no patience for negotiating: "It would be a great pleasure to me that it should go to England; but no more of *dealing* with the British Museum—the *Soanes* are the people for me."[24] Salt here took a page from Drovetti's book: he would offer his collection to his own nation first, but if they did not act quickly enough, he would happily sell it to the highest bidder, whoever that happened to be.

Coincidentally, Jean-François Champollion was in Turin—in the new Museo Egizio studying the Drovetti collection—when he heard that Salt's collection was for sale in nearby Livorno. He rushed to Livorno to see it for himself, and was delighted by what he found: "This collection is definitely superior to that of Drovetti . . . ," he reported. "The number of idols and objects in gold and silver is very considerable; the bronzes, of which many are more than two feet high, and decorated with gold and silver wire, are beyond all praise, and nothing similar has yet appeared in Europe." Driving his point home, Champollion continued: "The moment has come for France to console itself for the loss of the Drovetti collection by acquiring that of Mr. Salt. The price that is asked . . . is so small that I had to have it repeated many times; it would only be a matter of spending 150,000 francs, at most, to possess more or less what the King of Sardinia paid 450,000 to have."[25] Within just three months of seeing Salt's collection, Champollion got the go-ahead from the French government to negotiate a price with Santoni; and in February 1826, France bought Salt's collection for 250,000 francs (about £10,000 then, easily over half a million now).[26] "I rejoice with Your Excellency on the acquisition of such a beautiful collection, the equal of which cannot be found in any other museum . . . ," wrote Pietro Santoni to the minister of the king's household. "The owner, my intimate friend, . . . is happy to have satisfied his desire, that of knowing the collection [will be] placed in a setting that suits it."[27]

So it was that Henry Salt finally received his retirement money, not from the British government he had served for ten years, but from the French, whom he had been fighting the whole time. Yet even a calm return to Britain was to be denied him. Tensions in Greece—where pressure was mounting on Britain to intervene against the Egyptian forces fighting there—had come to such a head that Salt had to delay his departure in order to stay at his post. "I am thoroughly tired of Egypt," he moaned in May 1827, "and have a mass of sketches and notes sufficient to amuse me during the rest of my life, which, after what I have undergone, I cannot expect to be a long one."[28] Later that summer, he "had another of my old attacks." Salt was "still very weak" in October: "This has finally determined me not to protract my stay here, under any considerations, beyond April next. . . . I have sacrificed myself sufficiently for the Government." In the same letter, he told Pietro Santoni that he had sent off a third collection of antiquities that very day, "a very select one, and rich in interesting objects."[29]

Three weeks later, Henry Salt was dead. The climate, the disease, the strain, and the sadness: Egypt, it seemed, had killed him after all. His last days were tortured by violent, delirious fits, and fantasies of the supernatural. "Oh! Doctor, this is Frankenstein!" he cried in his last conscious moment.[30] And so he left Egypt, and life, haunted by the vision of another man's fatal experiment in discovery and refashioning.

## II. France Redux

With the arrival of Salt's 117 cases of antiquities in France, the balance of Egyptian collections tilted definitively in Paris's favor. It was a hint of things to come, in terms of France's profile in Egypt, and even in terms of French influence in North Africa as a whole. For this swing from British to French preeminence in antiquities seemed to underscore a trend in diplomatic matters as well. In 1821, after six years in Egypt pursuing his own private business, Bernardino Drovetti had been reinstated as the French consul. "Lawyer, soldier, Vice Consul, lover, husband, farmer, businessman, antiquarian, nothing has been able to satisfy M. Drovetti, his restless ambition will be his undoing," complained his immediate predecessor, a cantankerous old man who loathed him. In truth, though, Drovetti had been remarkably successful in most of these guises. His reappointment (with a promotion to the Legion of Honor to boot) confirmed how indispensable the old Bonapartist was as France's, even Bourbon France's, representative in Egypt. Drovetti was probably Muhammad Ali Pasha's closest European adviser. Making him consul helped ensure that France would in turn be Egypt's closest European friend.

Even in these post-Waterloo years, the hand of France seemed to be everywhere in Egypt. It guided what was perhaps in the long run to be Muhammad Ali's most significant "modernizing" scheme: cultivation of long-fibered Jumel cotton. The Lyonnais Louis Jumel himself managed Muhammad Ali's textile mill at Bulaq. Another conspicuous—and, to the British, alarming—site of French intervention was the Egyptian military, which from 1820 was completely restructured along European lines.[31] In 1822, the British traveler James Burton saw a "regiment of Arabs stationed at Farsiout now being instructed after the European mode. . . . They have European Muskets and bayonets and the drums are beaten à la Française, the Drum Major being a French Mameluke. The Officers are French and Italian."[32] The pasha's top military adviser was a Napoleonic veteran named Joseph Sève, whom Salt described as "a true heir of the Bonapartian school." According to Salt, other "French officers in the Pasha's service . . . certainly have done much but nothing in comparison with Col. Sève," who cemented his affiliation with Egypt in 1823 by converting to Islam. "[O]n turning Turk," he was:

> elevated to the rank of Bey (Suliman Bey). . . . I will not say that the Turks did it expressly . . . —but he received his Pelisse and advancement in the morning of Christmas-day, as if expressly to outrage the religion he had renounced. After all he is a fool for his pains—he has sold for preferment his birthright, and the Pasha may now cut off his head at his pleasure.[33]

The French presence in the Egyptian army was so pronounced that French newspapers gave "the soldiers who fought below the walls of Missolonghi [in Greece] the title of Gallo-Egyptians." This was a savage indictment, since allegations of atrocities committed by the Egyptians there provoked nigh-universal outrage in western Europe.[34]

In actual fact, as Drovetti was keen to show, there were only fourteen French officers in Muhammad Ali's army in 1826 (as well as sixteen Piedmontese, four Spaniards, and five Neapolitans)—but the numbers were rather beside the point.[35] It was to France that Muhammad Ali turned first, for everything from providing "56 musicians, to form two French-style military bands, and to teach native students," to hosting a group of forty-four young Egyptians to study in Paris, the first such educational exchange ever sent from the Middle East to Europe.[36] Gifts crossed between Paris and Cairo, such as a carriage and Gobelin tapestries for Muhammad Ali, and antiquities and the permission to dig for them for France.[37] As Salt saw it, "The alliance, as it may be termed, between His Highness and the Court of France is every day more closely drawn together and the plans of the French Government continually gaining ground."[38]

When Salt wrote this dispatch in 1826, those "plans of the French Government" involved encouraging Muhammad Ali to declare his independence from the sultan. France welcomed an autonomous Egypt as a potential ally and counterpoise to British and Russian interests in the region. But French and British relations with Muhammad Ali were beginning to turn on more than their own long-standing rivalry in Egypt. They would be enduringly reshaped by events rapidly unfolding in Greece.

Greece had become a province of the Ottoman Empire following the fall of Byzantine Constantinople to the Turks in 1453. By the late eighteenth century, encouraged in part by radical currents making their way across Europe, a patriotic movement began to take shape in Greece. In early 1821, revolution broke out across the mainland, with the goal of winning independence from the sultan. European powers were reluctant to get involved. After all, this was a colonial revolt, and though Britain had sponsored colonial uprisings in South America against its old imperial rival Spain, preserving the Ottoman Empire seemed essential for maintaining European peace. But from Russia to Britain to the United States, public sympathies were strongly with the Greeks. Philhellenes rushed to Greece to volunteer their support—famously Lord Byron, who died of fever at Missolonghi in 1824. In 1827 the Greeks turned to Britain for professional assistance, hiring a British general to command the Greek army, and engaging the services of the dashing admiral Lord Thomas Cochrane, who had previously helped Chile, Peru, and Brazil win their independence. The sultan Mahmud II, in the meantime, turned to his most powerful subordinate for help. Muhammad Ali had already served the sultan by defeating the Wahhabis in the Hijaz, and had been rewarded in 1818 when the sultan appointed Muhammad Ali's brilliant, bellicose eldest son, Ibrahim, as pasha of the province. In exchange for fighting in Greece, Muhammad Ali expected to receive more land and titles from the sultan, in either Greece or, his most coveted prize, Syria.

Commanded by the veteran Ibrahim, the Egyptian armies swept into Crete and Cyprus and handily asserted Ottoman dominance. In 1825, Ibrahim launched an invasion of the Peloponnesian peninsula, using his father's newly constructed navy, an armada of more than fifty ships. He left a bloody trail of slaughter behind him. At Missolonghi, on the Gulf of Corinth, a year-long siege ended in carnage in 1826, when Ibrahim's men slaughtered some four thousand fleeing Greeks. The event provoked a furor in western Europe. Eugène Delacroix, who had startled viewers at the Paris Salon of 1824 with his canvas of another Turkish outrage in Greece, *The Massacre at Chios,* promptly allegorized the scene in his painting *Greece on the Ruins of Missolonghi,* which was exhibited in Paris "au profit des Grecs."[39] (Delacroix would reprise his full-figured female "Greece" three years later in the bare-breasted allegory of Liberty in *Liberty Leading the People,* a celebration of the French revolution of 1830.) Before Missolonghi, European powers had held back from offering open support to the Greeks, preferring to maintain a delicate status quo with the Ottomans. Ibrahim's outrage now pushed them over the edge into formal alliance with Greece.

The year that Salt wrote back to Whitehall warning of France's support for Egyptian independence, 1826, saw Muhammad Ali in an excellent position to assert himself. His army occupied Greece, and his navy—constructed in the Bulaq shipyards with French advisers, and boasting five French-made warships—sat in the seas around the Peloponnesian peninsula. It also saw Britain and France caught in a bind. Each had long been vying to help Muhammad Ali extend and assert his power; now each was openly helping the cause of Greek independence—and thus openly opposing the Egyptian army and navy. Furthermore, if both Greece and Egypt gained independence, the stability of the Ottoman Empire as a whole would be severely compromised. Caught in the cross fire of Western interests, Muhammad Ali would find that his very strength precipitated his downfall. For while inside Egypt, Salt and Drovetti had vied with each other to promote their nations' interests, outside it, France and Britain joined forces to crush the pasha's power.

The collision of West and East occurred in the bay of Navarino, on the eastern shore of the Peloponnese. The Turco-Egyptian fleet that had gathered there in early September 1827 "is not," Muhammad Ali gloated to his son Ibrahim, "the sort of fleet you have seen hitherto. It is now a brilliant fleet, in modern style, and such as has never been seen before in the Muslim world."[40] The pasha knew that a confrontation with the pro-Greek European coalition was inevitable, but he confidently assumed that only a few of his ships would be lost. The European allied navy hovered at the mouth of the bay, hoping to bully the Egyptians into withdrawing.

But Ibrahim would not budge. On October 15, 1827, the French admiral who was commanding the pro-Greek coalition sent a letter to all the Frenchmen who were serving with the Egyptians on the other side. Leave the Egyptian navy now, he advised them, or else Frenchmen will be forced to fire against fellow Frenchmen. Five days later, the coalition fleet sailed into the bay, and—at anchor and close range—the two navies exchanged punishing fire for four hours. By evening, thanks to superior firepower from the allies, sixty ships and six thousand lives had been lost on the Egyptian and Ottoman side: a devastating wreckage, at least double that of the Battle of the Nile. Thus were Muhammad Ali's hopes destroyed, for the time being, by the very European nations that had helped promote them. In the event, neither Salt nor Drovetti was on hand to deal with this crisis in Anglo- and Franco-Egyptian relations: Salt was buried the day before news of the defeat reached Egypt; Drovetti was on sick leave in France.[41]

The Greek War forced France to scale back its support of Muhammad Ali's bid for independence, at least for the time being. But the pasha, undaunted by his defeat, quickly began to rebuild his navy, again with French support (further evidence of the double game European powers were playing). Shortly after Navarino—which Muhammad Ali was said, in retrospect, to blame more on Britain than on his French allies, who, he thought, had been pushed—Drovetti pressed a new scheme for expansion, and alliance with France, on his friend. He proposed that France undertake to control Algeria, the nearest North African state, not by invading and occupying the region directly, but rather by "engaging and aiding the Vice Roy to make the conquest of that state; His Highness having previously rendered himself master of the other two Regencies [Tripoli and Tunis] lying in his way!" This would let France enjoy most of the benefits of colonial occupation without its costs; and Muhammad Ali could push the limits of the Egyptian empire yet further. It was a bold proposal, but, Drovetti was convinced, by no means impossible. "Gigantic and even chimerical as this project appeared to my British Intellect," reported Salt's successor John Barker, "when the French Consul-Gen[era]l. expatiated on the details of its execution, all obstacles vanished."[42] (Why Drovetti chose to share his scheme with his British rival remains an open question.) Perhaps Drovetti knew that, decades earlier, Napoleon had considered invading Algeria, and that draft schemes were still to be found somewhere in the files of the Paris ministries. Whatever else, it was plain that for this Napoleonic veteran, at least, Egypt was just as vital to the expansion of the French Empire in the east as it had been to Napoleon himself thirty years before.

In the event, Egypt played no role in France's invasion of Algeria, in the spring of 1830. It would take almost twenty years of fitful war before French forces imposed authority and defeated the resistance movement led by the emir Abd el-Kader; but Algeria would soon be entirely assimilated into French control, first as a colony and later as a full-fledged *département* of France. Algeria was to the modern French Empire something like what India was to the British: the Eastern colony most closely tied to France; its first won and hardest lost. With the conquest of Algeria, France began once more to pursue territorial expansion overseas. Over the coming decades France would again build a transcontinental empire to rival Britain's, one stretching from Morocco to Madagascar, Senegal to Saigon; it would also become the leading European imperial power in the Middle East.

Yet while the French Empire that took shape after 1830 differed in many ways from the colonial undertakings of the Ancien Régime—most visibly, because of an increasingly detailed doctrine of the "mission civilisatrice"—there were also, as Drovetti's scheme suggested, long-standing precedents for it. The turn to North Africa was anchored in France's long history of involvement in the region, and in Egypt in particular. Arguably, France would never have moved to conquer Algeria had it not already established itself, in some sense, in Egypt. To an extent, the invasion of Algeria resembled Napoleon's invasion of Egypt: both were not new projects, but extensions of something old. Here was vivid testament to the strength and persistence of French imperial ambitions in the East, even across the decades of apparent quiescence reaching back to the Seven Years War.

Drovetti left Egypt in June 1829, with his "gigantic and even chimerical" vision of a conquering Franco-Egyptian force unfulfilled. But a month after his departure, the new French consul, Jean François Mimaut, described "a singular circumstance, . . . inspiring pointed reflections," that testified to the enduring bond between France and Egypt. It was a fine summer day, and Mimaut, as "Consul of the King of France," found himself "seated between the Viceroy and his son, on a fragment of the ancient ruins of Alexandria." Behind them was Pompey's Pillar, one of the few standing ancient monuments visible in Alexandria. In front of them was the supposed site of the now vanished Tower of Pharos, one of the seven wonders of the ancient world, on which Muhammad Ali had built a new palace. They had gathered there "to watch a parade of the troops returned from the Morea" in Greece. It was with delight and obvious emotion that Mimaut watched the men go past, "marching under four white flags [the flag of Bourbon France], and to the sound of the tune 'Vive Henri IV.' "[43]

At the time of Drovetti's departure for Europe, a sort of "special relationship" existed between France and Egypt that endured in the face of Britain's prominence in the Ottoman and Asian worlds as a whole. And though Britain and France might make common cause around international issues of mutual concern—such as Greek independence—in Egypt their political and cultural rivalry intensified. It might be politically impossible (and indeed, undesirable) for France to colonize Egypt outright. But it could still aspire to seize ancient Egypt instead. And that is just what Jean-François Champollion personally set out to do, in the biggest campaign of French collecting in Egypt since the savants.

## III. Preservers and Destroyers

In August 1828, Champollion "arrived . . . in this land of Egypt, which I have been sighing after for so long." The effects of Navarino, nine months after the event, were still plainly visible: Champollion found the port of Alexandria patrolled by European ships, some of which were preparing to evacuate Egyptian soldiers from the Peloponnese; and the harbor was filled with the sad remnants of the Egyptian fleet, being patched up to the extent that any repair was possible. ("This mélange of ships of every nation, friend and enemy at once, is a very odd sight, and manages to sum up the times," Champollion remarked.)[44] He came at the helm of a scholarly mission similar to Napoleon's, the *Mission Franco-Toscane*—so-called because the grand duke of Tuscany attached a few scholars to it, thus bringing another European nation to Egypt and to collecting. The group spent twelve months studying Egypt, working their way through the sites of Cairo and the Nile Valley (half their time was passed at Thebes and Luxor alone), making meticulous drawings and copying hieroglyphics. The *Description de l'Égypte*, Champollion never tired of pointing out, was riddled with errors; he aimed to supersede it.

But the central goal of the mission was to collect. Champollion had a mandate (though not as large a budget as he would have liked) to excavate and purchase antiquities on behalf of his Musée Charles-X; Drovetti secured *firmans* from the pasha for him to dig. Champollion's state-sponsored trip signaled the demise of Drovetti's entrepreneurial approach to collecting. (There also seems to have been some ill will between the two men, quite possibly because, compatriots though they were, they were also rival collectors.)[45] The era of the competing consuls had come to a close. Henry Salt was dead (Champollion was sorry not to have met him), and Drovetti, whose health was steadily failing, left Egypt permanently a few months after Champollion arrived.[46] A different culture of collecting was taking shape in Egypt, around new institutions and goals. Museums, universities, and scholarly groups in Europe (especially on the Continent) took an increasingly active role in collecting—which they retain to this day—by sponsoring archaeological expeditions. But the greater change was that, for the first time, Europeans began to talk of protecting, conserving, and registering antiquities, instead of just hauling them away like slaughtered big game. "It is to be hoped . . . that dilapidation is not the object of this visit to the magnificent monuments of Egypt," the *Asiatic Journal* archly observed, reporting on Champollion's expedition.[47]

It is no surprise that this barb should appear in the British press, for while Champollion acted out the French state's commitment to collecting, his most vocal opposition came, predictably, from Britons. In much the way that Champollion's scholarly approach replaced Drovetti's style of collecting, an unusual band of British expatriates in Egypt were approaching antiquities differently from Henry Salt. Immersing themselves in Egyptian culture, ancient and modern, these figures began to promote the cause of preservation, instead of collection. They articulated their case in explicit opposition to the exploits of Champollion and the French. Around the old Anglo-French rivalry, new dichotomies coalesced: between state-sponsored and private collecting initiatives, between going home and going native, and—most enduringly—between taking away and preserving in place.

If Champollion's expedition suggested how the nationalist edge of French collecting had been sharpened in the 1820s, these Britons stood in telling counterpoint to the kinds of collectors who had lived on empire's frontiers a generation earlier. While before the wars only a handful of enterprising Europeans had traveled to Egypt for pleasure, by the 1820s Egypt was becoming an exotic addition to many itineraries. British officers increasingly passed through the country on their way to or from India—a route that would become regularized in the later 1830s with the introduction of steamships. Gentleman antiquarians and aristocrats, such as the Earl of Belmore and his family, and Charlotte Clive's brother-in-law Algernon Percy, Lord Prudhoe (later Duke of Northumberland), followed in the footsteps of Viscount Valentia from fifteen years before. Artists and architects, attracted by the grand plate illustrations in the *Description de l'Égypte* and the vogue for neo-Egyptian design, went to Upper Egypt to draw, among them Joseph Bonomi, future director of the Soane Museum; and Frederick Catherwood, who would later become famous for his drawings of Mayan monuments in the Yucatán. (Catherwood's collaborator-cum-employer in Latin America, John Lloyd Stephens, had also visited ancient sites in the Middle East before going to Mexico.) In short, the British were coming, and in ever greater numbers. For all that France made a fetish out of all things Egyptian, from 1798 to 1850 Britons published more than twice as many travel books on Egypt—well over one hundred—as Frenchmen.[48]

Some of these travelers came planning to stay for just a few months, but ended up remaining for years. "I was to have been in England . . . in June or July 1823. That year, however, passed and two days before Christmas of 1835, I put my foot upon the quay at Dover," wrote James Burton, one of the most prominent British expatriates in Egypt.[49] Burton was the son of a rich property developer (James's brother was the well-known architect Decimus Burton), and was looking for something more exciting to do after studying at Cambridge than to train as a solicitor, which his father had urged. Cairo offered an alluring escape hatch from the restrictions and boring realities of life in Britain.[50] Another traveler who stayed far longer than he expected was Burton's friend John Gardner Wilkinson, a Harrow and Oxford man. Wilkinson had gone to Egypt at the instigation of the antiquarian Sir William Gell because it was a relatively unknown part of the ancient world and worth exploring by an enterprising gentleman scholar. He arrived in 1821, and went home a dozen years later.

Young, rich, well-educated, and generally well-born, these British expatriates were quite different—and conspicuously held themselves apart—from the Europeans who lived in Egypt as diplomats, merchants, or full-time employees of the pasha. Eschewing the self-contained "Frankish quarter" of Cairo, Burton, Wilkinson, and their friends settled in the twisted medieval

Expatriate life in the tombs, as depicted by Robert Hay.

alleys of the city, in tall stucco houses ornamented with turned wooden *mashrabiyya* balconies. They studied Arabic, wore Turkish clothes, and learned to eat with their hands. And in Cairo's notorious slave market, they bought women who often became their mistresses, and in some cases their wives—this at a time when abolitionist sentiment in Britain was running high. Their amanuensis in all things was Salt's dragoman, Osman Effendi. Osman was an ideal go-between. Born William Thomson in Perth, he came to Egypt with the British invading forces in 1807. One of the four hundred prisoners taken at the battle of El-Hamed, he converted to Islam and settled in Egypt permanently. (Before he joined Salt's service, Osman had been Burckhardt's faithful retainer; later, he also looked after Salt's illegitimate, half-English son.)

A slightly later glimpse into this milieu is provided by the beautifully detailed paintings of John Frederick Lewis, who lived in Cairo in the 1840s. But a splendid account of how Britons settled into this Oriental mode of life during the 1820s has been left by another notable expatriate, Robert Hay. Hay hailed from a Scottish family of long tradition and broad acres. He joined the navy as a boy of thirteen in 1812—first visiting the eastern Mediterranean on a naval cruise in 1818—but the deaths of two elder brothers (one of whom was killed at Waterloo) provided him, unexpectedly, with an inheritance and an estate. A talented artist, Hay decided to return to the East and compile a visual record of Egypt.[51]

On his first full day in Cairo, in November 1824, Hay wrote: "My first operation this morning was an attempt to get rid of a proper proportion of my hair as it is my intention to observe the dress of the Country." He then went to call on Henry Salt, where he met one of Salt's agents skulking in a corner, wearing a dirty robe pulled up to his chin, which "made me almost think it was a pig wrapped up in a bournoose, instead of an Englishman. Coffee was brought, à la Turk," after which Hay went off in Osman's care to visit James Burton. "On coming near Mr. B.'s House I saw one of his ladies looking out the window, for he lives like the turks in that respect"—shutting his womenfolk away from public view—"but he is not singular." Osman, whose "manners are perfectly of a turk" then escorted Hay home, "and I thought I could perceive from his answer to hints of mine, that he w[oul]d not be sorry to be in Auld Reekie [Edinburgh] again."[52]

Hay, however, very happily stayed in Egypt for ten more years, dividing his time between Cairo and Thebes, in the company of his Greek bride, Kalitza. By 1826, he found the European section of Cairo as alien as he had initially found the Arab ones, and disdained it: "I entered the frank quarter with the same feelings I would enter New Gate Prison—ashamed to own that I had any connection with them. Indeed so disagreeable is even the sight of the coat and hat to me, that I was sorry when anyone came to the house in that degraded garb."[53] On a later visit to Cairo, Hay shared a house with perhaps the biggest "Oriental" of all, Edward William Lane. Known as Mansoor to his friends, Lane lived in Egypt on and off between 1825 and 1849, learned Arabic to perfection, bought and later married a slave girl named Nefeeseh, and amassed material for several books on Egypt. Among them was the classic *Manners and Customs of the Modern Egyptians* (1836), which Lane lavishly illustrated with his own engravings.[54]

All this was "going native" (in the late Victorian phrase) to an extent that Henry Salt would never have dreamed of—and he did not entirely approve of it. In October 1824, Salt had posted a notice in Cairo "stating," as James Burton paraphrased it, "that he would not protect any British subjects who appeared in Turkish costume, or much to that effect."[55] Burton's summary was slightly exaggerated: in fact the notice had been put up in response to claims recently made on British protection by various Maltese—subjects of the British Empire—who worked for Muhammad Ali. "In engaging themselves in the Pasha's service," the Foreign Office instructed Salt, "they naturally diminish their Claim on the immediate protection of their own Government."[56] Burton and Wilkinson, however, who shared a house in the heart of medieval Cairo and made a point of dressing *à la Turque,* took Salt's announcement as a personal affront. They protested to the consul, who replied brusquely: "I cannot help strongly recommending to you to wear the European dress so long as you may stay in Egypt, or, otherwise, any unpleasant consequences, that may arise from your wearing the oriental dress, must rest with yourselves."[57] Burton and Wilkinson wrote angrily back. They wore Turkish clothes, as European travelers had done in Egypt for centuries, "in order to meet with no obstruction in our pursuits even in Cairo." Walking around in European dress was an invitation to trouble, they contended, which was why the pasha "offers the Turkish dress to those who are employed by him." In short, they were "fully persuaded as we always were that we are entitled by right as Englishmen to the protection of H[is] B[ritannic] M[ajesty's] Consul," no matter what clothes they wore, or in what manner they chose to live.[58]

There was definitely some snobbery in this exchange: Wilkinson and particularly Burton (who carried around Sir William Gell's "Saline Verses" in his notebook) were rather disdainful of Salt, their social inferior, and took obvious pleasure in challenging and condescending to him. But while the younger men enjoyed flaunting their unconventional living habits, the incident also revealed the limits of their identification with the Egyptian manners they were adopting—or exposed, at any rate, the persistence of a British core. This *was* a costume for them. Beneath it, they were still free-born Englishmen, able to come and go between the two guises as they chose. In this sense—and quite different from Polier and his friends in late-eighteenth-century Lucknow—Burton, Wilkinson, Lane, and their peers were practiced cultural voyeurs, watching Egypt in disguise.

Yet this Orientalist mode was only one aspect of their lives in Egypt. Many of these men immersed themselves in *ancient* Egypt as thoroughly as they did in modern Egypt. For long periods they lived in Thebes, the pharaohs' necropolis, embedded in a rocky ridge along the Nile, opposite Luxor. From a distance, Thebes is a gorgeous red-gold ribbon of stone, set back from the river by a lush plain of farmland, interspersed with date palms and mud-walled houses. Drawing nearer, you begin to notice small black dots puncturing the stone. Each is an entrance to a tomb: the mountain is honeycombed with the resting places of the ancient dead. On the far side of the ridge lies the magical Valley of the Kings, where the pharaohs were buried deep in underground labyrinths, packed with all the treasures and invocations they needed to comfort them in the afterlife. On the near side, facing the Nile, Egyptian noblemen were buried in more ordinary tombs, painted with scenes of daily life. Nowhere is ancient Egypt more stunningly preserved; and nowhere has it been more exhaustively studied and excavated.

It was here, facing the river, among the tombs of the nobles, that Henry Salt had built a house—the first to be erected on the Theban ridge in

The village of Gurna, in and around the ancient tombs.

centuries—in a village called Gurna. He stayed in it during his own visits to Thebes, and his principal agent, the Greek-born Yanni Athanasi, lived there permanently into the 1830s, supervising excavations. But Robert Hay and John Gardner Wilkinson went a step further than Salt. Like the Arab villagers of Gurna, the *gurnawi,* they took up residence inside the tombs themselves. Robert Hay lived in the tomb of Ramses IV; his artist friends made their encampment in the nearby tombs of Ramses V and VI. Wilkinson settled into a large tomb halfway up the ridge, and added walls and doors to convert the place into a sprawling house. Here, they devoted themselves to studying and recording the monuments, becoming Egyptologists in all but name. Benjamin Disraeli, visiting Egypt in 1831, spent "a week at Thebes with the advantage of the society of Mr. Wilkinson, an Englishman of vast learning . . . who can read you the side of an obelisk or the front of a pylon as we would the last number of the *Quarterly.*"[59] James Burton's notes on the Valley of the Kings, made during a long stay in 1825, were used in the 1990s to rediscover the tomb of the sons of Ramses II, the largest in the Valley.[60]

In March 1829, Jean-François Champollion and his *Mission Franco-Toscane* tied up at an ancient pier on the Luxor side of the Nile. They would stay in the area for half a year, mostly drawing and copying inscriptions in the Valley of the Kings and Gurna. It was during these months in Luxor that Champollion conceived what may have been the most grandiose French collecting scheme to date. In front of Luxor Temple stood two splendid obelisks, among the only ones still upright, and perhaps the finest. Champollion decided to bring one of them to France. In October 1828, Muhammad Ali had offered two small obelisks in Alexandria, "Cleopatra's Needles," to Britain and France, respectively. But "If the government wants an obelisk in Paris," Champollion insisted, "it is [a matter of] national honor to have one of those from Luxor."[61] Thanks to persistent French lobbying, Muhammad Ali agreed to the switch. In 1831, the French government dispatched a special mission under the direction of the improbably named Baron Isidore Justin Séverin Taylor to take one of the Luxor obelisks away, on a specially designed ship called the *Louqsor.* The obelisk was erected at the Place de la Concorde in 1833, where it still stands, in part as a monument to Champollion, who had died at the untimely age of forty-two the previous year.[62]

France proudly celebrated the event, but the British were scandalized by this act of appropriation. As the French carried monuments off to Paris with pomp and circumstance, opinion among the British expatriates began to coalesce around the idea of preserving antiquities in place. No longer was the Anglo-French antiquities contest simply about snatching trophies. It was overlaid with a competition between different national identities, expressed through opposing ideologies and methods of collecting. Wilkinson, who was in Thebes when the *Louqsor* was on its way, wrote to Hay: "We expect the French daily it has already given me a fit of the liver."[63] The British expatriates were disgusted, and by more than just the anger of defeat, of the kind Belzoni felt when Drovetti's men beat him to a prize discovery. They were outraged, at least in part, by the permanent disfigurement of an ancient site. A visitor to Paris may find it magnificent to see the obelisk in the Place de la Concorde, but to see the Luxor Temple with only one obelisk standing lopsidedly in front of it is like seeing somebody smile to reveal a missing front tooth. But the seizure of the obelisk was nothing new to Wilkinson and his friends. They had seen Champollion in action already, and they knew how ruthless he could be.

Champollion and his team spent the spring and summer of 1829 on the Nile's West Bank. On April 2, he held a party in honor of his little daughter Zoraïde's fifth birthday. (The pièce de résistance was to be "*jeune crocodile à la sauce piquante*," though unfortunately "it turned during the night—the flesh became green and putrid.")[64] The venue for the party was one of the rooms in the tomb of Seti I, still known as Belzoni's Tomb. Two months later, another and rather less jolly episode unfolded in the tomb. It was reported in full to James Burton by his friend, the artist Joseph Bonomi, who lived in Gurna making drawings with Robert Hay.

One day in June, an excavator working for the British came to Bonomi to tell him "that sawyers had arrived from Cairo to cut various pictures from Belzoni's tomb—he requested me to join with him and try to prevent Champollion from cutting and taking away what he [the excavator] considered belonged to the English." Bonomi instantly fired off a letter to Champollion:

Gourneh June 13th
1829

Sir,

I have been informed that certain people have arrived here in Gourneh by your orders to cut certain pictures from the tomb in the valley of Biban el Molook [Valley of the Kings] opened by Belzoni at the expence of the late English Consul Mr. Salt. If it be true that such is your intention I feel it my duty as an Englishman and a lover of antiquity to use every argument to dissuade you from so Gothic a purpose at least till you have permission from the present Consul General or Mohammed Ali.

Your most obedt. servt.
Joseph Bonomi

Champollion replied the next day (in French):

> Sir,
>
> I also fulfill a duty as a Frenchman to tell you that, not recognizing any authority in Egypt other than the Pasha, I do not need to ask anybody's permission, still less that of the British Consul. . . .
>
> [D]o not doubt, sir, that you will one day have the pleasure of seeing in the Museum of France some of the beautiful bas-reliefs of the tomb of [Seti I], this will be the only way to save them from imminent destruction [from the water damage to which the tomb was prone] and by putting this plan into action I am acting only as a true friend of antiquity <u>because I am taking away these monuments to conserve them and not to sell them.</u>
>
> I have the honor, etc. etc.
> J. Champollion le jeune

It was not an auspicious reply. Bonomi was furious, but there was nothing he could do. Then one of the Tuscan scholars came to suggest a compromise: the sawyers would proceed with slicing off reliefs for the Louvre, but they would also cut one off for the British Museum. This satisfied Bonomi, and he let the matter rest.[65]

James Burton, however, to whom all this was addressed, was far from pleased. He had already had an altercation with Champollion about an ancient trilingual inscription on a stone found lodged in a Cairo mosque. Burton had discovered the piece some months before, and considered it his, by right of discovery; but Champollion bluntly ignored this convention and cut the stone out of the mosque. "His appropriation of this tomb . . . to himself is just on a par with his conduct in the case of the Trilinguar inscription and if it is not purely French is at all events quite of the Napoleon school in which Monsr. Champollion has been educated," Burton raged to the British consul John Barker. As for his claim "that he carries away these monuments to preserve them," Burton continued, "Mr. Champollion might have preserved in its original state a monument that has stood the test of 30 or 40 centuries and would have done himself more honor in the eyes of the world."[66] Burton had already written to Bonomi to tell him to renounce the British Museum's claim to severed reliefs; Barker "entirely agree[d]" with him "in thinking Mr. Bonomi near wrong in either proposing or accepting on the part of the British Museum a portion of the sacrilegious spoils of the Tomb of the Kings."[67] But the dirty deed was done: the tomb was cut up. Of all the "monuments of every size" that Champollion brought back for his museum, he considered the reliefs from the tomb one of the two most "beautiful Egyptian objects ever sent to Europe. This must rightfully come to Paris and will follow me like a trophy of my expedition: I hope [it] will remain in the Louvre in memory of me *forever.*"[68]

The language invoked on both sides of the squabble would prove far more resilient than the tomb itself. A charitable reading would suggest that Champollion and Burton were both sincere in their apparent concern for preservation. Indeed, on leaving Egypt in 1829, Champollion addressed a memoir to Muhammad Ali urging him to protect several crumbling and endangered temples, and to stop the "barbarous devastation" and pillage of sites (particularly at Gurna and the Valley of the Kings) committed "by the ignorance and avidity of excavators or their employees": that is, by antiquities dealers and the Egyptian fellahin.[69] If one accepts both Burton's and Champollion's conservationist appeals at face value, then the dispute between the British and the French over the tomb points to a controversy that is still in progress. Is it acceptable to preserve something, as Champollion insisted he was doing, by removing it from a site where it is at risk? Or is it better to preserve something, as Burton contended, by finding a way to protect it where it is, in its own setting? Framed another way, does removing an object from its original location constitute an act of destruction in itself? These of course are exactly the same questions that still get raised over the Elgin Marbles in the British Museum, and over other contested objects around the world.

Such arguments, in the Egyptian context, were new. Yet there was an older element at play in the animosity between Burton and Champollion, reaching back to Burton's anger over the trilingual inscription "of which M. Champollion has robbed me!" (Burton and his friends were highly critical of Champollion's tendency, as they saw it, to claim credit for everything. "I fancy it would be better for the few travellers who are here, to distribute a list of their researches in alphab[etical] order . . . otherwise the results of their labours will be all the 'belles découvertes que j'ai fait,' " wrote Burton to Sir William Gell.)[70] These preservationist debates dressed the familiar, long-standing Anglo-French rivalry in new clothes. Burton, after all, was not categorically opposed to *all* collecting. Indeed, the episode of Belzoni's Tomb convinced him that "The very circumstance of Champollion having a second time appropriated to himself the property of another will be a plea on which to rest an application to the Pasha for securing one or both of the Luxor Obelisks for the English Government"—the very obelisk that Wilkinson and others were so outraged to see France remove some years later. In asking for the obelisk, Burton decided, "I do not think we can justly be accused of committing the same crime for which we reproach our antagonists." To his mind, cutting up the tomb (which was "British" anyway because of Belzoni's discovery) was an act of wanton destruction, different from taking away a monument that was standing out in the open.[71]

There was a final, rather troubling aspect to the emerging discourse of preservation. The pros and cons of Champollion's argument are plain. As he saw it, Egyptians were not looking after their own cultural property, so Europeans needed to step in and do it for them. To an extent, he was right. In an impassioned 1841 pamphlet arguing for preservation, the American consul in Egypt, George Gliddon, identified more than a dozen well-known sites that had been destroyed or seriously damaged since the French invasion, their stones taken and burned for lime, or carried off for the construction of Muhammad Ali's new saltpeter and indigo factories.[72] Like Champollion, Gliddon urged Western powers to take action to stop the destruction. Yet as virtuous as calls for preservation might seem, they were couched in exactly the same paternalistic terms that underlay the French imperial *mission civilisatrice* as a whole; or, for that matter, the policies of Anglicist administrators in contemporary India. It is no accident that this position should be taken by Champollion "l'Égyptien," who knew little of modern Egypt.

That charge could not be levied against the British advocates of preservation such as Hay and Burton, but the questions they raised are in some ways more perplexing. How does one reconcile the fact that it was these most "Orientalist" of Britons—whose relationship to modern Egypt seems to embody the condescending views so widely critiqued today—who were at the same time the most sympathetic advocates for preservation? Robert Hay, for instance, who lounged around his tomb home in Thebes in full Turkish garb, tirelessly fought against " 'spoiling Egypt of her Ancient Monuments!' "[73] He lamented the destruction of temples and tombs by Arabs and Europeans alike. Speaking about Salt's agent Yanni, Hay criticized the "love he acquired under Mr. Salt, for distroying tombs, under a false idea of preserving them, by attempting to cut the paintings off the walls." Anticipating the methods of modern archaeology, Hay also urged excavators that "every thing should be registered, . . . for I have reason to know that frequently things insignificant in appearance tho' interesting in other respects, have been cast aside; and eventually entirely lost sight of from the ignorance of those who possessed them."[74]

The most benign answer would be that Burton, Hay, Wilkinson, and the rest were fundamentally romantic, moved by pure love of Egypt, modern and ancient alike. However incomplete or imperfect their understanding, one could argue, their intentions were essentially good. The most insidious answer would be that they were, rather, the ultimate imperialists, appropriating both modern and ancient Egypt with an arrogant sense of entitlement. But a third reading seems most convincing. They may not have been collectors principally of objects, but they were collectors nevertheless: proto-Egyptologists and proto-anthropologists, recording archaeological data and cultural experience. And as collectors of this new kind, they, too, embarked on a kind of self-fashioning, living as renegades in self-imposed exile, intentionally flouting the restrictions of British society. Were they marginal men? Not in Britain, at least not to the extent that either Salt or Belzoni had been. But in a sense, they were using Egypt to play at being marginal or even, perversely, to reinvent themselves as marginal. On New Year's Day 1836, James Burton wrote to Robert Hay from his new home in St. Leonard's-on-Sea (a town developed by his father), with all the poignance of an imperial returnee from eighteenth-century India:

> I am still a triste ruminating arrival. I cannot yet conquer the effect of this drear climate, the privation of sun, this cheerless sky, these thick foushiferous [?] lung-tearing fogs, this parapluie, and flannel-doubled-indian-rubber-greatcoat-atmosphere. Moreover I find I have been living too long on claret and truffles, and that your English port and sherry and muggy ale induce gastric affections, that add wonderfully, I believe, to my gloomy state of mind, and magnify the annoyances of society.[75]

For him, certainly, return to England was an unhappy retreat: a return to "normal" life by a man who preferred to escape it.

What did it say about the expansion of European power that frontier zones like this one, on the edges of empire, had become places for the privileged to seek solace in being marginal, rather than for marginal figures to seek privilege? Oriental adventures of this kind had become accessible, and acceptable, to a much greater extent than they had been a generation or two earlier. British aesthetes and antiquarians spent time in Egypt in something of the way American college students might now spend summers digging wells in Central America: they were the human face of informal empire. At the same time, they looked for personal reinvention by adapting to cultural difference, in much the way some of their more marginal predecessors in eighteenth-century India had. Their gentlemanly experiments with self-fashioning pointed both to the durability of Britishness and imperial power, and to a continuing urge, and ability, among Europeans to embed themselves in Eastern societies.

By 1835, Wilkinson, Hay, and Burton had all returned to Britain; Champollion was dead; Drovetti had retired to Piedmont; and Belzoni and Salt lay buried in different parts of Africa. But together they had transformed the culture of collecting and empire in Egypt. From open Anglo-French war for Egypt itself, in 1801, had emerged a war for antiquities—and with it, a tension in European attitudes toward Egypt ancient and modern. New Western claims to stewardship over ancient Egypt in effect brought things full circle: from empire to collecting and back again. Preservation did not put an end to collecting. Instead it infused European claims on Egypt with paternalist justification. How precisely those currents converged would become manifest in the late 1830s, in Muhammad Ali's last decisive encounter with Britain and France.

## IV. Collecting Back

It was a telling sign of change that Henry Salt's successor as consul, John Barker, found it impossible to sell his collection of "a great many . . . valuable antiquities . . . , for their value not being known, no one likes to run the risk of buying them. The gout [taste] for Egyptian Antiquities seems to have gone by! The market seems to be overstocked."[76] So lamented his son Edward in 1831. Edward Barker was wrong at one level: the "gout" for antiquities infected ever larger numbers of European and American museumgoers, antiquarians, and tourists, who arrived at regular intervals, from the 1840s onward, on P&O steamships plying the route to India.[77] But entrepreneurial, high-profit, high-profile collecting belonged to the past. Now Western interest turned increasingly toward antiquities that could *not* be collected: Egypt's temples and tombs. Where the pasha had once been approached with requests for *firmans* to excavate, now he received petitions from Westerners asking him to prevent the destruction and looting of sites.

How did Muhammad Ali respond to calls for preservation, and to the shift in Western attitudes toward collecting they represented? He was at once ingenious and innovative. On August 15, 1835, the pasha issued an ordinance forbidding the export of antiquities altogether, and proposing the establishment of a museum in Cairo. A hall of the Ezbekiyya palace was cleared out to make way for the new collections, and an Egyptian director appointed in the person of Rifa'a al-Tahtawi, an intellectual rising star. Tahtawi had recently returned from five years in Paris, as part of the first educational exchange between Egypt and Europe, where he had been taken under the wing of the ex-savant Edmé-François Jomard. There Tahtawi had seen Egyptian antiquities in the galleries of the Louvre; in his memoir of his French sojourn, published in Cairo in 1834 and widely distributed, he observed that Egyptians should "preserve the ornaments and works which their ancestors have left them." Tahtawi later wrote a history of pre-Islamic Egypt and made concerted efforts to interest his countrymen in the pharaonic era.[78]

The ordinance was one of the first pieces of legislation passed by any country to preserve its cultural heritage, and a pivotal moment in the history of imperial collecting. With it, Egypt effectively declared its independence from European intervention in the antiquities sphere, and took charge of its ancient past.[79] It also laid claim to an important aspect of most national identities: the ability to package and control the nation's history. But like many forward-looking proposals, the ordinance encountered skepticism, and eventual failure. To the American consul George Gliddon, it seemed to be a "new act of Monopoly," which he believed the pasha had passed just to control the lucrative excavation business himself. Sir John Gardner Wilkinson delivered the opinion, which proved at the time to be correct, that "the formation of a museum in Egypt is purely Utopian."[80] "Years have rolled away, and *there is no Museum*, but that identical empty corridor at Cairo . . . ! The Exportation of antiquities remains to this hour a *Monopoly!*" opined Gliddon in 1841.[81] In 1842, Muhammad Ali granted permission to the Prussian Egyptologist Richard Lepsius to lead the largest state-sponsored research and collecting expedition since the French savants had swept through four decades before. Muhammad Ali's successors gave away the small holdings of the Ezbekiyya Museum to visiting dignitaries. Only in 1858 did Egypt successfully begin to regulate the antiquities trade, with the establishment of the Egyptian Museum and the Egyptian Antiquities Service—both directed by the French Egyptologist Auguste Mariette.[82]

Yet though Gliddon and others were quick to blame the failure of the 1835 ordinance on Muhammad Ali's inconstancy, the deeper causes lay elsewhere. For the fact remained that Westerners, not Egyptians, were and always would be the primary consumers of Egyptian antiquities. In many Muslim eyes, the monuments were idolatrous vestiges of the age before the Prophet—negligible at best, at worst offensive. Significantly, Muhammad Ali's proposed Egyptian Museum was intended to appeal to "travelers who visit this country," not to Egyptian visitors.[83] "I must tell you, entre nous," observed one British antiquarian to another in 1838, "that both His Highness and Boghos Bey care a vast deal less about Egyptian Antiquities and science than people in Europe may fancy. Ask Mr. Wilkinson, with my compliments, if this is not so."[84] For the pasha and his successors, antiquities mattered chiefly because Westerners wanted them: they could be sold or swapped—or preserved—for what Egypt's rulers wanted instead.

It is tempting to read the 1835 ordinance as Egypt's attempt to reclaim its own ancient past: a progressive piece of collecting back. To an extent, of course, it was. But what the ordinance ended up revealing in sharp detail was just how deeply politicized collecting in Egypt had become—and on three levels. Not only were antiquities fought over between European nations competing for prestige and influence. They were also pawns in a battle between Europe and Egypt itself, over who had the right and responsibility to possess and protect antiquities. Conflict over ancient Egypt, finally, acted as a substitute for control over modern Egypt, and increasingly served as legitimation for that control. To claim that Egyptians were unable to appreciate, understand, or look after their antiquities—and thus needed the West to intervene—was analogous to saying that Egyptians were unable to look after their own land and culture, and thus needed the West to intervene. (It is no coincidence that many of the Europeans lobbying for preservation were also involved in the campaign to abolish the slave trade in Egypt.[85] Both causes formed part of the West's greater civilizing mission.) Preservation stood as a surrogate for more overt forms of territorial occupation: it represented an effort to collect the sites and landmarks of ancient Egypt under Western control. So it seems no mere coincidence, then, that calls for preservation came to a head at much the same time as did a new European effort to lay claim to modern Egypt.

In spite of Britain and France's joint effort to check his progress, Muhammad Ali had bounced back after Navarino and continued to pursue expansionist conquests, with considerable success. By the late 1830s he ruled an empire that reached north to the borders of Anatolia, east to Yemen, and south into the Sudan. In May 1838, the pasha summoned the French and British consuls and announced his intention to seek formal independence for Egypt and Syria, which his son Ibrahim had ruled since 1833. Ibrahim backed up his father's demands with a resounding victory over the Ottomans at the battle of Nezib in June 1839; the Ottoman navy promptly defected to the Egyptians. Once again, Egypt held the fate of the Ottoman Empire in its hands.

This new "Eastern crisis" acutely troubled Britain's foreign minister Henry John Temple, third Viscount Palmerston, who personified British international policy in this period. Palmerston was deeply committed to preserving the Ottoman Empire, and he loathed and mistrusted Muhammad Ali almost as much as he feared Britain's emerging rival in the region, Russia. "I hate Mehemet Ali," he wrote, "whom I consider as nothing but an ignorant barbarian . . . I look upon his boasted civilization of Egypt as the arrantest humbug; and I believe that he is as great a tyrant and oppressor as ever made a people wretched."[86] What made matters worse was that the pasha was becoming a risk to the British Empire. If his expansion continued apace, he would soon control both major Middle Eastern overland routes to India, which had become especially important to Britain since the introduction of steam-powered shipping. Concern about Egyptian domination in the Red Sea had already led Britain to seize the Yemeni port of Aden from its Egyptian occupiers in 1839.[87] Finally, there was the ever-present specter of French intervention. "The public mind of France is taken possession of, by the idea of Egyptian colonization," claimed one British expert, who insisted that France still sought "the permanent domination of . . . Egypt, whether by the strategies of diplomacy or by war."[88] Working in the face of French opposition, Palmerston brokered an agreement between Europe's other powers to reverse Muhammad Ali's conquests. "I look upon the question for decision to be, whether England is to remain a Substantive Power, or is to declare herself a dependency of France," he pronounced. On July 15, 1840, Britain, Russia, Prussia, and Austria put their names to the Convention of London, demanding that Egyptian forces evacuate Syria, and outlining the measures they would take to force Muhammad Ali to comply.[89]

For several months, Muhammad Ali held out, hoping—not unreasonably—for French aid. "The policy of France in spiriting up the poor old man who governs this country, to resist all the overtures that have been made to him by England, was felt every day more and more," commented a Briton then in Egypt.[90] Throughout the last weeks of summer, Britain and France edged around the prospect of another war over Egypt. But the French king Louis-Philippe, whose soldiers were already fighting hard against Abd el-Kader in Algeria, opposed it; and Palmerston sent in gunboats to bring Muhammad Ali into line. In September, a force of British and Turkish troops landed near Beirut and began to advance against the Egyptians in Syria, capturing Acre. On November 15, 1840, the British squadron appeared off the coast of Alexandria. By the month's end, Muhammad Ali had signed a convention agreeing to abandon his colonies (with the exception of the Sudan) in exchange for being recognized as hereditary pasha of Egypt. Queen Victoria, whose first child was born six days later, joked that she might have to name her new daughter "Turco Egypto."[91] The crisis was over.

Egypt would never be an empire. It would also never be genuinely independent during the rest of the nineteenth century. Not only did the pasha remain a vassal of the Ottoman sultan, subject to annual tribute payments, but also new European regulations drastically constrained the Egyptian economy, and reduced the size of Egypt's army from one hundred thousand to eighteen thousand. Muhammad Ali died in 1849, not long before a planned visit to Britain. He left his heirs with a technocratic bureaucracy, a Westernized military, modern factories, and substantial agricultural capabilities; but he also left them a state in thrall to European diplomatic and economic strictures. Egypt had been locked into Britain's informal empire and condemned to a position of subjection that would only deepen with the building of the Suez Canal and Egypt's crippling debt to British and French creditors. In 1882, Egypt's economic and political dependence on Britain would culminate in social upheaval, revolution, and occupation by British troops.[92]

With the 1840 resolution of the "Eastern crisis," Britain solidified an imperial presence in the Middle East that would have been inconceivable just forty years earlier, and that demonstrated Britain's diplomatic and military preeminence in Europe, as well as British willingness to act in defense of imperial interests, even at the risk of new entanglements. It revealed Britain's persisting anxiety about France and increasing worry about Russia as catalysts for imperial action. Palmerston's personal animosity toward Muhammad Ali also captured the crude conviction of superiority in the heart of many British liberals. And Muhammad Ali did not succeed either in collecting his own empire or in "collecting back" the prestige of ancient Egypt. His two-tiered failure—to assert Egyptian authority over antiquities and to lay claim to an Egyptian empire—reflected Egypt's double bind to the West. Collecting antiquities formed part of a cultural posture that legitimated and facilitated the assertion of European power.

Taken together, the Egyptian monuments in the museums and public spaces of London and Paris—the Young Memnon, the sarcophagus of Seti I, the Luxor obelisk—have a somewhat depressing yet multilayered story to tell about collecting and empire on an Eastern frontier of European expansion. They speak of the people who brought them, many of them marginal figures, far removed from the bastions of culture and power in which the objects themselves now stand. They speak, too, of national rivalry, and of the long-standing tensions that brought them to these European capitals. And they attest to a way in which they helped shape images of Egypt in the West, and cultivated Western desires. If there were foreshadowings in their history of the formal imperialism that was to come in Egypt, there were also ghostly omens of its postcolonial future: a future in which Egypt would struggle to come to terms with its own colonized ancient past.

And what of the place from which the ancient treasures came? A glimpse at how European attitudes toward ancient Egypt made their mark on contemporary society can still be seen in one of the places where Salt, Drovetti, and Belzoni were most active. For on the Theban ridge in Gurna, the house that Salt built remained very much alive. When he had put it up in the 1810s, there were no other modern structures in the area. But within a short time, wooden beams and mud bricks began to rise around it: a new village of Gurna was tak-

The *gurnawi* digging for antiquities.

ing shape around Salt's house, on top of the ancient tombs. Economically as well as physically, modern Gurna was built at the intersection of Europe and the ancient past. The modern *gurnawi* made their livings by excavating and hunting for antiquities. In November 1826, Robert Hay set up his camera obscura in Gurna to draw a panorama of Thebes and Luxor. The image shows a busy built-up settlement with fellahin hard at work digging, clearing, and sifting for antiquities like farmers tending their native soil.[93] Salt's house survives to this day, but it is a ruin now, frequented more by goats than by people. Yet while the ruined house embodies the demise of one vision of collecting, it also calls attention to the emergence of another. Gurna has become a thriving modern village, devoted to the preservation and display (for Western tourists) of ancient Egyptian tombs.

European imperial interest worked to detach ancient from modern Egypt. Postcolonial Egypt has been left with the challenge of bringing both together into a common national frame. It has not been an easy fit. Gamel Abdul Nasser, for instance, the founding father of postcolonial Egypt, placed Arab identity at the heart of Egyptian nationhood, paying less mind to Egypt's pre-Islamic past. Indeed his Aswan High Dam, built in the 1960s in the name of modernity and progress, threatened to wipe away dozens of ancient temples under Lake Nasser. More recently, the sense of a gulf between modern Egyptian identity and Egypt's ancient heritage has deepened with the rise of religious activists seeking to replace Egypt's secular government with an Islamist régime. "I have killed Pharaoh!" yelled a member of the Muslim terrorist group Gama'a al-Islamiyya in 1981 when he shot President Anwar Sadat, who had made peace with Israel and the West.[94] A spate of attacks on Western tourists at pharaonic sites in the 1980s and 1990s directly challenged the cultural bond between the West and ancient Egypt, and threatened to destroy the Egyptian tourist trade, a mainstay of the nation's economy. Where this has come from is all too plain: a history of European intervention that sought to colonize Egypt by collecting its antiquities.

A chance glimpse of a final collected antiquity places a suggestive capstone on the history of empire and autonomy, collecting and preservation, in Egypt. The two most significant temples put at risk by the proposed Aswan Dam, Abu Simbel and Philae, were saved from destruction by a UNESCO project, funded in large part by the United States, which painstakingly moved them, stone by stone, to higher ground. In thanks for American assistance, Nasser presented the United States with another doomed structure, the Temple of Dendur, which now rests in the Metropolitan Museum of Art, in New York. It was as if nothing had changed since the early days of Muhammad Ali: antiquities could be traded for modern technology and Western development aid. So it is that Dendur sits in the Met, a box within a box. And on the walls of its small inner sanctum there is a curious vestige of an earlier imperial age, in the graffiti that pockmarks the ancient carvings. One inscription,

Pride or prejudice? A roadside sign on the way to the Valley of the Kings.

signed on the western wall and dated 1816, tells that DROVETI was here. But of course, Bernardino Drovetti would have known how to spell his own name—with two *t*'s—which means that this was written for him by somebody else. Thus the European collector left his mark on Egypt, but alas it was mistaken.

CONCLUSION

# *Collecting an Empire*

In the hot season of 1839, a middle-aged Englishwoman named Emily Eden accompanied her brother George to perhaps the most archetypically British spot in India. No place better merits clichés about the British Empire than Simla: the cool Himalayan hill station where imperial personnel and their families passed the stifling summer months ensconced in chalets and lodges straight out of some Highland idyll. "Twenty years ago no European had ever been here," Eden wrote to their sister,

> and there we were, with the band playing the "Puritani" and "Masaniello," and eating salmon from Scotland, and sardines from the Mediterranean . . . and all this in the face of those high hills, some of which have remained untrodden since the creation, and we, 105 Europeans, being surrounded by at least 3,000 mountaineers, who, wrapped up in their hill blankets, looked on at what we call our polite amusements. . . . I sometimes wonder they do not cut all our heads off, and say nothing more about it.[1]

It was a prophetic image. Less than twenty years later, the Mutiny-Rebellion of 1857 would make imaginings like this one—of the massed ranks of the ruled turning on the tiny corps of British rulers—cruelly real to British communities in India, and to a terrified reading public back home. Indeed, even before the year 1839 was out, Emily Eden's fantasy would edge closer to reality than she could know.

Her observation captured a critical way that the British Empire, in India as elsewhere, had by the early Victorian years transformed itself into something quite different from the cosmopolitan imperial society familiar from the eighteenth century. Fifty years earlier, Elizabeth Plowden had written in her Lucknow diary of cross-cultural families, collections, social gatherings, and power relations. Now Eden could describe a contained British microcosm, incongruously (and very recently) stuck into an Indian setting. Crucially, she could present an opposition, of a kind Plowden would have been hard-pressed to make, between white rulers and nonwhite ruled facing off against each other like animals and keepers at a zoo. Yet was it entirely clear which side was which? This glimpse of early-Victorian British India raises two key questions about imperial conquest and collecting that would hang over the nineteenth century and beyond. How would the British represent themselves to, and protect themselves from, the vast numbers of subjects they purported to govern? And how would the ruled respond to, or resist, these strange, salmon- and sardine-eating women and men in their midst?

When Queen Victoria assumed her throne in 1837, Britain had come to possess a substantial territorial empire in the East, and an imperial persona that was showing symptoms of becoming the rigidly hierarchical, racialized, and gendered imperial culture popularly associated with the late nineteenth century. Queen Victoria's empire would grow bigger, tougher, grander, and nastier than that of her grandfather George III. This empire was represented overseas by swashbuckling characters such as Cecil Rhodes and General Charles Gordon; represented for a reading public by the exotic fictions of Rudyard Kipling and H. Rider Haggard; and represented in the flesh by ceremonials such as the extravagant durbar held when Queen Victoria was named Empress of India. Britain was no longer marginal to France, or to Eastern imperial powers, to the extent it had been a century before. Britain had also refashioned itself in several ways. During the Napoleonic Wars a sense of British imperial mission had begun to coalesce: one that was martial, nationalist, paternalistic, moralistic, and racially pure. That sensibility worked to abolish slavery in the British Empire in 1833, but it also moved to "civilize" India and other parts of the world.[2] (The celebrated abolitionist William Wilberforce, for instance, was a poisonous anti-Hindu bigot.) Across the reaches of empire, ethnic and racial mingling was less common and less tolerated—not least because the consolidation of British power meant that there were fewer opportunities for marginal Europeans to seek fame and fortune in indigenous milieux; and fewer such arenas that could promise it to them.

And yet, imperial self-fashioning remained just that: a mask over a far messier reality. British power overseas remained conflicted and sometimes incomplete. Though the live danger of global war with France had disappeared, Britain continued to confront imperial dissent, resistance, and possible defeat. After Waterloo, as after the Seven Years War, Britain faced vastly increased territories and interests to protect and safeguard. The century from 1815 to 1914 often is portrayed as a period of peace for Britain, but the image quickly dissolves once overseas imperial conflicts are taken into account. These read like an imperial gazetteer: the Opium Wars in China (1839–1842 and 1859–1860); the Afghan Wars (1838–1842 and 1878–1880); the Sikh Wars (1842–1849); the Maori Wars (1860–1866); wars against the Zulu, Basuto, and Matabele in southern Africa (1879–1893); the Mahdist uprisings and conquest of the Sudan (1881–1898); and, most serious of all, the Indian Mutiny-Rebellion of 1857–1858 and the Boer War of 1899–1902. Because they were so scattered, often brief, and involved relatively small numbers of white British troops, these conflicts sometimes had the appearance of isolated skirmishes. Yet taken together, they make an obvious point: beneath the rhetoric of Victorian imperial triumphalism coursed persisting anxieties, insecurities, rivalries, and failures.

So, too, cultural identities for those living in the new heartlands of empire, and on its frontiers, could be negotiated across the lines of East and West. In India, for example, an Irish-born army officer called Charles Stuart joined a long genealogy of border-crossing collectors by forming the first major European collection of Hindu sculpture—most of it now in the British Museum—and by developing such an "intimacy" with "the natives of this country," in the words of one obituarist, that "his toleration of, or rather apparent conformity to, their ideas and prejudices, obtained for him the name of *Hindoo* Stuart."[3] Stuart died in 1828, and his tomb, deep in the shaded enclosures of Calcutta's Park Street Cemetery, takes the unusual form of a north Indian temple—tangible evidence of a life spent between cultures.[4] A tour around sites of British interest in the 1840s might introduce one to the Fynn family of Natal, whose members lived as chiefs among the Zulus; to the pakeha Maori of New Zealand, white Europeans adorned with Maori facial tattoos; to James Brooke, the "White Rajah" of Sarawak; or, of course, to lingering expatriates in Egypt, such as the painter John Frederick Lewis.[5] There were also systematic ways that cultural boundaries would continue to be crossed. The expansion of Britain's empire in India, for instance, meant that more and more sepoys were needed to police it—and that more and more traveled overseas to fight for it, as they had done in Egypt in 1801. By the end of the century, Indians would be garrisoning Egypt and Singapore, cutting sugarcane in Trinidad and Fiji, and running railroads in East Africa.[6]

These were more than just the last gasps of a fundamentally pre-Waterloo world, colorful exceptions to the hardening of imperial rule. They pointed as well to the future of the British Empire. For even as the empire gained definition as a single entity—in culture, discourse, administration, and territorial limits—so did the fissures, oppositions, and hybridities that seemed to challenge it from within. Not only would traces of the eighteenth-century world continue into the nineteenth. One could also already detect hints of late colonial and postcolonial tensions that would extend into the twentieth century and beyond.

Emily Eden herself stood at just one remove from an early Victorian act of conquest and collecting that crystallized earlier patterns and hints of future

"Hindoo" Stuart's temple-cum-tomb in the South Park Street Cemetery, Calcutta.

oppositions. Her brother George, Lord Auckland, was the governor-general of India. At the same time that the foreign secretary Palmerston worked to contain Egypt and protect British India from the Middle East, Auckland faced challenges to India's northwest, just beyond those "high hills" that looked down on his sister's lighthearted entertainment. Russia was making an ally of Persia; Persia was making war on Afghanistan; and Afghanistan bordered Company territory in India, and the Punjab, ruled by the powerful and independent Sikh Ranjit Singh. News had reached Auckland of direct Russian overtures to Afghanistan's ruler, the amir Dost Muhammad Khan.

Though some in Parliament and the East India Company objected to British expansion beyond what was considered to be India's natural western border, the River Sutlej, Auckland believed that the Russian threat in Afghanistan demanded action. He decided to depose Dost Muhammad Khan and replace him with the elderly ex-amir Shah Shujah, who had been living in India as a Company pensioner. In December 1838, a 15,000-strong force, the "Army of the Indus," marched over the Sutlej to restore Shah Shujah to his throne. The régime change seemed simple and successful: Dost Muhammad fled to Bokhara, and Shah Shujah rode triumphantly into Kabul in August 1839. But while the British troops settled into a genial round of ice skating, amateur theatricals, and cricket matches on the dusty plains, trouble approached: Dost Muhammad came back. In November 1841, a crowd stormed the house of the British resident Alexander Burnes and stabbed him to death. Akhbar Khan, Dost Muhammad's son, invited Burnes's senior colleague to negotiate a settlement, and then promptly murdered him. Terrified and traumatized, British commanders looked for the fastest way out. Accepting unconditional surrender and a promise of safe passage, the Army of the Indus retreated from Kabul on January 6, 1842, bound for British India.

Trekking through the Hindu Kush in January would have been an ordeal in itself, but things got much worse when Akhbar Khan, contrary to his promise, set upon the retreating forces. Thousands of Britons and Indians died in open fighting; thousands more from exposure. Others were picked off by bullets from the long-barreled *jezails* of marksmen in the hills around. Partway through the march, 120 British women and children were escorted back to Kabul as captives. They were relatively lucky. Of the 4,500 soldiers and 12,000 camp followers who snaked into the high mountain passes, just one man made it through alive: William Brydon, army surgeon, who staggered into the British camp at Jalalabad on January 13, 1842, to tell his awful tale.[7] Ten months afterward, British and Indian soldiers trudging through the same passes found the way "literally strewed with the horrid remains of men,— skeletons they could not be called, for in many the features were so hideously perfect, that little difficulty was experienced in recognising . . . those who had been known in life." As the gun carriages rolled over the bodies, their "wheels crushed the bones of those unburied masses, and the harsh, agonizing sound struck mournfully and direfully on the heart."[8] It had been the worst defeat in the history of Britain's eastern empire.

At about the same time that the pathetic figure of Dr. Brydon appeared at the gates of Jalalabad, slumped over his pony, a new governor-general, Lord Ellenborough, arrived in India determined (he told the Company Court of Directors) "*to restore peace to Asia.*"[9] He learned of the Kabul catastrophe the day he arrived, and promptly set about plotting the best way to get the rest of the troops, and the British captives, out of Afghanistan. One branch of the army was instructed to liberate Jalalabad; the other, commanded by General Sir William Nott, was to proceed via Ghazni, to Kabul. In part this was so the British could recapture the city, which had fallen in March.[10] In part it was to indulge in a conspicuous, and face-saving, act of collecting.

After a battle on the outskirts of Ghazni, the British entered the city on September 5, 1842. On Ellenborough's orders, they paused there long enough to remove the carved sandalwood gates from the tomb of Ghazni's legendary eleventh-century sultan Mahmud. Convention held that the gates originally belonged to the Temple of Somnath, in Gujarat, and that Mahmud had seized them on one of his devastating incursions into India. (Wilkie Collins's moonstone had also supposedly been looted from Somnath by one of Mahmud's men, before making its way to Seringapatam, and thence to Britain.) Mullahs at the site confirmed "that the carpet round the monument, the sandal-wood gates, and the marble animals had been brought to Ghuznee on elephants, as trophies from the temple of Somnauth."[11] Now they would be Britain's trophies instead. On September 9, army engineers lowered the great doors from their mountings. "The numerous fakeers attending the tomb, wept at their removal, as they accounted them their most valuable treasure," wrote a British cleric attached to Nott's brigade. "One can imagine their exclaiming with Micah, 'Ye have taken away our gods, and what have we more?' "[12] While the Afghans wept, British soldiers cheered on seeing these "proud and memorable trophies of our successes" borne away, "each on the carriage of a four-and-twenty pounder, dragged heavily by a herd of half-starved sleepy buffaloes."[13] On the general's orders, the citadel of Ghazni was entirely destroyed; and the army resumed its march toward Kabul on September 10.

As a piece of propaganda and showmanship alone, the seizure of the gates made a striking statement. The British army had just sustained its worst-ever defeat in the East, but Ellenborough grabbed these "just trophies" of Britain's "successful marches" to help polish tarnished laurels. Inverting the usual relationship between conquest and collecting, the Somnath gates offered a symbol that replaced imperial authority, not a symbol of its assertion. Trophy-taking disguised the *lack* of imperial power—in much the way that it had for Napoleon in Egypt.

The "Somnath gates" in the Red Fort, Agra.

But a more dramatic gesture of imperial self-fashioning was to follow. Ellenborough issued a public proclamation to "all the Princes and Chiefs, and People of India" announcing that he would return the doors triumphantly to Somnath and restore them to their rightful Hindu owners. Thus, after centuries in the hands of Muslim infidels, he announced, "the insult of eight hundred years is at last avenged."[14] This targeted appeal to Hindu interests reflected an important transition in British rule: the Company's evolution from a state within and alongside the Mughal Empire, to a state that superseded it and reached out to India's religious majority. Fifty years earlier, Company servants had immersed themselves in Indo-Persian courts, and lived and collected like Mughal nobles. Now, though the shell of the Mughal Empire remained, and would last until 1858, the East India Company had emerged as India's single most significant ruler, and it governed a substantial population composed (like its army) chiefly of Hindus. By declaring Britain to be, specifically, the protector of Hindu India, Ellenborough also in effect declared British supremacy.

But his play for Hindu sympathies proved highly unwelcome to many. The minister with Nott's brigade, for instance, was none too pleased to watch a "child-like parade with the old gates of Soomnaut," on the army's triumphal return to Ferozepore, and judged "Lord Ellenborough's line of policy, . . . both unwise and unbecoming the representative of a christian nation, . . . and painfully at variance with that devout acknowledgment of God's providence and goodness which had generally characterised his lordship's proclamations."[15] More significantly, by reaching out to Hindus in this way, Ellenborough also appeared to be delivering an affront to Muslims, who now more than ever were feared and branded as "fanatics." Ellenborough's gesture proved so contentious that it triggered a motion of censure in Parliament. The historian and liberal MP Thomas Babington Macaulay castigated the governor-general for interfering "in disputes among the false religions of the East," and for having the audacity to prefer Hinduism—"the most degrading and most corrupting of all forms of worship"—to the monotheistic, and to him more palatable, Islam. Macaulay promoted a version of British rule that bestowed clean administration, security of property, civil rights, and, some hoped, "true religion"—giving (according to another leading liberal, Lord John Russell) "the millions of natives forming that vast empire" a kind of life "which they never could have been in before their conquest." In the liberal imagination, Britain should play the part of civilizer, standing impartially above Indian cultures and imposing British ways on them all.[16]

Ellenborough, on the other hand, chose to refashion himself, and the British imperial government, in a transcultural vein, appealing to religious constituencies from within. In a characteristically graphic passage, Macaulay suggested that Ellenborough donned personalities like cloaks: "His plan of governing with success seems to have been that of turning himself as fast as he can into the various characters of Hindoo, Rajah, Mussulman, and omnipotent governor, and that alone supplies ample reason for his recall." (Ellenborough had also, in the process, behaved like the hated Napoleon: the proclamation was "neither English nor oriental," Macaulay decided, but "an imitation of those trashy rants . . . from the proconsuls of France in the time of the Directory.") This strand would be taken up at the century's end by the splendidly paternalistic viceroy Lord Curzon, who made much of casting Britain as a strictly neutral protector of India's "national" past, Hindu and Muslim alike.[17] But of course what Ellenborough had also done was to articulate a sense that this distinction existed at all: that Hindus and Muslims were necessarily opposed, that their interests needed to be balanced against each other, and managed with care from on high.[18] That sense of communal division would permeate (and, for many, legitimate) British rule in India, and has provoked politics of prejudice and repeated outbreaks of violence in postcolonial South Asia.

Among Britons, then, the controversy over the gates presented two visions of what British imperial rule could or should stand for, and a divided picture of Indian society. But for better or worse, the gates' procession through India did not excite the attention some had expected. "The general feelings among the Hindus who visit our Trophy, is that of curiosity, and not of religion . . . ," said Ellenborough's aide-de-camp, who accompanied the gates on their journey. "The Mahomedans do not seem to care the least about them, and the only people who take offence at our march, are the Missionaries in Calcutta." By then they had reached Agra, where "The weather is now becoming hot, so much so that Lord Ellenborough has determined to place the Gates in the Fort of Agra, until the commencement of next cold season, when he resumes our march to Guzerat."[19] But Parliament forbade Ellenborough from moving the gates farther. One person suggested that they go to "the British Museum, or some other place, where they may be looked on as curious relics, without any amazing respect for their holiness."[20] Another proposed that they go to the Indian Museum in Calcutta, "the metropolis of our empire," where "as trophies of our victory over the Affghans who had so signally discounted us" their "political importance" might be appreciated.[21] But in Agra they were to remain. Their authenticity, which had always been in doubt, has been definitively disproven. They now stand behind battered glass doors in a small room in the Red Fort, where a modern Archaeological Survey of India sign explains that they are there "EITHER AS A WAR TROPHY OF THE BRITISH CAMPAIGN OF 1842, OR AS A SAD REMINDER OF THE HISTORIC LIES OF THE EAST INDIA CO." In their dusty irrelevance, the gates demonstrate how the British Empire itself has become the museum piece, a relic of history.

Objects have a tremendous capacity for acquiring competing meanings, and different interpretations over time. If Britain used foreign objects to underscore, and sometimes define, its imperial persona, then how might imperial subjects use objects to respond to foreign rule? A suggestive answer leads back into the alleyways of north Calcutta, to the place where this book began. It was there, in 1835, in the tight lanes of the Chor Bhagan quarter, that a young Bengali patrician called Rajendro Mullick broke ground for his new house. Five years later, with the sweat of five thousand laborers, the house was finished: all three stories of it, fronted with long Corinthian galleries, crowned by a heavy Palladian pediment. The massive Antwerp mirrors that panel the walls of the ballroom were put in place before the room was done, since they were too large to move through any door. It was said that ninety different kinds of marble inlaid the floors, which gave the house its name: the Marble Palace.[22]

This was no ordinary house, nor was it built to be one. Mullick's father had died when Rajendro was a baby, leaving the infant a massive inheritance and feuding relatives eager to get their hands on it. The Court of Wards entrusted the boy to an Anglo-Irish guardian, Sir James Weir Hogg. (Hogg's own son Stuart designed Calcutta's New Market, just off Chowringhee, a splendid piece of Victorian red-brick Gothic, complete with a clock tower.) Hogg exposed Rajendro to the curriculum of a young English gentleman: Greek, Latin, and English grammar. He also imbued his ward with the idea that a proper gentleman should collect art. When Rajendro turned sixteen, he decided to put his lessons into action. The Marble Palace, drawn up partly by European architects, was designed from the outset to be a showcase for Rajendro's collection, and it soon displayed an extraordinary array of art, ranging from Rubens, Reynolds, and Titian to "a large and full sized bronze figure of an English Cow presented to the Mullicks by Sir Elijah Impey." In the words of an early-twentieth-century Indian guide, "a galaxy of bronze and marble statues in the best style—classical, mythological and heraldic—adorn the corridors and recesses"; in one room stands a figure of the Queen Empress herself, draped in heavy robes, carved out of solid oak.[23]

As a collection of Western art in India, the Marble Palace was not, in and of itself, a novelty. Mullick was an heir of sorts to Asaf ud-Daula, who had blended an Indo-Muslim tradition of royal collecting with the habits of European connoisseurs; and to Tipu Sultan, who had also sought out European objects, particularly mechanical ones. An even closer parallel to Mullick was the young maharaja Serfoji II of Tanjore, who established a European-style cabinet of curiosities in the 1810s under the influence of his own European guardian, the German Pietist missionary Christian Friedrich Schwartz.[24] Some years later, Rajendro Mullick would tie himself into that princely tradition by acquiring objects directly from the last nawab of Awadh, Wajid Ali Shah, who had been exiled to Calcutta after the Mutiny-Rebellion of 1857.

But the Marble Palace diverged from princely collections in a signal respect, and not just because Mullick was not a ruler. It was not formed in order to advertise the Mullick family's magnificence per se. Mullick self-consciously set out to educate the public (or at least, a select portion of it) by inviting them through the iron gates to look at his art and learn about European tastes. The Marble Palace in this sense was a glorious pretender: a mock-up of a European gentleman's house, built to instruct an Indian audience in the strange manners of the people who lived among and governed them. Thanks to its wider mission, the Marble Palace counts as India's "first museum of western art," specifically designed for public appreciation and education. It also represented another kind of collecting back, to set alongside contemporary Egyptian attempts to collect back their own heritage: this was a know-thy-enemy approach to art and culture.[25]

Rajendro Mullick fitted into a tradition of individuals collecting and re-inventing themselves in empire's embrace. History has not always treated them kindly. Where European border crossers like Charles "Hindoo" Stuart have been consigned to the anonymous ranks of the "gone native," Westernized Indians such as Mullick are often chastized for "collaborating" or "assimilating," or for being foolish apers, lacking the taste of the real masters. At first glance, Mullick might seem to personify the colonial Indian elite envisaged by T. B. Macaulay (again) in his "Minute on Indian Education," written in the same year that construction of the Marble Palace was begun. In it (along with his infamous assessment that "a single shelf of a good European library was worth the whole native literature of India and Arabia"), Macaulay advances the view that Britain should set out to create "a class of persons Indian in blood and colour, but English in taste, in opinions, in morals, and in intellect." This colonial elite would work as "interpreters" of British rule to the wider Indian public, a buffer class of sorts between "us and the millions whom we govern."[26]

Yet though Mullick worked dedicatedly at being "English in taste," and even at "interpreting" those tastes for his countrymen, he was Indian in far more than "blood and colour." Though he had a European guardian, he also had a formidable mother, who took an active part in planning her son's education so as to make sure he never lost touch with his Hindu roots. (To protect her modesty, the devout widow would conduct her conversations with Hogg through a bamboo screen.) Mullick must have been the only schoolboy of his times to study the Vedas alongside his Homer. He remained deeply devout throughout his life. One reason he never traveled to Europe, for instance, was because of the Hindu prohibition against crossing the ocean. He left orders that after his death no fewer than eighty-six special *pujas* be performed at the house each year—in a worship hall decked with effigies of Greek and Roman gods. Mullick also maintained the practice, started by his father and continuing still, of providing free meals at the house to six hundred paupers every day. And while the main, public portion of the "palace" was given over to extravagance and opulence, in the family quarters above, austerity reigned: there were wooden floors instead of marble. For its owner, too, austerity was the rule: Mullick dressed simply and without jewels, maintained a strict vegetarian diet, and eschewed lavish entertainments. Luxury and Western style were for public consumption only.

At one level, of course, the Marble Palace paid tribute to the ascendancy of British power in India: Mullick turned to European culture for the same reasons Antoine Polier and his peers once approached the Mughals. But the Marble Palace also offered a sharp riposte to Macaulay. This was not hollow mimicry. The house represented an attempt to reap the best of both worlds. Mullick could project a public face in keeping with the European gentlemanly tradition in which Hogg had trained him, while at the same time, if somewhat behind the scenes, maintaining the religious orthodoxy of his Hindu forebears. Here, too, refinement met realpolitik. Mullick believed his compatriots should be familiar with the culture of their European rulers, and with an aesthetic tradition he delighted in; yet this was not to come at the expense of Indian culture. There may have been more self-promotion—or self-contradiction—in the compromise than he cared to admit. But the house bears witness to an enduring lesson: cultural exchange is a two-way street, and cultural identities are not an either-or proposition.

Perhaps the best sense of how much these episodes in imperial collecting anticipated trends that would continue well into the nineteenth century can be found in the work of Rudyard Kipling, who penned so many of imperial Britain's favorite tales, verses, and mottoes. Published in 1901, the year the Queen died, Kipling's novel *Kim* tells the adventures of a boy, the eponymous Kim, caught up in Britain's competition with Russia for control of India's northwest frontier. Surely the best-known novel of British India, if not of the British Empire as a whole, *Kim* opens with a splendid evocation of collecting and empire:

> He sat, in defiance of municipal orders, astride the gun Zam-Zammah on her brick platform opposite the old Ajaib-Gher—the Wonder House, as the natives call the Lahore Museum. Who hold Zam-Zammah, that "fire-breathing dragon," hold the Punjab; for the great green-bronze piece is always first of the conqueror's loot.[27]

Brown-skinned, barefoot, swearing fluently in Hindustani, Kim in fact is white; he secures his position on the cannon's barrel by shoving away a Muslim boy and a Hindu boy in turn, with "some justification . . . since the English held the Punjab and Kim was English." In the narrative that unfolds, Kim will turn his inside knowledge of India to the service of imperial power, by becoming a spy in the Anglo-Russian "Great Game." He also turns himself inside out, discovering an original *sahib* self (Kimball O'Hara) lurking beneath that dusky, Indianized skin. Written by the author of such imperial catchphrases as "the white man's burden" and "East is East and West is West," *Kim*—a story of going un-native—seems to embody the self-confidence and ethnic arrogance associated with the British Empire at its late-nineteenth-century apex. In Kipling's telling, Kim sits on the cannon as Britain sits on the Punjab: a single object anchors the imperial order; conquest and collecting march in step.

But this apparently seamless correspondence covers a more blurry reality. For like so many "imperialists" on the edges of empire, Kim hails from the margins of white society. Not English at all, he is the son of a poor, drunken Irish soldier, is raised by a "half-caste" opium addict, and speaks English with a foreign accent. And in much the way that Kim (to quote a chapter epigraph) has "two / Separate sides," the objects in the novel, too, have double meanings.[28] The Ajaib-Gher is both Indian "Wonder House" and British-run museum. In the book's next scene, the Tibetan lama who will later guide Kim through the byways of North India, tours the museum galleries with their British curator. The two men marvel together over a collection of Gandharan Buddhist sculpture, admiring two things in one: sacred relics for the lama, beautiful artifacts for the curator. Perhaps it is no accident that this heavily Greek-influenced art itself attests to an episode of East-West convergence, Alexander the Great's march toward India. Objects, like people, can transcend cultural boundaries.

Not many people read *Kim* anymore, and aspects of the novel may seem archaic to those who do. Yet Kipling's sensitivity to nuances of cultural contact help render it in other ways surprisingly fresh. The themes of its opening pages—conquest, collecting, and cultural crossing—are the themes that this book has traced through earlier European encounters with the East; they suggest how relevant various collisions, crossings, and anxieties remained even at Kipling's high imperial moment. Looking behind apparent emblems of power, such as the Somnath gates, or discovering points where the colonized might appropriate, and reinterpret, the symbols of the colonizers, such as the Marble Palace, shines light on an empire that even at its heyday remained both more culturally fluid and less secure than commonly supposed. Britain's eastward expansion in the eighteenth and early nineteenth centuries forged a global, territorial empire involving direct rule over millions of obviously foreign subjects. As Britain collected an empire, it classified imperial subjects—and objects—along ethnic, religious, and social lines. But this was also, crucially, an embracing empire, in which imperial subjects, on both sides of power divides, found their own ways of subverting or manipulating those categories to enduring effect.

Britain's imperial history was never simply a two-sided saga of colonizers versus colonized, and not only because those categories remained contested within the borders of empire itself. Empires are built in opposition to one another. Throughout the generations chronicled here, rivalry between Britain and France had formative consequences for the shape of what would for a time be the world's two largest overseas empires. By the 1850s, Britain and France each controlled substantial Eastern territories, through coherent imperial styles; their empires both reflected, and helped constitute, distinctive British and French national identities. The differences between them were in some ways as great as the distance between their core colonies, French Algeria and British India. Algeria was conquered by outright invasion, joined to France with full *département* status, and relinquished only after one of the twentieth century's bloodiest wars of decolonization. India was acquired piecemeal over decades, governed by a range of ad hoc institutions, and hastily evacuated with violent consequences for the nations it left behind, India and Pakistan, but only vicarious wounds for Britain itself. Looking at British and French imperial histories together helps counteract the temptation to see empires in black and white. And a still more shaded picture emerges from considering how their origins, and subsequent trajectories, were actually linked and entwined.

Empires are also built on top of one another. Soon it would be Russia and the United States that posed the most serious challenges to British world power; while France, of course, would find its greatest rival in neighboring Germany. In much the way that Britain and France built their power in the East on the backs of earlier empires, the Mughals and Ottomans, so the United States and Soviet Union would fill the imperial voids left by British and French decolonization after World War II. Terminology changes, but the postcolonial world plainly remains a world of imperial ambitions. Recognizing how more recent empires have inherited worldviews, problems, and policies from their predecessors can go a long way toward understanding how they do or do not, and should or should not, function in changed times.

Every empire, and every collection, holds the ingredients of its own dissolution. Britain's imperial collecting foreshadowed at least three features of the postcolonial aftermath. One was the fraught legacy of imperial collecting left in India and Egypt. Empire bound up sites and objects in the definition of imperial, national, and communal identities. It is no coincidence, then, that postcolonial violence has found focal points in material remains, whether it is terrorist attacks on Western tourists in the Nile Valley, or Hindu rioters pulling down the Babri Masjid at Ayodhya. A second omen concerned the postcolonial fragmentation of Britain itself, and Britain's incorporation into other larger wholes. Decolonization can be linked to devolution—the autonomy that has been recently extended to Britain's component regions of Scotland and Wales—to calls for further integration with the rest of Europe, and to the growing ethnic diversity of London and other British cities. But it has also brought rising hostility toward immigration and "others" of all stripes, xenophobic opposition to European integration, and heated controversy over how Britain should relate to the United States. Parallel debates in France serve as a reminder that these effects are by no means unique, even if they carry specific national resonances.

The third and final legacy of the history of empire and collecting traced here is both the most tangible and the most seductive to imaginative interpretation. It lives in the corridors of Western art galleries and great houses; in the stones of edifices such as the Victoria Memorial Hall in Calcutta, a marble wedding cake of a museum built with the "voluntary" contributions of Indian princes and merchants; in a half-ruined mansion in the back lanes near Cairo's Sayyida Zeinab Mosque, where the French savants once stayed; or in the (broken) clock at the Cairo Citadel, given to Muhammad Ali in return for the Luxor obelisk. It lives in objects, and the ways people see them. All perspectives are conditioned, of course, and one person's treasure may be another's stolen goods. But collecting, like empire-building, represents an enduring human inclination to preserve and combine, as well as to order and control. One can only hope that the embracing and tolerant forms of collecting objects will outweigh the violence of collecting empires.

# *Acknowledgments*

This book has been researched and written on four continents, and my debts are accordingly vast. The topic started life as a paragraph in an application essay, scribbled out during my senior year in college. My first acknowledgment goes to those who saw something in it, and gave me a fellowship to study at the University of Cambridge. There, Chris Bayly superintended my first foray into this subject and turned me into an aspiring imperial historian along the way. He has remained a supremely generous mentor ever since.

The project evolved into a Ph.D. dissertation at Yale University, where I was fortunate to learn about history in an academic environment that values narrative writing. Paul Kennedy assisted my progress at various points; and in Britain the omniscient Peter Marshall kindly sifted through uncertain drafts and still less certain thoughts. Special gratitude goes to John Merriman for sharing his exuberant love of France, for teaching me how to think about French history, and for his unstinting encouragement and confidence. I am indebted most of all to Linda Colley, and not only for her wisdom, good humor, and patience. She has profoundly influenced the way I think and write about history, in part by giving me tremendous freedom to find my own voice, and in part by presenting, in her own work, one of the finest models of historical research and writing I know.

I wrote this book during two years at the Society of Fellows at the University of Michigan, where I received a warm welcome from James Boyd White and from the Department of History. Michigan's lively intellectual community proved to be a great setting in which to rework this project, and I have drawn much insight and pleasure from conversations with Geoff Eley, Dena Goodman, David Hancock, Kali Israel, Barbara Metcalf, Tom Metcalf, Farina Mir, Sonya Rose, Damon Salesa, and Tom Trautmann. But my best thanks go to all my fellow Fellows, whose companionship, both academic and social, contributed immeasurably to my experience in Ann Arbor. I am also grateful to Chuck McCurdy and my colleagues in the Department of History at the University of Virginia for their continuing support.

Writing a book consumes a lot of other people's time, patience, and money. Every research grant I received as a student was greedily welcomed, especially the Andrew W. Mellon and Jacob K. Javits Fellowships that funded me through graduate school. Every librarian and archivist who answered my questions is warmly remembered, particularly Jeremy Rex-Parkes and Estelle Gittins at Christie's, London, and the unfailingly helpful staff of the Oriental and India Office Collections at the British Library. Rosie Llewellyn-Jones and Anne Buddle generously shared their expertise on Lucknow and Seringapatam, respectively. My experience of Egypt was transformed by the hospitality and insights of Kent and Susan Weeks. And above all, I would not have been able to write this without a host of peers, colleagues, and friends, who have provided everything from editorial suggestions and company in the archives, to much-needed distraction from them. Warmest thanks go to Tim Barringer, Anna Dale, Michael Dodson, Jeevan Deol, Douglas Fordham, Durba Ghosh, Tobias Jersak, Lorenz Luthi, Elisa Milkes, John Monroe, Arabella Pike, Mridu Rai, Marco Roth, Neil Safier, Wendie Schneider, Rachel Sturman, Rachel Teukolsky, Robert Travers, Stephen Vella, Patrick Walsh, and Jay Winter.

Some personal debts must be singled out. The first is to Anna Morpurgo Davies, who has always made a home for me in England, for lending me her Oxford house during my research year in Britain. My research visit to India was also a homecoming of sorts, thanks to the warm welcome I received from my relatives there. William Dalrymple infused a timely bit of life into this project by making me chase down the de Boignes, and has become a valued friend and model. And some unlucky few have done more than their fair share of bucking me up and cheering me on: Duncan Chesney, on five continents; Josiah Osgood, for some twenty years; Nasser Zakariya, who bravely read the entire book in draft; and Julie Zikherman, who knew me when. Megan Williams read and refined the manuscript at a critical stage, with sharp logic, wit, and martinis from Ann Arbor to Argentina. Jesse Scott first heard about Giambattista Belzoni on a train through the Tuscan hills in the summer of 1997. Since then she has patiently heard and improved most of my ideas, whether on cargo ships, in cafés, on epic walks, or, most impressively, in cyberspaçe. Kirk Swinehart, my kindred spirit and comrade-in-arms, has walked these ways with me since my first weeks in graduate school. I simply cannot imagine what this book would have been without our friendship, or how much less fun would have been fitted in between the lines.

I do know, though, that this book would not be in print without the efforts of the magisterial Andrew Wylie, who took a gamble on a callow young academic; or of Sarah Chalfant and Michal Shavit, who helped shepherd me through the publishing labyrinth. To Carol Janeway at Knopf I deliver *hommages* for her warm and wise counsel. At Fourth Estate, Mitzi Angel has been a terrific source of moral and critical support, and I appreciate her and Caroline Michel's enthusiasm for this project. I also want to thank Clive Priddle for his assistance at a pivotal juncture.

But my last and most heartfelt thanks are reserved for my family: for my grandparents, whose stories drew me into history; my big brother Alan, for scouting out the way ahead; and my parents, Sheila and Jay, my first and best models. It is not just that they gave me constant encouragement, frequent room and board, and essential editorial advice. They also instilled the insatiable taste for travel, for art, for reading books, and for writing them. This is the result, and it is dedicated to them, with admiration and love.

# *Note on Sources*

Because the notes provide a thorough running list of references, I have not included a formal bibliography. Full citations are given in each chapter at the first mention of a source.

The primary research presented here rests chiefly in two major types of archival material: diplomatic and administrative documents, and private papers. I have used official documents, in the case of India, chiefly to fill out unexplored corners in an already detailed secondary literature, and to investigate state- and Company-sponsored collecting. Though my research on India draws more on the Oriental and India Office Collections of the British Library than on any other single archive, the Archives Nationales in Paris contain many unexpected treasures for the historian of eighteenth- and nineteenth-century South Asia. In the case of Egypt, for which secondary literature is considerably less extensive than for India, I have used the dispatches written by British and French diplomats between 1750 and 1840 (now held in the Public Record Office, the Archives Nationales, and the Ministère des Affaires Étrangères) to lay the foundations of my discussion. These letters are crucial sources on the shaping of European policy in the region. Equally important for my purposes, they present a detailed, fascinating, and much underutilized chronicle of life on the ground in a sphere of informal empire.

The second set of materials I used in depth—collections of private papers in the British Library, the Bibliothèque Nationale, and some regional repositories in Britain and France—is by nature more diffuse. Diaries and personal letters by Europeans who traveled overseas provide rich testimony about the encounter of cultures, people, and objects; and surviving account books and inventories are of course essential for recovering details of particular collections. In some instances, papers such as those of Robert Hay and James Burton, in the British Library, contain specific and detailed information about collecting. In other cases, notably for Lucknow, I have used private papers to flesh out the wider world in which collectors, whose individual paper trails may otherwise be lost, operated and lived.

Inevitably one may ask how "representative" the sampling of imperial collectors offered here is, and how widespread the practice was. An investigation of Bengal wills and inventories for the later eighteenth century suggested that about one in twenty Europeans died with small "collections" of Indian art and artifacts—a few weapons, perhaps, or a set of "Hindoostanee" paintings—in their possession. Presumably at least the same percentage, if not more, of those who returned to Europe brought some sort of artifacts with them. The number of Europeans traveling to Egypt was much smaller; and because collecting in this period was linked to excavation and tended to be conducted on a monumental scale, it is not difficult to gain a pretty complete picture of collecting in the Nile Valley. Salt, Drovetti, and Belzoni were among its key players. Harder to gauge is the scale of the market in small antiquities, aimed at travelers, that was spreading in early-nineteenth-century Egypt; but of course one must distinguish between souvenir-buying and collecting in the sustained manner undertaken by the individuals I have discussed.

In order to assess the extent and range of collecting from India and Egypt in Britain, I decided to look at the best existing record of the British art market across this period: the archive of Christie's auction house in London. Founded in 1766, Christie's (unlike Sotheby's, which is somewhat older) preserves a complete run of its sale catalogues, fully annotated with prices, names of buyers, and often names of sellers. By studying all Christie's sales up to 1835, I was able to turn up a few clusters of Indian and Egyptian objects, and the names of some prominent or regular buyers. But the relative absence of material was much more illuminating than its presence: the "market" for Indian and Egyptian objects in London remained very limited, and distinctly marginal to the market for Old Master paintings, prints, books, European antiquities, or even wine, which alone easily accounted for more sales in these decades than did exotic objects. These findings helped crystallize my decision to focus on individual collectors overseas, who obviously played a crucial role in the importing of objects to Europe. (There is no historic analogue of Christie's and Sotheby's in France, where since the early eighteenth century, auctions were administered by so-called *commissaires-priseurs,* who were individually licensed by the state. This system is now being dismantled in light of European Union regulations.)

I explored two other kinds of collecting in some detail before deciding to set them aside. State-sponsored surveys—notably those performed by Francis Buchanan and Colin Mackenzie in India, and by the French savants in Egypt—constituted a form of imperial collecting, without a doubt. The Mackenzie Papers in particular yield a rich, layered record of collecting in India through the dozens of reports sent to Mackenzie by his "native agents" in the field. But though the aims and results of these official collections support my larger argument about the relationship between collecting and imperial self-fashioning, these state enterprises are in other respects quite different from the individual stories presented here. Another domain related, but ultimately tangential, to this book is the subject of manuscript collecting and scholarly "Orientalism." Important collections of Indian and Egyptian coins, medals, inscriptions, and texts were beginning to be formed in this period. A study of these genres of collection would have led me away from personal histories, however, and toward a more familiar terrain of European scholarly societies and contemporary intellectual journals such as *Asiatic Researches* and the *Journal Asiatique*. In short, both surveys and Orientalist collections raise questions that lie beyond the scope of this study—and which have been well treated by others elsewhere.

Finally, although this book has focused on individuals rather than institutions and museums, these latter are important sources in their own right. My visits to public and private collections in Britain, France, India, and Egypt have played a major part in helping me reconstruct the material worlds of imperial collectors, and the larger public spheres in which they lived. Without them, I would not have come to this subject in the first place. They are powerful testaments to the immediacy of the themes I have sought to trace here.

# *Notes*

The following abbreviations are used in the notes:

| | |
|---|---|
| Add. MSS | Additional Manuscripts, British Library, London. |
| ADS | Archives Départementales de la Savoie, Chambéry. |
| AE | Ministère des Affaires Étrangères series, Archives Nationales, Paris. |
| AN | Archives Nationales, Paris. |
| BL | British Library, London. |
| BNF | Bibliothèque Nationale de France, Paris. |
| CCC | Correspondance Consulaire et Commerciale series, Ministère des Affaires Étrangères, Paris. |
| *DNB* | *Dictionary of National Biography*, eds. L. Stephen and S. Lee, 66 vols. (London, 1885–1901). |
| FO | Foreign Office records, Public Record Office, Kew. |
| MAE | Ministère des Affaires Étrangères, Paris. |
| MAR | Ministère de la Marine series, Archives Nationales, Paris. |
| NAF | Nouvelles Acquisitions Françaises, Department of Western Manuscripts, Bibliothèque Nationale, Paris. |
| NAS | National Archives of Scotland, Edinburgh. |
| NLW | National Library of Wales, Aberystwyth. |
| OIOC | Oriental and India Office Collections, British Library, London. |
| PRO | Public Record Office, Kew. |
| SHAT | Service Historique de l'Armée de la Terre, Vincennes. |
| SRO | Scottish Record Office, Edinburgh. |
| WO | War Office records, Public Record Office, Kew. |

## INTRODUCTION

1. Linda Colley, *Captives: Britain, Empire and the World 1600–1850* (London: Jonathan Cape, 2002), pp. 4–10. The population anxiety was eased only by the first British census, undertaken in 1801.

2. I am influenced here by Pierre Bourdieu, *Distinction: A Social Critique of the Judgment of Taste,* trans. Richard Nice (Cambridge, Mass.: Harvard University Press, 1984). The links between collecting and gentility have been investigated in detail by many scholars of early modern Europe: Lisa Jardine, *Worldly Goods: A New History of the Renaissance* (New York: W. W. Norton, 1996); Paula Findlen, *Possessing Nature: Museums, Collecting, and Scientific Culture in Early Modern Italy* (Berkeley: University of California Press, 1994); Thomas DaCosta Kaufmann, *The Mastery of Nature: Aspects of Art, Science, and Humanism in the Renaissance* (Princeton, N.J.: Princeton University Press, 1993).
3. The binary terms set out in *Orientalism* (New York: Pantheon, 1978) have been modified by many scholars, including Said himself, in *Culture and Imperialism* (New York: Alfred A. Knopf, 1993), pp. xxiv–xxvi. *Cf.* Ann Laura Stoler and Frederick Cooper, "Between Metropole and Colony: Rethinking a Research Agenda," in Frederick Cooper and Ann Laura Stoler, eds., *Tensions of Empire: Colonial Cultures in a Bourgeois World* (Berkeley: University of California Press, 1997), pp. 1–37; Catherine Hall, *Civilising Subjects: Metropole and Colony in the English Imagination, 1830–1867* (Chicago: University of Chicago Press, 2002), pp. 15–18; Kathleen Wilson, *The Island Race: Englishness, Empire and Gender in the Eighteenth Century* (London: Routledge, 2002), pp. 4–5; Antoinette Burton, *At the Heart of the Empire: Indians and the Colonial Encounter in Late Victorian Britain* (Berkeley: University of California Press, 1998), pp. 20–23.
4. I do not mean here to censure Jan Morris's "Pax Britannica" trilogy (Volume 1: *Heaven's Command*), which presents probably the most vivid, detailed historical chronicle of the British Empire at its height.
5. Consider, for instance, the closing words of Angus Calder's otherwise brilliant *Revolutionary Empire: The Rise of the English-Speaking Empires from the Fifteenth Century to the 1780s* (London: Phoenix, 1998), a firm Marxist indictment of British imperialism: "After Cook, it seemed that the British would go everywhere. . . . The younger Pitt and his colleagues, like the classes whose support they mobilised, believed that markets must be captured, and could be captured, all over the globe. Despite the loss of the North American colonies, Britain was stronger than ever before. Not far behind brave explorers and honest if foolish missionaries, Manchester cotton would follow Birmingham guns" (p. 535).
6. I would certainly come in for the criticisms levied by Nicholas Dirks, *Castes of Mind: Colonialism and the Making of Modern India* (Princeton, N.J.: Princeton University Press, 2001), pp. 309–13.
7. Linda Colley, *Britons: Forging the Nation, 1707–1837* (New Haven: Yale University Press, 1992); John Brewer, *The Sinews of Power: War, Money and the English State, 1688–1783* (New York: Vintage, 1989); Kathleen Wilson, *The Sense of the People: Politics, Culture, and Imperialism in England, 1715–1785* (Cambridge, UK: Cambridge University Press, 1995); Jeremy Black, *Natural and Necessary Enemies: Anglo-French Relations in the Eighteenth Century* (London: Duckworth, 1986); Clive Emsley, *British Society and the French Wars, 1793–1815* (London: Macmillan, 1979).

8. J. R. Seeley, *The Expansion of England* (Chicago: University of Chicago Press, 1971), p. 12.
9. David Armitage, *The Ideological Origins of the British Empire* (Cambridge, UK: Cambridge University Press, 2001).
10. Anthony Pagden, *Lords of All the World: Ideologies of Empire in Spain, Britain and France c.1500–c.1800* (New Haven: Yale University Press, 1995), pp. 126–29. Many French theorists were equally suspicious of a Spanish-style empire of conquest and, for that matter, of their own state: Montesquieu's *Lettres Persanes,* published in 1721, fictionalized a visit by two Persian ambassadors to Paris as a way of critiquing the despotic institutions of absolutist France.
11. Colley, *Britons,* pp. 321–24; Benedict Anderson, *Imagined Communities,* 2nd ed. (London: Verso, 1993), pp. 109–11.
12. But see Uday Mehta, "Liberal Strategies of Exclusion" in Cooper and Stoler, eds., *Tensions of Empire,* esp. pp. 59–62—who detects an exclusionary strand in Locke and demonstrates how in Victorian liberal thought, a society's level of "civilization" could become a prerequisite for inclusion. See also Bernard Semmel, *The Liberal Ideal and the Demons of Empire: Theories of Imperialism from Adam Smith to Lenin* (Baltimore: Johns Hopkins University Press, 1993); Eric Stokes, *The English Utilitarians and India* (Oxford: Oxford University Press, 1959); Thomas R. Metcalf, *Ideologies of the Raj* (Cambridge, UK: Cambridge University Press, 1995), pp. ix–x, 28–42.
13. Quoted in Muriel E. Chamberlain, *Lord Palmerston* (Cardiff: GPC, 1987), p. 74.
14. This is what Partha Chatterjee influentially termed the "rule of colonial difference." Partha Chatterjee, *The Nation and Its Fragments* (Princeton, N.J.: Princeton University Press, 1993). Inclusion could of course sharpen hierarchical distinctions based on race or class; see Catherine Hall, "The Nation Within and Without" in Catherine Hall, Keith McClelland, and Jane Rendall, *Defining the Victorian Nation: Class, Race, Gender, and the British Reform Act of 1867* (Cambridge, UK: Cambridge University Press, 2000), pp. 179–233.
15. The phrase comes from Rudyard Kipling, whose 1899 poem "The White Man's Burden" was in fact addressed to Americans, on the subject of the U.S. occupation of the Philippines.

## CHAPTER ONE: CONQUESTS

1. I have drawn my account chiefly from Francis Parkman's magisterial *Montcalm and Wolfe* (New York: Modern Library, 1999), pp. 398–414; and Fred Anderson, *Crucible of War: The Seven Years' War and the Fate of the Empire in British North America, 1754–1766* (London: Faber and Faber, 2000), pp. 344–62. *Cf.* Simon Schama, *Dead Certainties* (*Unwarranted Speculations*) (New York: Vintage, 1992), pp. 3–39, 66–70. The competing accounts of Wolfe's death are judiciously summed up in A. Doughty and G. W. Parmelee, *The Siege of Quebec and the Battle of the Plains of Abraham,* 6 vols. (Quebec: Dussault and Proulx, 1901), III, pp. 201–37. As Bruce Lenman observes, Parkman (like Ben-

jamin West) played up the significance of the battle as part of a generally triumphalist, patriotic reading of the Seven Years War—an interpretation that endures. (Bruce Lenman, *Britain's Colonial Wars 1688–1783* [New York: Longman, 2001], pp. 153–55.)

2. This was by no means the first time that Britain erupted in patriotic rejoicings around a broadly "imperial" victory: Admiral Vernon's defeat of the Spanish at Portobello, in 1739, inspired a massive public outpouring. (Vernon was celebrated across the Atlantic, too, in the name of the Washington family manor, Mount Vernon.) But Wolfe's victory may have been all the more gripping as it was performed not by the beloved navy but by the much-maligned army. Stephen Brumwell, *Redcoats: The British Soldier and War in the Americas, 1755–63* (Cambridge, UK: Cambridge University Press, 2002), pp. 54–57; Kathleen Wilson, *The Sense of the People: Politics, Culture and Imperialism in England, 1715–1785* (Cambridge, UK: Cambridge University Press, 1998), pp. 140–65.
3. Though Edward Penny's 1763 version of the same scene—a composition bearing several similarities to West's—also used modern dress. Schama, pp. 21–39.
4. The 1929 *Cambridge History of the British Empire* divided its subject in these terms, for instance; "First" and "Second" are still often used as shorthand labels for the British Empire before and after the American Revolution. For reevaluations of this periodization, see P. J. Marshall, "The First British Empire," and C. A. Bayly, "The Second British Empire," in Robin Winks, ed., *Oxford History of the British Empire, Vol. V: Historiography* (Oxford: Oxford University Press, 1999), pp. 43–72.
5. Though see Jean Meyer et al., *Histoire de la France coloniale: Des origines à 1914* (Paris: Armand Colin, 1991) and Jean Martin, *L'Empire renaissant 1789–1871* (Paris: Denoël, 1987) for an outline of key events of the period.
6. See Todd Porterfield, *The Allure of Empire: Art in the Service of French Imperialism 1798–1836* (Princeton, N.J.: Princeton University Press, 1998) for an excellent exposition of this theme in general, and the place of Egypt across regimes in particular.
7. Samuel Purchas, *Hakluytus Posthumus or Purchas His Pilgrimes, Contayning a History of the World . . .*, 20 vols. (Glasgow: James MacLehose and Sons, 1905), Part I, IV, pp. 334–39.
8. William Foster, ed., *The English Factories in India 1618–21* (Oxford: Clarendon Press, 1906), pp. viii, 38–40.
9. Philip Lawson, *The East India Company* (London: Longman, 1993), p. 20.
10. Alexander Hamilton, *A New Account of the East Indies . . .*, 2 vols. (Edinburgh, 1727), quoted in P. T. Nair, ed., *Calcutta in the Eighteenth Century* (Calcutta: Firma KLM, 1984), p. 4.
11. "A Voyage to Calcutta in 1761," quoted in Nair, ed., p. 134. This writer reported that "Of 84 rank and file, which our company consisted of on our arrival, we had but 34 remaining in three months." Captain Hamilton, visiting Calcutta in the first decade of the century, commented that 460 of 1,200 Europeans had been buried in four months.

12. The poignant and tragic story of the dragoman, Étienne Roboly, can be followed in the archives of French consular correspondence, AN: AE B/I/109. The allegation that Roboly was in fact an Armenian, and had taken service with France without the sultan's permission, does seem to have been justified; though his treatment was not, and indeed was one of the outrages later cited by French lobbyists to argue for an invasion of Egypt. It is not surprising that the dragoman—the quintessential man on the margins—was also a collector, desperate to send pieces of classical sculpture (and prove his loyalty?) to Louis XV.
13. The Company's late-seventeenth-century expansionism, promoted particularly by Sir Josiah Child and supported by James II, was mostly erased under the "trade to conquest" narrative that made Plassey the starting point of a newly militant era in Company history. For a detailed account of these earlier maneuvers, see Philip J. Stern, "'One Body Corporate and Politick': The Growth of the English East India Company-State in the Later Seventeenth Century" (Ph.D. dissertation, Columbia University, 2004).
14. Robert Harms, *The Diligent: A Voyage Through the Worlds of the Slave Trade* (New York: Basic Books, 2002).
15. Alan Taylor, *American Colonies* (New York: Penguin, 2001), p. 132.
16. J. F. Richards, *The Mughal Empire* (Cambridge, UK: Cambridge University Press, 1993), pp. 253–81; Muzaffar Alam, *The Crisis of Empire in Mughal North India: Awadh and the Punjab 1707–1748* (New Delhi: Oxford University Press, 1986). This period used to be characterized as one of "decline"; more recent interpretations have stressed that it was the very *success* of the old imperial system at promoting regional autonomy that led to its unraveling.
17. Robert Orme, *A History of the Military Transactions of the British Nation in Hindoostan*, 2 vols. (London, 1763–1778), II, p. 47.
18. Michael Edwardes, *Plassey: The Founding of an Empire* (London: Hamish Hamilton, 1969), p. 65; Linda Colley, *Captives: Britain, Empire, and the World 1600–1850* (London: Jonathan Cape, 2002), pp. 255–56. The sensationalism was started by one of the survivors, John Zephaniah Holwell, *A Genuine Narrative of the deplorable deaths of the English gentlemen, and others, who were suffocated in the Black-Hole in Fort-William, at Calcutta . . .* (London, 1758). Holwell gives the—undoubtedly exaggerated—figure of 23 survivors, from a group of 146.
19. Orme, II, pp. 127–35.
20. Captain Edmund Maskelyne, "Journal of the Proceedings of the Troops Commanded by Lieutenant Colonel Robert Clive on the Expedition to Bengal," OIOC: MSS Eur Orme 20, p. 35.
21. "Letter from Mr. Watts to his father giving an account of events in Bengal from the treaty concluded with Seerajah Doulet on the 6th of February to August 13 [1757], including Changernagore, the battle of Plassey, etc.," OIOC: MSS Eur Orme 20, p. 109. Orme gives rather higher numbers in his *History*, II, p. 173.
22. On the conspiracy, see Edwardes, pp. 111–29; and Mark Bence-Jones, *Clive of India* (London: Constable, 1974), pp. 119–32.

23. "Letter from Mr. Watts . . . ," p. 111.
24. Orme, II, pp. 179–84.
25. The last flowering of French activity in Indian courts was in the Punjab: Jean-Marie Lafont, *La Présence française dans le royaume sikh du Penjab, 1822–1849* (Paris: École Française de l'Extrême Orient, 1992); Jean-Marie Lafont, *French Administrators of Maharaja Ranjit Singh* (New Delhi: National Book Shop, 1986).
26. C. A. Bayly, *Indian Society and the Making of the British Empire* (Cambridge, UK: Cambridge University Press, 1988), pp. 47–52.
27. John Splinter Stavorinus, quoted in Nair, ed., p. 163.
28. Percival Spear, *The Nabobs: A Study of the Social Life of the English in Eighteenth-Century India* (New Delhi: Oxford University Press, 1998; 1st pub. 1932), p. 30.
29. Mrs. Nathaniel Kindersley, quoted in Nair, ed., p. 145.
30. Suresh Chandra Ghosh, *The British in Bengal: A Study of the British Society and Life in the Late Eighteenth Century* (New Delhi: Munshiram Manoharlal, 1998), pp. 96–109.
31. T. B. Macaulay, *Macaulay's Essays on Clive and Hastings*, ed. Charles Robert Gaston (Boston: Ginn and Co., 1910), pp. 89–90. The essay is a review of Sir John Malcolm's three-volume hagiography, commissioned by Clive's son Edward, and Macaulay is here paraphrasing Malcolm.
32. Philip Lawson and Jim Phillips, " 'Our Execrable Banditti': Perceptions of Nabobs in Mid-Eighteenth-Century Britain," in Philip Lawson, *A Taste for Empire and Glory: Studies in British Overseas Expansion* (Aldershot: Variorum Collected Studies Series, 1997), XII, pp. 225–41.
33. P. J. Marshall, *Bengal the British Bridgehead* (Cambridge, UK: Cambridge University Press, 1987), p. 18; Macaulay, p. 78.
34. Quoted in Lawson and Phillips, p. 238.
35. For the Walpole quote and evocations of this splendid landing, see A. Mervyn Davies, *Clive of Plassey* (New York: Scribners, 1939), pp. 326–27, and Bence-Jones, pp. 188–89.
36. Margaret Clive to John Carnac, May 6, 1761, OIOC: MSS Eur F 128/27.
37. See Clive's financial journals from 1763 to 1774 in NLW: Robert Clive Papers, F2/1–14. For conversions from eighteenth-century pounds sterling to modern equivalents, I have used the multiplication factor of eighty suggested by Roy Porter, *English Society in the Eighteenth Century*, 2nd ed. (London: Penguin, 1990), p. xv.
38. Robert Clive to Henry Vansittart, February 3, 1762, quoted in Lucy S. Sutherland, *The East India Company in Eighteenth-Century Politics* (Oxford: Clarendon Press, 1952), p. 86*n*.
39. Henry Strachey to Robert Clive, February 8, 1774, quoted in Bence-Jones, p. 298.
40. Of all Clive's activities in Britain, his political career is the only aspect that historians have chronicled in detail. See Sutherland, pp. 81–137; H. V. Bowen, *Revenue and Reform: The Indian Problem in British Politics, 1757–1773* (Cambridge, UK: Cambridge University Press, 1991), pp. 169–86.

41. He won narrowly at the polls, but lost on appeal—together with the £3,000 it cost him to run. The division list is given in Linda Colley, "The Mitchell election division, 24 March 1755," *Bulletin of the Institute of Historical Research* XLIX (1976): 80–107.
42. L. B. Namier, *The Structure of Politics at the Accession of George III*, 2 vols. (New York: Macmillan, 1957), II, pp. 320–32, 352–63. Namier complained that "Clive's biographers follow him on his conquest of an empire in Asia, and do not dwell on his capture of a Parliamentary borough at home" (p. 352*n*). This oversight has been amply corrected by Philip Lawson and Bruce Lenman, "Robert Clive, The 'Black Jagir', and British Politics," in Lawson, *A Taste for Empire and Glory*, XI. For a breakdown of nabob political factions, see James M. Holzman, "The Nabobs in England: A Study of the Returned Anglo-Indian, 1760–1785" (Ph.D. dissertation, Columbia University, 1926), pp. 103–16.
43. P. J. Cain and A. G. Hopkins, *British Imperialism, 1688–2000* (New York: Longman, 2002), pp. 22–37.
44. Bence-Jones, pp. 189, 203, 257, 265.
45. Namier, II, pp. 293–97. Even in this age of rotten boroughs, Bishop's Castle was "notoriously corrupt" (p. 304).
46. NLW: Robert Clive Papers, EC2/1.
47. Andrew Wilton and Ilaria Bignamini, eds., *The Grand Tour: The Lure of Italy in the Eighteenth Century* (London: Tate Gallery Publishing, 1996). Something of the scale of the practice is captured by John Ingamells, *A Dictionary of British and Irish Travellers in Italy 1701–1800* (New Haven, Conn.: Yale University Press, 1997).
48. Iain Pears, *The Discovery of Painting: The Growth of Interest in the Arts in England, 1680–1768* (New Haven, Conn.: Yale University Press, 1988), pp. 207–9.
49. Ibid., pp. 101–2; Christie's statistics are based on my own tabulation.
50. Robert Clive to Henry Strachey, May 15, 1771, OIOC: MSS Eur F 128/93.
51. Robert Clive to Henry Strachey, May 15, 1771, OIOC: MSS Eur F 128/93. In one of Clive's several letters to Strachey of that day, he wonders "whether Chas. Clive could not be of some use in ascertaining the Value and Condition of Sir James Wright's Pictures."
52. On Clive's wardrobe: Malcolm, II, pp. 181–83.
53. According to the Christie's auctioneer's books, Clive bought nine paintings for £362 4s. 6d. at the high-profile sale of a collection formed by the speculator Robert Ansell, on February 15–16. But the ledger of Clive's accountant shows a further payment of £1,086 15s. to "Mr. Christie for Pictures" on February 18, which means that the vast majority of Clive's acquisitions were made by others bidding on his behalf. West and Patoun were also present at the sale. (Christie's: Auctioneer's Books, January–March 1771. NLW: Robert Clive Papers, F 12/11.)
54. Robert Clive to Henry Strachey, May 15, 1771, OIOC: MSS Eur F 128/93.
55. Robert Clive to Henry Strachey, May 16, 1771, OIOC: MSS Eur F 128/93.
56. "A Capital and Valuable Collection of Italian, Flemish, and Dutch Pictures, Fine Bronzes, etc. Collected by A Gentleman [i.e., Peter Demasso] Well known to the Vertu, for his Knowledge, and refined Taste," Christie's, March

8–9, 1771. Before 1760, according to Pears, well under 5 percent of paintings sold for more than £40 (p. 216).

57. Clive's accounts show a payment in this amount to "H. Hoare Esqr. Cost and Charges of 2 Pictures by Vernet" on June 16, 1773. NLW: Robert Clive Papers, H9/7.
58. Bence-Jones, pp. 295–96. Some of these purchases, at Christie's and elsewhere, can be traced in the cash books of Clive's accountant, Edward Crisp. The last volume lists "Customs and Charges on 2 Pictures and 4 Cases of Figures and Marbles," acquired on Clive's trip to Italy in 1774 (NLW: Robert Clive Papers, H9/9). On his visit to Florence that year, Clive met Johan Zoffany, who said Clive wanted "a picture similar to what I am now painting of the Tribuna, but poor man, he could not go to the expense" (Ingamells, p. 221).
59. Quoted in Bence-Jones, p. 266. He notes that the £507 3s. Clive paid for the Claude "was not excessive considering that Claude was then the highest-priced painter on the English market," which may be true, but it certainly would have made the painting one of the most expensive on the London art market in a decade.
60. J. H. Plumb, *Sir Robert Walpole*, 2 vols. (London: Cresset Press, 1956–60), II, pp. 85–87.
61. Though in a rare moment of aesthetic judgment, he pronounced Vernet "the most delightful Landscape Painter I ever saw." Robert Clive to Henry Strachey, October 6, 1771, OIOC: MSS Eur F 128/93.
62. Robert Clive to Henry Strachey, May 26, 1771, OIOC: MSS Eur F 128/93. Connoisseurs disagreed over the merits of some of his pictures; see Bence-Jones, pp. 265–66.
63. The portrait stayed in the Clive family until 1929, when the Earl of Powis presented it to the Corporation of Shrewsbury; it is currently on display in Powis Castle. I am grateful to Margaret Gray of the National Trust for this information.
64. "Had it been in my Power, I should e'en now have sent Meer Jaffier a present of a well drawn Picture of Lord Clive. . . . I have not had it my Power to get my Lord's Picture drawn any thing like him in London, but at Bath there is a man who takes the most surprizing Likenesses, and to whom my Lord has long promised me to sit, when next he has opportunity. . . . Gratitude induced us to think of sending the old Nabob this Present as a mark of our lasting Sense of his Favors." Margaret Clive to John Carnac, February 27, 1764, OIOC: MSS Eur F128/27.
65. Samuel Foote, *The Works, with Remarks and an Essay by Jon Bee (1830)*, 3 vols. (New York: Georg Olms Verlag, 1974), III, pp. 215–17, 222–26, 236. In this connection the best example to cite from Clive's career would be the establishment of the Lord Clive Fund, a charity for disabled Company soldiers and widows. Clive founded the trust with a suspect legacy of £70,000, left to him by Mir Jafar.
66. Bence-Jones, pp. 285, 287.
67. For the deaths of Clive, and a perverse suggestion that he may have been murdered, see Robert Harvey, *Clive: The Life and Death of a British Emperor* (London: Hodder & Stoughton, 1998), pp. 367–76.

68. Clive's will specifies that certain items be kept for Edward. I have drawn this, and what follows, from the inventories in NLW: Clive Papers, T4/1. The "Indian Curiosities" were inventoried on March 17, 1775, and valued at £1,154.
69. Some of Robert Clive's Indian objects have been definitively identified in the Powis Castle collection. See Mildred Archer, Christopher Rowell, and Robert Skelton, *Treasures from India: The Clive Collection at Powis Castle* (New York: Meredith Press, 1990).
70. Bence-Jones, p. 243; Robert Clive to George Grenville, July 21, 1767, NLW: Robert Clive Papers, CR4/1.

## CHAPTER TWO: CROSSINGS

1. John Prinsep, quoted in J. P. Losty, *Calcutta City of Palaces: A Survey of the City in the Days of the East India Company, 1690–1858* (London: British Library, 1990), p. 36.
2. William Hodges, *Travels in India during the years 1780, 1781, 1782, and 1783* (London, 1794), p. 14.
3. "Some account of the transactions in the Province of Oud from the 1st April to the end of June 1776," OIOC: MSS Eur Orme Vol. 91.
4. Matthew Edney, *Mapping an Empire: The Geographical Construction of British India, 1765–1843* (Chicago: University of Chicago Press, 1997), p. 9.
5. I have compiled these statistics from the "General Register of the Military on the Coast of Coromandel 31 December 1766," OIOC: L/Mil/11/109; "Register of the Honorable Company's Effective European Troops on the Coast of Coromandel as they stood on the 31st December 1800," OIOC: L/Mil/11/120. Religion is not listed, but county of origin is; the majority of Irish troops came from the counties of the south.
6. Estimates range from 100,000 to 400,000, even before Plassey: P. J. Marshall, *Bengal the British Bridgehead* (Cambridge, UK: Cambridge University Press, 1987), p. 24; Geoffrey Moorhouse, *Calcutta: The City Revealed* (London: Phoenix, 1998), p. 40.
7. "List of Inhabitants etc. who bore arms at the seige of Calcutta, with their fate, whether killed or wounded July 1, 1756," OIOC: MSS Eur Orme 19, pp. 61–64.
8. OIOC: Clive Collection, MSS Eur G37/18, piece 9. This is a rare document, since the British did not compile regular lists of British civilians and protégés in Calcutta until later in the century. Marshall suggests that the names given here were male heads of household (p. 23).
9. Many inventories also give full records of estate sales, with buyers' names and prices. Only sales by Armenians did not seem to be attended by buyers from outside the community. For the years 1761–1770, see OIOC: P/154/62–69.
10. Michael H. Fisher, *Indirect Rule in India: Residents and the Residency System, 1764–1858* (New Delhi: Oxford University Press, 1998), pp. 43–69.
11. OIOC: L/Mil/9/103, Embarkation Lists, 1778–84. The Company had three recruiting stations in Ireland at this time, two of them south of Ulster. C. A.

Bayly, *Imperial Meridian: The British Empire and the World, 1780–1830* (London: Longman, 1989), p. 127.

12. R. M. Bird, *Dacoitee in Excelsis; or, the Spoliation of Oude, by the East India Company . . .* (London, 1857), p. 21.
13. C. U. A. Aitchison, ed., *A Collection of Treaties, Engagements, and Sunnuds Relating to India and Neighbouring Countries, Vol. II: Northwestern Provinces, Oudh, Nipal, Bundelcund and Baghelcund* (Calcutta, 1876), pp. 74–78; Purnendu Basu, *Oudh and the East India Company, 1785–1801* (Lucknow: Maxwell Co., 1943), pp. 101–2.
14. Quoted in Desmond Young, *Fountain of the Elephants* (London: Collins, 1959), p. 101.
15. Jean Deloche, ed., *Voyage en Inde du Comte de Modave, 1773–76* (Paris: École Française d'Extrême Orient, 1971), p. 170.
16. Abdul Halim Sharar, who believed that "as any community or nation progresses, its diet is the most salient guide to its refinement," is especially eloquent on food: Abdul Halim Sharar, *Lucknow: The Last Phase of an Oriental Culture*, trans. E. S. Harcourt and Fakhir Hussain (New Delhi: Oxford University Press, 1975), pp. 155–68.
17. Thomas Twining, *Travels in India a Hundred Years Ago* (London, 1893), p. 312.
18. Muhammad Faiz Bakhsh, *Tarikh-i-Farahbakhsh*, trans. William Hoey, *Memoirs of Delhi and Faizabad* (Allahabad, 1889), p. 24.
19. Warren Hastings to John Macpherson, December 12, 1781, quoted in Richard B. Barnett, *North India Between Empires: Awadh, the Mughals, and the British, 1720–1801* (Berkeley: University of California Press, 1980), pp. 204–5.
20. For an itemization of some of Asaf ud-Daula's expenditures, see "Estimate of the Expences of the Nabob Vizier for the Fussellee Year 1192 [1783–84]," BL: Hastings Papers, Add. MSS 29,093. On a more anecdotal note, see William Blane, *An Account of the Hunting Excursions of Asoph ul Doulah, Visier of the Mogul Empire, and Nabob of Oude* (London, 1788); Captain Charles Madan, *Two Private Letters to a Gentleman in England, from His Son who Accompanied Earl Cornwallis on his Expedition to Lucknow in the Year 1787* (Peterborough, 1788); and "Account of Lucknow," in *Asiatic Annual Register*, vol. 2 (London, 1800), "Miscellaneous Tracts," pp. 97–101.
21. Abu Talib Khan, *Tahzih ul-ghafilin*, trans. William Hoey, *History of Asafu'd Daulah Nawab Wazir of Oudh* (Allahabad, 1885; repr. Lucknow: Pustak Kendra, 1974), pp. 73–74.
22. Twining, pp. 309–10.
23. Pigeon-rearing and kite-flying were among the activities banned by the Taliban in 1996, for encouraging "wicked consequences." Asne Seierstad, *The Bookseller of Kabul* (Boston: Little, Brown, 2003), p. 81.
24. Sharar, pp. 198–201, 94. Sharar also perceptively observed one reason for the popularity of animal fighting in this emasculated city: "Unable to display deeds of valour one looks for them through the medium of fighting animals. One enjoys watching courageous acts and seeks acclaim by causing others to watch animal combat. This is what happened in Lucknow" (p. 116).
25. Mir Taqi Mir, *Zikr-i Mir: the autobiography of the eighteenth-century Mughal*

*poet, Mir Muhammad Taqi 'Mir', 1723–1810*, trans. C. M. Naim (New Delhi: Oxford University Press, 1999); Carla Petievich, *Assembly of Rivals: Delhi, Lucknow and the Urdu Ghazal* (New Delhi: Manohar, 1992).

26. Juan R. I. Cole, *The Roots of North Indian Shi'ism in Iran and Iraq: Religion and State in Awadh, 1722–1859* (Berkeley: University of California Press, 1988). Sharar called it "the Baghdad and Cordoba of India and the Nishapur and Bokhara of the East" (p. 94).
27. Amir Hasan, *Palace Culture of Lucknow* (New Delhi: B. R. Publishing, 1983), p. 183.
28. Rosie Llewellyn-Jones, *A Fatal Friendship: The Nawabs, the British, and the City of Lucknow* (New Delhi: Oxford University Press, 1985).
29. L. F. Smith, "A letter to a friend containing a historical sketch of the late Asuf-ud-Dowlah, Nawab of Oude (1 March 1795)," quoted in Mildred Archer, *India and British Portraiture, 1770–1825* (London: Sotheby Parke Bernet, 1979), pp. 142–43.
30. C. A. Bayly, *Rulers, Townsmen, and Bazaars: North Indian Society in the Age of British Expansion, 1770–1870* (Cambridge, UK: Cambridge University Press, 1983), p. 102. On the structure itself, see Neeta Das, *The Architecture of the Imambaras* (Lucknow: Lucknow Mahotsav Patrika Samiti, 1991), pp. 64–71.
31. Mir Taqi Mir, quoted in Ishrat Haque, *Glimpses of Mughal Society and Culture* (New Delhi: Concept Publishing, 1992), p. 69.
32. Sharar, p. 48.
33. Sharar and Basu note the practice, and the couplet is cited in Hasan, p. 181.
34. Rosie Llewellyn-Jones, "European Fantasies and Indian Dreams," in Violette Graff, ed., *Lucknow: Memories of a City* (New Delhi: Oxford University Press, 1997), p. 51.
35. See C. A. Bayly, ed., *The Raj: India and the British, 1600–1947* (London: National Portrait Gallery, 1990), p. 116; Mary Webster, *Johan Zoffany* (London: National Portrait Gallery, 1976), pp. 77–78.
36. I take implicit exception here with Beth Fowkes Tobin's reading of British Indian portraits of the period as undermining, contradicting, or threatening an evolving ideology of British imperial dominance. As this picture so emphatically illustrates, the political, social, and cultural landscape of Lucknow was enormously complex; and "the British" were by no means its masters. See Beth Fowkes Tobin, *Picturing Imperial Power: Colonial Subjects in Eighteenth-Century British Painting* (Durham, N.C.: Duke University Press, 1999), pp. 110–38.
37. Diary of Elizabeth Plowden, OIOC: MSS Eur F 127/94, March 4, 1787.
38. Ibid., April 17, 1788; November 22, 1787.
39. Ibid., September 18, 1788.
40. Ibid., March 20, 1788; 8 October 1788.
41. Quoted in Walter F. C. Chicheley Plowden, *Records of the Chicheley Plowdens* (London: Heath, Cranton, & Ouseley, 1914), pp. 173–74.
42. See "Cases of Ozias Humphry and Mr. Paul at Lucknow," BL: Wellesley Papers, Add. MSS 13,532; and John Brewer, *The Pleasures of the Imagination: English Culture in the Eighteenth Century* (New York: Farrar Straus Giroux, 1997), pp. 316–18.

43. Claude Martin to Elizabeth Plowden, June 5, 1796, OIOC: MSS Eur C 149. (This is, incidentally, Martin's only surviving letter to a woman.)
44. When selling his collection to the East India Company Library in 1807, Richard Johnson told Charles Wilkins that "the choicest pictures [cost me] from 20 to 150 rupees on each" (quoted in Mildred Archer and Toby Falk, *Indian Miniatures in the India Office Library* [London: Sotheby Parke Bernet, 1981], p. 27). On the opposite end of the price scale, Elizabeth Plowden said that "Cowper told me he had once in his possession a Persian Book valued at ten Thousand Rs. which when he went to England he presented to the King. . . . [W]hat made it curious was that each Letter was written within the inside tracing of leaves flowers etc. in small beautiful characters and the intermediate leaf between each letter were beautiful paintings and round the leaves that were written on a variety of borders in a most elegant stile of painting chiefly flowers" (Plowden Diary, October 10, 1787).
45. Sharar, p. 103.
46. Archer and Falk's *Indian Miniatures in the India Office Library* is a catalogue raisonné of the Johnson collection. His Lucknow commissions are Cats. 346–61; Cat. 431 was completed in Hyderabad.
47. Rosane Rocher, "British Orientalism in the Eighteenth Century: The Dialectics of Knowledge and Government" in Carol A. Breckenridge and Peter Van der Veer, eds., *Orientalism and the Postcolonial Predicament: Perspectives on South Asia* (Philadelphia: University of Pennsylvania Press, 1993), p. 237.
48. Plowden Diary, December 13, 1787. On Polier's Orientalism, see also Muzaffar Alam and Seema Alavi, *A European Experience of the Mughal Orient: The I'jaz-i Arsalani (Persian Letters, 1773–1779) of Antoine-Louis Henri Polier* (New Delhi: Oxford University Press, 2001), pp. 50–56.
49. Polier, quoted in Georges Dumézil, ed., *Le Mahabarat et le Bhagavat du Colonel de Polier* (Paris: Gallimard, 1986).
50. Raymond Schwab, *The Oriental Renaissance: Europe's Rediscovery of India and the East, 1680–1880*, trans. Gene Patterson-Black and Victor Reinking (New York: Columbia University Press, 1984); Jean-Marie Lafont, *Indika: Essays in Indo-French Relations, 1630–1976* (New Delhi: Manohar, 2000). Schwab's book remains perhaps the most eloquent celebration of Orientalist intellectual achievements, as well as a rare study of French Indology.
51. Polier to Hastings, July 15, 1786, BL: Hastings Papers, Add. MSS 29,170.
52. S. Chaudhuri, ed., *Proceedings of the Asiatic Society of Bengal, Vol. 1: 1784–1800* (Calcutta: Asiatic Society, 1980), p. 390.
53. Many portraits of eighteenth-century Europeans by Indian painters show them in Western dress—such as the Mughal gouache of Warren Hastings sitting on a chair (reproduced in Bayly, ed., *The Raj*, p. 115). Another Lucknow collector, John Wombwell, was also painted in his *jama* by a local artist; the image is reproduced in William Dalrymple, *White Mughals: Love and Betrayal in Eighteenth-Century India* (London: HarperCollins, 2002).
54. The original volume is in the Bibliothèque Nationale, and has been edited and translated by Muzaffar Alam and Seema Alavi as *A European Experience of the Mughal Orient* [hereafter cited as *I'jaz*]. See also G. Colas and F. Richard, "Le

Fonds Polier à la Bibliothèque Nationale," in *Bulletin de l'École Française d'Extrême Orient* 73 (1984): 112–17.

55. *I'jaz*, pp. 108–9, 111, 125–26, 149–50.
56. Ibid., pp. 261–62.
57. Ibid., pp. 296–97.
58. Ibid., pp. 164–65; 266–67.
59. "Went after dinner into his Zinannah to see Col. Poliers family." Plowden Diary, January 23, 1788; November 10, 1788.
60. The best scholarly treatment of this fraught subject is Durba Ghosh, "Colonial Companions: *Bibis, Begums,* and Concubines of the British in North India, 1760–1830" (Ph.D. dissertation, University of California at Berkeley, 2000). For a detailed portrait of an Anglo-Indian love affair at this time, see Dalrymple, *White Mughals.*
61. *I'jaz*, pp. 153–56.
62. *I'jaz*, p. 285. Polier's second son, Baba Jan (John), was evidently too young to write to his father.
63. I have relied here and in many places below on the splendid biography of Martin by Rosie Llewellyn-Jones, *A Very Ingenious Man: Claude Martin in Early Colonial India* (New Delhi: Oxford University Press, 1992).
64. Ibid., pp. 155–76.
65. "Inventory of the Effects of the late Major General Claud Martin," OIOC: L/AG/34/27/24, Bengal Inventories, 1801, Vol. 1.
66. "Inventory . . ."; Deloche, ed., *Voyage en Inde du Comte de Modave . . .*, p. 106.
67. "Tribunus," quoted in Llewellyn-Jones, *A Very Ingenious Man*, pp. 149–50.
68. Martin to Raikes and Company, August 13, 1796; May 25, 1798. I am indebted to Dr. Llewellyn-Jones for transcriptions of these letters, held in the Archives du Rhône, Lyon. They have now been published in her *A Man of the Enlightenment in Eighteenth-Century India: The Letters of Claude Martin 1766–1800* (New Delhi: Permanent Black, 2003).
69. Rosie Llewellyn-Jones, "Major General Claude Martin: A French Connoisseur in Eighteenth-century India" in *Apollo Magazine*, Vol. 145 (March 1997): 17–22.
70. Quoted in Llewellyn-Jones, *A Very Ingenious Man*, p. 87.
71. Twining, p. 311.
72. "Account of Lucknow," p. 100.
73. L. F. Smith, quoted in Archer, *India and British Portraiture, 1770–1825*, pp. 142–43.
74. Clifford Geertz, "Centers, Kings and Charisma: Reflections on the Symbolics of Power," in J. Ben David and T. N. Clark, eds., *Culture and Its Creators* (Chicago: University of Chicago Press, 1977), pp. 150–71.
75. "Account of Lucknow," p. 101.
76. Milo Cleveland Beach and Ebba Koch, *King of the World* (London: Azimuth Editions, 1997).
77. Pramod J. Jethi and Christopher W. London, "A Glorious Heritage: Maharao Lakhpatji and the Aina Mahal," and Amin Jaffer, "The Aina Mahal: An Early Example of 'Europeanerie,' " *Marg* 51 (2000): 12–39.

78. Daniel Johnson, quoted in Llewellyn-Jones, *A Very Ingenious Man*, p. 133.
79. George Annesley, Viscount Valentia, *Voyages and Travels in India, Ceylon, the Red Sea, Abyssinia, and Egypt, in the Years 1802, 1803, 1804, 1805, and 1806*, 3 vols. (London, 1809), I, p. 156. Frederick Arnott brought a stock of European guns "Commissioned by Mr. Arnott for the Nabob at his express desire and a stipulated sum . . . agreed on." His inventory also included a number of curiosities that would have been sold to Asaf-ud-Daula or his courtiers, like "2 Large Ivory Immaum Barrahs," "192 China Toys and 62 Tumbling Boys," and "2 China Temples." ("Cases of Ozias Humphry and Mr. Paul at Lucknow," BL: Add. MSS 13,532.)
80. *I'jaz*, p. 326.
81. Basu, p. 4.
82. Twining, pp. 311–12.
83. Valentia, I, pp. 164–65.

## CHAPTER THREE: COMPROMISES

1. The figure is offered by Rosie Llewellyn-Jones, *A Very Ingenious Man: Claude Martin in Early Colonial India* (New Delhi: Oxford University Press, 1992), p. 102.
2. Polier to Hastings, July 15, 1786, BL: Hastings Papers, Add. MSS 29,170, ff. 129–30.
3. Walter F. C. Chicheley Plowden, *Records of the Chicheley Plowdens* (London: Heath, Cranton, & Ouseley, 1914), p. 160.
4. Figure cited in Linda Colley, *Captives: Britain, Empire, and the World 1600–1850* (London: Jonathan Cape, 2002), p. 251.
5. Epitaphs in Park Street Cemetery of Eliza Forsyth (1821), Lawrence Gall (1806), Richard Becher (1782), and Harriet Hunt (1801); Charlotte Becher's epitaph is at St. John's Church (1759).
6. Warren Hastings to Marian Hastings, November 20, 1784, BL: Hastings Papers, Add. MSS 29,197, f. 101.
7. Georges Dumézil, ed., *Le Mahabarat et le Bhagavat du Colonel de Polier* (Paris: Gallimard, 1986), p. 19.
8. Claude Martin to Elizabeth Plowden, June 5, 1796, OIOC: MSS Eur C 149. Marie de Polier says that he "brought and legitimized the children, that he had had with different Indian women" (p. xxxii).
9. Unless otherwise stated, I have drawn the account of what follows from Marie de Polier, *Mythologie des Indous*, 2 vols. (Paris and Roudolstadt, 1809), I, pp. i–xliii.
10. Polier to Warren Hastings, December 21, 1776, BL: Hastings Papers, Add. MSS 29,138, f. 43.
11. Richard Cobb, *Reactions to the French Revolution* (Oxford: Oxford University Press, 1972); D. M. G. Sutherland, *France 1789–1815: Revolution and Counter-revolution* (Oxford: Oxford University Press, 1986), pp. 286–92.
12. Pierre Polier grew up to be an adventurer, like his father: he became an officer

under Napoleon, won the Legion of Honor, married a Russian princess, and discovered diamond mines in Siberia. Eugène and Émile Haag, *La France Protestante*, 9 vols. (Paris, 1846–59), VIII, p. 276.

13. Martin to Elizabeth Plowden, June 5, 1796, OIOC: MSS Eur C 149. He had heard of the tragedy by October 1795, when he wrote to his London agents, "I am extremely affected for the death of Colonel Polier, whose character deserved a better fate" (Claude Martin to Raikes and Company, October 4, 1795).
14. Benoît de Boigne [hereafter BDB] to Cockerell and Traill, July 2, 1797, ADS: Fonds de Boigne, Letter-book "Copy of Letters from the day of my Landing at Deal in England 31 May to June 1797." When I consulted the de Boigne papers in April 2001, they were in the process of being catalogued for the first time. I am unable to provide reference numbers for quoted items, but have given dates and authors wherever possible.
15. Claude Martin to Elizabeth Plowden, June 5, 1796, OIOC: MSS Eur C 149.
16. Unless otherwise stated, I have drawn all biographical information on de Boigne from Desmond Young, *Fountain of the Elephants* (London: Collins, 1959) and Marie-Gabrielle de Saint-Venant, *Benoît de Boigne (1751–1830): Du général au particulier,* Mémoires et documents de la Société Savoisienne d'Histoire et d'Archéologie XCVIII (Chambéry: Société Savoisienne d'Histoire et d'Archéologie, 1996). The latter, written by a de Boigne descendant, is the only work since Young's to be based directly on the de Boigne papers.
17. [G. M. Raymond], *Mémoire sur la Carrière militaire et politique de M. le Général de Boigne . . . , Seconde Édition* (Chambéry, 1830), p. 45.
18. Nothing is known of de Boigne's whereabouts between his release in 1774 and his appearance in Egypt in 1777. One theory has it that he spent part of this time in Russia, scouting out an overland route to India for the empress Catherine. Herbert Compton, *A Particular Account of the European Military Adventurers of Hindustan, 1784–1803* (Karachi: Oxford University Press, 1976; 1st pub. 1892), pp. 18–19; *cf.* Young, pp. 298–304.
19. Seema Alavi, *The Sepoys and the Company: Tradition and Transition in Northern India 1770–1830* (New Delhi: Oxford University Press, 1995), pp. 216–20.
20. I have drawn these names (with the exception of Boyd) from a list in the de Boigne papers dated July 1, 1792, of the sale of the effects of Lieutenant Fleury Martin; of the twenty-five officers' names listed, seven are Indian. Several of the Europeans mentioned above receive notice in the Appendix to Compton's *Military Adventurers. . . .* Boyd wrote to de Boigne later that year to ask for a commission. (John P. Boyd to de Boigne, October 10, 1792, ADS: Fonds de Boigne.) De Boigne drew some of his officers, such as the talented Scottish officer George Sangster, from the disbanded corps of the Breton mercenary René Madec.
21. William Blane to BDB, January 5, 1790, ADS: Fonds de Boigne.
22. Saint-Venant, pp. 36–40.
23. Hamilton and Aberdein, de Boigne's Calcutta agents, sent him a violin, a pair of horns, a flute, a bass clarinet, and a "hoboe," along with a bandmaster named Leander: "All our endeavours to procure french horn men were in vain.

But as Leander is a compleat musician and brings several different sorts of Instruments along with him, he will very soon be able to train a band of Boys to any instruments you may like. The French horn, in particular, he says, is very quickly learn't." (Hamilton and Aberdein to BDB, October 26, 1789, ADS: Fonds de Boigne.)

24. As it happens, a heavily fictionalized incarnation of de Boigne scampers through Vikram Chandra's novel *Red Earth and Pouring Rain* (London: Faber and Faber, 1995).
25. BDB to Lord Macartney, April 9, 1782, quoted in Young, pp. 42–43.
26. *Cf.* Saint-Venant, who stresses that beneath his fluctuating allegiances, "Boigne était d'abord un Savoyard" (p. 19).
27. Jean-Marie Lafont, *Indika: Essays in Indo-French Relations, 1630–1976* (New Delhi: Manohar, 2000), pp. 177–204.
28. Saint-Venant, pp. 22, 53.
29. Joseph Queiros to BDB, April 5, 1792, ADS: Fonds de Boigne.
30. Quoted in Young, pp. 162–69.
31. William Blane to BDB, October 19, 1792, ADS: Fonds de Boigne. Blane was writing from Lucknow, where he was surgeon to Asaf ud-Daula. He saw a fair amount of de Boigne in England, where Blane apparently lived "in some style at Wickfield Park" (Young, p. 214); though Claude Martin was surprised to hear "that Blane who pretend to Science and high Polite Life and society would have gone to live in Scotland, and not in the Midle of art and Science London and Suppose he is Gone to Emprove his professions and his fortune, as I understand Scotland is a Country where one live Cheap, and in which there is some famous phisician" (Martin to Elizabeth Plowden, June 5, 1796, OIOC: MSS Eur C 149).
32. Contemporary account quoted in Young, p. 174.
33. Inventory entitled "Marque D. B. des Malles laissées a Hambourg chez les Banquiers W. M. Jean Beremberg, Gossler et Compes," ADS: Fonds de Boigne.
34. Young casually dismisses all this as "odds and ends of the kind which the returning resident of India wonders, on arrival in Europe, why he ever bothered to have packed" (p. 186).
35. When I saw these letters in the spring of 2001, they were bunched together in a small and rather battered black metal chest. I refer here to a volume of translations in the de Boigne papers prepared in 1870 by Syed Abdoolah, "Professor of Oriental Languages and late Translator and Interpreter to the Board of Administration for the Affairs of the Punjab," Nos. 12 and 17 (from Madho Rao Scindia); 20 (from Shah Alam); 30 (from "the Empress"); 83 (referring to de Boigne's Persian titles); and 94 (a 1789 *sanad,* granting de Boigne thirty-six villages).
36. The drawing, and de Boigne's correspondence with Colonel John Murray about restoration, is reproduced in Jérôme Boyé, ed., *L'Extraordinaire aventure de Benoît de Boigne aux Indes* (Paris: Éditions C & D, 1996), pp. 123–30.
37. An inventory in the de Boigne papers entitled "Effects and Goods my Property as being in my Possession and the value worth or brought for Camp 1 Ablvel 1207 or 13 November 1798" includes "Delhy Sword Koran's passages," "Cam-

aone with Hindoo Gods," and various daggers with animal hilts (as well as a microscope and five clocks). The date given on this document is somewhat perplexing—and undoubtedly incorrect—since in November 1798 de Boigne was living in London.

38. List of "Armes indiennes" itemized with inventory of "Marque D. B. des Malles laissées a Hambourg chez les Banquiers W. M. Jean Beremberg, Gossler et Compes," ADS: Fonds de Boigne. Some of these items, including the commander's batons, are illustrated in Boyé, ed.
39. BDB to Messrs. Duntzfelt, Meyers and Co., July 2, 1797, ADS: Fonds de Boigne, "Copy of Letters from the day of my Landing at Deal in England 31 May to June 1797."
40. Quoted from a bond in the de Boigne papers by William Palmer to de Boigne, signed and dated at Futtyghur, March 5, 1794, which diverts the interest of 136 rupees *per annum* on Palmer's debt to provide for these girls.
41. Power of attorney to Joseph Queiros, dated May 28, 1796, Lucknow, ADS: Fonds de Boigne. Claude Martin was to handle the payment of their pensions.
42. BDB to Hamilton and Aberdein, July 2, 1797, ADS: Fonds de Boigne, "Copy of Letters from the day of my Landing at Deal in England 31 May to June 1797."
43. BDB to Cockerell and Traill, July 2, 1797, ADS: Fonds de Boigne, "Copy of Letters from the day of my Landing at Deal in England 31 May to June 1797."
44. BDB to Duntzfelt, Meyers and Co., July 2, 1797, ADS: Fonds de Boigne, "Copy of Letters from the day of my Landing at Deal in England 31 May to June 1797." Denmark was unlucky for de Boigne: learning of the great Copenhagen fire of 1795, he said "I have 30 thousand pounds at Copenhagen, the conflagration of which place is to give me much subject of apprehension till information from my Agents is obtained." BDB to William Palmer, January 17, 1796 (draft), ADS: Fonds de Boigne.
45. BDB to Messrs. Duntzfelt, Meyers and Co., July 2, 1797; BDB to Cockerell and Traill, July 2, 1797.
46. BDB to Duntzfelt, Meyers and Co., July 2, 1797; BDB to Captain Tennent, July 14, 1797; BDB to Hamilton and Aberdein, July 2, 1797.
47. The will is included in "Statement of General Bennet de Boigne's Property as Existing at this Day 15 August 1797," ADS: Fonds de Boigne. In this document the children are named as "Ally Bux, to be Baptised John Baptiste," and "Banoo Jaun, to be do. Helena."
48. BDB to Cockerell and Traill, October 27, 1797.
49. BDB to Fairlie, Guilmore and Co., January 26, 1798.
50. Young, pp. 193–94; Saint-Venant, p. 92.
51. Claude Martin to BDB, May 28, 1798, quoted in Rosie Llewellyn-Jones, ed., *A Man of the Enlightenment in Eighteenth-Century India: The Letters of Claude Martin, 1766–1800* (New Delhi: Permanent Black, 2003), p. 369.
52. Adèle d'Osmond de Boigne, *Mémoires de la Comtesse de Boigne,* . . . 2 vols. (Paris: Mercure de France, 1999), I, pp 152–53. In her memoirs Adèle does not give the first name of the "Monsieur Johnson" who introduced them, but she is surely referring to Richard Johnson, de Boigne's banker and confidant—

whom de Boigne appointed in 1799 to serve as a trustee for Nur, and whose house de Boigne frequented during his early months in London. The marriage broker was Daniel O'Connell (uncle of his more famous namesake, the Irish nationalist), a "wild goose" who had commanded de Boigne in the Clare regiment thirty years before.

53. Undated draft of a letter from BDB to Adèle, probably late 1798, quoted in Saint-Venant, p. 85.
54. Listed in "Goods wanted from Mde de Boigne being my own property," c. 1800, ADS: Fonds de Boigne.
55. She likely learned about them soon after her marriage. De Boigne wrote to his brother Joseph in 1801, "it is a good thing for me that my legal wife should have delicate sentiments . . . [toward] this Indian woman." Quoted in Saint-Venant, p. 87.
56. D'Osmond de Boigne, I, pp. 155–57.
57. "Estimation of my fortune at this day 20 October 1798 . . . ," ADS: Fonds de Boigne. At this time he was paying £500 per year to the d'Osmonds, and an annuity of £400 to Adèle.
58. These receipts are in the de Boigne papers.
59. Young, p. 232.
60. BDB to Duntzfelt, Meyers and Co., July 17, 1797; November 13, 1797.
61. Martin to BDB, September 29, 1798, quoted in Llewellyn-Jones, ed., *A Man of the Enlightenment*, p. 375.
62. Martin to BDB, August 20, 1799, quoted in ibid., p. 389.
63. Ibid., p. 390.
64. "Last Will and Testament of Claude Martin, 1 January 1800," OIOC: L/AG/34/29/12, Bengal Wills, 1800. It is unlikely that Martin was actually embalmed, but he could very well have been doused in spirits. When I visited the crypt of Constantia (now La Martinière school) in November 1999, the principal took pains to assure me that the air, though rather musty, was quite clean and healthy.
65. Llewellyn-Jones, *A Very Ingenious Man*, pp. 145–47. Martin's distinctly foreign English is here evident in his description of Europe as a "country," for the French *contrée* (region). He has been recognized as a Briton posthumously, at least: he is included in the new edition of the *DNB*.
66. The house is described in detail in Rosie Llewellyn-Jones, *A Fatal Friendship: The Nawabs, the British and the City of Lucknow* (New Delhi: Oxford University Press, 1985), pp. 140–46.
67. Martin to Elizabeth Plowden, June 5, 1796, OIOC: MSS Eur C 149.
68. I have drawn these details from the Constantia inventory ("Inventory of the Effects of the late Major General Claud Martin," OIOC: L/AG/34/27/24, Bengal Inventories, 1801, vol. 1) and Llewellyn-Jones, *A Very Ingenious Man*, pp. 184–85.
69. Martin to BDB, February 16, 1800, quoted in Llewellyn-Jones, ed., *A Man of the Enlightenment*, p. 396.
70. Martin to Elizabeth Plowden, June 5, 1796, OIOC: MSS Eur C 149.
71. Martin to Raikes and Co., October 4, 1795, quoted in Llewellyn-Jones, ed., *A Man of the Enlightenment*, p. 277.

72. "Tribunus," quoted in Llewellyn-Jones, *A Very Ingenious Man*, p. 205.
73. Llewellyn-Jones, *A Very Ingenious Man*, p. 220.
74. Martin to BDB, May 28, 1798, quoted in Llewellyn-Jones, ed., *A Man of the Enlightenment*, p. 371. Llewellyn–Jones attributes the quote "après moi la fin du monde" to Voltaire, p. 315.
75. George Annesley, Viscount Valentia, *Voyages and Travels in India, Ceylon, the Red Sea, Abyssinia, and Egypt, in the years 1802, 1803, 1804, 1805, and 1806*, 3 vols. (London, 1809), I, pp. 143–48; Captain Charles Madan, *Two Private Letters to a Gentleman in England, from His Son who Accompanied Earl Cornwallis on his Expedition to Lucknow in the Year 1787* (Peterborough, 1788), pp. 57–58.
76. Michael Fisher, *A Clash of Cultures: Awadh, the British, and the Mughals* (New Delhi: Oxford University Press, 1987), pp. 114–41. I certainly do not mean to suggest that cultural hybridity disappeared from Awadh. On the contrary, as Ghazi ud-Din's coronation ceremony demonstrated—he was enthroned on an extravagant Indo-Persian *musnud*, wearing robes likely designed by the British artist Robert Home, crowned by the Shiite mujtahid, and serenaded by "God Save the King"—it was in some ways as evident as ever. But by this stage neither Mughal nor Awadh rule went much beyond the symbolic. This belonged at least as much to the India of Curzon's gorgeously neo-Mughal Delhi durbars (1903 and 1911), as to the city of Colonel Mordaunt's cockfights.
77. John Pemble, *The Raj, the Indian Mutiny, and the Kingdom of Oudh, 1801–1859* (New Delhi: Oxford University Press, 1979); Veena Talwar Oldenburg, *The Making of Colonial Lucknow* (Princeton, N.J.: Princeton University Press, 1984), pp. 3–61.
78. Lafont, *Indika*, pp. 103–5.
79. "Extract from a Letter from the Honourable Court of Directors, dated the 15th of May 1798," in *Asiatic Annual Register*, vol. 1 (London, 1799), "Chronicle," pp. 107–8.
80. Ray Desmond, *The India Museum* (London: HMSO, 1982). For these early acquisitions, see OIOC: MSS Eur D 562/17. These are among the founding collections of the British Library's own Oriental manuscripts division. The origins of the British Library Oriental collections thus contrast strongly with those of the Bibliothèque Nationale, which had been built up since the time of Colbert through a succession of state-sponsored collecting missions.
81. "Extract from a Letter . . . ," *Asiatic Annual Register*, pp. 107–8.
82. "A Catalogue of the Very Valuable Collection of Rare and Curious Persian and other Mss. and a few Books, of the late Nathaniel Middleton, Esq. Dec. . . . ," February 9, 1808; "A Catalogue of a most Valuable Collection of Oriental Manuscripts, the Property of a Gentleman, Late in the East India Company's Service . . . ," March 9, 1809; "A Catalogue of a Very Valuable Collection of Persian, and a few Arabic, Mss. Selected Many Years Ago, in the East, by Archibald Swinton, Esq. . . . ," June 6, 1810. A similar event auction was held by the heirs of Sir John Carnac's manuscript collection, at Phillips in 1804. I have drawn information on buyers from the annotated auctioneer's books of these sales held in the Christie's archive, London.
83. Lucian Harris, "Archibald Swinton: A New Source for Albums of Indian

Miniatures in William Beckford's Collection," *Burlington Magazine* (June 2001): 360–66. These albums are now in the Museum für Indische Kunst, in Berlin.

84. BDB to William Palmer, January 17, 1796, ADS: Fonds de Boigne.
85. Young, p. 236; Saint-Venant, pp. 94–95. The letter from Napoleon to de Boigne no longer exists—if, indeed, it ever did. But Napoleon was known to be planning such an invasion, and he certainly consulted with several veteran French officers from Indian armies.
86. Young, pp. 213–14. For the annuity, BDB to Messrs. Edwards, Templer and Co., March 3, 1802, ADS: Fonds de Boigne.
87. BDB to a friend, quoted in Saint-Venant, p. 96; Young, pp. 243, 256–57.
88. These letters are quoted in Young, pp. 241–43.
89. A daguerreotype of Charles is reproduced in Boyé, ed., p. 142.
90. The memoirs were published in 1907 and influenced Marcel Proust, who reviewed them in *Le Figaro* under the title "Le snobisme et la postérité." (Editor's introduction in D'Osmond de Boigne, I, p. xv.)
91. Evan Cotton, "The Begum of Sussex: The Strange Tale of de Boigne's Indian Wife," *Bengal Past & Present* 46 (1933): 91–94; Durba Ghosh, "Colonial Companions: *Bibis, Begums,* and Concubines of the British in North India, 1760–1830" (Ph.D. dissertation, University of California at Berkeley, 2000), pp. 158–59; Young, pp. 292–97; Rosie Llewellyn-Jones, *Engaging Scoundrels: True Tales of Old Lucknow* (New Delhi: Oxford University Press, 2000), p. 93.
92. Llewellyn-Jones, *A Very Ingenious Man,* pp. 216–17.
93. Valentia, I, p. 166.
94. He did adopt a half-Indian boy named Zulfikar, whom he sent to school in Calcutta "for to learn to read and write English as also to learn the Christian Religion that he might chuse either the one or the Musulman or any he may chuse he preferred the Christiand and he was christened in Calcutta Church by the name of James." Martin provided well for James and his Indian relatives, but he did not make the boy his heir. ("Last Will and Testament of Major-General Claude Martin," Article 9.)
95. "Last Will and Testament . . . ," Article 32. The first students were European and Anglo-Indian only, though Martin did not specify that this should be so. Emily Eden, visiting Constantia in 1837 ("a sort of castle in a fine jungle park"), said that Martin had left it to the public so that "Any European in want of change of air might go with his family and live there for a month, and beyond the month, unless another family wanted it. This would be a great convenience to the few English in Oude, particularly to poor officers; so of course, for thirty years, the Supreme Court has been doubting whether the will meant what it said it meant, and the house has been going to decay; but it is now decided that people may live there, and it is all to be repaired." Emily Eden, *Up the Country* (Oxford: Oxford University Press, 1930), pp. 58–59.
96. Linda Colley, "Going Native, Telling Tales: Captivity, Collaborations, and Empire," *Past & Present* 168 (August 2000): 181–82. The presence of Britons in these armies has been routinely downplayed by such writers as Herbert Compton, whose *Particular Account of the European Military Adventurers of Hindustan . . .* (1892) remains one of the most thorough sources on the subject.

97. On Company reintegration of Thomas and Skinner, see Alavi, pp. 232–50.
98. Between 1795 and 1807 at least eight French India hands submitted memorandums on the subject to the central government. AN: AE B/III/459 and AF/IV/1686.

CHAPTER FOUR: INVADING EGYPT

1. Simon Schama, *Citizens: A Chronicle of the French Revolution* (New York: Vintage, 1990), pp. 668–69.
2. John Aikin, M.D., *Annals of the Reign of King George the Third*, 2 vols. (London, 1816), I, p. 465.
3. George III to William Pitt, February 2, 1793, quoted in J. Heneage Jesse, *Memoirs of the Life and Reign of King George the Third*, 3 vols. (London, 1867), III, p. 201.
4. Alan Forrest, *The Soldiers of the French Revolution* (Durham, N.C.: Duke University Press, 1990), pp. 68–83. In the Seven Years War, the French government called for 270,000 men; at its height, some 330,000 fought in line units. Lee B. Kennett, *The French Armies in the Seven Years War* (Durham, N.C.: Duke University Press, 1967), p. 77.
5. J. E. Cookson, *The British Armed Nation, 1793–1815* (Oxford: Clarendon Press, 1997), pp. 66, 95. A report to Parliament in May of that year indicated that 482,000 men were willing to fight, and 176,000 were already in the militia. Linda Colley, *Britons: Forging the Nation 1707–1837* (New Haven: Yale University Press, 1992), p. 293. At the beginning of the Seven Years War, by contrast, the British Army numbered about 35,000, growing to 100,000 by its end. Fred Anderson, *Crucible of War* (London: Faber and Faber, 2000), p. 560.
6. Michael Broers, "Cultural Imperialism in a European Context? Political Culture and Cultural Politics in Napoleonic Italy," *Past & Present* 170 (2001): 152–80; Stuart Woolf, "French Civilization and Ethnicity in the Napoleonic Empire," *Past & Present* 124 (1989): 96–120.
7. Paul Kennedy, *The Rise and Fall of the Great Powers* (New York: Random House, 1989), pp. 115–39.
8. Michael Duffy, "World-Wide War and British Expansion, 1793–1815," in P. J. Marshall, ed., *Oxford History of the British Empire, Vol. II: The Eighteenth Century* (Oxford: Oxford University Press, 1998), pp. 184–207; Jeremy Black, *Britain as a Military Power, 1688–1815* (London: UCL Press, 1999), pp. 241–66. Of course by this time, too, Britain's imperial military presence was far greater than its establishment on the Continent, which was limited to the garrison at Gibraltar.
9. Again, the traditional demarcation of "First" and "Second" British Empires, divided by the American Revolution, ought to be revised. C. A. Bayly, "The First Age of Global Imperialism, c. 1760–1820," *Journal of Imperial and Commonwealth History* 26 (1998): 28–48; C. A. Bayly, *Imperial Meridian: The British Empire and the World, 1780–1830* (London: Longman, 1989), pp. 100–132; Stuart Woolf, "The Construction of a European World-View in the Revolutionary-Napoleonic Years," *Past & Present* 137 (1992): 72–101.

10. See especially: Colley, *Britons*, pp. 283–319; Bayly, *Imperial Meridian*, pp. 160–63; Duffy, "World-Wide War"; and P. J. Marshall, " 'Cornwallis Triumphant': War in India and the British Public in the Late 18th Century," in Lawrence Freedman, Paul Hayes, and Robert O'Neill, eds., *War, Strategy and International Politics: Essays in Honour of Sir Michael Howard* (Oxford: Clarendon Press, 1992), pp. 57–74.
11. Cookson, pp. 153–81. In an earlier crisis of recruitment, the Catholic Relief Act of 1778 had been passed to facilitate enlistment of Irish and Highland Scottish troops.
12. Duffy, p. 202.
13. Alfred Fierro, André-Palluel-Guillard, and Jean Tulard, *Histoire et dictionnaire du Consulat et de l'Empire* (Paris: R. Laffont, 1995), pp. 376–77.
14. "Extract of a Letter from Signior Brandi, at Alexandria, dated 5th July 1779," encl. in Sir Robert Ainslie to Viscount Weymouth, August 17, 1779, OIOC: Factory Records, Egypt and Red Sea, G/17/5, f. 237.
15. "Translation of a Hatti Sheriff, addressed to the Government of Egypt," enclosed in Richard Scott to Laurence Sulivan, July 6, 1780, OIOC: G/17/5, ff. 292–95.
16. Printed pamphlet entitled "The Humble Petition of George Baldwin [to the East India Company Court of Directors]," April 23, 1783, OIOC: G/17/5.
17. John O'Donnell to Sir Robert Ainslie, August 5, 1779, OIOC: G/17/5, ff. 260–66.
18. I have compiled my account from John O'Donnell to Sir Robert Ainslie, August 5, 1779, OIOC: G/17/5; Eliza Fay, *Original Letters from India* (New York: Harcourt, Brace and Company, 1925), pp. 90–99; and "Narrative of the Sufferings of M. de St Germain and his Companions in the Deserts of Egypt," BL: Hastings Papers, Add. MSS 29,232, ff. 305–6. Probably referring to the same episode (though a similar incident unfolded shortly afterward concerning another merchant ship, the *St. Helena*), the French consul in Alexandria reported that "many young Indians" of the crew were "extremely mistreated," made to convert to Islam and forcibly circumcised. (Consul Taitbout to Ministry of the Marine, August 3, 1779, AN: AE/BI/112.)
19. "Extract of a Letter from Signior Brandi, at Alexandria, dated 5th July 1779," encl. in Sir Robert Ainslie to Viscount Weymouth, August 17, 1779, OIOC: G/17/5, f. 238.
20. Sir Robert Ainslie to Peter Michell, October 17, 1780, OIOC: G/17/5, ff. 305–10.
21. Rosemarie Said Zahlan, "George Baldwin: Soldier of Fortune?" in Paul Starkey and Janet Starkey, eds., *Travellers in Egypt* (London: Tauris, 2001), p. 24. Further schemes for opening communications between India and Britain via Suez can be found in OIOC: G/17/6, including the journal of Captain Mark Wood, who carried dispatches to India through Egypt in the summer of 1779. While in the East, Baldwin also met and married the dazzling Smyrna-born Jane Maltass, who in 1782 sat in Eastern dress for a magnificent portrait by Sir Joshua Reynolds; the portrait fetched £3.36 million at Sotheby's in July 2004.

22. [George Baldwin], "Speculations on the Situation and Resources of Egypt, 1773 to 1785," OIOC: G/17/5, ff. 48–50, 57.
23. [George Baldwin], "Reflections concerning the Communication by way of Suez to India. How it came to be overset; and why it is necessary; and how it is possible to restore it," encl. in Richard Scott to Laurence Sulivan, July 6, 1780, OIOC: G/17/5, ff. 289–91.
24. Experimental overland voyages were also made by this route: see "Journal of a Passage by Sea and Land from Bengal in the East Indies to England undertaken by Henry Doidge, Edward Ives, John Pye and three of their Servants" (1757–1759), NLW: Robert Clive Papers, SF3/1. This was later described in Edward Ives, *A Voyage from England to India in the Year MDCCLIV* . . . (London, 1773).
25. Henry Dundas et al., to Carmarthen, PRO: FO/24/1, f. 3; Foreign Office to Baldwin, June 20, 1786, PRO: FO/24/1, f. 33.
26. Baldwin to Dundas, September 16, 1788, OIOC: G/17/6, f. 201.
27. Baldwin to Dundas, October 21, 1787, OIOC: G/17/6, f. 183.
28. In a 1775 bulletin on the "État géneral des françois etablis dans les trois Echelles d'Egypte," for instance, the French consul Mure listed seventy French men, women, and children in the three towns. AN: AE B/III/290, f. 118.
29. Magallon lost a considerable part of his fortune in the wake of the 1786 Ottoman campaign to reassert control in Egypt; he later became French consul. On the Magallons and their losses, see e.g., Magallon to Ministry of Foreign Affairs, March 27, 1789; and Bertrand to Ministry of Foreign Affairs, January 2, 1793, MAE: CCC Cairo 25.
30. François Charles-Roux, *Les Origines de l'expédition d'Égypte* (Paris: Plon-Nourrit, 1910). See also his *Autour d'un route: l'Angleterre, l'isthme de Suez et l'Égypte au XVIIIème siècle* (Paris, Ploun-Nourrit, 1922); *L'Isthme et le canal de Suez* (Paris: Hachette, 1901); *Le Projet français de commerce avec l'Inde par Suez sous le règne de Louis XVI* (Cairo: Institut Français d'Archéologie Orientale, 1929). These documents are chiefly to be found in the archives of the Ministry of the Marine (AN: Mar B/7/433, 440, 452, 462); see also SHAT: 1/M/1677 and MAE: Mémoires et Documents, Égypte 1 and 21. The historiographical oversight is especially significant in view of what remains the most prominent reading of Napoleon's invasion in Anglo-American scholarship, Edward Said's *Orientalism*, which attributes the inspiration behind the expedition chiefly to the writing of the philosophe traveler Constantin Volney.
31. Sartine to de Tott, April 14, 1781, AN: Mar B7/440. The importance of discretion was stressed, since de Tott had a reputation for having "talked a little too much about his mission."
32. "Compte rendu de la mission secrète du Baron de Tott," 1779, AN: Mar B7/440; Charles-Roux, *Les Origines*, pp. 70–82.
33. See e.g., "Note pour M. de Boynes," May 1774, AN: Mar B7/433.
34. Baron de Tott, "Examen de l'État Phisique et Politique de l'Empire Ottoman, et des vues qu'il détermine relativement à la France" (undated), AN: Mar B7/440.
35. "Observations de M. de St. Didier sur l'Égypte," AN: Mar B7/440.

36. Grenville to Dundas, February 8, 1793, quoted in Zahlan, pp. 34–35.
37. George Baldwin, "Essay on the Plague," July 12, 1791, OIOC: G/17/6, f. 246.
38. George Baldwin to Benoît de Boigne, June 14, 1823, ADS: Fonds de Boigne.
39. George Baldwin, *Mr. Baldwin's Legacy to His Daughter*, 2 vols. (London, 1811), II, p. i.
40. George Baldwin, *La Prima Musa Clio* (London, 1802).
41. Baldwin to Dundas, October 9, 1799, OIOC: G/17/6, ff. 268–69.
42. Charles Magallon, "Mémoire sur l'Égypte presenté au Ministre des Relations Extérieures de la République Française," February 9, 1798, MAE: Mémoires et Documents Égypte 21.
43. Henry Laurens, *L'expédition d'Égypte 1708–1801* (Paris: Éditions du Seuil, 1997), pp. 34–36, 42.
44. Somewhat anticlimactically, however, all the works of art except the horses of San Marco remained boxed in their wooden cases. Andrew McClellan, *Inventing the Louvre* (Cambridge, UK: Cambridge University Press, 1994), pp. 117–23.
45. Duffy, p. 190.
46. See "Projets contre l'Angleterre, dans les quels le Gal. Bonaparte laisse parler ses vues sur l'Egypte," AN: AF/IV/1687, Dossier II, Pièces 18–19.
47. Alain Blondy, *L'Ordre de Malte au XVIIIème siècle: des dernières splendeurs à la ruine* (Paris: Bouchene, 2002), pp. 372–73.
48. *Correspondance de Napoléon I,* 32 vols. (Paris, 1858–69), IV, p. 256.
49. Dominique Vivant Denon, *Voyage dans la basse et la haute Égypte* (Paris: Gallimard, 1998), p. 71. The later, romanticized version is usually cited: "Forty centuries are looking down on you!"
50. Laurens, p. 126. Bourienne arrived just after the battle: "[W]e saw the banks of the Nile strewed with heaps of bodies, which the waves were every moment washing into the sea. This horrible spectacle . . . led us to infer, with tolerable certainty, that a battle fatal to the Mamelukes had been fought." Quoted in Shmuel Moreh, trans. and ed., *Napoleon in Egypt: Al-Jabarti's Chronicle of the French Occupation, 1798* (Princeton, N.J., and New York: Markus Wiener, 1993), p. 142. [Hereafter cited as Al-Jabarti.]
51. Laurens, p. 128.
52. Al-Jabarti, p. 38.
53. Nelson to St. Vincent, June 17, 1798, BL: Nelson Papers, Add. MSS 34,907, f. 32. A word on dates: considerable inconsistency surrounds the precise dating of various events in the campaign, which is perhaps not surprising given that three different calendars were in use: Muslim, Revolutionary, and Gregorian. I have adhered to the chronology in Laurens.
54. Nelson to St. Vincent, July 12, 1798.
55. Jean-Joel Brégeon, *L'Égypte française au jour le jour 1798–1801* (Paris: Perrin, 1991), pp. 106–7; Laurens, pp. 56–57; Denon, pp. 51–54; C. F. La Jonquière, *L'Expédition d'Égypte,* 5 vols. (Paris, 1899–1907), II, p. 279. Dates vary.
56. Napoleon blamed Admiral Brueys for keeping the fleet in the bay rather than bringing it safely into port, and Admiral Villeneuve for incompetent conduct in battle. For a powerful contradiction see Alan Schom, *Napoleon Bonaparte* (New York: HarperCollins, 1997), pp. 132–44.
57. Brégeon, p. 109.

58. See the primary account by Lachadenède in La Jonquière, II, pp. 396–400. Like many sailors, he could not swim, but survived the rest of the battle by clinging to a floating piece of timber.
59. La Jonquière, II, p. 419.
60. Schom, p. 142; Napoleon, *Campagnes d'Égypte et de Syrie*, introd. Henry Laurens (Paris: Imprimerie Nationale, 1998), p. 121.
61. Nelson to St. Vincent, June 17, 1798, BL: Nelson Papers, Add. MSS 34,907, f. 32.
62. Laurens, pp. 130–32, 200–202.
63. La Jonquière, II, p. 65.
64. Brégeon, pp. 274–75.
65. Saladin Boustany, ed., *The Journals of Bonaparte in Egypt 1798–1801, VIII: Bonaparte's Proclamations as Recorded by Abd al-Rahman al-Jabarti* (Cairo: Dar al-Maaref, 1971), pp. 1–3.
66. "Diary of an anonymous French officer, 1798–99," BL: Nelson Papers, Add. MSS 34,942, f. 83.
67. Ibid. f. 84. This account is not intrinsically unbelievable: Rosetta was the most pro-French city in Egypt. According to the young engineer Édouard Villiers du Terrage, "I was told that the reduction of Rosetta was due to the proclamations brought by the [Muslim] slaves we liberated at Malta. Before their arrival, they wanted to kill all Europeans. But after the reading of the proclamations, everyone changed face." Édouard Villiers du Terrage, *Journal et souvenirs sur l'expédition d'Égypte (1798–1801)* (Paris, 1899), p. 51.
68. Laurens, pp. 98–101.
69. Al-Jabarti, pp. 24–33.
70. *Cf.* Albert Hourani's reading: "No doubt there was something in this of political propaganda, but there was also an admiration for the achievements of Muhammed (a subject to which Napoleon returned in later life), and a certain [Enlightenment rationalist] view of religion." Albert Hourani, *Islam in European Thought* (Cambridge, UK: Cambridge University Press, 1991), p. 15.
71. "Mémoire politique de Mr. Mure sur l'Égypte," SHAT: 1/M/1677.
72. *Courier de l'Égypte* No. 1 (12 Fructidor VI), reprinted in Saladin Boustany, ed., *The Journals of Bonaparte in Egypt 1798–1801, IV: Courier de l'Égypte* (Cairo: Dar al-Maaref, 1971); *Campagnes . . .*, p. 148.
73. Laurens, p. 158; *Campagnes . . .*, p. 149.
74. Mona Ozouf, *Festivals and the French Revolution*, trans. Alan Sheridan (Cambridge, Mass.: Harvard University Press, 1988).
75. *Courier de l'Égypte* Nos. 8–10 (6, 10, 15 Vendémiaire VII); Patrice Bret, *L'Égypte au temps de l'expédition de Bonaparte 1798–1801* (Paris: Hachette, 1998), pp. 167–70.
76. On Ottoman propaganda, see Laurens, pp. 195–202.
77. Al-Jabarti, p. 62.
78. Boustany, ed., VIII, p. 19. Unfortunately the opening speech was largely unintelligible to its auditors—their Arabic speakers, al-Jabarti complained, were Bedouins, and their Turks low-born peasants. Laurens, p. 204.
79. Laurens, pp. 208–12; André Raymond, *Égyptiens et français au Caire 1798–1801* (Cairo: IFAO, 1998), pp. 110–12, 124–26.

80. *Campagnes . . .*, p. 163.
81. Al-Jabarti, p. 71.
82. Étienne Geoffroy Saint-Hilaire, *Lettres écrites d'Égypte . . .* (Paris: Hachette, 1901), p. 113.
83. Laurens, pp. 210–14.
84. *Courier de l'Égypte* No. 21 (25 Frimaire VII), reprinted in Saladin Boustany, ed., *The Journals of Bonaparte in Egypt 1798–1801, IV: Courier de l'Égypte* (Cairo: Dar al-Maaref, 1971).
85. This paragraph is based on the passage in *Campagnes . . .*, pp. 144–48.
86. Laurens, pp. 284–85.
87. Jean Tulard, ed., *Dictionnaire Napoléon* (Paris: Fayard, 1987), p. 451.
88. Boustany, ed., VIII, pp. 32–33.
89. Al-Jabarti, p. 97.
90. Laurens, pp. 246–48.
91. Laurens, pp. 288, 539n. The letters from the sharif of Mecca are translated in Silvestre de Sacy, *Chrestomathie Arabe, ou, Extraits de divers écrivains arabes . . .*, 3 vols. (Paris, 1826–27), III, pp. 319–27.

## CHAPTER FIVE: SEIZING SERINGAPATAM

1. For the original French proceedings of the Seringapatam Jacobin Club, see OIOC: MSS Eur K 179. I have quoted here from the contemporary translation prepared by the East India Company (OIOC: P/345/38, Madras Military Proceedings, June 11, 1799) and reprinted in M. Wood, *A Review of the Origin, Progress, and Result of the Decisive War with the Late Tippoo Sultaun, in Mysore . . .* (London, 1800). Several sources, including Mark Wilks, *Historical Sketches of the South Indian History . . .*, 2 vols. (London, 1817), misdate the proceedings to 1798. Its members were not, as Wilks claims, the volunteers from Mauritius. Some of them, rather, may have been the workers who had come in 1789.
2. *Cf.* Lynn Hunt, *Politics, Culture, and Class in the French Revolution* (Berkeley: University of California Press, 1984), pp. 52–86. Investigating Jacobins abroad would be especially profitable in light of Hunt's argument that Jacobinism was strongest on the peripheries of France. Many of its exporters in the merchant marine were, of course, natives of France's peripheries.
3. G. B. Malleson, *Final French Struggles in India . . .* (London, 1878), pp. 158–251; Jean-Marie Lafont, *La Présence française dans le royaume Sikh du punjab 1822–49* (Paris: École Française d'Extrême Orient, 1992), pp. 77–116.
4. See for instance Francis Robson, *Life of Hyder Ally* (London, 1786) and the "Incomplete draft (1785) of an account of the Mysore War 1780–84" (OIOC: MSS Eur K 116) that he seems to have consulted.
5. Anonymous letter dated June 2, 1799, "Camp at Gariahguanelly," OIOC: MSS Eur B 276, f. 5.
6. "Narrative of the Mysore War of 1799 by Lt. Col. P. A. Agnew addressed to Mr. Ewart Physician Genl. on Ceylon and dated January 1800," OIOC: MSS Eur D 313/5, f. 7.

7. Kate Teltscher, *India Inscribed: European and British Writing on India, 1600–1800* (New Delhi: Oxford University Press, 1995), pp. 229–55; Linda Colley, *Captives: Britain, Empire, and the World 1600–1850* (London: Jonathan Cape, 2002), pp. 269–307.
8. Maistre de la Tour, *The History of Nawab Hyder Ali Khan and of His Son Tippoo Sultan* (Jaipur: Printwell, 1991), p. 35.
9. Maistre de la Tour, pp. 37–38.
10. "Nottes sur l'Inde. D'après un Voyage fait pendant les années 1769, 1770, 1771 et 1772 par M. Hugau Capitaine de Dragons. Année 1775. Première Partie," AN: AF IV 1686, Secrétaire d'État Impériale, Relations Extérieures: Perse et Indes, 1806–1810, p. 11.
11. Francis Buchanan, who visited Seringapatam on an East India Company survey a year after its capture, was distinctly contemptuous of the "immense, unfinished, unsightly, and injudicious" fort, and claimed, unjustly, that: "Tippoo seems to have had too high an opinion of his own skill to have consulted the French who were about him; and adhered to the old Indian style of fortification, labouring to make the place strong by heaping walls and cavaliers one above the other." Francis Buchanan, *A Journey from Madras Through the Countries of Mysore, Canara, and Malabar . . .*, 3 vols. (London, 1807), I, p. 62.
12. Maistre de la Tour, p. 42, pp. 77–79; Hasan, p. 237.
13. The Ottomans had used European military advisers since Mehmet the Conqueror's day—in this period, Baron de Tott supervised Abdul Hamid I's arsenal; French officers trained Selim III's Nizam-i-Çedid; and Mahmud II's reformed troops wore French uniforms. Muhammad Ali of Egypt reorganized his army with the help of the Napoleonic veteran Colonel Joseph Sève. In Persia, Britain and France vied with each other to place advisers in the court of Fath Ali Shah—an early taste of the Great Game and cold war methods to come.
14. Josias Webbe to General Harris, July 6, 1798, quoted in R. Montgomery Martin, ed., *The Despatches, Minutes, and Correspondence, of the Marquess Wellesley, K. G.*, 5 vols. (London, 1836), I, p. 75 [hereafter cited as *Despatches. . . .*].
15. Napoleon to Executive Directory, April 14, 1798, *Correspondance de Napoléon I*, 32 vols. (Paris, 1858–69), I, p. 84.
16. Quoted in Maurice Besson, "Un Partisan Savoyard aux Indes: De Motz de la Sale de Lallée" in *Revue d'histoire des colonies* 22 (1934): 60. Malleson wrongly identifies Lallée as a nephew of the (in)famous Lally, commandant of Pondicherry, and as a predecessor of Raymond in Hyderabad. This Lallée joined the Compagnie des Indes army c. 1758, after a failed career as a monk, was held prisoner in London from 1763 to 1765, then returned to India and evidently served in native courts until his death, c. 1799. A similar patriotic assertion can be found in a scheme presented to Napoleon in 1804 by a former mercenary called Loustaunau, who was moved by "the desire to be useful to my country [patrie]" to suggest and offer help with a French invasion of India. ("Plan Submitted to Napoleon for an Invasion of India," OIOC: MSS Eur D 458.)
17. A. W. C. Lindsay, ed., *Lives of the Lindsays . . .*, 3 vols. (London, 1849), III, p. 258.

18. Quoted in Mohibbul Hasan, *History of Tipu Sultan* (Calcutta: Bibliophile, 1951), p. 15.
19. Quoted in Anne Buddle, ed., *The Tiger and the Thistle: Tipu Sultan and the Scots in India* (Edinburgh: National Galleries of Scotland, 1999), p. 16.
20. "Incomplete draft (1785) of an account of the Mysore War (1780–84)," OIOC: MSS Eur K 116, f. 84.
21. When I visited the Daria Daulat Bagh in December 1999, the descriptive label provided by the Archaeological Survey of India was something of an artifact itself, and bears citing in full: "The lower part of this panel illustrates battle of Polilur. The procession of Haider Ali and Tipu Sultan is on one side and at centre depicts Colonel Baillie's Defeat with the special prominance [*sic*] to the explosion and to the consternation of the British square along with native cavalry and French troops. Colonel Baillie is in a palanquin carried by six native soldiers as he is wounded and biting his pointing finger. General Bird and Colonel Fletcher are on horse-back, side by side are shown in more confusion in the battle of defeat. On the left hand top portion of the square is the massive explosion of the tumbril. Dressed with elongated hat, cross belted red overcoat, white breeches, black shoes and white belted British soldiers protecting their leader Colonel Baillie with musket is prominent in this panel. A lot of chaos, horror on the faces of the warriors is equalled on the faces of their horses. The British square is attacked by cavalry troops of Tipu Sultan and French army from all directions. On the extreme right top of the panel is standing Mons. Laly holding gorgeous instrument (telescope?). His uniform and cocked hat are almost as magnificent as his leadership. The native warriors are dashing forward with swords drawn and a few with bows and arrows. Few soldiers are being trampled to death. There are heads without bodies and vice versa. The bravery, ferocity, confusion and fear are very realistically depicted in this painting."
22. Lewin Bentham Bowring, *Haidar Ali and Tipu Sultan, and the Struggle with the Musalman Powers of the South* (New Delhi: Asian Educational Services, 1997; 1st pub. 1899), p. 206. "A most amusing caricature," Bowring styled it.
23. "Anonymous letter dated 2 June 1799 . . . ," OIOC: MSS Eur B 276, f. 11.
24. Charlotte Florentia Clive, *Journal of a voyage to the East Indies, and during a residence there, a Tour, through the Mysore and Tanjore countries &c. &c. and the Return Voyage to England*, OIOC: WD 4235, f. 90.
25. "Sketch of a Journey to Seringapatam and Mysoor," NAS: Seaforth Muniments, GD 46/17/39, f. 8.
26. J. Michaud, *History of Mysore Under Hyder Ali and Tippoo Sultaun*, trans. V. K. Raman Menon (New Delhi: Asian Educational Services, 1985; 1st pub. 1801), pp. 105–6.
27. Being recognized in this way by the caliph gave Tipu a crucial stamp of legitimacy as he asserted his independence from the Mughal emperor. See Kate Brittlebank, *Tipu Sultan's Search for Legitimacy: Islam and Kingship in a Hindu Domain* (New Delhi: Oxford University Press, 1995), pp. 57–81. Initially Tipu's ambassador, Gholam Ali Khan, was instructed to continue on to Versailles, and even London, but Tipu recalled him from Constantinople first.

Gholam Ali instead proceeded to Alexandria, Cairo, and Mecca—carried the whole way in a silver chair, since he was ill (Hasan, pp. 128–38; Wilks, II, p. 361). George Baldwin noted with alarm that "Tippoos Ambassadour engaged during his stay here, by large bounties as many European Seamen as were willing to go with him, and among the rest a number of English Sailors who had been dismissed from a ship sold at Constantinople." Baldwin to FO, June 21, 1788, PRO: FO 24/1, Foreign Office In-Letters, Egypt 1786–1796.

28. For a detailed account of the embassy and Tipu's instructions, see Hasan, pp. 116–27.
29. Hasan, pp. 377–78. See also William Kirkpatrick, trans., *Select Letters of Tippoo Sultaun to Various Public Functionaries* . . . (London, 1811), pp. 369–78 and 454–55.
30. Hasan, pp. 117–18.
31. Michaud, p. 85.
32. Hasan, p. 119; the gouache "The Ambassadors and their Entourage Walking in the Park at St Cloud, 1788" is reproduced in Buddle, ed., p. 30.
33. Michaud, p. 85.
34. Buddle, ed., p. 29; Marcelle Brunet, "Incidences de l'ambassade de Tipoo-Saib (1788) sur la porcelaine de Sèvres," *Cahiers de la Céramique* 24 (1961): 281. A button engraved with the profile of one of the ambassadors fetched almost £4,000 at auction at Christie's in June 2000.
35. *Conversation de l'ambassadeur de Tipoo-Saib, avec son interprète* (Paris, 1788); *Lettres de l'un des ambassadeurs de Typoo-Saïb, où il est beaucoup parlé des affaires du royaume de Gogo* . . . (Paris, 1789). Michaud also repeatedly drew parallels between Tipu and Louis XVI, though with the loyal royalist's aim of defending the latter.
36. Numbers in Hasan, p. 122.
37. Buddle, ed., pp. 29–31. Wilks adds that "the embassadors returned in a state of feud, originally excited on the occasion of receiving some valuable presents by order of Louis XVI." The slighted Muhammed Osman Khan retaliated by accusing his colleagues of "being indecorously captivated by the beauty of female infidels, and even accepting presents of forbidden liquors" (Wilks, II, p. 361). According to Michaud, the ambassadors could not stop raving about the wonders of France, which so angered Tipu that he had two of them summarily executed, "and no-one talked about the riches of France any more" (Michaud, p. 87).
38. "Correspondence between Tipu Sultan and the King of France, and their subordinates," OIOC: MSS Eur K 135.
39. Hasan, pp. 182–85. Kirmani says that Tipu rejected a French offer of one thousand troops in 1791, under the malign influence of self-serving courtiers. Mir Hussain Ali Khan Kirmani, *History of Tipu Sultan: Being a Continuation of the Neshani Hyduri*, trans. Col. W. Miles (Calcutta: Susil Gupta, 1958; 1st pub. 1864), p. 85.
40. Memorandum, March 25, 1797; Tipu to Executive Directory, August 30, 1798, OIOC: P/354/38.
41. Mahmud Husain, trans., *The Dreams of Tipu Sultan* (Lahore: Pakistan Histori-

cal Society Publications, [n.d.]), pp. 81–82. This is a full translation of a Persian manuscript in which Tipu recorded thirty-seven dreams over the years 1785–98. It was taken by the British in 1799 with the rest of Tipu's library and is now in the British Library, OIOC: MSS Ethé 3001.

42. Hasan, p. 287; Wilks, II, pp. 635–36.
43. OIOC: P/354/38. The British gleefully translated numerous documents on this misbegotten embassy after the fall of Seringapatam.
44. "Je vous prie de m'envoillé par la viseau un Citoyen poyr faire mes Ecritures en Français, le Citoyen Ripaud ne se porte pas bien et il n'est pas Ecrivains," Tipu to Malartic, Germinal, An V, OIOC: I/1/12. A few surviving notes from Ripaud betray a quite wonderful glimpse of what French looks like when spelled phonetically.
45. Ambassadors to Tipu, April 30, 1798, OIOC: P/354/38. They sent him seven casks of clove and nutmeg trees "under Charge of a Guard, to take care of them, with a letter, and an account particulars of the names of the trees, which we translated from the account, given by the European."
46. "Rapport officiel du chef de brigade Chappuis, commandant les forces française envoyées par le gouverneur général Malartic, auprès de Tipoo Sultan," BNF: MSS NAF 9374, f. 32.
47. Wilks, II, p. 645.
48. "Rapport officiel . . . ," f. 33. Chapuis gives a rare account of Tipu's behavior at this time, and I have drawn on it for other details in this paragraph.
49. Tipu to Wellesley, December 18, 1798, *Despatches* . . . , I, p. 381.
50. Wilks, II, p. 679.
51. The contemporary British reading public certainly enjoyed them, too: *Copies of Original Letters from the Army of General Bonaparte in Egypt, Intercepted by the Fleet Under the Command of Admiral Lord Nelson* (London, 1798), including (very loose!) English translations, went through at least ten editions in 1798 alone, and inspired one of James Gillray's most brilliant satires, eight "Intercepted Drawings" of the French in Egypt. The volume ends with a translation of Napoleon's "Proclamation to the Egyptians."
52. These letters, dated 1798–99, were written by French officers who had been killed. NAS: Maxtone Graham of Cultoquhey, GD 155/1261, Papers of Thomas Graham.
53. Napoleon to Tipu, 7 Pluviose VII [January 26, 1799], OIOC: P/354/38.
54. Silvestre de Sacy, *Chrestomathie Arabe, ou, Extraits de divers écrivains arabes* . . . , 3 vols. (Paris, 1826–27), III, p. 325.
55. Iris Butler, *The Eldest Brother: The Marquess Wellesley, 1760–1842* (London: Hodder & Stoughton, 1973), pp. 100–109.
56. "Minute of the Governor-General to the Secret Committee," August 12, 1798, *Despatches* . . . , I, p. 185.
57. "Extract Letter from the Earl of Mornington to the Resident at Hyderabad dated 9th November 1798," OIOC: I/1/12, p. 674.
58. Wilks, II, p. 689.
59. "Minute . . . ," *Despatches* . . . , I, p. 159.
60. Reports of the Battle of the Nile soon followed, but Wellesley did "not yet

think it impossible that the desperate and enterprizing spirit of Buonaparte, exasperated by the new and increasing difficulties which surround him, may attempt to push forward a force to Malabar . . ." (Wellesley to E. Clive, November 5, 1798, *Despatches . . .*, I, p. 322). After all, losing a fleet in the Mediterranean did not directly impinge upon Napoleon's ability to sail into the Red Sea—a point made in contemporary pamphlets. See "Reply to Irwin: or, the Feasibility of Buonaparte's Supposed Expedition to the East, Exemplified. By an Officer in the Service of the East India Company" (London, 1798).

61. As Edward Ingram has argued, "British India under Wellesley acted as a revolutionary state, not formulating a policy in response to local conditions but trying to create the conditions necessary for the attainment of his objectives." Edward Ingram, *Commitment to Empire: Prophecies of the Great Game in Asia 1797–1800* (Oxford: Clarendon Press, 1981), pp. 117–18.
62. Wellesley to Court of Directors, March 20, 1799, *Despatches . . .*, I, p. 501.
63. For a forceful exposition of Wellesley's warmongering and the French threat, see Ingram, Chapter 5, esp. pp. 189–91.
64. "Journal (1790–92) of Lt.-Col. Francis Skelly," OIOC: Skelly Papers, MSS Eur D 877/2, ff. 23–24.
65. Skelly to N. Davison, February 8, 1790, OIOC: MSS Eur D 877/4. The liberation of Tipu's harem was the subject of a Thomas Rowlandson cartoon published in 1799 (reproduced in Colley, *Captives*, p. 294).
66. Quoted in William Dalrymple, *White Mughals: Love and Betrayal in Eighteenth-Century India* (London: HarperCollins, 2002), p. 180.
67. Lt.-Col. Benjamin Sydenham to W. Kirkpatrick, May 15, 1799, PRO: Cornwallis Papers, 30/11/209, f. 6. Firsthand accounts of Seringapatam such as this tend to say far more about the aftermath of the battle than about the fighting itself.
68. Alexander Beatson, *A View of the Origin and Conduct of the War with Tippoo Sultaun . . .* (London, 1800), p. civ.
69. Kirmani, p. 125.
70. "Narrative of the Mysore War of 1799 by Lt. Col. P. A. Agnew . . . ," OIOC: MSS Eur D 313/5, f. 7.
71. Kirmani, p. 129.
72. Ibid., p. 124.
73. "Rapport officiel du chef de brigade Chappuis . . . ," BNF: MSS NAF 9374, f. 36.
74. "Anonymous letter . . . ," OIOC: MSS Eur B 276, ff. 6–7.
75. Michaud, p. 57.
76. W. Kirkpatrick to Wellesley, July 26, 1799, OIOC: MSS Eur E 196, f. 5. He published his own heavily annotated and heavily edited sample in 1811. A sad reminder of how easily the historical record could be manipulated can be found in a letter to Kirkpatrick from his brother, James Achilles, resident in Hyderabad. Sending William some of Tipu's Persian papers, James adds that he had many others burned, since the residency office was too cluttered. (J. A. Kirkpatrick to W. Kirkpatrick, September 11, 1801, OIOC: Kirkpatrick Papers, MSS Eur F 228/13, f. 158. My thanks to William Dalrymple for this reference.)

77. See originals in OIOC: P/354/38. They were immediately reprinted by Wood and used extensively by Wilks and Beatson (Brittlebank, pp. 10–11).
78. Lachlan Macquarie, "Original Account of Siege of Seringapatam," OIOC: Home Misc. 814.
79. Benjamin Sydenham to William Kirkpatrick, May 15, 1799, PRO: Cornwallis Papers, 30/11/209.
80. David Price, *Memoirs of the Early Life and Service of a Field Officer on the Retired List of the Indian Army* (London, 1839), p. 429.
81. Edward Moor, *A Narrative of the Operations of Captain Little's Detachment* (London, 1794), pp. 24–32.
82. Price, pp. 434–35.
83. Kirmani, p. 128.
84. Ibid., p. 127.
85. A. Wellesley to R. Wellesley, May 8, 1799, in Arthur Wellesley, 2nd Duke of Wellington, ed., *Supplementary Despatches and Memoranda of Field Marshal Arthur Duke of Wellington, K. G.*, 6 vols. (London, 1858), I, p. 212.
86. Edward Moor, *Oriental Fragments* (London, 1834), p. 40.
87. Price, p. 435.
88. This is the most widely told such story—the vendor is variously described as a soldier in the Seventy-fourth, a drummer, and a grenadier. (Price, p. 435; Moor, p. 41; *Narrative Sketches of the Conquest of Mysore* . . . [London, 1800], pp. 105–6.)
89. For a table of prize shares, see Wellington, ed., I, pp. 223–24. Numbers are given in star pagodas, which were worth about eight shillings at the time.
90. Philip Guedalla, *The Duke* (London: Wordsworth Editions, 1997), p. 91.
91. Wellington, ed., I, p. 242. He did eventually accept the insignia of the Order of St. Patrick, made out of captured jewels and presented by the army.
92. Even the Court of Directors was disgusted by the "enormous disproportion in the scale of shares" and singled out Harris's payment for criticism: his £140,000, they argued, should have been shared among all the commanders—that is, by East India Company commanders as well (Court of Directors to Fort St. George, August 24, 1804, OIOC: Home Misc. 83, ff. 543–44). The distribution of the prize was the subject of a protracted and bitter dispute, in part because the money had to be divided among the three armies of the Company, the Crown, and the nizam of Hyderabad. The greatest scandal concerned the Prize Commission's attempt to exclude two detachments from the prize, on the grounds that they were too far from the action on May 4. (See OIOC: Board's Collections, F/4/100/2034. Copies and related papers are in OIOC: Home Misc. 83; OIOC: L/Mil/5/159; and BL: Wellesley Papers, Add. MSS 13641.) Individual payments could take years in coming: dividends were being paid out at the time of the Peninsular Wars, and after Waterloo the prize commissioners were still calling in debts from the 1799 prize sales. The saga of payments can be followed in OIOC: Board's Collections, F/4/230/5258 and 5258A; F/4/278/6325 (includes prize roll); and F/4/355/8377. For claims by individual officers, see F/4/292/6615 and F/4/8953; for debts owed to the Prize Commission, F/4/11473.

93. Wolfe at Quebec would be an obvious precedent, however. For other earlier celebrations of imperial victory, see Kathleen Wilson, "Empire, Trade, and Popular Politics in Mid-Hanoverian Britain: The Case of Admiral Vernon," *Past & Present* 121 (1988): 74–109; and P. J. Marshall, " 'Cornwallis Triumphant': War in India and the British Public in the Late 18th Century," in Lawrence Freedman, Paul Hayes, and Robert O'Neill, eds., *War, Strategy and International Politics: Essays in Honour of Sir Michael Howard* (Oxford: Clarendon Press, 1992), pp. 57–74.
94. Pauline Rohatgi, "From Pencil to Panorama: Tipu in Pictorial Perspective," in Buddle, ed., pp. 39–52.
95. Among original sources for this pamphlet are the anonymous letter dated June 2, 1799, "Camp at Gariahguanelly" (OIOC: MSS Eur B 276) and the "Description of various Articles found in the Palace of Seringapatam and sent to England as presents to the Royal Family and to the Court of Directors," written at Wellesley's behest by Lt. Benjamin Sydenham (OIOC: Home Misc. 255).
96. Abu Talib Khan, *The Travels of Mirza Abu Taleb Khan, in Asia, Africa, and Europe, during the Years 1799, 1800, 1801, 1802, and 1803* . . . trans. Charles Stewart, 2 vols. (London, 1810), II, pp. 95–96.
97. C. A. Bayly, *Imperial Meridian: The British Empire and the World 1780–1830* (London: Longman, 1989), p. 114.
98. C. A. Bayly, "Ireland, India and the Empire 1780–1914," *Transactions of the Royal Historical Society* VI (2000): 377–97.
99. Commissioners for the Affairs of Mysore to Richard Wellesley, June 25, 1799, and June 30, 1799, OIOC: Home Misc. 255. The British relentlessly stressed (and partly constructed) the "legitimacy" of the Wodeyars both as a ruling dynasty and as Hindus, in contrast to the Muslim "usurpers" Haidar and Tipu.
100. See Nicholas Dirks, *Castes of Mind: Colonialism and the Making of Modern India* (Princeton, N.J.: Princeton University Press, 2001), pp. 81–123; Bernard S. Cohn, "The Transformation of Objects into Artifacts, Antiquities and Art in Nineteenth-Century India," in *Colonialism and Its Forms of Knowledge* (Princeton, N.J.: Princeton University Press, 1996), pp. 76–105; Thomas Metcalf, *Ideologies of the Raj* (Cambridge, UK: Cambridge University Press, 1995), pp. 113–59; Benedict Anderson, *Imagined Communities*, 2nd ed. (London: Verso, 1991), pp. 163–85.

## CHAPTER SIX: THE OBJECTS OF VICTORY

1. *Narrative Sketches of the Conquest of Mysore* . . . (London, 1800), p. 99.
2. The same cannot be said of the first Indian object actually placed on public display: a black siltstone Vishnu in the Ashmolean, presented by William Hedges in 1685. Richard Davis, *The Lives of Indian Images* (Princeton, N.J.: Princeton University Press, 1997), p. 143.
3. Ray Desmond, *The India Museum* (London: HMSO, 1982). For early guidebook descriptions, see *Old Humphreys Walks in London and Its Neighborhood*

(London, c. 1804) and E. W. Brayley, J. N. Brewer, and J. Nightingale, *A Topographical and Historical Description of London and Middlesex*, 5 vols. (London, 1814). It figures as the "Man-Tyger-Organ" in John Keats's poem "The Cap and Bells, or the Jealousies, a Faery Tale" (1819–20).

4. *Cf.* the hyperbolic rendition in *Narrative Sketches*: "this characteristic emblem of the ferocious animosity of the modern Bajazet against the British nation" (p. 100). Mildred Archer suggests that Tipu's Tiger depicts the killing of Sir Hector Munro's son Hugh by a tiger in the Sunderbans; certainly a composition very similar to Tipu's Tiger is reprised in the Staffordshire figurine "The Death of Munrow" (c. 1815). Mildred Archer, *Tippoo's Tiger* (London: HMSO, 1959).
5. Alexander Beatson, *A View of the Origin and Conduct of the War with Tippoo Sultaun* . . . (London, 1800), pp. 153–54.
6. Kate Brittlebank, "*Sakti* and *Barakat:* The Power of Tipu's Tiger," *Modern Asian Studies* 29 (1995): 257–69. The cypher appears to read "bismillah" and "Muhammad"—not, as many have thought, "asad allah al-ghalib." Mohammad Moienuddin, *Sunset at Srirangapatam: After the Death of Tipu Sultan* (New Delhi: Orient Longman, 2000), pp. 140–41.
7. Davis, pp. 173–84; Moienuddin, pp. 42–44. The slogan is particularly notable in view of the contemporary British opinion that "the natives of Hindoostan make no distinction between a lion and a tiger" (Beatson, pp. 155–56).
8. George Annesley, Viscount Valentia, *Voyages and Travels to India, Ceylon, the Red Sea, Abyssinia, and Egypt, in the Years 1802, 1803, 1804, 1805, and 1806*, 3 vols. (London, 1809), I, p. 236.
9. David Price, *Memoirs of the Early Life and Service of a Field Officer on the Retired List of the Indian Army* (London, 1839), pp. 444–45; Wellesley to Court of Directors, August 14, 1799, OIOC: Home Misc. 255. Colonel Gent, who had bought the *huma* bird for about £2,500 at the prize sales, loyally relinquished it to the Company for only £1,760.
10. Valentia, I, p. 61. Other gifts to the royals included some of Tipu's armor and weapons for the Prince of Wales and the Duke of York; and, for King George III, "Three Chetas or Hunting Tygers, with a hunting Cart, two trained Bullocks, & every other Article necessary for hunting the Cheta in England, in the same manner as the Royal hunt of the Sultan was conducted at Seringapatam. These are accompanied by six Native Huntsmen, three from Tippoo's Service." But the cheetahs were probably in no more condition to hunt than the king. ("Note of the Articles sent, in charge of Major Davis, to the Chairman of the Honorable Court of Directors," OIOC: Home Misc. 255.)
11. Iris Butler, *The Eldest Brother: The Marquess Wellesley, the Duke of Wellington's Eldest Brother* (London: Hodder & Stoughton, 1973), pp. 212, 225.
12. A. Wellesley to R. Wellesley, August 19, 1799, *Supplementary Despatches* . . . , I, p. 289.
13. C. A. Bayly, "The British Military-Fiscal State and Indigenous Resistance," in Lawrence Stone, ed., *An Imperial State at War: Britain from 1689 to 1815* (London: Routledge, 1994), p. 348; Davis, p. 156.
14. R. Wellesley to A. Wellesley, June 19, 1799, in Arthur Wellesley, 2nd Duke of Wellington, ed., *Supplementary Despatches and Memoranda of Field Marshal Arthur Duke of Wellington, K. G.*, 6 vols. (London, 1858), I, p. 246.

15. Sydenham to William Kirkpatrick, May 15, 1799, PRO: Cornwallis Papers, 30/11/209, f. 6.
16. Price, p. 429. Almost two centuries later the mustache turned up again in the possession of one Mrs. Pepper in British Columbia, who wrote to the Victoria and Albert Museum offering it for sale.
17. *Narrative Sketches . . .*, pp. 86–87. This particular story may well be fiction, but in fact nobody knows who killed Tipu Sultan—"in all probability," it was supposed, because Tipu's jewels, "now become the spoil of the fortunate soldier . . . are too precious to be hastily acknowledged." Fictional claimants to the title include the boy hero of G. A. Henty's *The Tiger of Mysore* (1895), and, more recently, Bernard Cornwell's serial adventurer Richard Sharpe (*Sharpe's Tiger*, 1998).
18. See "Further Proceedings relative to the sums due by Individuals on account of purchases at the Seringapatam Prize Sales" in OIOC: F/4/476/11,473.
19. For the locations of Seringapatam objects today, see Anne Buddle, ed., *Tigers Round the Throne* (London: Zamana, 1990); Denys Forrest, *Tiger of Mysore: The Life and Death of Tipu Sultan* (London: Chatto and Windus, 1970), pp. 354–61; Moienuddin, *passim;* and binders on Tipu in the Victoria and Albert Museum, Indian and South-East Asian Section. On Beckford's hookah, Derek E. Ostergard, ed., *William Beckford 1760–1844: An Eye for the Magnificent* (New Haven: Yale University Press, 2001), pp. 338–39.
20. James Hevia, *English Lessons: The Pedagogy of Imperialism in Nineteenth-Century China* (Durham, N.C.: Duke University Press, 2003), pp. 74–118. A third of the British forces who participated in the war (and prominently in the looting) were from India. The high commissioner, the Earl of Elgin—whose father, while serving as ambassador in Constantinople, had acquired the "Elgin Marbles"—became viceroy of India, and died in office in 1863.
21. *Narrative Sketches . . .*, pp. 100–101. This passage is lifted directly from the anonymous letter cited below, which was reprinted as "Curious Particulars Relative to the Capture of Seringapatam," in the *Asiatic Annual Register*, vol. 1 (London, 1799).
22. Kate Brittlebank, *Tipu Sultan's Search for Legitimacy: Islam and Kingship in a Hindu Domain* (New Delhi: Oxford University Press, 1997), pp. 114–19.
23. *Narrative Sketches . . .*, p. 98.
24. Anonymous letter dated June 2, 1799, "Camp at Gariahguanelly," OIOC: MSS Eur B 276, f. 9.
25. *Narrative Sketches . . .*, pp. 99–100.
26. Price, p. 446. Price estimates the library had "3 to 4000 volumes." Charles Stewart, who compiled the catalogue of Tipu's manuscripts for the East India Company, claimed that "Very few of these books had been purchased either by Tippoo or his father. They were part of the plunder brought from Sanoor, Cuddapah, and the Carnatic" (p. iv). But a study of the owners' seals and price markings in Tipu's manuscripts suggests that their provenances were varied, and that Tipu was an active buyer on the book market—just like his contemporaries in Lucknow. I am grateful to Dr. Jeevan Deol for assistance on this point.
27. Charles Stewart, *A Descriptive Catalogue of the Oriental Library of the Late Tippoo Sultan of Mysore . . .* (Cambridge, 1809). A further sixty-one titles were

sent to the Asiatic Society of Bengal, via the College at Fort William. See "List of Books for the Asiatic Society," OIOC: MSS Eur E 196, ff. 67–70; P. Thankappan Nair, ed., *Proceedings of the Asiatic Society, Vol. 2: 1801–1816* (Calcutta: Asiatic Society, 1995), pp. 147–49.

28. Both girls later furthered their grandfather's dynastic ambitions exactly as he would have wished: Henrietta Clive (1786–1835) married Wales's foremost gentleman, Sir Watkin Williams Wynn; Charlotte (1787–1866) married Hugh Percy, third Duke of Northumberland, in 1817, and was governess to the Princess Victoria from 1830 to 1837. Lord Greville found Charlotte's husband to be "a very good sort of man, with a very narrow understanding, an eternal talker, and a prodigious bore," but her brother-in-law Algernon, the fourth duke, was scholarly and a significant collector of Egyptian antiquities. Greville quote in Mildred Archer, et al., *Treasures from India: The Clive Collection at Powis Castle* (New York: Meredith Press, 1987), p. 137.

29. Charlotte Florentia Clive, *Journal of a voyage to the East Indies, and during a residence there, a Tour, through the Mysore and Tanjore countries &c. &c. and the Return Voyage to England*, OIOC: WD 4235, p. 38. [Hereafter cited as Clive Journal.] Quotes from this journal are sometimes wrongly attributed to her mother.

30. Clive Journal, pp. 61–62, 76–77, 90–96.

31. Valentia, for instance, likened it to Herefordshire, while Lady Hood found the Kaveri "a noble river, rapid and rocky, and under the Zenana windows as broad as the Thames at Fulham."

32. Henrietta (daughter) to Edward Clive, March 20, 1800, NLW: Clive Papers, Correspondence 2324.

33. Quoted in Richard Altick, *The Shows of London* (Cambridge, Mass.: Harvard University Press, 1978), p. 23.

34. J. C. Beaglehole, ed., *The* Endeavour *Journal of Joseph Banks 1768–71*, 2 vols. (Sydney: Angus and Robertson, 1962), I, p. 5; and Patrick O'Brian, *Joseph Banks* (Chicago: University of Chicago Press, 1993), pp. 26–27.

35. Richard Drayton, *Nature's Government: Science, Imperial Britain, and the "Improvement" of the World* (New Haven: Yale University Press, 2000), pp. 42–47.

36. Henrietta to Edward Clive, January 28, 1802, NLW: Clive Papers, Correspondence 463.

37. Henrietta to Edward Clive, February 18, 1802, NLW: Clive Papers, Correspondence 466.

38. She was assisted by two founders of the Company collection, William Roxburgh, director of the Calcutta Botanical Garden, and Benjamin Heyne (who she thought "mineralizes better than he packs up"), commissioned with the geological and botanical portion of the Mysore survey.

39. Henrietta and Charlotte to Edward Clive, March–October 1800, NLW: Clive Papers, Correspondence 2323–35; Clive Journal, p. 185.

40. In Britain at the time having pets was largely a genteel preserve; interests in good breeding, among animals and people, seemed to go together. The first big menagerie toured Britain in 1805. Harriet Ritvo, *The Animal Estate: The En-*

*glish and Other Creatures in the Victorian Age* (Cambridge, Mass.: Harvard University Press, 1987), pp. 84–97, 207.

41. N. B. Edmonstone to Thomas Pattle, February 23, 1803, BL: Add. MSS 19,346, f. 7. Mildred Archer calls Valentia "the first and only grand tourist to visit India," though I think the title is debatable: Mildred Archer and Ronald Lightbown, *India Observed: India as Seen by British Artists, 1760–1860* (London: Victoria and Albert, 1982), p. 87.
42. About all of which he was characteristically rude. The raja of Benares, e.g., "begged my acceptance of an old sword which Mr. Neave declared he said had belongd to Firrochsere. . . . I have however a little doubt respecting the whole transaction as it was arranged with a certain confusion and mystery. . . . Nor is the blade of that value for so splendid a sovereign to have used the Hilt was copper gilt The scabbard was green velvet" (BL: Add. MSS 19,345, f. 38).
43. Quoted in Archer et al., p. 27.
44. And the only one I have come across. Collecting by British women in India tended to follow the conventions of contemporary British collecting culture; thus, for instance, Elizabeth Plowden and Margaret Fowke "collected" Indian songs in the 1780s. A closer precursor to Lady Clive would be Lady Mary Impey, who accompanied her husband, Sir Elijah, to Calcutta in the 1770s, and patronized Indian artists and Company School painters there.
45. See the catalogue raisonné of the collection: Archer et al.
46. J. Kirkpatrick to W. Kirkpatrick, September 16, 1801, quoted in William Dalrymple, *White Mughals,* p. 281*n*.
47. Archer et al., p. 27.
48. Stuart Semmel, "Reading the Tangible Past: British Tourism, Collecting, and Memory after Waterloo," *Representations* 69 (2000): 9–37.
49. "Sketch of a Journey to Seringapatam and Mysoor," NAS: Seaforth Muniments, GD 46/17/39, p. 9.
50. "Sketch . . . ," p. 11.
51. Quoted in *DNB,* XVIII, p. 1255.
52. Clive Journal, p. 102.
53. Ibid., f. 26; quote in Archer et al., p. 29.
54. "Note of the Contents of the Case belonging to the Right Honble. Lord Clive," OIOC: Clive Collection, MSS Eur G 37/18. The list is placed with Robert Clive's papers, but various references contained within it make clear that the Lord Clive in question is Edward. The list can be dated to 1788, since the portraits are known to have been commissioned on the Clives' visit to Italy in that year. (*Powis Castle* [London: The National Trust, 2000], p. 26.)
55. Quoted in Archer et al., p. 25. Even Edward's parents had despaired of him at times. As his mother frankly confessed in 1766, "I think him deficient in many things for a boy of his age." "But," she acknowledged, "his heart is good," and Edward did try his hardest, writing to his father from Eton—in such labored handwriting it looks like he was scratching on stone—"I shall endeavour to render myself worthy of your love and affection by improving and cultivating my mind with whatever is useful." (Margaret to Robert Clive, November 12, 1766; Edward to Robert Clive, November 6, 1766, NLW: Robert Clive Papers, CR 12/3.)

56. Quoted in Butler, p. 201.
57. Quoted in Archer et al., p. 25.
58. Quoted in Butler, p. 201.
59. Edward to Henrietta Clive, December 2, 1801, BL: Powis Papers, Add. MSS 64,105, ff. 31–32.
60. Edward to Henrietta Clive, May 29, 1802, BL: Add. MSS 64,105, ff. 54–55.
61. Edward to Henrietta Clive, May 9, 1803, BL: Add. MSS 64,105, f. 110.
62. The Clives' choice of images of Vishnu the Preserver, rather than, for example, Shiva the Destroyer, "suggests a distinct awareness and preference on the part of the collector" (Archer et al., p. 112).
63. Edward to Henrietta Clive, May 29, 1802, BL: Add MSS 64,105, ff. 54–55. He does not indicate which "God" this is: two of the major temples at Kanchipuram are Shaiva, but there is also a Vaishnava temple, and given his collecting tastes, Clive may have made his presentation in this one.
64. Clive Journal, p. 111.
65. Archer et al., p. 95. We have little evidence, however, about how and where the Indian collections were displayed during the Clives' lifetimes.
66. Valentia, I, p. 165.
67. Duffy, p. 201.
68. Rosemary Said Zahlan, "George Baldwin: Soldier of Fortune?" in Paul Starkey and Janet Starkey, eds., *Travellers in Egypt* (London: Tauris Parke 2001), pp. 36–37.
69. R. Wellesley to David Baird, February 10, 1801, in R. Montgomery Martin, ed., *The Despatches, Minutes, and Correspondence, of the Marquess Wellesley, K. G. . . .*, 5 vols. (London, 1836), II, pp. 451–52. Arthur Wellesley was slated to join the expedition, too, but a bout of illness at Bombay kept him grounded. As it happened, the ship he was due to sail on was lost en route: "Never was an attack of fever more opportune than that which prevented the future conqueror of Napoleon from taking part in this expedition" (G. B. Malleson, *Final Struggles of the French in India . . . With an Appendix Containing an Account of the Expedition from India to Egypt in 1801* [London, 1878], p. 271).
70. Henry Laurens, *L'expédition d'Égypte 1798–1801* (Paris: Éditions du Seuil, 1997), pp. 269–98.
71. Quoted in Jean Tulard, *Napoléon: ou le mythe du sauveur*, 2nd ed. (Paris: Fayard, 1987), p. 99.
72. Dominique Vivant Denon, *Voyage dans la basse et la haute Égypte* (Paris: Gallimard, 1998), p. 342.
73. Despite the fiascos of the campaign, he masterfully drew on the mystique of his "Oriental" adventure for propaganda purposes: Annie Jourdan, *Napoléon: Héros, empereur, mécène* (Paris: Aubin, 1998); Todd Porterfield, *The Allure of Empire: Art in the Service of French Imperialism* (Princeton, N.J.: Princeton University Press, 1998), pp. 43–79; *cf.* Darcy Grimaldo Grigsby, "Rumor, Contagion, and Colonization in Gros's *Plague-Stricken of Jaffa* (1804)," *Representations* 51 (1995): 8–10, 24–37.
74. General Hely-Hutchinson to Lord Hobart, August 16, 1801, PRO: WO/1/345.

75. Étienne Geoffroy Saint-Hilaire, *Lettres écrites d'Égypte . . .* (Paris: Hachette, 1901), pp. 92, 152.
76. Édouard de Villiers du Terrage, *Journal et souvenirs sur l'expédition d'Égypte (1798–1801)* (Paris, 1899), p. 241.
77. Diary of Captain Charles Fitzmaurice Hill, Sixteenth Grenadiers, OIOC: MSS Eur D 108, p. 36.
78. Sir Sidney Smith to Admiral Keith, September 28, 1800, PRO: WO/1/344.
79. Koehler to Grenville, July 15, 1800, and November 17, 1800, PRO: FO/78/27.
80. I have based these two paragraphs on the details and arguments of Piers Mackesy's splendidly informative *British Victory in Egypt, 1801: The End of Napoleon's Conquest* (London: Routledge, 1995).
81. James M'Gregor, *Medical Sketches of the Expedition to Egypt, from India* (London, 1804), p. 5. For partial records of outfitting and embarkation, see OIOC: G/17/7, ff. 296–349. For a return of troops at the end of the campaign, see Baird to Lord Hobart, September 4, 1801, PRO: WO/1/345.
82. Hill Diary, pp. 74–80.
83. Comte Louis de Noé, *Mémoires relatifs à l'expédition anglaise de l'Inde en Égypte* (Paris, 1826), p. 142.
84. Hill Diary, pp. 87–88.
85. Anthony Maxtone to Helen Maxtone, September 4, 1801, NAS: Maxtone Graham of Cultoquhey, GD 155/874/19.
86. Baird to Hely-Hutchinson, September 24, 1801, PRO: WO/1/345.
87. Denon, p. 187. He would have been surprised to learn that the existing structure was in fact built by the Romans, foreign occupiers, in the first century B.C.
88. "Military Journal of John Budgen Esq. Captain Eighty-fourth Regiment, Aid [*sic*] de Camp on the Staff of General Sir David Baird during Service at the Cape, India and Egypt from Feb 7th 1796 to Feb 14th 1802," OIOC: MSS Eur A 102, ff. 53–54.
89. Budgen Diary, f. 54.
90. Edward Daniel Clarke, *Travels in Various Countries in Europe, Asia and Africa*, 6 vols. (London, 1810), Part 2, vol. II, pp. 57–58.
91. These travels are the subject of Brian Dolan, *Exploring European Frontiers: British Travellers in the Age of the Enlightenment* (London: Macmillan, 2000).
92. Clarke, Part 2, II, pp. 57–58.

## CHAPTER SEVEN: RIVALS

1. Jean-Jacques Fiechter, *La Moisson des dieux* (Paris: Julliard, 1994); Peter France, *The Rape of Egypt: How the Europeans Stripped Egypt of Its Heritage* (London: Barrie and Jenkins, 1991); Brian M. Fagan, *The Rape of the Nile: Tomb Robbers, Tourists, and Archaeologists in Egypt* (London: Macdonald and Jane's, 1975).
2. Edward Daniel Clarke, *The Tomb of Alexander* (London, 1805), pp. 38–39.
3. James Greig, ed., *The Farington Diary: August 28, 1802, to September 13, 1804* (New York: George H. Doran, 1923).

4. Michael Duffy, "World-Wide War and British Expansion, 1793–1815," in P. J. Marshall, ed., *Oxford History of the British Empire, Vol. II: The Eighteenth Century* (Oxford: Oxford University Press, 1998), p. 196.
5. "Articles de la Capitulation proposée par Abdoulahy Jacques François Menou Général en Chef de l'armée française actuellement à Alexandrie. A Messieurs les Generaux des armées de Terre et de mer de sa majesté brittannique et de la Sublime Porte formant le Blocus d'Alexandrie, en date du 12 fructidor an 9 de la Republique française (30 aout 1801)," PRO: WO/1/345, p. 450.
6. Étienne Geoffroy Saint-Hilaire, *Lettres écrites d'Égypte* . . . (Paris: Hachette, 1901), p. xxiv.
7. Édouard de Villiers du Terrage, *Journal et souvenirs sur l'expédition d'Égypte (1798–1801)* (Paris, 1899), p. 319.
8. Saint-Hilaire, pp. xxiii–xxv.
9. J. Christopher Herold, *Bonaparte in Egypt* (London: Hamish Hamilton, 1962), p. 387.
10. Saint-Hilaire, pp. xxiv–xxv.
11. Clarke, quoted in Brian Dolan, *Exploring European Frontiers: British Travellers in the Age of Enlightenment* (London: Macmillan, 2000), p. 136.
12. Saint-Hilaire, p. xxv. The feud between the savants and the British is described in Yves Laissus, *L'Égypte, une aventure savante 1798–1801* (Paris: Fayard, 1998), pp. 396–400; and Henry Laurens, *L'Expédition d'Égypte 1798–1801* (Paris: Éditions du Seuil, 1997), p. 465. *Cf.* Saint-Genis, "Description des Antiquités d'Alexandrie et de ses environs," in *Description de l'Égypte: Antiquités, Descriptions*, 24 vols. (Paris: Panckoucke, 1820–30), V, pp. 181–82.
13. "List of objects ceded by the French," BL: Add. MSS 46,839, ff. 12–13. See also M. L. Bierbrier, "The Acquisition by the British Museum of Antiquities Discovered During the French Invasion of Egypt" in W. V. Davies, ed., *Studies in Egyptian Antiquities: A Tribute to T. G. H. James*, British Museum Occasional Paper 123 (London: British Museum, 1998), pp. 111–13.
14. See note 2. In fact, the sarcophagus is that of one of the last pre-Ptolemaic pharaohs, Nectambo II—though before hieroglyphics were deciphered there is no way Clarke could have known this. The site of Alexander's grave is more widely believed to be in Alexandria's Mosque of Nabi Danial. (Anthony Sattin, *The Pharaoh's Shadow* [London: Indigo, 2000], pp. 24–29.)
15. Quoted in Laissus, p. 397. My translation.
16. Clarke, p. 38*n*. William Richard Hamilton's *DNB* entry fancifully states that "He procured an escort of soldiers, and, in spite of the danger of fever, rowed out to the French transport and insisted on carrying off the precious monument" (*DNB*, VIII, p. 1119).
17. Leslie Greener, *The Discovery of Egypt* (New York: Dorset Press, 1966), pp. 46–81; Anthony Sattin, *Lifting the Veil: British Society in Egypt 1768–1956* (London: J. M. Dent, 1988), pp. 7–19; Donald M. Reid, *Whose Pharaohs?: Archaeology, Museums, and Egyptian National Identity from Napoleon to World War I* (Berkeley: University of California Press, 2002), pp. 27–28; Jean-Marie Carré, *Voyageurs et écrivains français en Égypte, t. 1: des pélerins du Moyen Âge à Méhémet-Ali* (Cairo: IFAO, 1956), pp. 39–78.

18. Greener, pp. 39–41; Max Rodenbeck, *Cairo: The City Victorious* (New York: Vintage, 1998), pp. 33–34.
19. Jean-Marcel Humbert, Michael Pantazzi, and Christiane Ziegler, eds., *Egyptomania: L'Égypte dans l'art occidental 1730–1930* (Paris: Réunion des musées nationaux, 1994), pp. 220–35.
20. This is the implication, for instance, in Jean Tulard's classic *Napoléon, ou le mythe du sauveur* (Paris: Fayard, 1987), pp. 95–96. The association of the campaign with scientific achievement began as early as the 1830s, with the *Histoire militaire et scientifique de l'expédition d'Égypte*, 10 vols. (Paris, 1830–36). More recently, the savants were celebrated by a bicentennial exhibition at the Muséum d'Histoire Naturelle; see the catalogue, *Il y a 200 ans, les savants en Égypte* (Paris: Nathan, 1998).
21. Anna Piussi, "Images of Egypt during the French Expedition (1798–1801): Sketches of a historical colony" (D.Phil. dissertation, Oxford University, 1992). *Cf.* Todd Porterfield, *The Allure of Empire: Art in the Service of French Imperialism 1798–1836* (Princeton, N.J.: Princeton University Press, 1998).
22. The original version of the preface (and the frontispiece) was submitted to Napoleon for corrections on the Eighteenth Brumaire 1809; his changes were not substantial, but they subtly refined events to suit his Eastern policy of the moment. For the Panckoucke edition of 1821, all references to Napoleon were erased (no small feat), and the book reads as a patriotic hymn to France in the abstract. (J.-J. Champollion-Figeac, *Fourier et Napoléon: L'Égypte et les Cent Jours, Mémoires et Documents Inédits* [Paris, 1844]; and Piussi, p. 177.)
23. *Cf.* Reid, pp. 31–36.
24. Edward Miller, *That Noble Cabinet: A History of the British Museum* (Athens: Ohio University Press, 1974); Arthur MacGregor, ed., *Sir Hans Sloane: Collector, Scientist, Antiquary, Founding Father of the British Museum* (London: British Museum Press, 1994).
25. Inventories in folder "Early British Museum Register Pages, Department of Egyptian Antiquities," British Museum: Department of Egyptian Antiquities. In its early years, the museum possessed four human mummies: one from the Sloane collection, two donated by the Letheullier family in 1756, and a fourth given by Edward Wortley Montague to George III. One, probably a Letheullier mummy, was dissected in 1792 by a doctor from the University of Göttingen. (Paper presented by M. L. Bierbrier at ASTENE conference, London, July 8, 2000.)
26. The definitive history is William St. Clair, *Lord Elgin and the Marbles: The controversial history of the Parthenon sculptures*, 2nd ed. (Oxford: Oxford University Press, 1998).
27. Clarke, pp. 24, 29.
28. I have drawn biographical information on Drovetti chiefly from Ronald T. Ridley, *Napoleon's Proconsul in Egypt: The Life and Times of Bernardino Drovetti* (London: Rubicon, 1998).
29. Afaf Lutfi al-Sayyid Marsot, *Egypt in the Reign of Muhammad Ali* (Cambridge, UK: Cambridge University Press, 1984), pp. 36–50.
30. George Annesley, Viscount Valentia, *Voyages and Travels to India, Ceylon, the*

*Red Sea, Abyssinia, and Egypt, in the Years 1802, 1803, 1804, 1805, and 1806,* 3 vols. (London, 1809), III, p. 466.

31. Greig, ed., *The Farington Diary,* pp. 174–75. "State reasons prevented His being introduced to the King publickly," Farington noted, but an "accidental" encounter between the two was planned in the Windsor Castle guardroom.
32. Missett to FO, September 29, 1806, PRO: FO/24/2, f. 134.
33. Lt.-Col. MacLeod to his father, March 27, 1807, NLS: MS 19,302, f. 142.
34. "Extract of a letter from a British officer a Prisoner in the Citadel of Grand Cairo May 9 1807," NLS: MS 19,304, f. 61.
35. NLS: MS 19,304, ff. 57–59; Fraser to Drovetti, May 7, 1807, in Silvio Curto and Laura Donatelli, eds., *Bernardino Drovetti Epistolario (1800–1851)* (Milan: Cisalpino-Goliardica, 1985), p. 15.
36. The claim that the soldiers were "sold as slaves" all over Egypt comes from Mungo Park, *The Journal of a Mission to the Interior of Africa in the Year 1805 . . .* (London, 1815), pp. civ–cv. The same source goes on to say that "the ransoms paid for the redemption of the captives differed very considerably; the prices varying from between twenty and thirty pounds to more than one hundred pounds sterling for each man. But it is observable, on comparing the different rates, that the highest ransoms were paid for those who must be considered, from their names, to have been natives of Scotland; and who, it may be presumed, were more *valuable* than the rest from being more orderly and intelligent." Park, it hardly needs mentioning, was a Scot.
37. Roussel to Ministry of Foreign Affairs [hereafter cited as Ministry], July 22, 1817, MAE: CCC Aléxandrie [hereafter cited as Alex.], vol. 19.
38. He appears as "Boulanger de la Nation" on the "État général des françois etablis dans les trois Echelles d'Egypte 1775," AN: AE B/III/290, f. 118.
39. Joseph Balthalon to Ministry, 29 Fructidor XII, MAE: CCC Alex. 17.
40. Fiechter, pp. 23–25. This affair—which fills a good one hundred pages of consular correspondence—receives only passing notice in Ridley's biography of Drovetti (p. 37). This seems unduly brief considering what consequences the affair must have had for Drovetti's life and career in Egypt.
41. Ridley surmises from Fraser's statement that Rosine "and Drovetti were married obviously by 1807" (p. 368), but the 1818 wedding is noted in MAE: CCC Alex. 19.
42. Pillavoine to Ministry, March 6, 1820, MAE: CCC Alex. 20.
43. Jean-Marie Carré, *Voyageurs et écrivains français en Égypte, I: Des pèlerins du Moyen Âge à Méhémet-Ali,* 2nd ed. (Cairo: IFAO, 1956), pp. 170–87. Chateaubriand wrote up his journey in *Itinéraire de Paris à Jérusalem* (1811).
44. Ridley, p. 43; Fiechter, pp. 27–28.
45. Valentia, III, pp. 394, 432–33.
46. Missett to FO, March 25, 1812, PRO: FO/24/4, f. 26.
47. Fiechter, pp. 36–38; Carré, pp. 195–96. Boutin became good friends with the Drovettis, and relied on Bernardino for intelligence, news, and advice: see his letters in Curto and Donatelli, eds., *Epistolario,* pp. 35–65 *passim;* and his brother's letter to Drovetti, pp. 127–28. Boutin was killed by bandits in Syria in 1815.
48. Ridley mistakenly dates "the earliest evidence for Drovetti's interest in antiqui-

ties" to February 1812, when he arranged the dissection of a mummy for Lady Hester Stanhope (p. 57).

49. Missett to FO, March 22, 1806, PRO: FO/24/2, ff. 113–14.
50. J. J. Halls, *The Life and Correspondence of Henry Salt, Esq. F. R. S. . . .*, 2 vols. (London, 1834), I, pp. 45–47, 58.
51. Ibid., I, pp. 136–37.
52. The connection was Salt's uncle the Reverend Thomas Simon Butt, who held the living of Arley, the Mountnorris estate in Staffordshire. Ibid., I, pp. 65, 129.
53. Quoted in Deborah Manley and Peta Rée, *Henry Salt: Artist, Traveller, Diplomat, Egyptologist* (London: Libri, 2001), p. 25. Salt's account of his excursion was included in Valentia's *Voyages*.
54. "Proceedings in the Court of King's Bench, *ex parte* George Viscount Valentia, 1796" (Kidderminster, 1799), pp. 6–7.
55. Quoted in Nigel Leask, *Curiosity and the Aesthetics of Travel Writing, 1770–1840: "From an Antique Land"* (Oxford: Oxford University Press, 2002), p. 182.
56. "Trial for Adultery. The Whole Proceedings on the Trial of John Bellenger [*sic*] Gawler, Esquire, for Criminal Conversation with Lady Valentia, in the Court of King's Bench, before Lord Kenyon" (London, 1799), p. 51.
57. Quoted in Manley and Rée, p. 64.
58. Salt to Valentia, April 13, 1815, and May 2, 1815, BL: Add. MSS 19,347, ff. 136–38; Salt to FO, May 21, 1825, PRO: FO/78/135, f. 155.
59. Charles Ronald Middleton, *The Administration of British Foreign Policy 1782–1846* (Durham, N.C.: Duke University Press, 1977), pp. 244–53.
60. Banks to Castlereagh, April 13, 1815, PRO: FO/24/6, f. 83.
61. Halls, I, p. 485.
62. PRO: FO/24/6, f. 66.
63. "List of gifts bought from Theops. Richards and Son," July 17, 1815, PRO: FO/24/6, f. 90. The full name of Salt's would-be bride is not known; he discusses her rejection of him and his disappointment in a letter to Bingham Richards, April 2, 1817, BL: Add. MSS 19,347, f. 181.
64. Valentia to Salt, July 9, 1815, BL: Add. MSS 19,347, f. 141.
65. Salt to Valentia, July 19, 1815, BL: Add. MSS 19,347, f. 143.
66. Valentia to Salt, July 9, 1815, BL: Add. MSS 19,347, f. 141.
67. Andrew McClellan, *Inventing the Louvre* (Cambridge, UK: Cambridge University Press, 1994), pp. 198–200. Only about half the booty, in the event, was actually returned.
68. Henry Salt to Lord Valentia, October 7, 1815, quoted in Halls, I, pp. 425–27. The original of this, and Salt's other letters to Valentia, are in BL: Add. MSS 19,347. Halls censored parts of Salt's letters; in those cases, I have quoted from originals.

## CHAPTER EIGHT: REMOVALS

1. Missett to FO, June 18, 1814, PRO: FO/24/5, f. 13.
2. Afaf Lutfi al-Sayyid Marsot, *Egypt in the Reign of Muhammad Ali* (Cambridge, UK: Cambridge University Press, 1984), p. 72.

3. Marsot, pp. 198–203; Salt to FO, June 15, 1816, PRO: FO/24/6, ff. 110–12.
4. David Landes, *Bankers and Pashas: International Finance and Economic Imperialism in Egypt* (Cambridge, Mass.: Harvard University Press, 1958), p. 75. For a Foucauldian critique of Muhammad Ali's methods, see Timothy Mitchell, *Colonising Egypt* (Cambridge, UK: Cambridge University Press, 1988), esp. pp. 34–62.
5. Salt to Mountnorris, December 28, 1816, quoted in J. J. Halls, *The Life and Correspondence of Henry Salt, Esq. F. R. S. . . .*, 2 vols. (London, 1834), I, p. 469.
6. Ibid.
7. Ibid.
8. Missett to FO, August 27, 1814, PRO: FO/24/5, f. 27.
9. Ministry of Foreign Affairs to Drovetti, September 24, 1814; Drovetti to Ministry, December 10, 1814, MAE: CCC Alex. 18.
10. Thédenat, who had been working in French Mediterranean consulates for thirty years, entered the profession by an eventful route. Originally from Languedoc, he started out as a clerk in Livorno and Cadiz, but fled Spain after a torrid affair with his cousin's wife. En route to Marseilles, his ship was attacked by North African corsairs; he was taken captive and bought by the bey of Mascara. After three and a half years, Thédenat was freed and returned to Europe. It was his fluency in Spanish, Italian, and Arabic that led him into the consular service. Marcel Emerit, ed., *Les Aventures de Thédenat: Esclave et ministre d'un Bey d'Afrique* (*XVIIIème siècle*) (Algiers: Société Historique Algérienne, 1948).
11. Salt to Mountnorris, December 28, 1816, quoted in Halls, I, p. 469.
12. Roussel to Ministry, July 22, 1817, MAE: CCC Alex. 19.
13. Salt to Mountnorris, December 28, 1816, BL: Add. MSS 19,347, ff. 176–77.
14. Ibid.
15. Comte de Forbin, *Voyage dans le Levant en 1817 et 1818* (Paris: 1819), p. 226.
16. Roussel to Ministry, July 22, 1817, MAE: CCC Alex. 19.
17. Roussel to Ministry, December 19, 1817, MAE: CCC Cairo 26.
18. The most thorough biography of Belzoni in English is Stanley Mayes, *The Great Belzoni: Archaeologist Extraordinary* (London: Putnam, 1959). See also Marco Zatterin, *Il gigante del Nilo: storia e avventure del grande Belzoni, l'uomo che svelò i misteri dell'Egitto dei faraoni* (Milan: Mondadori, 2000); and Maurice Willson Disher, *Pharaoh's Fool* (London: Heinemann, 1957). Belzoni's plan on arriving in Malta was to proceed to Constantinople and find work there.
19. Ismael Gibraltar helped lead the Turco-Egyptian invasion of the Peloponnese in 1825. He was also friendly with the antiquarian Sir William Gell, who encouraged several young Britons to study and travel to Egypt. Jason Thompson, *Sir Gardner Wilkinson and His Circle* (Austin: University of Texas Press, 1992), p. 32–33.
20. There is a contemporary drawing in the British Museum of Belzoni performing this act, reproduced in Mayes and Disher.
21. Not much is known about Sarah, who has with little or no basis been described both as Irish and as a woman of Amazonian proportions. Recent research suggests that she was born Sarah Banne or Bane in Bristol in 1783; she died in Jersey in 1870 (Zatterin, pp. 30, 267–69). She supplemented Belzoni's *Narrative*

with a "Short Account of the Women of Egypt, Nubia, and Syria," on which see Billie Melman, *Women's Orients: English Women and the Middle East, 1718–1918* (London: Macmillan, 1992), pp. 180–82.

22. Mayes, p. 72.
23. Giambattista Belzoni, *Narrative of the Operations and Recent Discoveries in the Pyramids, Temples, and Tombs, and Excavations, in Egypt and Nubia . . .*, 2nd ed. (London, 1821), p. 24.
24. On Burckhardt, see Katherine Sim, *Desert Traveller: The Life of Jean Louis Burckhardt* (London: Phoenix Press, 2000).
25. Belzoni, p. 96; BL: Add. MSS 19,347, ff. 167–68.
26. Halls, I, pp. 491–92.
27. Belzoni, p. 25.
28. Ibid., p. vi.
29. Soon after he arrived in Egypt, Belzoni wrote to Drovetti several times for help in dealing with the pasha. (*Epistolario*, pp. 76–79, 82–83.)
30. Sending a copy of the book to his friend Peter Lee, the vice-consul in Alexandria, Belzoni wrote, "you will find many errors in it, particularly according to the sistem of that country Egypt which is not allways political to speak the Trooth, but I have wrot it for Ingland" (Belzoni to Peter Lee, December 29, 1821, BL: James Burton Papers, Add. MSS 25,658, ff. 1–2). Interestingly, the book was promptly translated into French with only minimal modifications to the pervasively anti-French tone; and the German and Italian editions were prepared from this in turn (Mayes, pp. 255–56).
31. Belzoni, p. 39.
32. Ibid., pp. 110–11. Belzoni always refers to Rifaud by some variant of the name "Jacques."
33. Ibid., p. 126.
34. Donald M. Reid, *Whose Pharaohs?: Archaeology, Museums, and Egyptian National Identity from Napoleon to World War I* (Berkeley: University of California Press, 2002), p. 40.
35. Roussel to Ministry, February 24, 1817, MAE: CCC Alex. 19. "I would reply," he said, "that the French army dispersed throughout Egypt with so many enemies on its hands, did not have the time to condescend to the desire of the savants who wanted to transport it; while the English army, all united in Alexandria, and having lots of means at its disposal, tried ineffectually to take away one of the two obelisks of Cleopatra . . . and couldn't even move it."
36. Belzoni, p. 135.
37. Halls, II, pp. 32–33.
38. Salt to FO, October 12, 1817, PRO: FO/78/79, ff. 64–65; Rear-Admiral Sir Charles Penrose to FO, December 9, 1817, PRO: FO/78/89, f. 82.
39. Salt to Mountnorris, August 7, 1818, quoted in Halls, I, p. 494.
40. G. Belzoni, *Narrative of the Operations and Recent Discoveries in the Pyramids, Temples, and Tombs, and Excavations, in Egypt and Nubia . . .*, 3rd ed., 2 vols. (London, 1822), I, p. 224.
41. Belzoni, 2nd ed., p. 349.
42. Ibid., pp. 230–36.
43. Jean-Jacques Fiechter, *La Moisson des dieux* (Paris: Julliard, 1994), pp. 40–41.

44. Roussel to Ministry, January 22, 1817, MAE: CCC Alex. 19; Roussel to Ministry, December 19, 1817, MAE: CCC Cairo 26.
45. Pillavoine to Ministry, August 14, 1819, MAE: CCC Alex. 20.
46. Forbin, p. 267.
47. Belzoni, pp. 248–49.
48. Ibid., p. 354.
49. The contest for the obelisk did not end there. Bankes and Drovetti were still disputing its ownership a year later, but they refused to take their case as far as Muhammad Ali, because they were "afraid that His Highness would take it himself so as not to displease anybody and that this difference would give him reason in future to refuse the slightest permission to dig. This fear has reduced Mr. Drovetti to silence and given Mr. Bankes the freedom to send the obelisk to England" (Pillavoine to Ministry, October 23, 1819, MAE: CCC Alex. 20). Belzoni had also very nearly lost it entirely: while he tried to load it onto the boat, the obelisk slipped into the Nile—from which, luckily, it was retrieved.
50. Belzoni, pp. 364–67.
51. Ibid., p. 436. The French consul, for his part, grumbled at the "jealous humor of antiquaries" that had caused such trouble. Pillavoine to Ministry, August 14, 1819, MAE: CCC Alex. 20.
52. Belzoni, p. 437.
53. Belzoni to Peter Lee, December 29, 1821, BL: James Burton Papers, Add. MSS 25,658, ff. 1–2.
54. Salt to Mountnorris, December 28, 1816, quoted in Halls, I, pp. 472–73.
55. Salt to Mountnorris, December 20, 1817, BL: Add. MSS 19,347, ff. 194–95.
56. Salt to Mountnorris, August 7, 1818, BL: Add. MSS 19,347, f. 227.
57. Ibid., ff. 225–27.
58. BL: James Burton Papers, Add. MSS 25,661, f. 33. Salt's recent biographers valiantly defend him from Gell's charges: Deborah Manley and Peta Rée, *Henry Salt: Artist, Traveller, Diplomat, Egyptologist* (London: Libri, 2001), p. 215.
59. Robert Richardson, M.D., *Travels Along the Mediterranean, and Parts Adjacent; in Company with the Earl of Belmore, During the Years 1816–17–18 . . .*, 2 vols. (London, 1822).
60. Manley and Rée, pp. 125–32.
61. Dr. Robert Richardson, quoted in Manley and Rée, p. 135.
62. Salt to Mountnorris, January 18, 1818, quoted in Halls, II, pp. 51–53.
63. Belzoni, p. 387.
64. Halls, II, pp. 16–17.
65. Their biographers have taken up their causes: Mayes, pp. 190–91; Manley and Rée, pp. 137–38.
66. Halls, II, pp. 25, 17.
67. Belzoni, pp. 38–39.
68. Halls, II, pp. 27, 19.
69. Belzoni to Sir Joseph Banks, November 14, 1818, BL: Add. MSS 19,347, f. 237.
70. Nigel Leask, *Curiosity and the Aesthetics of Travel Writing, 1770–1840: "From an Antique Land"* (Oxford: Oxford University Press, 2002), pp. 102–110, 123–28.

71. William St. Clair, *Lord Elgin and the Marbles: The Controversial History of the Parthenon Sculptures* (Oxford: Oxford University Press, 1998), p. 181.
72. Salt to Mountnorris, August 7, 1818, BL: Add. MSS 19,347, f. 227.
73. "Copy of Paper sent by Henry Salt to Sir Joseph Banks being the list of articles offered for sale to the British Museum with the prices," BL: Add. MSS 19,347, ff. 236–37; Salt to W. R. Hamilton, June 10, 1818, quoted in Halls, II, pp. 299–301.
74. Halls, II, pp. 299–300.
75. Ibid., pp. 301, 302*n*. Halls, who was a professional painter, defended Elgin in terms that show how, by the early 1830s, the reputation of both the man and the Marbles had been revised in Britain: "This nobleman had the honour of bringing into England, and probably of rescuing from the destructive ravages of barbarians, one of the finest collections of Grecian sculpture, and of the purest aera, which any European nation can boast. . . . What ought to have been done in the first instance, was at length adopted: the evidence of competent judges was resorted to, and the antiquities were finally purchased by a grant from parliament of thirty-five thousand pounds, about one half of the sum which it had altogether cost his Lordship in assembling the collection" (pp. 301–2*n*). Halls also, unlike his friend Salt, opposed the repatriation of art from the Louvre in 1815.
76. Banks to Salt, February 14, 1819, quoted in Halls, II, pp. 303–4. There was more than a little bitterness in an awkward verse Salt later wrote, that antiquities "Might furnish out amusement for a year / To one whose nerves could dare withstand the sneer / Of carping critic, prompt with eager haste / To sweep the wretch away for such ignoble taste" (Halls, II, p. 416).
77. W. R. Hamilton to Salt, February 16, 1819, quoted in Halls, II, p. 305.
78. Salt to Banks, May 28, 1819, quoted in Halls, II, pp. 305–6.
79. Salt to Mountnorris, June 1, 1819, BL: Add. MSS 19,347, ff. 251–54.
80. W. R. Hamilton to Mountnorris, September 30, 1819, BL: Add. MSS 19,347, f. 263.
81. Rt. Hon. Charles Yorke to Sir Joseph Banks, November 5, 1819, quoted in Halls, II, p. 318.
82. Salt to Mountnorris, June 25, 1820, BL: Add. MSS 19,347, f. 315.
83. Salt to Mountnorris, May 14, 1822, BL: Add. MSS 19,347, f. 353.
84. Manley and Rée, pp. 206–9; Halls, II, pp. 338–86; Bingham Richards to Mountnorris, September 5 and 24, 1822, BL: Add. MSS 19,347, ff. 356–59.
85. Salt to Richards, May 26, 1822, quoted in Halls, II, p. 322.
86. Leask, p. 137.
87. Mayes, pp. 240–44.
88. James Stevens Curl, *The Egyptian Revival: An Introductory Study of a Recurring Theme in the History of Taste* (London: G. Allen & Unwin, 1982), p. 124; Richard Altick, *The Shows of London* (Cambridge, Mass.: Harvard University Press, 1978).
89. Mayes, p. 261.
90. *A Catalogue of the Valuable Collection of Antiquities, of Mr. John Belzoni, in Egypt, Nubia, etc. Which Will be Sold by Mr. Robins, at the Egyptian Hall, Pic-*

*cadilly, on Saturday, the 8th of June, 1822, at Twelve o'Clock* (London, 1822). The copy of this catalogue in the British Library is partially annotated with prices.

91. Dorothy Middleton, "Banks and African Exploration," in R. E. R. Banks et al., eds., *Sir Joseph Banks: A Global Perspective* (Kew: Royal Botanic Gardens, 1994); Mungo Park, *Travels in the Interior Districts of Africa: performed under the direction and patronage of the African Association in the years 1795, 1796 and 1797* (London, 1799); Mungo Park, *The Journal of a Mission into the Interior of Africa, in the year 1805* (London, 1815); *The Narrative of Robert Adams* (London, 1816). One can still join a camel caravan that runs from Zagora in southwestern Morocco to Timbuktu in about forty days.
92. Sarah Belzoni to Jane Porter, September 8, 1823, BL: Add. MSS 35,230, f. 71.
93. Quoted in Mayes, p. 284.
94. Annie Coombes, *Reinventing Africa: Museums, Material Culture, and Popular Imagination in Late Victorian and Edwardian England* (New Haven: Yale University Press, 1994), pp. 7–28.
95. Mayes, pp. 285–87.
96. Ibid., pp. 293–95.
97. [Sarah Atkins], *Fruits of Enterprize . . .*, 2nd ed. (London, 1822), pp. 149–50.
98. Bela Bates Edwards, *Biography of Self-Taught Men* (Boston, 1832).
99. City of Belzoni Web site, http://www.belzoni.com, visited June 2004.
100. Atkins, pp. 48, 17, 154.

## CHAPTER NINE: RECOVERIES

1. The mythic interpretation of Champollion was set out in a 1906 German biography by Hermine Hartleben, *Jean-François Champollion, sa vie et son oeuvre 1790–1832* (Paris: Éditions Pygmalion/Gérard Watelet, 1983).
2. Vicomte de la Rochefoucauld, "Rapport au Roi," May 15, 1826, AN: Maison du Roi, O/3/1418.
3. J.-F. Champollion, *Lettres écrites d'Égypte et de Nubie en 1828 et 1829* (Paris: 1833), pp. 12–13.
4. Anonymous memorandum on formation of Musée Charles-X (1826), AN: O/3/1418.
5. Jason Thompson, *Sir Gardner Wilkinson and His Circle* (Austin: University of Texas Press, 1992), pp. 229–30.
6. This was one of the worst acts of vandalism of the period. Champollion objected, and used his knowledge of hieroglyphics to prove that the zodiac did not date from distant pharoanic times, as many had thought, but had in fact been put up—like the temple itself—by a more recent Roman emperor of Egypt. Once this was revealed, the Comte de Forbin, director-general of Museums, petitioned the Ministry of the Interior for a refund of the 75,000 francs the museums had invested in the zodiac. "This is not the place to discuss the unreflecting manner in which this sale took place. The fact is that the appropriate price for this monument cannot now be higher than 10,000 francs" (Forbin to King's Household, December 22, 1826, AN: O/3/1417).

7. Pillavoine to Ministry of Foreign Affairs, September 28, 1819, 29 November 1819, and May 6, 1820, MAE: CCC Alex. 20. Drovetti told the French consul that he was "only selling his cabinet to pay 200,000 piasters he owes the Pasha."
8. Pillavoine to Ministry, March 7, 1821, MAE: CCC Alex. 21.
9. Jomard to King's Household, October 30, 1824, AN: O/3/1414.
10. Todd Porterfield, *The Allure of Empire: Art in the Service of French Imperialism 1798–1836* (Princeton, N.J.: Princeton University Press, 1998), pp. 81–116.
11. It was also an amnesty for Champollion personally, a Bonapartist through and through, who had been hounded out of an earlier job because of his political sympathies. His elder brother and guardian, Jean-Jacques Champollion-Figeac, introduced him to Napoleon in 1815, when the deposed emperor passed through Grenoble on his way to Paris. The emperor "listened with interest to the exposition of his projects . . . ," recalled Champollion-Figeac, "[T]he Coptic dictionary especially attracted his attention: 'Bring all that to Paris,' he told me, 'we will have it printed; it will be a lot easier than the Chinese Dictionary.' " J.-J. Champollion-Figeac, *Fourier et Napoléon: L'Égypte et les cent jours, mémoires et documents inédits* (Paris, 1844), p. 232.
12. Salt to Mountnorris, August 7, 1818, BL: Add. MSS 19,347, f. 233.
13. Salt to Nathaniel Pearce, September 19, 1819, quoted in J. J. Halls, *The Life and Correspondence of Henry Salt, Esq. F. R. S. . . .*, 2 vols. (London, 1834), II, p. 146. The French consul Pillavoine was one of the witnesses (Pillavoine to Ministry of Foreign Affairs, October 23, 1819, MAE: CCC Alex. 20).
14. Deborah Manley and Peta Rée, *Henry Salt: Artist, Traveller, Diplomat, Egyptologist* (London: Libri, 2001), pp. 182–86.
15. Salt to Mountnorris, June 25, 1820, BL: Add. MSS 19,347, f. 313.
16. Salt to Mountnorris, May 14, 1822, BL: Add. MSS 19,347, f. 353.
17. Salt to Bingham Richards, July 25, 1820, BL: Add. MSS 19,347, f. 333.
18. Halls, II, p. 148.
19. Salt to FO, April 28, 1824, PRO: FO/78/126, f. 236.
20. Robert Hay, quoted in Jason Thompson, *Sir Gardner Wilkinson and His Circle* (Austin: University of Texas Press, 1992), p. 87.
21. [Henry Salt], *Egypt, A Descriptive Poem, with Notes, by a Traveller* (Alexandria, 1824). This was the first English book printed in Alexandria. The text is reprinted in Halls, II, pp. 388–420.
22. Henry Salt, *Essay on Dr. Young's and M. Champollion's phonetic system of Hieroglyphics . . .* (London, 1825).
23. Salt to Richards, June 18, 1825, quoted in Halls, II, p. 245.
24. Salt to Richards, quoted in Halls, II, p. 250.
25. Champollion to the Duc de Blacas, July 24, 1825, AN: O/3/1418. (Blacas was French ambassador in Naples.)
26. The chief objections raised to buying Salt's collection came from advocates of a rival collection, formed by one Joseph Passalacqua. How Passalacqua assembled this collection is hard to know, since little mention is made of him in the British and French memoirs, diaries, and letters I have seen. He had an exhibition at 52, Passage Vivienne, just steps away from the old Bibliothèque Nationale. Between 1825 and 1827 he repeatedly pressured the French govern-

ment to buy his items, dropping his price with increasing desperation from 140,000 francs to 50,000 francs plus a pension. He published a catalogue, with learned dissertations by savants such as Geoffroy Saint-Hilaire, to help his case; and Saint-Hilaire read a report on the Passalacqua collection to the Académie Royale des Sciences in November 1826. The catalogue makes clear that—unlike the collections of Salt and Drovetti, which placed special emphasis on massive and monumental pieces—Passalacqua's collection was devoted instead to a reconstruction of ancient Egyptian life. (*Catalogue raissonné et historique des Antiquités découvertes en Égypte par J. Passalacqua* . . . [Paris, 1826]. Proposals to government and Saint-Hilaire's report are in AN: O/3/1417, 1418 and 1419). The collection was ultimately bought by Prussia, and Passalacqua was made its curator. (Donald Malcòm Reid, *Whose Pharaohs?: Archaeology, Museums, and Egyptian Identity from Napoleon to World War I* [Berkeley: University of California Press, 2002], p. 45.)

27. Santoni to Duc de Doudeauville, March 23, 1826, AN: O/3/1418.
28. Salt to Richards, May 12, 1827, quoted in Halls, II, pp. 268–69.
29. Salt to Santoni, October 7, 1827, quoted in Halls, II, pp. 275–76.
30. Manley and Rée, p. 269.
31. Khaled Fahmy, *All the Pasha's Men: Mehmed Ali, His Army, and the Making of Modern Egypt* (Cambridge, UK: Cambridge University Press, 1997).
32. Diary of James Burton (1822–23), November 27, 1822, BL: Burton Papers, Add. MSS 25,624, ff. 132–33.
33. Salt to FO, February 8, 1824, PRO: FO/78/126, f. 226.
34. Drovetti to Ministry, April 7, 1826, MAE: CCC Alex. 22.
35. He included a list in his April 7, 1826, dispatch, which is reprinted in Ronald T. Ridley, *Napoleon's Proconsul in Egypt: The Life and Times of Bernardino Drovetti* (London: Rubicon, 1998), p. 308.
36. Malivoire to Ministry, April 4, 1826, MAE: CCC Cairo 26; Drovetti to Ministry, March 4, 1826, MAE: CCC Alex. 22.
37. Salt to FO, November 10, 1824, PRO: FO/78/126, ff. 265–66; Chateaubriand to Muhammad Ali, March 9, 1824, MAE: CCC Alex. 21. It should be noted that Muhammad Ali was always careful to woo Britain with gifts, too. In 1826 he sent giraffes to both Charles X and George IV; and his gift of an obelisk to France was matched by the presentation of Cleopatra's Needle to Britain. Salt to FO, October 27, 1826, PRO: FO/78/147, f. 137; Michael Allin, *Zarafa: A Giraffe's True Story, from Deep in Africa to the Heart of Paris* (New York: Walker, 1998). The Windsor giraffe was more sickly than its Paris-bound cousin, and died after two years (Manley and Rée, p. 253 and p. 297, note 11). George IV, having "learnt . . . that Deer and Kangaroos are animals not to be found in Egypt," thought they "might be a present likely to be valued by His H[ighne]ss" (FO to Salt, October 5, 1826, PRO: FO/78/160, f. 47).
38. Salt to FO, April 4, 1826, PRO: FO/78/147, f. 72.
39. Hugh Honour, *Romanticism* (London: Icon Editions, 1979), p. 230.
40. Quoted in David Brewer, *The Flame of Freedom: The Greek War of Independence, 1821–1833* (London: John Murray, 2001), p. 321.
41. Brewer, pp. 325–36; Ernle Bradford, *Mediterranean: Portrait of a Sea* (London: Penguin, 2000), pp. 491–94; Manley and Rée, p. 273; Ridley, pp. 148–52.

42. Barker to FO, August 18, 1829, PRO: FO/78/184, ff. 205–6. *Cf.* H. H. Dodwell, *The Founder of Modern Egypt: A Study of Muhammad Ali* (Cambridge, UK: Cambridge University Press, 1931), pp. 97–104.
43. Mimaut to Ministry of Foreign Affairs, July 7, 1829, MAE: CCC Alex. 23.
44. Champollion, p. 20.
45. Drovetti wrote to Champollion in May 1828 to dissuade him from making the trip, given the tense state of relations between France and Egypt in the wake of Navarino. The letter missed Champollion, who set off anyway; Drovetti was caught by surprise by Champollion's arrival, but gave him a warm welcome. Champollion later suspected, however, that the talk of political turbulence had been exaggerated: "All that was, at base, no more than a self-interested calculation. The antiquities dealers were all quaking at the news of my arrival in Egypt with the intention of excavating. A cabal was thus formed when it came to the matter of issuing of *firmans* for my digs. . . . His Highness declared he did not want to give *firmans* except to his friends Drovetti and Anastasi." Drovetti resolved the matter by ceding his own personal concessions to Champollion. (Champollion, pp. 44–45.)
46. Thompson, pp. 125–26.
47. *Asiatic Journal and Monthly Register* 26 (London, 1828), p. 346.
48. Reid, p. 43; Manley and Rée, pp. 213–23; Anthony Sattin, *Lifting the Veil: British Society in Egypt, 1768–1956* (London: J. M. Dent, 1988); Paul Starkey and Janet Starkey, eds., *Travellers in Egypt* (London: Tauris Parke, 1998).
49. James Burton to Robert Hay, January 1, 1836, BL: Hay Papers, Add. MSS 38,094, f. 93.
50. Neil Cooke, "James Burton: The Forgotten Egyptologist," in Starkey and Starkey, eds., pp. 85–94. Burton later changed his name to Haliburton, under which he is listed in the *DNB*.
51. Selwyn Tillett, *Egypt Itself: The Career of Robert Hay of Linplum and Nunraw, 1799–1863* (London: SD Books, 1984).
52. Diary of Robert Hay, November 23, 1824, BL: Hay Papers, Add. MSS 31,054, ff. 81–83.
53. Diary of Robert Hay, April 1826, BL: Hay Papers, Add. MSS 31,054, f. 115.
54. Leila Ahmed, *Edward W. Lane: A Study of His Life and Works and of British Ideas of the Middle East in the Nineteenth Century* (London: Longman, 1978), pp. 23–49. Robert Hay stayed with Lane in Cairo in 1826, and was impressed by the degree to which he had assimilated himself. "He like most of the travellers at present in Egypt, wears the Turkish costume, and even eats as they do wh. only a few do. . . . I must confess I think it a proper thing for all Eastern travellers to learn to do like the natives to avoid being thought awkward when perhaps they are obliged to dine or eat in their company but, to do so when there is no real necessity seems to me little short of ridiculous as no one but a Turk who has been accustomed to eat with his fingers all his life and to see those round him do the same can possibly prefer it to the less clumsy way of feeding oneself with the fork, knife and spoon" (Diary of Robert Hay, February 22, 1826, BL: Hay Papers, Add. MSS 31,054, ff. 106–7).
55. Burton, quoted in Manley and Rée, p. 233.
56. FO to Salt, March 26, 1824, PRO: FO/78/126, ff. 213–14.

57. Salt to Burton and Wilkinson, November 8, 1824, BL: Burton Papers, Add. MSS 25,658, f. 8.
58. Burton and Wilkinson to Salt, November 18, 1824, BL: Burton Papers, Add. MSS 25,658, ff. 11–12; Thompson, pp. 45–47.
59. Quoted in Thompson, p. 104. Another visiting dignitary was Sir Hudson Lowe, Napoleon's jailer, who turned up among the tombs asking to be shown the sights before leaving later in the day. "How infinite must be the man's taste be who can see All Thebes in one day!!!" said Robert Hay. Needless to say, the days of Thomas Cook Tours were still some distance off. (Diary of Robert Hay, May 18, 1826, BL: Hay Papers, Add. MSS 31,054, f. 130.)
60. Kent Weeks, *The Lost Tomb* (New York: William Morrow, 1998). The Web site of the Theban Mapping Project is packed with information about the history of excavations in the valley: http://www.thebanmappingproject.com, visited June 2004.
61. Champollion, p. 249.
62. J.-J. Champollion-Figeac, *L'Obélisque de Louqsour transporté à Paris* (Paris, 1833). For the Taylor expedition, see BNF: MSS NAF 9444.
63. Wilkinson to Hay, June 26, 1831, BL: Hay Papers, Add. MSS 38,094, f. 21.
64. Champollion, p. 276.
65. Translation and emphasis mine. James Burton to John Barker, August 3, 1829, BL: Burton Papers, Add. MSS 25,658, f. 50.
66. Burton to John Barker, August 3, 1829, BL: Burton Papers, Add. MSS 25,658, ff. 50–52.
67. Barker to Burton, August 15, 1829, BL: Burton Papers, Add. MSS 25,658, f. 56.
68. Champollion, pp. 408–9.
69. Ibid., pp. 443–48. Robert Hay movingly wrote of one temple, pulled down for its stones on the instructions of the local bey: "Hearing of the rapid destruction of the remains of the temple of Hermopolis I determined to see it before it was totally removed from the list of Egyptian Antiquities, as that wd. be its fate in all likely hood by the time I returned, and now three columns remaind standing. Accordingly taking our Camera lucidas to take one of the last views that wd. be taken of this ruin, as we thought, we set out. . . . We had just arrived in time to see the melancholy end of the temple! My disappointment was great when I saw prostrate on the ground what I had expected would have been left to shew future travellers what Hermopolis was—and I could scarcely believe my eyes that this was the spot where stood the eleven massive columns that I had before seen and drawn. It almost seemed from the spot where I stood, as if the very ground had been swept!" (Diary of Robert Hay, April 24, 1826, BL: Hay Papers, Add. MSS 31,054, ff. 117–8.)
70. Burton to Sir William Gell, May 23, 1829, BL: Add. MSS 50,135, f. 19.
71. Burton to Barker, August 3, 1829, BL: Burton Papers, Add. MSS 25,658, ff. 51–52.
72. George R. Gliddon, *An Appeal to the Antiquaries of Egypt on the Destruction of the Monuments of Egypt* (London, 1841).
73. Robert Hay to *Albion* (newspaper), June 8, 1835, BL: Hay Papers, Add. MSS 29,859, f. 32.
74. Robert Hay to Edward Hawkins, August 25, 1835, British Museum: Depart-

ment of Western Asiatic Antiquities, Departmental Correspondence, 1826–67 (New Series), vol. 1.

75. Burton to Hay, January 1, 1836, BL: Hay Papers, Add. MSS 38,094, f. 93.
76. Edward Barker to John Ffiott Lee, December 17, 1831, BL: Add. MSS 47,490, f. 120.
77. The overland route had found its new George Baldwin in Lieutenant Thomas Waghorn, who worked tirelessly (and in the face of official opposition) to establish steamer service to India through the Red Sea. His efforts were rewarded in 1841, when Muhammad Ali awarded a concession to the British to dock in Suez (Afaf Lutfi al-Sayyid Marsot, *Egypt in the Reign of Muhammad Ali* [Cambridge, UK: Cambridge University Press, 1984], p. 252).
78. Reid, pp. 52–54, 108–12.
79. Ibid., pp. 54–58. The Greek Archaeological Service was founded in 1833, and the first law about the export and control of antiquities passed there in 1834. Maria Avgouli, "The First Greek Museums and National Identity," in Flora E. S. Kaplan, ed., *Museums and the Making of "Ourselves": The Role of Objects in National Identity* (London: Leicester University Press, 1994), pp. 246–65.
80. Quoted in Reid, p. 58.
81. Gliddon, *An Appeal to the Antiquaries*, pp. 130–31.
82. Reid, p. 58; on Mariette, 99–108.
83. Reid, p. 56. To this day, foreign tourists vastly outnumber Egyptians at Cairo's Egyptian Museum, and at archaeological sites.
84. Robert Coster to John Ffiott Lee, January 24, 1838, BL: Add. MSS 47,490, f. 190.
85. R. R. Madden, *Egypt and Mohammed Ali, Illustrative of the Condition of His Slaves and Subjects, etc.* (London, 1841), pp. 110–98.
86. Quoted in Kenneth Bourne, *Palmerston: The Early Years 1784–1841* (New York: Macmillan, 1982), p. 576.
87. Marsot, pp. 240–45.
88. Quoted in Madden, p. 102.
89. Dodwell, pp. 183–91; Bourne, pp. 577–94, quote p. 593.
90. Madden, p. 9.
91. Marsot, pp. 245–46; Bourne, pp. 595–620, quote p. 616.
92. Marsot, pp. 249–56; Juan R. I. Cole, *Colonialism and Revolution in the Middle East: Social and Cultural Origins of Egypt's 'Urabi Movement* (Princeton, N.J.: Princeton University Press, 1993).
93. The original drawings are in the Hay Papers in the British Library, but a reproduction has recently been put up in Gurna, not far from where Hay made it. My thanks to Caroline Simpson for information about Hay's panorama.
94. Reid, p. 295.

CONCLUSION

1. Emily Eden, *Up the Country* (Oxford: Oxford University Press, 1930), pp. 293–94.
2. A classic summary of the Victorian imperial frame of mind is offered in

Ronald Robinson and John Gallagher, *Africa and the Victorians: The Official Mind of Imperialism*, 2nd ed. (London: Macmillan, 1981), pp. 1–5.

3. *Asiatic Journal and Monthly Register*, vol. 26 (July–Dec. 1828), London, pp. 606–7.
4. On Stuart and other white border crossers of his period, see William Dalrymple, *White Mughals: Love and Betrayal in Eighteenth-Century India* (New York: Viking, 2002), pp. 23–43, 391–92; and my "Collectors of Empire: Objects, Conquests and Imperial Self-Fashioning," *Past & Present* 184 (2004): 130–33.
5. Jan Morris, *Heaven's Command: An Imperial Progress* (London: Faber and Faber, 1973), pp. 64, 142, 175.
6. Thomas R. Metcalf, "Empire Recentered: India in the Indian Ocean Arena," in Gregory Blue, Martin Bunton, and Ralph Croizier, eds., *Colonialism and the Modern World* (London: M. E. Sharpe, 2002), pp. 25–39.
7. Sir John Kaye, *History of the War in Afghanistan* . . . , 2 vols. (London, 1851), II, pp. 218–50.
8. Captain J. Martin Bladen Neill, *Recollections of Four Years' Service in the East with H. M. Fortieth Regiment* . . . (London, 1845), pp. 272–73.
9. "Lord Ellenborough's Speech, Before Departing for India, at the dinner given in his honour by the Court of Directors of the Honourable East India Company, November 3, 1841," in R. C. E. Abbott, 3rd Baron Colchester, ed., *History of the Indian Administration of Lord Ellenborough* (London, 1874), p. 169.
10. J. A. Norris, *The First Afghan War 1838–42* (Cambridge, UK: Cambridge University Press, 1967), pp. 391–416.
11. Lt. James Rattray, *Scenery, Inhabitants, and Costumes of Afghaunistan* . . . (London, 1847), plate 18.
12. Rev. I. N. Allen, *Diary of a March through Sinde and Affghanistan, with the troops under the command of General Sir William Nott, K. C. B., and sermons delivered on various occasions during the campaign of 1842* (London, 1843), p. 277.
13. Neill, p. 244; Rattray, plate 18.
14. J. H. Stocqueler, *Memoirs and Correspondence of Major-General Sir William Nott, G. C. B.*, 2 vols. (London, 1854), II, pp. 111–12; Albert H. Imlah, *Lord Ellenborough* (Cambridge, Mass.: Harvard University Press, 1939), pp. 79–119.
15. Allen, p. 371.
16. Debate of March 9, 1843, Hansard, *Parliamentary Debates*, 3rd ser., vol. LXVII, pp. 513–706.
17. Mridu Rai, "Contested Sites: Religious Shrines and the Archaeological Mapping of Kashmiri Muslim Protest, c. 1900–47," *Past & Present*, forthcoming.
18. Romila Thapar, "Somanatha: Narratives of a History," in *Narratives and the Making of History: Two Lectures* (New Delhi: Oxford University Press, 2000), pp. 24–50.
19. William Herries to John Herries, February 18, 1843, OIOC: MSS Eur C 149.
20. "The Affairs of India. Private Correspondence," *The Times*, March 14, 1843. My thanks to Stephen Vella for this and other references in *The Times*.
21. "Miscellaneous Extracts from the Papers," *The Times*, October 24, 1843.
22. I am indebted to Hirendro Mullick for information on Rajendro's education,

and for a comprehensive tour of the collection. Disappointingly, the Hogg papers in the British Library appear not to contain any information about Hogg's Bengali pupil (OIOC: Hogg Collection, MSS Eur E/342).

23. Dinabandhu Chatterjee, *A Short Sketch of Rajah Rajendro Mullick Bahadur and His Family* (Calcutta: G. C. Day, 1917), pp. 61–63. On elite Bengali art patronage at this time, see Tapati Guha-Thakurta, *The Making of a New 'Indian' Art: Artists, Aesthetics and Nationalism in Bengal, c. 1850–1920* (Cambridge, UK: Cambridge University Press, 1992); and Partha Mitter, *Art and Nationalism in Colonial India, 1850–1922: Occidental Orientations* (Oxford: Oxford University Press, 1994).
24. Indira Vishwanathan Peterson, "The Cabinet of King Serfoji of Tanjore: A European Collection in Early Nineteenth-Century India," *Journal of the History of Collections* xi (1999): 71–93.
25. I disagree here with Geoffrey Moorhouse's statement, in an otherwise excellent description of the Marble Palace, that "This is not a museum. It is a home, though you are very welcome to wander around it freely between the hours of ten and five for nothing more than your signature in the visitor's book." Geoffrey Moorhouse, *Calcutta* (London: Phoenix, 1998), p. 23.
26. T. B. Macaulay, "Minute on Indian Education," in T. B. Macaulay, *Poetry and Prose* (Cambridge, Mass.: Harvard University Press, 1967), pp. 722, 729.
27. Rudyard Kipling, *Kim*, introd. Edward Said (London: Penguin, 1989), p. 49.
28. Ibid., p. 179.

# *Index*

(Page references in *italic* refer to illustrations.)

# *Illustration Credits*

19 Yale Center for British Art, Paul Mellon Collection
38 Courtesy of Shrewsbury Museums Service, U.K.
46 By permission of the British Library, WD 4148
54 Author's collection
58 Yale Center for British Art, Paul Mellon Collection
66 Courtesy of Victoria Memorial, Kolkata
68 Private collection
72 Author's collection
85 By permission of the British Library, OMS OR 4761
91 Author's collection
103 Author's photograph
108 Author's collection
120 Yale Center for British Art, Paul Mellon Collection
134 Réunion des Musées Nationaux/Art Resource N.Y.
139 By permission of the British Library, Add. MSS 34,942
146 Cliché Bibliothèque Nationale de France, Paris
150 V&A Images/Victoria and Albert Museum
155 Yale Center for British Art, Paul Mellon Fund
158 © Otto Money (photography by AIC Photographic Services)
169 By permission of the British Library, P430
174 By permission of the British Library, P779
178 V&A Images/Victoria and Albert Museum
180 National Trust Photo Library/Erik Pelham
185 By permission of the British Library, OMS I.O. Islamic 3565
188 By permission of the British Library, WD 4235
191 National Trust Photo Library/Erik Pelham
201 Yale Center for British Art, Paul Mellon Collection
202 Courtesy of Harvard College Library
217 Author's collection
219 By permission of the British Library, Add. MSS 46,839
220 Courtesy of Special Collections, University of Michigan Library
223 DT46.F8 1809, Special Collections, University of Virginia Library

P.S.

Ideas, interviews & features . . .

## About the author



## About the book



## Read on

# Q and A with Maya Jasanoff

**Martin, Polier and de Boigne all lead fantastic lives, yet the pull of the place that was once 'home' is ever-present. Where is home for you and why?**
The East Coast of the US is where I feel most comfortable. But after I went to college my family moved away from the town I grew up in, and I've lived in four different places in the US since then, as well as in Britain and France. So for me, 'home' is not a single spot so much as a combination of places where I live and work, where I have family and friends, and where I feel settled and relaxed in a familiar environment. I like the idea that you can be at home in many places, or that different settings can each supply elements of what you consider to be home. I think expats like Martin and Polier must have shared a bit of this sensation: their homes were in at least two places at once.

**The book is dedicated to your parents and you describe them as border crossers. How did their background and life influence your own choices?**
My parents crossed borders most conspicuously by marrying each other (my mother is from Bengal, my father from Brooklyn), at a time when such couples were quite rare. They are both academics, who value the life of the mind above much else, and who break paradigms in their own work. And they also have a passion for foreign travel, which very much shaped my childhood. One obvious way I was

influenced by them was to end up following a career path determined first and foremost by my own curiosity and inclinations. I also grew up fairly unfazed about finding myself in strange or foreign settings, or being surrounded by languages I don't understand. Above all, because my own ethnicity is mixed, I think that – for better and worse – I find it hard to see things in black and white.

**You travel across many countries and a hundred years in the book, but which place or object inspired you to write it?**
I still have the diary I kept from my first trip to Europe at the age of five, in which I recorded visiting the Victoria and Albert Museum and seeing 'a tiger ciling a englishman' [sic]. So Tipu's Tiger made an early impact on me – probably just as its captors would have wished. I was also fascinated by Egyptian objects, particularly mummies, in the British Museum and the Louvre. But I think what really inspired me to write this book was not just seeing things in European and American museums, it was having the chance to see them *in situ* as well, in Egypt and in India. This is surely what sparked my interest in how objects, like people, can be displaced and recontextualized across continents.

> 'What really inspired me to write this book was not just seeing things in European and American museums, it was having the chance to see them *in situ* as well, in Egypt and in India.'

**Have you always wanted to be a writer or did you have other ambitions as a child?**
The first career I seriously considered (aged eight) was archaeology, and more ▶

Author photo © Duncan McColl Chesney

LIFE AT A GLANCE

**BORN**

Cambridge, Massachusetts, 1974

**EDUCATED**

Harvard (BA), Cambridge (MPhil), Yale (PhD)

**CAREER**

Research fellow for two years at the University of Michigan, now Assistant Professor, University of Virginia

**LIVES**

Charlottesville, Virginia

## Q and A with Maya Jasanoff *(continued)*

◂ specifically Egyptology. So apparently the idea of excavating the past, in some manner, appealed to me even then. I toyed with various other career possibilities in college (notably in theatre), but at base I have always loved stories, fiction and non-fiction, and I knew that prose narrative had to play a part in whatever I did. At first I thought I might study literature, because I so enjoyed reading novels. What convinced me to be a historian instead was that I could read *and* write stories: much more fun.

**This is a very accessible book and yet you are an academic: did you deliberately set out to write something for the general public, rather than your peers, or do you consider the distinctions between academic and non-academic writing to be false?**
I think the distinction is certainly overdrawn. Of course in any academic discipline there are debates, discoveries and discussions that are of particular interest to specialists; that is one reason we have journals, conferences and scholarly monographs, all of which help ground our profession. On the other hand, historians study plenty of subjects that general readers might also find interesting, and I see no reason why one can't try to address 'scholarly' questions in terms that informed non-academics can engage with. I think it is wrong to insist on some fixed separation between one kind of writing and the other, leaving 'readable' books to non-academics to write. If anything, experts should write accessibly more often: they know the most

important questions to ask and how to accumulate and assess evidence of all different kinds; they are also professional teachers, who communicate their findings to student audiences all the time. Having venues for academic exchange is crucial – but there is no excuse for insisting that academics can *only* write for other academics.

**In the conclusion you make clear that Lucknow's attitude of embracing other cultures was more conducive to tolerance than the British Empire's later incarnation as a ruling power imposing on India. Do you think there are still political lessons to be learnt from this?**
Yes. I certainly don't think that tolerance can solve everything, and it has to come from all sides to work. But I also don't think that one political culture can be effectively imposed on another unless it has the capacity to adapt, and this often requires understanding something about local conditions. One thing I learned while working on this book is that the widely held view that associates empires with intolerance – with hard imposition of one dominant culture over all others – is too pat. For one thing, power can of course be resisted in all kinds of ways. For another, the culture of seemingly dominant powers is not always as monolithic as one might think. It is also worth noting that empires are intrinsically inclusive, often more than nation-states, and that nation-states have historically been far more destructive to the interests of minority communities than empires have been. ▶

‘Experts should write accessibly more often: they know the most important questions to ask and how to accumulate and assess evidence of all different kinds; they are also professional teachers, who communicate their findings to student audiences all the time.’

## Q and A with Maya Jasanoff *(continued)*

> One thing I learned while working on this book is that the widely held view that associates empires with intolerance – with hard imposition of one dominant culture over all others – is too pat.

◂ **Have you, like your subjects, ever been a collector and, if so, of what?**
Not really: I've never managed to be dedicated or single-minded about collecting any particular thing. The one exception might be that I do in some sense 'collect' travel experiences. I have been to around forty countries so far, and I have thousands of photographs from my trips, and a lot of travel diaries. I also like to pick up unusual objects. So while I don't have an expanding collection of any single genre of item, my house is by now filled with everything from teaspoons to armchairs that I have acquired on my travels. If I share something with some of the collectors in this book, maybe it is that I feel I do have a personal connection with the objects that surround me.

**Who are the writers that you admire most and who have influenced your work?**
My writing has been most influenced by the work of narrative historians, from nineteenth-century greats like Francis Parkman to the splendid trilogy on the British Empire by Jan Morris. I particularly admire Simon Schama, who has a brilliant capacity to bring places and people to life, to synthesize detailed arguments, and to wrap it all up in breathtaking prose. I've probably learned the most about the craft of writing history, though, by reading French historiography: whether micro-histories by Emmanuel LeRoy Ladurie and Natalie Zemon Davis, or wonderfully sweeping *annaliste* accounts like Fernand Braudel's *Mediterranean* or Marc Bloch's *French Rural*

*History*, or the terrifically quirky, vibrant studies by Richard Cobb.

**What are you writing now?**
I am working on a book about Loyalists – people who remained loyal to Britain during the American Revolution – who became refugees and exiles during and after the war. White, black and (Native American) Indian, these Loyalists moved across the British Empire: to Canada, the Caribbean, Sierra Leone, South Asia and beyond. Surprisingly few people today, especially in America, know about the Loyalist diaspora and just how substantial and wide-ranging it was. But the founding moments of the United States look somewhat different when you reckon that about one in thirty people fled the emerging nation. The Loyalist exiles are also significant for the history of the British Empire, where they become real imperial pioneers by settling new territories. Finally, Loyalist experiences relate to a phenomenon with which we are still dismally familiar today: their exodus constituted the largest refugee crisis yet faced by the British Empire. ■

‘I do in some sense “collect” travel experiences. I also like to pick up unusual objects. My house is now filled with everything from teaspoons to armchairs that I have acquired on my travels.’

## TOP TEN BOOKS ABOUT CROSS-CULTURAL ENCOUNTERS

Robert Byron
***The Road to Oxiana***

Bruce Chatwin
***The Viceroy of Ouidah***

Joseph Conrad
***Lord Jim***

John Demos
***The Unredeemed Captive***

Amitav Ghosh
***In an Antique Land***

Graham Greene
***The Quiet American***

V. S. Naipaul
***The Loss of El Dorado***

George Orwell
***Burmese Days***

Jonathan Spence
***The Memory Palace of Matteo Ricci***

Jonathan Swift
***Gulliver's Travels***

# A Writing Life

**When do you write?**
Early morning into early afternoon. If I'm having a really good day I'll write or revise late at night, too.

**Where do you write?**
Mostly in my study at home, which has lots of light and faces a splendid magnolia tree.

**Why do you write?**
Because I can't think of anything I'd rather do! And it is a critical part of my job.

**Pen or computer?**
Computer – though on a few memorable occasions, pen, on yellow legal pads.

**Silence or music?**
Usually silence, though sometimes NPR or (if I am in Britain) Radio 4.

**What started you writing?**
I kept travel diaries from the age of five; maybe that had some influence. I discovered how much I really loved writing history when I was writing my MPhil dissertation in the summer of 1997.

**How do you start a book?**
I tend to start by writing about an incident that has grabbed me, whether or not it is at the beginning of the story, and develop things from there. I do not use structured outlines, although I do have a sense of what will go in each chapter before I start.

**And finish?**
In a hurry under deadline pressure!

**Do you have any writing rituals or superstitions?**
Not really, except about schedule. If my momentum is broken during the course of a morning then I can't get it back. If I have one good day then the next one will be bad. If I write one chapter quickly the next one will be slow. That sort of thing.

**Which living writer do you most admire?**
For history, Simon Schama.

**What or who inspires you?**
Seeing new things.

**If you weren't a writer, what job would you do?**
I am a professor, which suits me because it involves other things – such as human contact! – in addition to writing.

**What's your guilty reading pleasure or favourite trashy read?**
The Lucia novels, by E. F. Benson.

# A Tourist with a Twist

*by Maya Jasanoff*

It is one thing to visit a place and later be inspired to learn and write about it. It is quite another to spend years researching and reading about a setting before seeing it for yourself. This book is the product of both kinds of experience, of travels old and new.

Perhaps the key place which I wondered about, without ever having seen it, was Alexandria, Egypt. My curiosity took off in the summer of 1999, which I spent holed up in Parisian archives, poring over the correspondence of French diplomats in Egypt. During long days immersed in their letters, I began to live vicariously with the French community in eighteenth-century Alexandria. I knew the layout of their compound, with its fifteen apartments, offices, shop and chapel. I followed their conflicts with the Ottoman authorities and with each other; I read tales of adultery, insanity, captivity. When I emerged bleary-eyed each evening, they shadowed me on my walk home: as I squeezed past the garment racks in a street of Chinese textile shops, I thought about them dealing in hides and cotton in Alexandria's warehouses. When I bought my demi-baguette at a local bakery, I wondered what sorts of bread the French baker in Cairo had produced. Above all, I tried to imagine Alexandria itself, full of resonance, yet entirely unknown to me.

I had visited Egypt at the age of eight, and the trip left powerful if unstructured impressions – such as the rose-coloured highlights of the desert as it looked from the window of a small plane, flying to Abu Simbel just before dawn. With my first-ever camera, I photographed a statue of Horus in a temple courtyard so brightly lit by the sun in parts, and so heavily shaded in others, that it was as if the world had gone monochrome. In the afternoons I played with my brother, pretending that our cabin on a Nile cruise boat was a spaceship. But I had not been back since; I barely remembered anything beyond ancient ruins, and I had never visited Alexandria. After months of experiencing Egypt through the curled script of 200-year-old letters, my desire to return was stronger than ever.

I wanted to sail to Alexandria, ideally from Marseilles, and retrace the route that for centuries joined the cities in a Mediterranean circuit of commodities, languages and peoples. I was disappointed to learn that the passenger ferry service to Alexandria had recently stopped: so much for living history. Instead, in the spring of 2001, I flew from Paris to Cairo – doing in hours what Napoleon (for instance) had done in weeks. This capital-to-capital flit puts France and Egypt in sharper cultural juxtaposition than one would have experienced in the days of sail. It has also turned Alexandria, once the major point of entry for foreign tourists, into an outpost. This echoes a larger transformation in the city's position. Alexandria has been a cosmopolitan crossroads since antiquity; and even as recently as two generations ago up ▶

## A Tourist with a Twist *(continued)*

◀ to 30 per cent of the city's population hailed from non-Arab or non-Muslim ethnic and religious backgrounds. But following a wave of nationalizations in 1956, most of Alexandria's minority communities were forced or encouraged to leave. Practically overnight, the population became almost entirely Egyptian Arab. Where once I might have had some trouble encountering a native Arabic-speaker in central Alexandria, now I felt like the only foreigner to spend more than a night there.

Yet while the population might have changed, the Europeanized cityscape remained. I stayed in a grand, decrepit building facing the harbour, the Hotel Crillon. (Aptly, the famous Hotel de Crillon, in Paris, fronts on to the obelisk on the Place de la Concorde.) It was one of many art deco apartment blocks lining the waterfront, with dusty elevator cages and marble staircases with battered brass railings. I sauntered between the scrubby palm trees on Midan al-Tahrir, with its late nineteenth-century equestrian statue of Muhammad Ali Pasha. I sat in cafés frequented by the smart set of the 1930s, and ploughed my way through Laurence Durrell's *Alexandria Quartet*. One day my reading was interrupted by afternoon prayers, led by a man with a microphone on the Midan Saad Zaghloul. In short, I saw how the city's old multi-ethnic spaces had been put to new uses by its Egyptian Arab residents. It was an aspect of cosmopolitanism that no archives could reveal.

While my trip to Alexandria had been prefigured by years of formal study, my visit to Calcutta built on long-standing acquaintance. I encountered India with the instinctive confidence of a part-native: my mother comes from Calcutta, and I have been visiting India regularly since before I can remember. This intimacy has let me engage with the place in ways that most tourists do not; and thanks to repeated family trips, I have also seen more parts of the subcontinent than most. Yet this familiarity is also deceptive. I speak no Indian languages, and in key respects I *am* a tourist, a privileged outsider who can drop in at will, spectate, then vanish. Until embarking on this project, what little I knew of Indian history was the sort of thing you might learn from a guidebook, or (in my case) a grandparent.

I began to study the history of British India almost by accident, thanks to an influential supervisor in my first year of graduate study. Before then I had known Calcutta as my mother's native city, bursting with great-aunts who force-fed us sweets, and with sari shops where my mother would replenish her wardrobe till the next visit. Through my reading I came to see it from what was, to me, the 'other' side – the British one. I learned about what life was like for a 'griffin' starting out with the East India Company, about the cargoes coming in and out of the Hooghly, about meetings of the Asiatic Society of Bengal. But for all that I trawled through my memory for glimpses of old British Calcutta, I drew a blank. The ▶

## A Tourist with a Twist *(continued)*

◀ city I knew and the city I studied seemed like two different places. So it was with tremendous excitement, and some trepidation, that I visited Calcutta in 1999, by myself for the first time, and with newly informed eyes.

Whereas in the past I had not really been a tourist there at all, now I enjoyed the sense of being a tourist with a twist. I was staying in a private apartment in a residential area, where a maid came up every morning and magically emerged from a soi-disant kitchen with a pot of tea. Each evening I took a taxi and used my few words of Bengali to give directions to the home of my closest relatives in the city, who gave me splendid home-cooked meals. At the same time, my daytime exploits – such as visiting the Marble Palace – were the kinds of things some of my relatives (like many locals) could never imagine doing themselves. I rode the subway, which many of them would not; even worse, I sometimes walked. I ate street food in preference to patronizing the hushed, darkened, air-conditioned establishments on Park Street. I ventured into parts of town nobody I knew would have occasion to visit. In essence, my research led me to look at a familiar city in an unfamiliar way – and by combining the two views, I was able to gain a more shaded perspective on empire and its legacies than archives (or family stories) might alone have provided.

I had imagined Alexandria from documents. I knew Calcutta through personal experience long before I had read about its history. But ultimately, I discovered much the same in both places: juxtapositions of past and present that play out on many levels, including those of my own memory and awareness. In more ways than one, researching this book brought me into contact with worlds near and far, and let me savour the best of both. ■

Read on

# If You Loved This, You Might Like . . .

***Empire: How Britain Made the Modern World***
Niall Ferguson
The story of the rise and fall of the British Empire, focusing on profit, trade and missionaries.

***A History of Britain III: The Fate of Empire 1776–2001***
Simon Schama
Simon Schama's *A History of Britain* was praised for its accessible approach to the subject. In this, the final part of the trilogy which began in 3000 BC, Schama focuses particularly on Britain's colonial influence on two countries, India and Ireland.

***Captives: Britain, Empire and the World 1600–1850***
Linda Colley
One of the most respected narratives about the impact of the British Empire, Colley's book tells the story from a previously unknown perspective, that of British subjects imprisoned abroad, in countries that their own rulers sought to conquer.

***The Ordinary Person's Guide to Empire***
Arundhati Roy
After winning the Booker Prize for *The God of Small Things*, Roy gave up fiction for polemic. In this collection of essays and speeches she considers the impact of modern empire, specifically the US invasion of Iraq.

***White Mughals***

William Dalrymple

When James Achilles Kirkpatrick, the British Resident at the court of Hyderabad, falls in love with, then marries, Khair-un-Nissa, a Hyderabadi princess, he must change religion and consider his allegiances. Dalrymple tells the story of a nineteenth-century love which challenged expectations and empire.

# Find Out More

Museums are, by their very nature, repositories of plunder, their collections often evidence of successful expeditions and colonizations. Here are details of some of those mentioned in *Edge of Empire.*

***The British Museum***
*Great Russell Street, London*
*www.thebritishmuseum.ac.uk*
Visit many of the items mentioned in this book, including the Elgin Marbles, along with many other imperial 'gains'.

***Sir John Soane Museum***
*13 Lincoln's Inn Fields, London*
*www.soane.org*
Along with the alabaster sarcophagus of Seti I in the basement (see p. 250), this museum contains many other fascinating Greek, Roman and English sculptures, as well as paintings by Canaletto and an impressive collection of timepieces. The house itself, in which the museum was established, is fascinating.

***The Metropolitan Museum of Art***
*1000 Fifth Avenue, New York*
*www.metmuseum.org*
The Temple of Dendur (see pp. 305–6) is one of the most incredible 'exhibits' visible in any museum in the world.